WITHDRAWN

THE AFGHAN SYNDROME

The Afghan Syndrome
How to live with Soviet Power

Bhabani Sen Gupta

Sena Cāṇakya

Exclusive Distributor
for USA and CANADA
Advent Books, Inc.
141 East 44th Street
New York, NY 10017

VIKAS PUBLISHING HOUSE PVT LTD

VIKAS PUBLISHING HOUSE PVT LTD
Regd. Office: 5 Ansari Road, New Delhi 110002
H.O. Vikas House, 20/4 Industrial Area, Sahibabad 201010
Distt. Ghaziabad, U.P. (India)

COPYRIGHT © BHABANI SEN GUPTA, 1982

ISBN 0-7069-1349-3

1V2G5415

This study was undertaken and completed with a senior fellowship of the Indian Council for Social Science Research.

DS
371.2
S46
1982

Printed at Roopak Printers, K-17, Navin Shahdara, Delhi 110032 (India)

Dedicated to
*   Dr Nihar Ranjan Ray,*
*   Historian, who died recently*
*   Dr Asok Mitra,*
*   Demographer*
*   Mr G Parthasarathi*
*   Diplomat and Educational Administrator*
who made it possible for me to launch on an
academic career rather late in life

Contents

	Foreword	*ix*
One	*The Intervention*	1
Two	*Afghanistan: Friend or Victim?*	30
Three	*The Theory of Linkage*	48
Four	*The USSR: Emergent Global Power*	66
Five	*Moscow: Diplomacy of Intervention*	84
Six	*India: Diplomacy of "Crisis Defusion"*	106
Seven	*Pakistan: Diplomacy of Survival*	141
Eight	*China: Diplomacy of Insecurity*	160
Nine	*Towards Denouement*	179
Ten	*Asian Perceptions of Soviet Power*	199
Eleven	*How to Live with Soviet Power*	223
	Notes	251
	INDEX	291

Foreword

This is not a book on Afghanistan. It is a study of the Soviet Union in the context of Soviet military intervention in Afghanistan in December 1979. Even more precisely, it is a book on the manifestation of the Soviet Union as a global power and the world's reluctant, tormented manner of adjusting itself to that traumatic development. The international order is fundamentally different with the USSR emerging as a functional global superpower. This book raises the question that is likely to dominate international politics in the 1980s: How to live with Soviet global power?

It does not presume to answer that question. But by analysing and interpreting the responses of the principal actors in the Afghan drama to the thunder of Soviet global power, it offers silhouettes of answers that various nations tentatively made to that question. Finally, it dwells on the dilemmas faced by Uncle Sam in recognising Cousin Ivan as an equal in the global arena. If this study has a hypothesis, it is that the USSR has affirmed its emergence as a global power, and the world will, over time, adjust itself to this hard fact of life.

Perhaps it is right that this study should have been undertaken by an Indian who claims an ability to look out on the world with objectivity. The focus of the current superpower "confrontation" is on the "arc of crises" which takes in its geopolitical sweep the area in which India is situated. It was not accidental that the first shock of the exercise of Moscow's global power had to be absorbed by countries belonging to the geostrategic region of Southwestern and South Asia. India and Pakistan were among the countries immediately and directly involved in the crisis created by the Soviet intervention in Afghanistan. How the world is to live with the USSR as a global power is a question that must be answered more promptly and less ambiguously by the countries residing in the "arc of crises" than by others in the third world. How these countries answer the question will determine to a large extent the answer that finally emits from the United States.

This study was completed while the author was on a senior fellowship from the Indian Council for Social Science Research. It is an offshoot of a forthcoming study of the problems and prospects of regionalism in South Asia, funded by ICSSR.

In writing this volume, I have drawn upon a large quantity of secondary material, in addition to a huge amount of primary sources. I have benefited from the critical comments of participants in a seminar on the Soviet intervention in Afghanistan at the Institute of Defence Studies and Analysis early January 1980; I should like to thank the Institute's then Director, P.R. Chari, a cautious and perceptive student of strategic affairs. I also benefited from a seminar held in the spring of 1980 at the Military Studies Department of Allahabad University, at which my paper on the U.S. response to the Soviet intervention was expertly commented on by several scholars as well as by T.N. Kaul, former Indian ambassador to the United States, who chaired the seminar. The ninth chapter of this volume was read as a paper at the Second International Congress of Soviet and East European Studies held in the autumn of 1980 at Garmisch-Partenkirchen, Western Germany. I am grateful to Dr Deiter Braun, deputy director of the Foreign Policy Research Centre at Ebenhausen, near Munich, for critically reading portions of the manuscript and for inviting me to make a presentation on the main theme of the book at a faculty meeting at the institute. I am grateful to Michael Kauffman, Delhi-based correspondent of *The New York Times* for reading portions of the manuscript with a critical eye and friendly affection. Finally, I must record my sense of gratitude to my colleagues at the Centre for Policy Research, New Delhi, particularly its affable and erudite director, Dr V.A. Pai Panandikar, for numerous acts of help and cooperation.

My infinite thanks go to S.B. Dasgupta for his tireless research and secretarial assistance. Finally, a grateful hug for a wife who has been bearing stoically for many years with a husband who is weird enough to attempt a scholarly book every other year.

Centre for Policy Research   BHABANI SEN GUPTA
Diplomatic Enclave
New Delhi 110021, India

CHAPTER ONE

The Intervention

Thou com'st in such a questionable shape...
Hamlet, 1, iv, 42

On 27 December 1979, 40,000 Soviet troops intervened in Afghanistan to protect a Marxist regime teetering on the edge of collapse. The Soviet action signalled a new epoch in world politics. An epoch in which the world must reckon with the emergence of the Soviet Union as a global, interventionist superpower. From the fifties right up to the end of the Vietnam war, only one world power, the United States of America, had been cast in that role. Now, with the intervention in Afghanistan, a country outside the Soviet bloc and the socialist system, the USSR heralded its arrival on the stage of global politics as a co-equal of the United States. The second superpower capable of directly and effectively intervening in conflicts in the third world, and with demonstrated will to intervene.

The Soviet action could not have been occasioned more menacingly as far as its rival and adversary, the US, was concerned. For the United States the time had been out of joint and it did not seem that the man in the White House, Jimmy Carter, had been born to set it right. The Shah of Iran, America's trusted and pampered ally in the strategically important Persian Gulf, had fallen, and Iran had been taken over by a bitterly anti-US religious revolutionary leader of 79. The youth cohorts of the Ayatollah Rohullah Khomeini had seized the American embassy in the heart of Tehran (for many years, the heart *of* Tehran) and taken 50 or more US employees as hostages demanding that the US hand over the deposed Shah, then a patient in a New York hospital, to the revolutionary regime for trial for his crimes against the Iranian people. Crowds milling in front of the US embassy in Tehran were daily shouting slogans like "Death to Carter", and brandishing banners like "Khomeini Struggles, Carter Trembles." In Pakistan, a long-term ally, a mob had just stormed and set fire to the American embassy at Islamabad, killing two US citizens, with the Pakistani armed police looking away. Angry crowds had thrown rocks through the windows of a US consulate in Ismir, Turkey. Outside the American embassy in Dacca, capital of Bangladesh, a country into which the US had pumped, since the assassination of Sheikh Mujibur Rahman and the installation of a military regime, more economic aid than it could digest,[1] another crowd chanted "Down with American Imperialism." As Jimmy Carter found himself a hostage of a surfeit of misfortunes in Asia, many Americans seriously questioned the quality of his leadership and these doubts were shared by America's dismayed allies in Western Europe, particularly France and Western Germany. To make things worse for Carter, his candidacy for the Democratic party's nomination for a second term as President was challenged by Senator Edward Kennedy, on the score of the incumbent's weak-kneed leadership. The Soviet intervention in Afghanistan, then, occurred in America's worst winter of discontent. A cornered President was instantly tempted to try to turn it to a glorious summer of American muscle and teeth.

In New Delhi, a care-taker government under Chowdhuri Charan Singh was waiting in utter exhaustion for the electorate to choose a new regime in less than a week. Prime Minister Charan Singh, who, in the preceding summer, had pulled down the Janata government with clandestine help from Mrs. Indira Gandhi, was as familiar with the intricacies of international politics as a buffalo with the philosophy of Kant. He was bewildered by the Soviet intervention in Afghanistan, an event whose meaning he had neither the ability nor the will nor indeed the necessity to comprehend. In Pakistan, the military dictator, General Zia ul-Huq, stood discarded by the civilised world because of his cynical hanging of former Prime Minister, Zulfikar Ali Bhutto; his visage the target of the sullen anger of a nation, repeatedly cheated on the promise of restoration of civilian democratic rule. Neither Pakistan, nor Iran with its high revolutionary fevers, was healthy enough to absorb the shock of the Soviet action in Afghanistan.

Some analysts interpreted Carter's pugnacious response to the Soviet military intervention in Afghanistan as a declaration of Cold War II. If it were so, the focal point of the new cold war, and of a probable superpower confrontation, was, in Carter's own words, "the area running from the Middle East through the Persian Gulf to South Asia." Not far from the area running from Turkey to Greece, the southern flank of Europe, which had served as the launching pad of Cold War I in 1946-47. In July 1980, when Carter's Cold War II seemed to have lost much of its fuel, and the superpowers seemed to be crawling back to the half-sunk ship of detente, the prestigious Stockholm-based International Peace Research Institute (SIPRI) warned that a third world war could still break out in this decade as a result of superpower confrontation in the Persian Gulf region.*

In a world which had basked for a decade in the warmth of detente, the Soviet intervention in Afghanistan could not produce monolithic cold-warish images. It was seen differently by different governments and elite groups all over the world—in the realm of international communism, in the third world, in the Western alliance, indeed even within the United States itself. In the immediate wake of the Soviet action, extra-hard images instantly minted in the White House seemed to clash with softer, somewhat indulgent images timidly and briefly nursed on the seventh floor of the State Department building at Foggy Bottom. The White House images mingled easily with the prevailing dominant elite mood in the United States; became, in no time, the dominant American view; carried immediately to the far corners of the planet on the omnipotent electronic wires of the mass media; it also became, and remained for several months, the dominant world view.

WORLD VIEW OF SOVIET ACTION

The White House vision of the Soviet military intervention in Afghanistan, however, was not born in a vacuum. The collapse of the monarchy in Iran in February 1979 was America's severest political, strategic and economic setback since World War II, far outweighing what the US had actually lost on the charred paddies of Vietnam. To the Carter Administration, the American loss of Iran was, in itself, a major Soviet gain though the Soviets had no clout in aroused Iran, nor were they involved in the collapse of the Shah's regime.[2]

---

*The London-based International Institute for Strategic Studies took a somewhat less pessimistic view of the Iran-Afghan crises. "For the United States it meant that she could no longer rely on the local states to ensure stability on their own and would now need to become more directly involved with maintaining security in the region. This could lead not only to further weakening of the domestic authority of local regimes but also to increased risks of confrontation between the major powers, the Soviet Union and the United States." *Strategic Survey, 1979*, London, IISS, 1980, p. 42.

The White House initiated a series of strategic and political initiatives in 1979 aimed simultaneously at protecting vital US and Western interests in the Gulf-Middle East region, minimising losses in Iran, and meeting any overt Soviet military move southward towards Iran.

Soon after the downfall of the Shah, the Pentagon prepared the most comprehensive study to date of the comparative military advantages and disadvantages of the two superpowers in the Persian Gulf region. The conclusion reached in the study was that the US forces could not stop a Soviet thrust towards the Gulf through Iran except by using tactical nuclear weapons.[3] As soon as the hostage crisis broke out, American military planners went to work so that military forces could respond swiftly to any presidential order to intervene with force to rescue the Americans detained in Tehran.[4] In November-December 1979, Carter determined to increase the 1981 military budget by 5 per cent, ordered the streamlining of the Rapid Deployment Force (RDF) for use in future crises in the third world; despatched special aides to Saudi Arabia, Oman, Somalia and Kenya to seek access to military—specially naval—bases; and asked Defence Secretary Harold Brown to make his long-awaited trip to Peking thus symbolically inaugurating an era of Sino-US military cooperation. Carter's national security adviser, Zbigniew K. Brzezinski, sculptor of much of the president's response to the Soviet action in Afghanistan, observed in mid-December that the Rapid Deployment Force "will give us the capability to respond quickly, effectively and perhaps preemptively in those parts of the world where our vital interests might be engaged and where there are no permanently stationed American forces."[5] A report in the *New York Times* about the same time made it clear that the RDF was not necessarily meant exclusively to respond to Soviet military expansion. It might be made available to Egypt if Sadat's insecure regime were menaced by Libya, to Saudi Arabia in the event of a military threat from Iraq or Iran, and to Thailand if it were invaded by the Vietnamese from Kampuchea.[6] Earlier, on December 2, Hedrick Smith reported in the columns of the *New York Times* that the Iranian crisis was causing Washington to shed its reluctance to engage in intervention for the protection of American interests in the third world, with certain Congressional elements "prepared in principle to endorse military intervention even in friendly countries if Western interests were threatened."*

*Carter had authorised the creation of RDF as far back as August 1977; progress had been slow; at a news conference on 21 June, 1979, the US Army

Carter predictably linked the Soviet armed intervention in Afghanistan with the general crisis in the Persian Gulf region, for which, too, he held Moscow partly responsible. He described the Soviet action as the "greatest threat" to peace since World War II, a hyperbole that reflected more faithfully the abrasive mood of the American elite than the chronology of crises since 1945. "My opinion of the Russians has changed most drastically in the last week (more) than in the previous 2½ years before that," Carter confessed, and was taken to task by the media for his "striking naivety." Carter's pronouncements in the first week of January 1980 set the framework of US perceptions of the Soviet action in Afghanistan. The Soviet "invasion" of Afghanistan, he said, was a "deliberate effort by a powerful atheist government to subjugate an independent Islamic people." A Soviet-occupied Afghanistan threatened both Iran and Pakistan and was a "stepping stone to their possible control over much of the world's oil supplies," he added. The Soviet action was "a quantum jump in the nature of Soviet behaviour. And if they get through this with relative political and economic impunity, it will have serious consequences on the world in years to come," he warned. In order not to let this happen, Carter announced a number of "punishments." He suspended the sale of 17 million tonnes of US grain to the USSR and also of advanced technology; severely curtailed Soviet fishing privileges in American waters as well as cultural exchange programmes; and hinted that the US might boycott the Moscow Olympics. To shore up Afghanistan's neighbours, Carter said that the United States, "along with other countries will provide military equipment, food and other assistance" to help Pakistan defend its independence.[7]

American response to Carter's response to the Soviet troops movement into Afghanistan was less than uniform. Support came from the bulk of the foreign policy-making elite within and outside the US government. The Carter line was strongly backed by Drew Middleton, one of the leading American military analysts. In an article in the *New York Times* of 6 January, Middleton pointed out that there were no military forces in the immediate area that were collectively, much less individually, capable of deterring the Soviet Union. Assu-

---

Chief of Staff, General Bernard W. Rogers, said that the drafting of plans for the formation of a "Quick Strike Force of 110,000 men was progressing. The planning process was accelerated under the impact of hostage crisis of November.

ming that the United States and its allies did nothing, Russian forces could make further moves into Iran or Pakistan and command the entrance and exit to the Persian Gulf. China was willing to help but its military strength was committed to the northern frontier and it lacked advanced military technology. "There are doubts in Washington about China's capabilities. Anti-tank and anti-aircraft missiles would be required to slow down, if not halt, a Russian blitzkrieg. The Chinese regular army does not have enough of these weapons for its own forces." To some analysts in Washington, Middleton added, a turbulent Iran appeared to be most vulnerable to further Russian intervention. The effectiveness of the Iranian army of 285,000 including three armoured divisions, had been sapped by the execution or flight of a high percentage of officers and non-commissioned officers and a consequent breakdown in discipline. The American and British technicians who were training Iranians in the use of F14 fighters from the United States and Chieftain tanks from Britain had departed. The Iranian airforce probably could put only 10 per cent to 12 per cent of its combat aircraft in the air. The navy's surface combatants, after a brief and fruitless excursion in the Persian Gulf in December, were unable to get under way now for lack of spare parts and skilled maintenance personnel. Many American civilian and military analysts felt that Pakistan appeared to be the focus for investment that eventually might deter the Soviet Union. "They say this with full knowledge of that country's military difficulties." Pakistan's problem was not in the morale and effectiveness of its soldiers and pilots but the obsolescence of many of its weapons and the shortage of spare parts.

"Pakistan and Afghanistan share a rugged frontier that should make transferring the munitions of war difficult. A more reasonable objective for United States military policy would be to supply Pakistan with modern fighter aircraft, tanks, anti-tank and anti-aircraft missiles and armoured personnel carriers. The chief political drawback seen by some officials in Washington is that such a step would frighten India and possibly move that country closer to the Soviet Union, thus shifting the power balance in Asia even more toward Russia."

The dissenting viewpoint was put forth by the ace columnist of the *New York Times*, James Reston. "It is important not to exaggerate the Afghan tragedy," cautioned Reston. The Carter rhetoric, Reston claimed, was hedged by too many ifs, which only showed that "it is not the considered view of this government that Moscow is actually engaged in a reckless rampage to control the fuel and sealanes around the Persian Gulf."

The generally accepted analysis in Washington of the Soviet move, Reston claimed, was that "Moscow feared the overthrow of a Marxist government in Kabul and its replacement by a militant Islamic regime that, with the kind of religious fervour now sweeping in Iran, might infect and inflame the large Islamic population on the Soviet side of the Afghan-Iran borders.... It is not general war over the oil fields we have to fear but a more divided and dangerous world, with bigger defence budgets (now costing the nations over $ 600 billion a year), more inflation and less help for the poorest members of the human family. This is the larger tragedy of Afghanistan."[8]

THE CARTER DOCTRINE

Brushing aside the dissenting voices on both shores of the Atlantic, Carter crafted a strategic doctrine to contain Soviet expansionism in the 1980s. The Carter doctrine, embodied in the President's State of the Union message to Congress delivered on January 24, thus took its place among the five presidential doctrines framed in the United States since World War II. Each presidential doctrine sought to contain communist, especially Soviet power. However, from the Truman doctrine to the Pacific doctrine of Gerald Ford, there was a steady, albeit tortuous, progress from containment to coexistence, from a sharp East-West polarisation to a tentative balancing of near-equal strategic power. The Truman doctrine divided the world into two parts, one part united under communism and the other fragmented in its freedom and dependent on American leadership and American resources. Most of the beliefs and assumptions embedded in the Truman doctrine proved "either wrong, exaggerated, or impermanent," observed Professor Thomas C. Schelling with more than 20 years' historical hindsight. In any case, the Sino-Soviet schism which became unmistakably visible in 1963, brought to an end the period in which the Truman doctrine had even "limited validity."[9]

The Eisenhower doctrine of 1957, embodied in a congressional resolution, pledged America's military might to the "preservation of the independence and integrity of the nations of the Middle East." But US military might would only "assist any nation or group of nations requesting assistance against armed aggression from any country controlled by international communism." John Kennedy and

Lyndon Johnson did not promulgate their own doctrines, but carried out, in a gathering ambience of superpower understanding, the essentials of the Eisenhower doctrine. Richard Nixon, on the other hand, proclaimed a new era of negotiation instead of confrontation, and in the doctrine that bears his name, transferred to America's allies the main burden of defending their own lands and regimes. Nixon's defence secretary, Melvin Laird, explained that the Nixon doctrine and its supporting national security strategy "strikes a balance between what America should do and what our friends can do."[10] In the Persian Gulf region, Nixon and Kissinger built up the Shah of Iran and the monarchy of Saudi Arabia as the primary defenders of interests shared by the local ruling elites, the United States, Western Europe and Japan. Nixon, then, based his strategic doctrine not on the available power of the United States, but on its usable power in a world that had become multipolar and in which the power of both giants was getting increasingly diffused.

The Carter doctrine was proclaimed without serious consultations with allies and clients and with scant regard for the sensibilities of America's partners, not to speak of countries who wish to remain unentangled with superpower conflicts. The core of the Carter doctrine was a 50-word declaration: "Any attempt by any outside force to gain control of the Persian Gulf region will be regarded as an assault on the vital interests of the United States of America, and it will be repelled by use of any means necessary, including military force." The first striking departure from the Eisenhower doctrine is that there is no mention of international communism. The clear implication is that the United States will use military force, if necessary, to repel a bid to "gain control" of the Gulf region even by a local power tied closely to the Soviet Union. James Reston asked in his column in the *New York Times* whether the US would make war on a hypothetical regime in Tehran controlled by the Tudeh Party or other Iranian leftists, that might ask for, and receive, Soviet military help. Besides, what did "gain control of the Persian Gulf" precisely mean? asked Reston. Did it mean gaining control of the *entire* Gulf region or of any of the oil-producing countries? Would the US make war only with an expansionist Russia or also with leftwing forces in the region with strong ties with the USSR? Reston remarked that Carter was "jumping too far too fast" at a time when "a great many people" in the US and elsewhere "do not share his estimate that the Soviets have made a calculated military move in

Afghanistan nor dominate the oilfields ands ealanes of the Middle East."[11]

In his message to the Congress, President Carter stood his doctrine primarily on America's own military power; it was indeed a unilateral renewal of military globalism. However, Carter spelt out five specific limbs of the doctrine's architecture: (1) the Rapid Deployment Force that was being quickly assembled; (2) enhanced naval presence in the Indian Ocean and acquisition of base facilities in the Gulf and northeast African littoral; (3) a commitment to the defence of Pakistan and transfer of significant quantities of arms and dollars to that country; (4) strong military and political ties with other countries in the region; and (5) a "collective security framework" for the region under US auspices. Carter offered his doctrine with the label "A Framework of Regional Cooperation." The implication of this label was that the U.S. did not intend to wage a global cold war with the Soviet Union, as Secretary Vance made clear in March.[12] The intention was to contain the Soviet Union in the Persian Gulf region, not to take it on globally. Apart from the question whether the United States could wage a limited, regional cold war without giving up its pursuit of limitation of strategic arms, it was clear that even for the limited objectives of the Carter doctrine, the US needed the cooperation of the regional powers. Carter himself confessed to a group of Congressional leaders as, even in its first blush, his doctrine raised as many frowns as smiles:

> I don't think it will be correct
> for me to claim that at
> this time, or in future,
> we expect to have enough
> military strength and enough
> military presence there to
> defend the region unilaterally.[13]

The Carter doctrine, in essence, claimed for the United States the right to intervene in the Arabia-Persian Gulf-Southwest Asian region to protect and defend world capitalist interests just as the Brezhnev doctrine claims for the USSR the right to intervene with force to defend Marxist regimes belonging to the world socialist system. The two doctrines, then, confer an awesome doctrinal justification on the superpower confrontation of the 1980s. The great contrast between the two doctrines is that while the Brezhnev doctrine limits Moscow's interventionist commitments to the region adjacent to the USSR—the Afghan intervention extended the commitment for the first time beyond Eastern Europe but still kept it confined to the immediate southern flank of the Soviet Union—the Carter doctrine committed US military power to be used thousands of miles away from the American shores. One major problem of fulfilling this commitment was the doctrine's failure to enthuse local or regional actors. The Islamic revolutionary regime in Iran was intensely anti-American and viewed the display of US muscle in the region with extreme antipathy and anxiety. The Saudi Arabian regime publicly turned away from the Carter doctrine; in private, asked for a political price Carter was unable to pay—US support for an autonomous state for the Palestinians. Edward Luttwak, a hawkish strategic analyst based at Georgetown University, was "doubtful if the United States could get active support of the neighbouring countries for the Afghan rebels," nor did he think it likely that the Soviet Union would become the target of Muslim hostility everywhere.[14] The *New York Times* cautioned early January that "there is no firm terrain on which to build Carter's new wall of containment. Military pacts and bases will not stand up well in the region's political, ethnic and religious storm. Importing American power will arouse as many radicals as it will reassure conservatives, without resolving their conflicts. Military aid may temporarily sustain some strongman, like Pakistan's General Zia, but it will also produce Colonels like Quddafi. Economic aid can help, but it is no guarantee of political stability."[15] A month later, the *Indian Express* correspondent in Washington reported:

> So far the Persian Gulf States are by no means enthusiastic (about the Carter doctrine). Indeed Kuwaiti and United Arab Emirate newspapers have expressed a fear that the Carter doctrine may lead to the seizure of their oilfields at some future date. They are undoubtedly interested in checkmating the Russians but they are also committed to recovering from Israel the occupied lands and Jerusalem. They also want to hold the rest of the world to ransom by raising oil prices periodically. This puts limits on the extent of their cooperation with the United States.[16]

The multilateral promise of the Carter doctrine—a regional security system under US leadership, and substantial cooperation from allies in the industrialised world—remained unrealised. The West Europeans showed a coolness towards the doctrine that chilled the hearts of many Americans and drew forth, at the beginning of March, a public admonishment even from the suave and professional Cyrus Vance.[17] The Carter doctrine failed to unite the US foreign policy elite and became a strident issue in the presidential election campaign. Even well-known hawks like Senators "Scoop" Jackson and Patrick Moynihan urged Carter to be more cautious in his promises and commitments. In the first week of February, the State Department seemed to have abandoned the idea of a regional security arrangement. The department's spokesman told reporters that the US was *not* trying to put together a NATO or CENTO-type alliance in the Persian Gulf region because "such an alliance will not be useful." Instead, it would have "different types of *bilateral* relationships with individual countries of the region."[18]

THE VIEW FROM WESTERN EUROPE

The West European perceptions of the Soviet armed intervention in Afghanistan did not mirror those of the United States. West Europeans were, however, caught in the horns of an anguished dilemma: if they said what they really felt, the Western alliance would be severely strained, while if they faithfully echoed the voice of America, their own emerging European identity would have to be sacrificed, and with it, the coveted gains of detente. They therefore resorted to multiple ambivalances which provoked James Reston to observe on January 25 that what America's allies were saying in public and what they were saying in private "are entirely different."[19]

Each West European government condemned the Soviet action, was outraged by it, but none except the Tory regime of Great Britain believed that recall of the cold war, economic sanctions and boycott of the Moscow Olympics were the right response.[20] Strategic experts were divided on the defensive-offensive perception of the Soviet intervention. French strategic experts like Helene Carrere d'Encausse and Andre Fontaine saw it mainly as a defensive reflex of Soviet foreign policy—the Russians acting more out of fear than ambition. There was speculation in the West European press that the upsurge of cold war sentiments in the United States had strengthened the hawks in the Kremlin and that the hawkish group consisting of

Defence Minister Ustinov, KGB Chief Andropov, Foreign Minister Gromyoko, ideologue Suslov and senior Politbureau member Kirilenko gave the final push to the idea of going into Afghanistan, while a reluctant and somewhat cornered Brezhnev just went along, if he was not actually overruled.[21]

Six months after the Soviet intervention, Flora Lewis reported in the *New York Times* from Paris:

> Despite a chorus of verbal protests ... there is still no agreed Western assessment of what it really means, let alone what should be done about it. The one consensus is that the Russians should be persuaded not to go any further.
>
> France and Germany appear to be doing a hesitation waltz together, but for somewhat different reasons. West Germany feels that the future of Berlin and eased relations with East Germany and Eastern Europe are hostages to reasonable relations with Moscow; at the same time, its own security requires solidarity with the United States. France, almost by reflex, has insisted on showing some distance from Washington, veering suddenly from several years of complaint that the United States is too indecisive to noting the danger of American overreaction and, as usual, offering a balancing role. The smaller countries are watching the bigger ones uneasily. Whether from wishful thinking, experience or sagacity, America's partners are not ready to take it for granted that detente is dead and that there is no choice but to hunker down for cold war.[22]

SCRAMBLED IMAGES IN SOUTH ASIA

The Soviet armed intervention in Afghanistan shook all the national capitals in the South Asian neighbourhood. Each government recognised it to be an event of the utmost political-strategic import—for its own country, for the region and for the world. However, the South Asian perceptions of the intervention and of the interventionist power—the USSR—were a scramble of contrary images, each sketched with fluids of national interests as these were seen by the ruling elite, each fed by the region's deep-rooted strategic divisions and rivalries.

The Soviet ambassador to India, Yuri M. Vorontsov, took up his diplomatic office in New Delhi in April 1978 when the Janata government looked deceptibly stable. Like his predecessors, Vorontsov is a member of the central committee of the Communist Party of the Soviet Union (CPSU); he speaks English fluently with a strained "Oxford" accent. Vorontsov called on Ram Sathe, Foreign Secretary in the Indian external affairs ministry (who is the ministry's highest bureaucratic official) at his own initiative around midnight on 28 December, 1979, and handed him a message from the Soviet government informing the Government of India that, at the request of the Afghan leadership, Moscow had sent to Afghanistan a limited contingent military force to enable Kabul to resist external aggression and interference. The despatch of Soviet troops, the statement added, was in terms of the Soviet-Afghan treaty of peace and friendship as well as Article 51 of the UN Charter providing for individual or collective self-defence in the case of an external armed attack. In the brief conversation that followed between a bewildered Ram Sathe and a steel-jawed Vorontsov, the ambassador likened the Soviet action to the Indian armed intervention in Bangladesh in 1971. Sathe could not immediately reach the Indian foreign minister, S.N. Mishra, who was electioneering in Bihar. He got in touch with the cabinet secretary who got in touch with the interim prime minister, Charan Singh. An official statement issued a few hours later said that the government of India had taken note of the events in Afghanistan since December 21 and had been kept informed about them by its mission in Kabul. It had also received a message from the Soviet government. "Consistent with the Government of India's commitment to principles of non-alignment, it supports the sovereign right of the Afghan people to determine their own destiny free from foreign interference. The Government of India's attitude to such situation is well known. India has always opposed any outside interference in the internal affairs of one country by another. It is also the Government of India's earnest hope that no country or external power would take steps which might aggravate the situation and that normalcy would be restored there early."

In reply to reporters' questions, an official spokesman said that the Government knew that Hafizullah Amin was not in power in Afghanistan. The Indian ambassador had not seen his successor, Babrak Karmal, recently.* In reply to a question whether India supported or

---

*The sequence of events leading to the Soviet intervention in Afghanistan is given in the next chapter.

opposed the entry of Soviet troops into Afghanistan, the spokesman said "We are not supporting or opposing anyone. We are still observing the situation. We are assessing whether the Soviet assumption that they extended their help and assistance on the request of the duly constituted authorities in Kabul, is right or wrong." Answering more questions, he said "I do not know who invited the Soviets. We are awaiting analytical assessment from our embassy in Kabul. We have, however, taken note of the justification given by the Soviet Union."[23]

National election in India was less than a week away. It was too late for the Afghanistan issue to become a bone of electoral contention. In the last round of campaigning, political leaders hardly mentioned the Soviet intervention. The parties opposing Mrs Gandhi's return to power hesitated to speak of a threat to India's security lest this might direct the voter's mind to a "strong" government in New Delhi and therefore to Indira Gandhi. Mrs Gandhi herself preferred not to play up the Soviet factor but to draw the electorate's attention to the instant US move to rearm Pakistan making that country an advance base of Washington's confrontation with Moscow. Instructively, the elite English press in India saw the Afghan crisis essentially as it was seen by Mrs Gandhi. Only one major daily, *The Hindu*, of Madras, in South India, called the intervention "clear military aggression on the part of the Soviet Union against the small nation of Afghanistan" and found it "reprehensible on two counts: first, for its blatant violation of national sovereignty supposed to be guaranteed in international law and by the UN Charter; secondly, as a manifestation of superpower bullying that threatens peace (in that it triggers new tensions and offers fresh precedents for violating the peace) as well as regional security."[24] At the other end of the peninsula, the *Tribune*, based in Chandigarh, capital of Punjab, saw the USSR taking control of Afghanistan's Marxist revolution, strengthening its position in Afghanistan vis-a-vis Iran and Pakistan, and setting in motion "a political and military earthquake of which the end-result cannot be foreseen just yet."[25] None of the major New Delhi English dailies labelled the intervention an aggression. More than any other major English daily, the *Times of India*'s editorials mirrored the splintered Indian images of Afghanistan after the Soviet intervention. On December 29, the paper doubted if the Russians had "masterminded the present coup" conceding, at the same time, that "it could not have taken place without their help." Three days later it was "clear" to the newspaper that "the Russians are determined to tighten their hold on (Afghanistan) in order to bring it firmly within the Soviet orbit of influence." Hafizullah Amin, it believed, had started plotting with Pakistan to "jeopardise Soviet gains in Afghanistan," thereby giving a certain credence to the Soviet justification for intervention. The January 1 editorial ended with a reassuring conclusion that "Afghanistan is still some way from becoming a captive Soviet satellite." In a signed article, the paper's editor, Girilal Jain, vacillated between an "offensive" and an "defensive" vision of the Soviet intervention. "The Soviet takeover in Kabul is as unprincipled and brutal as its invasion of Hungary in 1956 and of Czechoslovakia in 1968 and the American bombing of North Vietnam. Kampuchea and Laos. ... The Kremlin has wilfully overthrown the Amin regime and it has used its own troops for the purpose. ... On the contrary, it is possible that the Kremlin has got sucked into Afghanistan for defensive considerations—the case is not convincing but it can be made—and that it will be only too glad to find a modus vivendi with Pakistan if only the latter stops active assistance to the Afghan insurgents. Islamabad's behaviour has been quite provocative."[26]

The *Indian Express* took a mellower view of the Soviet action. "There is no need to credit Moscow with all kinds of malevolent intentions. It is enough that they have placed themselves in a better position to intervene in a region where disaffected minorities like the Baluchis and the Kurds could yield rich opportunities. These are possibilities which must cause at least as much concern in India as the possible threat from Pakistan's newly acquired weaponry."[27]

The *Hindustan Times* saw the two superpowers equally responsible for the Afghan crisis. "If Soviet intervention is to be condemned, so must also be the American. What is more, any strengthening of the Pakistan army as a part of the power game will only revive the tensions on this sub-continent. Of course, the danger to Pakistan from the west is now real. This danger is not so much of invasion as of sap and mine, the erosion of its authority in the Pathan and Baluchi areas. So there is every reason to feel nervous. But perhaps all such consequences can be limited and the tension on the sub-continent avoided if Afghanistan is viewed as a victim of foreign intervention rather than as an extension of the 19th century diplomacy and if, therefore, effort is directed towards a Soviet pullout at the earliest."[28]

Even as Soviet troops were moving into Afghanistan, India was more perturbed by the image of Pakistan being rapidly and strongly rearmed by the United States. On December 30, Prime Minister

Charan Singh received a letter from President Carter drawing India's attention to the seriousness of the Soviet action but making no reference to his decision, already reported in the press, to lift the embargo on the transfer of arms to Pakistan. The same day the Indian Government expressed its concern at the US decision to supply arms to Pakistan. A senior official in the external affairs ministry told the US ambassador that the supply of arms to Pakistan in the past had invariably increased tensions in South Asia; it could not be otherwise now. India and Pakistan were still going through a protracted process of normalisation of relations shattered by the war of December 1971. Supply of US arms to Pakistan could only hurt that process as well as delay the restoration of normalcy in Afghanistan. On the same day, Charan Singh sent for the Soviet ambassador and told him that the presence of Russian troops in Afghanistan would have far-reaching adverse consequences for the South Asian region, and expressed the hope that Moscow would recall its troops as soon as possible. "India cherished its traditional close relationship with Afghanistan and would like its independence and nonalignment to be stronger." On January 2, Charan Singh, in his reply to Jimmy Carter, expressed India's "total opposition" to the American decision to transfer arms to Pakistan. Charan Singh expressed concern that the United States "should relapse into its old misguided policy" of arming Pakistan in response to a "temporary phase of developments in Afghanistan." The supply of arms to Pakistan would have the least relevance to the larger interests of the subcontinent at a time when, after decades of suspicion and animosity interspersed with two armed conflicts between India and Pakistan, bilateral relations had been improving steadily. The US decision would undermine a potential nonaligned initiative (which should include Pakistan) to remedy the Afghan developments.

The January 1980 parliamentary election in India brought Mrs Indira Gandhi back to power in a surprise landslide victory, and she took charge of India's response to the Afghan crisis even before she was sworn in as Prime Minister. After the Soviet Union vetoed an American move in the Security Council to censure the intervention, the US and its friends took the issue to the General Assembly, where a 17-nation resolution, moved, among others, by Pakistan and Bangladesh, asked for immediate withdrawal of all foreign troops from Afghanistan. Under instructions cabled from New Delhi, the Indian envoy at the UN made a short statement on January 11 which stunned many delegations. Without approving or supporting the Soviet intervention, the Indian delegate said that India had received "assurances" from Moscow that the intervention had been at the specific request of Afghanistan and that Soviet troops would be withdrawn whenever Kabul asked for it; India, he added, had no reason to disbelieve the assurances of a "friendly country." India was "concerned" about the attempts of "outside powers to interfere in the internal affairs of Afghanistan by training, arming and encouraging subversive elements to create disturbances" in that country. India was vitally interested in the peace, security, independence and nonalignment of Afghanistan.

Mrs Gandhi took a regional view of the Afghan crisis rather than a spatial global view which prevailed in the United States, China and Pakistan. Seen from the pure regional angle, the strategic divide in South Asia is between Pakistan and India; Pakistan's traditional allies are the United States and China, India's the USSR. In the interest of regional stability and balance of power, what was needed, in Indira Gandhi's view, was to contain the Afghan crisis, not to aggravate it and enlarge its context and scope. It would be necessary to obtain the withdrawal of the bulk of the Soviet forces from Afghanistan within a specific time-frame. But this would not be possible if the insurgency was internationalised and if Pakistan were converted into a base for Sino-US military operations against the Soviets in Afghanistan. Mrs Gandhi's policy also implied that while India could live with a Marxist Afghanistan passing into the orbit of the Soviet bloc, it could hardly live with a Pakistan rearmed by the US and China, even less with a Pakistan destabilised and perhaps dismembered by the intermeshing impact of great power confrontation and internal conflict. Mrs Gandhi's way to stabilise the situation and enforce a certain element of caution in the actions of Pakistan, the US and China was to unequivocally reaffirm the strategic linkage between India and the Soviet Union in the event of a major conflict building up in South Asia.[29]

Having reaffirmed the Indo-Soviet strategic linkage, Mrs Gandhi maintained a measure of distance from Moscow. India abstained from voting on the 17-nation resolution in the UN Assembly. Mrs Gandhi made it clear in fragments of pronouncements that she had not supported or approved the Soviet intervention; she stressed her opposition to all foreign intervention and the presence of foreign troops in third world countries. Mrs Gandhi's government opened channels of diplomatic dialogues with several countries within and outside the region with a view to exploring the possibility of an initiative that would induce the Soviets to pull out the bulk of their troops from Afghanistan within a relatively short time.

PAKISTANI PERCEPTIONS

Pakistan was the country where the impact of the Soviet military movement into Afghanistan produced the largest trauma and the deepest perplexities. Pakistan had been involved in whatever had been going on in Kabul in December 1979 between president Hafizullah Amin and the outside world to get the Soviets out of Afghanistan. Nearly half a million Afghans had taken refuge in Pakistan since the revolution of April 1978; thousands of them were actively engaged in an armed insurgency against the pro-Soviet regime. That Pakistan was training and arming a large number of insurgents and permitted other powers, notably the United States, China and Egypt, to feed the rebels with arms and ammunitions had been common knowledge.[30] However, General Zia-ul-Huq, leader of Pakistan's ruling military junta and self-appointed President of the republic, did not have the least expectation of a rapid Soviet takeover of the Afghan revolution. In the closing days of 1979 he suddenly found Soviet military power breathing hotly down Pakistan's neck, bringing about a complete change in the balance of political, military and social power in South-western Asia.

Even before Gen. Zia was able to sort out his scrambled images of the Soviet intervention right across the door from Pakistan, he found that President Carter had already offered him military assistance and made his country an advance base of international resistance to Soviet expansionism. Gen. Zia also saw Peking enthusiastically backing the US. And he also witnessed India's refusal to go beyond mild cosmetic criticism of the Soviet action. The strategic scenario looked to Gen. Zia ominously similar to the one the last military dictator of unbroken Pakistan, General Yahya Khan, had to face in 1971—a resolute Soviet-Indian lineup against a feeble and uncertain Pakistan-US-China axis. The axis did not reassure Gen. Zia that he could openly combat the Soviet Union in Afghanistan.

If the Soviet intervention in Afghanistan posed an unprecedented threat to Pakistan, Carter's reflexive offer of military and economic aid immediately cast Gen. Zia in an important international role, and ended his isolation from the community of polite and civilised governments. Gen. Zia clutched at his unexpected luck, but was far from anxious to provoke the Soviet Union too much. His government's first official reaction to the Soviet action was somewhat cautious. In a statement issued on December 29, it expressed its "gravest concern" at the Soviet intervention, "all the more" because the victim was an Islamic nation. It called for the immediate withdrawal of Soviet troops. "Unofficially," however, Pakistan saw the action as "part of a grand Soviet design to establish hegemony in South Asia," and regarded it as a "direct threat to the security of Pakistan, Iran and other neighbouring countries."[31] Gen. Zia hastened to build up his case for massive US military and economic aid, making it clear, at the same time, that he would not invite "visible US presence" in Pakistan lest this might provoke militant Islamic elements in and outside the country. In the first week of January, it became clear that Gen. Zia was engaged in the hardest-ever bargaining with Washington in Pakistan's entire career as an ally of the United States; he was not ready to shortsell his country. The wire services broadcast Pakistan's doubts about America's credibility as an ally, and fears that Soviet "occupation" of Afghanistan would lead to Pakistan's finlandisation, if not to something worse. On the other hand, the Indian ambassador, K.S. Bajpai was called to the foreign office to listen to a long expression of "sincere regret" that India should take a dark view of American military aid flowing into Pakistan, ignoring Pakistan's great security predicament.

Gen. Zia's bargaining position vis-a-vis the Carter administration was weakened from the beginning by the bitter controversy the bid to rearm Pakistan raised among the American foreign policy decision-making elite as well as by his regime's political and economic travails. The initiative to transfer arms to Pakistan stemmed from the national security establishment and left the State department rather cold. Immediately after Carter announced his decision, it was attacked by the *New York Times*. In an editorial written before the results of the Indian election were announced, the paper observed that it did not automatically follow from the 1959 US-Pakistan security agreement[32] that America must enter into "open-ended arms sales to a divided country ruled by an erratic Islamic fundamentalist." Gen. Zia was "so unsure of his hold that he has postponed elections four times. He has been unable to quell Baluchi and Pathan insurgents and has filled the prisons with dissidents. Where and at whom would he aim American weapons?" After asking this searing question, the editorial warned the administration of even a more serious dimension of the transfer of arms to Pakistan. If Indira Gandhi were elected to power "then India is likely to use American arms aid (to Pakistan) as a pretext for speeding its own nuclear weapons programme and seeking Soviet ties to counter Pakistan and its ally, China."[33]

To the caution sounded by the *New York Times* was added the voice of one of the most knowledgeable American analysts of Indo-Pakistan affairs, a man who had created some international sensation by reporting on the two-year-long bloody civil war that raged in Pakistan in the latter half of the seventies between the government forces and political dissidents in Baluchistan. Selig Harrison, senior research associate of the Carnegie Peace Foundation, strongly warned the Carter administration not to lean too much on Pakistan while responding to the Soviet action in Afghanistan. He said that a "misconceived and oversized" military package to Pakistan would have "self-defeating consequences."

> Domestically it would strengthen the already disproportionate power enjoyed by the military in Pakistan. Internationally it would needlessly arouse Indian fears that Islamabad is seeking to use the Afghan crisis to bolster its power vis-a-vis New Delhi. In seeking to shore up Islamabad, the United States should consult closely with Indian leaders, recognising that India is the preeminent power in South Asia and that a breach between New Delhi and Washington over the issue of US aid to Pakistan would only play into the hands of Moscow.

Selig Harrison pointed out that the "Punjab-dominated Zia-ul-Huq regime has so far failed to take even a modicum of the political and economic steps needed to neutralise separatist sentiment in Baluch and Pushtun areas and thus to facilitate their effective military defence if this should become necessary." The willing cooperation of the Baluchi and Pushtun leaders "would be essential in mobilising any effective tribal cooperation with the Pakistan military in anticipation of Soviet-supported separatist adventures. In the absence of a political settlement, there is a great danger that US weaponry would be used not against Soviet-supported subversion but against Baluch and Pushtun dissident groups fighting for their legitimate rights as Pakistanis." Harrison recalled that this was precisely what happened between 1973 and 1977 when tensions between Islamabad and Baluchistan province "exploded."[34]

The arguments against appointing Gen. Zia-ul-Huq a Western policeman in Southwestern Asia were so strong that even Henry K. Kissinger, the US media's oracle-man on foreign policy and world affairs, who had predictably lent his support to the proposal to rearm Pakistan, conceded late January that no amount of US arms transferred to Pakistan would mean much in South and Southwestern Asia if India elected to move closer to the Soviet Union.[35]

CHINA AND THE AFGHAN CRISIS

In the last week of January, a Soviet analyst accused China of rendering substantial help to the Afghan insurgents. "The coordination of actions and practical collaboration between Washington and Peking had become more obvious in connection with the events in Afghanistan. After the victory of the April revolution, China's ruling circles began to act at one with the United States and its agents in Afghanistan. They coordinated in every way the pooling of such pro-Peking organisations as Sholee Javid and reactionary groups acting on the territory of the Democratic Republic of Afghanistan under the CIA wing. The counterrevolutionary mutiny at Herat and anti-government actions in other regions of Afghanistan were staged with the joint participation of Chinese and American secret services. Chinese instructors together with US military advisers are training Afghan rebels in special camps set up on Afghan territory. Like the USA, Peking also supplies Afghan insurgents with armaments and other equipment."[36]

The Soviet military lurch into Afghanistan looked as menacing to the Chinese rulers as did the successful Vietnamese military intervention into Kampuchea to install the Háng Semrin regime. The Chinese saw in both a menacing expansion of Soviet "hegemonism" at a time when the United States was losing its hold of strategically important geopolitical regions like the Persian Gulf. Four days after the Soviet intervention in Afghanistan, the Russian ambassador was called to the Chinese foreign office to be given a strong note of protest. Peking also "demanded" the immediate withdrawal of Soviet troops. "Afghanistan is China's neighbour and therefore the Soviet armed invasion of that country poses a threat to China's security," the Chinese note said. "This cannot but arouse the grave concern of the Chinese people."[37]

The *People's Daily* pointed out in an editorial that this was the first major use of Soviet troops outside the Soviet community. "This indicates that the Soviet Union will make full use of the military clauses of the so-called friendship and cooperation treaties it signed with a number of countries to conduct military interference so as to farther the path of expansionism."[38]

The Chinese Communist newspaper in Hongkong, *Ta Kung Pao*, expected the Soviet Union to "eventually carve out a separate Baluchistan as one of its satellites in South Asia."[39]

Moscow Explains Action

The first Soviet explanation of the military intervention came in the columns of *Pravda* on 31 December, 1979. Analyst A. Petrov reporting on "important events that have taken place in the life of the Afghan people in recent days," said that imperialist interference in Afghanistan had jeopardized "the very existence of the Republic." The April revolution had been made "with the minimum losses" showing not only that the previous regime was "outdated" but also that the programme of the People's Democratic Party "was backed by the broad masses which supported the revolution as their own vital cause." However, "the external imperialist forces entered into a direct collusion with the internal counterrevolutionary forces" to destabilize the young Afghan democratic republic. Petrov suggested that the United States, having lost its influence in Iran, sought to "subjugate the Afghan people and also the people of other countries of the region."

In 1978-79, Petrov continued, the Afghan government requested the Soviet Union "many times" for military support to suppress the external interference. The Soviet government restrained itself hoping that the activities of the counterrevolutionaries would not go beyond a certain limit. At the same time, the Soviet Union made "no secret that it would not allow Afghanistan to be turned into a bridgehead for the preparation of imperialist aggression against the Soviet Union." However, imperialist interference in Afghanistan became more and more serious and reached a climax when Hafizullah Amin assumed power after overthrowing and killing President Nur Mohammed Tarakki. "In conditions when interference from outside and terror unleashed by Amin within the country created a real threat to the democratic system, there were patriotic forces in Afghanistan which rose not only against foreign aggression but also against the usurper. Relying on the support of the people, they removed Amin, and revolutionary law and order was restored in the country."

At this stage, the Afghan government "made again an instant request" for Soviet military help. Moscow decided to grant this request and to send to Afghanistan "a limited Soviet military contingent that will be used exclusively for assistance to rebuff the armed interference from outside. The Soviet contingent will be completely pulled out of Afghanistan when the reason that necessitated such an action no longer exists." Petrov said that the decision to extend military help was taken under Article 4 of the 1978 Soviet-Afghan treaty of friendship.*

Petrov claimed that the Soviet action was taken also under the provisions of Article 51 of the UN Charter. Petrov went on to say that the Soviet Union and Afghanistan had had close friendly relations for many decades and Moscow had given considerable help to Afghanistan to build its economy and to progress in the social field. "To deny Afghanistan the assistance which it asked for now would mean to nullify the entire experience of our good and honest cooperation with that country, to leave Afghanistan alone to face the imperialist forces that are determined to deprive the Afghan people of the opportunity of enjoying their rights and freedom to the full extent."

In a second commentary on 5 January 1980, *Pravda* responded to a number of measures already taken by the United States to punish the Soviet Union for its military action in Afghanistan. The commentary said that it was not Afghanistan which was interfering in the domestic affairs of Pakistan but vice versa. The United States appeared to be very concerned about its own commitments and interests, "but what about the commitments and interests of other countries? Proceeding from a kind of strange logic, Washington openly claims that the interests and rights of all the others must take a second place as compared to the American interests and rights and that the former should be taken into consideration only so far

---

*This article says: "Acting in the spirit of the traditions of friendship and goodneighbourliness, as well as the United Nations Charter, the parties to the treaty will consult each other and, with mutual consent, will take appropriate measures to ensure the security, independence and territorial integrity of both countries. In the interests of reinforcing the defence potentials of the parties to the treaty, they will continue to develop cooperation in the military sphere."

as it benefits the USA." Repeating the charge of persistent and increasing external assistance to counterrevolutionary forces in Afghanistan, *Pravda* maintained that "the main flow of arms and mercenaries used by the imperialists in the struggle against democratic Afghanistan takes place through Pakistani territory. In Pakistan are located the main bases of anti-Afghanistan reaction seeking to drown Afghanistan's popular revolution in blood and make the country a bridgehead of hostile actions against the USSR." Pakistan had been repeatedly warned against interference in Afghanistan and its leaders were given enough time to stop the intervention. They did not do so. *Pravda* said, "The Soviet military assistance rendered to Afghanistan does not pursue any other aim except helping a friendly country to exercise the right to individual and collective self-defence in repulsing imperialist aggression from outside." It repeated the earlier assurance that Soviet troops would be withdrawn when the reason for their despatch no longer existed.

Two days later *Tass* issued a statement commenting on President Carter's televised speech of January 4. It said the statement was "couched in the verbiage of the cold war and is permeated with the pirit of the cold war." It was "not at all in keeping with the responsibility which the United States as a big power is called upon to bear for the maintenance of world peace and security." It rather looked like the statement of an electoral candidate: "By all indications, election considerations, consideration of courting chauvinistically minded circles carry a considerable weight in the President's statement."

The *Tass* statement also referred to the American threat of economic blockade of Iran if Tehran did not release the hostages. *Tass* said, "Washington clearly cannot stomach the revolution made by the Iranian people and their intention to oppose the imperialist policy of threats and diktat."

Regarding the sanctions against the Soviet Union announced by President Carter, *Tass* said the USSR had never sought economic, commercial and cultural ties with the United States as a favour but only as a matter of mutual advantage. "If the United States intended to influence in some way the Soviet Union and its foreign policy, this is a hopeless undertaking. Such attempts flopped in the past and they will flop now." *Tass* added that the Carter statement lacked "political balance" and overestimated the real "potentialities of those states with regard to which the United States plans to take some other steps. No one in the United States should have any doubt that the Soviet Union will be able to uphold its lawful interests, the interests of its allies and friends."

On January 13 Brezhnev himself outlined the most authoritative Soviet position on Afghanistan in reply to questions put by *Pravda*. He said that "from the very first day" the Afghan revolution "encountered external aggression, crude interference from outside." Thousands and tens of thousands of insurgents, armed and trained abroad, whole armed units were sent into the territory of Afghanistan. "In effect, imperialism, together with its accomplices, launched an undeclared war against revolutionary Afghanistan." A point was reached under Amin's "treachery" when Afghanistan was about to lose its independence or be turned into an imperialist military bridgehead on the southern border of the Soviet Union.

> In other words, the time came when we no longer could not but respond to the request of the government of friendly Afghanistan. To have acted otherwise would have meant leaving Afghanistan prey to imperialism, allowing aggressive forces to repeat in that country what they had succeeded in doing, for instance, in Chile, where the peoples' freedom was drowned in blood. To act otherwise would have meant to watch passively the establishment on our southern border of a seat of serious danger to the security of the Soviet state. . . .It was no simple decision for us to send military contingents to Afghanistan. But the Party's central committee and the Soviet government acted in full awareness of their responsibility and took into account the entire sum total of circumstances. The only task assigned to the Soviet contingents is to assist the Afghans in repulsing the aggression from outside. They will be fully withdrawn from Afghanistan once the reasons that made the Afghan leadership request their introduction disappear. . . .We are helping new Afghanistan on the request of its government to defend the national independence, freedom and honour of the country from armed aggressive action from outside.

Brezhnev asserted that the events in Afghanistan were not the true cause of the present complication of the international situation. "If there were no Afghanistan, certain circles in the United States, in NATO, would have surely found another pretext to aggravate the situation in the world." Brezhnev maintained that it was difficult to count the number of treaties and accords between Washington and Moscow that had been arbitrarily and unilaterally violated lately by the Carter administration. "Of course, we will manage without these and other ties with the United States. . . . Unilateral measures taken by the United States are tantamount to serious miscalculations in politics. Like a boomerang, they will hit back at their initiators, if not today, then tomorrow."

Brezhnev said that the attitude of Europe to detente was vastly different from that of the United States. "The cardinal interests of European peoples are inseparably connected with detente. The Europeans have already come to know its beneficial results from their own experience. . . . It is impossible to believe that there can be states in Europe who would wish to throw away the fruits of detente. . . . The western states, and the United States as well, need detente in Europe by no means to a lesser extent than the socialist countries, than the Soviet Union."

Taking its cue from Brezhnev's statement, *Pravda* in an editorial on January 29 spewed indignation and anger at the US response to Moscow's action in Afghanistan.

By what right does the United States assume the role of a supreme arbiter on such questions as how other peoples should build their lives, in accordance with what principles and values should they establish their national order? An answer is given to this: By right of the strong whom all the rest must obey. Unceremoniously the US government proclaims various areas of the globe as spheres of vital interests of the USA. In the process it is becoming increasingly clear that there has been a tendency for some time to advance these spheres directly to the Soviet borders. Washington, it seems, proceeds from the assumption that it is enough to declare Iran, Afghanistan and other countries or areas thousands of kilometres away from the American shores as zones of America's vital interests—to be more precise, of the biggest monopolies and the military industrial complex of the USA—for everybody to accept this . . . . At no time since the peak of the cold war has the cult of brute force been professed so openly. Carter has declared that America should be prepared to pay any price that may be required to remain the strongest country in the world. The document clearly reveals Washington's course of disrupting the existing approximate parity of forces between the USSR and the United States, of achieving American military superiority.

These authoritative Soviet pronouncements sketched the Soviet self-image as well as Soviet images of the United States and of the global balance of power at the turn of the decade of the eighties.

The Soviet leaders now saw the USSR clearly as a co-equal power of the United States. In their vision, the socialist system had gained in economic, political and military strength during a period of continuing decline of the world capitalist system. The global balance of power had therefore shifted decisively in favour of socialism. The USSR was no longer the junior superpower. The United States had been forced to concede strategic parity to the USSR; it must also concede parity of influence in the vital geostrategic regions of the world, especially in those areas in which the Soviet Union too had vital interests. In other words, the United States could no longer claim regions like the Persian Gulf and the Middle East as exclusively its own, or the West's areas of vital interests. Soviet might and power demanded worldwide equality, not just equality in the strategic field.

By defending with military force the Marxist revolution in Afghanistan, the Soviet Union signalled two important messages to the rest of the world. First, the countries comprising the world socialist system—its members, associate members and "observer" status members—could depend on the USSR for military protection; therefore, no external power must attempt to destabilise them. Secondly, the vanguard of the third world or nonaligned movement now consisted of the socialist states like Vietnam and Cuba, and states with socialist orientation such as Ethiopia, Angola, Yemen and Afghanistan. This vanguard pushed the moderate middle-of-the-road nations like India somewhat to the background and spearheaded the struggle to make nonalignment a "natural ally" of the world socialist system. These vanguard states, each one of which had a security-oriented friendship treaty with the USSR, could also depend on Moscow for protection from external threat.

In Soviet perception, the Afghan operations were entirely defensive; their objective was to secure a neighbouring friendly state and a Marxist revolution, as well as the sensitive southern flank of the Russian state from external intervention. At the same time, Moscow recognised the intermeshing of events in Iran and Afghanistan. The

Soviet pronouncements implied that just as the United States was trying to operate a comprehensive strategy for Iran, Afghanistan, the Persian Gulf and Pakistan with a view to regain strategic dominance of the region, so was the USSR operating a comprehensive strategy for the entire area with a view to reducing American influence, enhance Moscow's own, and turn the regional balance of power in favour of the socialist system.

The strategic designs of the two adversary superpowers engaged in one of the most important strategic regions of the world, creating a drama of global reach and consequence. This seminal engagement would now interact with the drift and scale of Middle Eastern tensions and conflicts, mingle with the strategic rivalries and animosities deeply rooted in the soil of the subcontinent, feed, and be fed by, the Sino-Soviet cold war. Would it lead to the first frontal collision between the superpowers, unleash a "limited nuclear war", or even World War III? Or would it lead tortuously and zigzaggedly to an understanding between the two global contenders on how to control third world conflicts and arrest any drift to global suicide?

The Soviet pronouncements seemed to reassure the world that while Moscow would stand firmly by the Marxist regime in Afghanistan, and withdraw its troops only on its own terms, it would not meet American venturism with its own venturism, but with strength, patience and peace offensives. The pronouncements made it amply clear that, in Soviet eyes, the United States was no longer the leader of the Western bloc. Detente had delinked Western Europe from the United States to a large extent. To a lesser extent, detente had also split the American foreign policy elite. The cold war elements appeared to dominate the decision-making process in a volatile presidential election year. But the election fevers would subside, and Washington would return, reluctant but wiser, to the battered road to strategic arms control, as it did in 1977. More, the Soviets seemed to be confident that the United States would get coiled in the contradictions between confronting and containing the USSR and keeping alive the SALT process, between fueling and massive armament programme and dealing with recurring economic crises with their inevitable social and political consequences.

Afghanistan, then, signalled a new phase in the dynamic relationship between the USSR and the US that has dominated world politics since 1945. The "Afghan Syndrome" heralded the self-assertion of the USSR as a *global* superpower. Suddenly, the relationship burst the framework of strategic parity the SALT process was painstakingly trying to put together as the infrastructure of detente or peaceful coexistence. The Soviets demanded global parity, and found the United States in no mood to concede.

Inevitably, then, Afghanistan brought the world on the threshold of a new US-Soviet confrontation. It was not a repeat of the confrontation that triggered the cold war in the late forties. The "total circumstances" which Brezhnev claimed the politbureau had taken fully into account before ordering Soviet troops into Afghanistan, were different from those Stalin had to face in the last five years of his life. The new confrontation found both adversaries stronger *and* weaker than they had been in the late forties and fifties. Its outcome was therefore less predictable than that of the first confrontation.

CHAPTER TWO

Afghanistan: Friend or Victim?

> Modern Afghanistan is indeed a purely accidental geographic unit, which has been carved out of the heart of Central Asia by the sword of conquerors or the genius of individual statesmen. —Lord Curzon, quoted in C. Collin Davies, *The Problem of the North-West Frontier: 1890-1908*, Cambridge, 1932, p. 153.

The generation of men and women that has grown up in the world since World War II has little knowledge of how Afghanistan dominated relations between two empires—the British in the south and the Russian in the north—for well over a hundred years spanning three centuries. Geography placed the central Asian kingdom precariously between the competition and conflicts of two swelling imperial themes. Associated with the modern history of Afghanistan are the names of the great empire builders of Britain—Gladstone and Disraeli, Dufferin, Landsdowne, Lytton, Ripon, Kitchner, Grey, Curzon and Churchill. During this entire period, the fate of Afghanistan was closely linked with the fate of Iran. The course of Russo-British rivalry for Afghanistan was greatly influenced by the drift and scale of war-and-peace diplomacy of the European powers. British power and might was cushioned on the empire, of which India was not only the largest and most precious jewel but also the strategic heart. Britannia ruled the seas, but the Indian empire was most vulnerable from the historical invasion routes in the northwest; athwart these routes lay Afghanistan. The British were determined to secure these invasion routes from Russia; they were also anxious to avoid a war with the Czar over Afghanistan. The two imperial powers never did actually collide over Afghanistan. However, a clash did occur between Afghans and Russians in March 1885 at Pul-i-Khatun, near Panjdeh, along the Afghan frontier. The Afghan force had to retire with heavy losses, leaving Panjdeh to the Russians. A British-Indian force, stationed nearby, did not stir; did, in fact, retreat to a safer spot.

Gladstone, who was Prime Minister, spat fire, obtained from a roused House of Commons a vote of credit of six and a half million pounds to meet the situation created by the Russian victory at Panjdeh. The British public cried out for war. The Russian public matched the bellicosity of the British. However, diplomatic negotiations led to the final establishment of the northwestern frontier of Afghanistan. The British made a major concession; the Russian frontier now extended to the very threshold of Afghanistan. The Afghan ruler approved of the transaction; but the Afghans began to nurse serious doubts if they could ever expect Britain to defend Afghanistan in a war with Russia. To live in peace with Russia became since then a cardinal principle of Afghanistan's external relations.[1]

Afghanistan's survival as an independent nation is to be ascribed more to the dynamics of the competing British and Russian imperialisms than to the diplomatic or political skills of its rulers. Among the British empire builders, at least two, Curzon and Churchill, wanted at one time or another to annex Afghanistan to the Indian empire. More than 100 years ago, in the seventies of the last century, the Russians wanted Britain to concede that Afghanistan was a buffer state between the two empires. The British refused. The term "buffer state" did not enter the vocabulary of protracted Anglo-Russian diplomatic negotiations, though other concepts like "neutral zone" and "neutral territory" did. In the agreement of 1873, Afghanistan was not recognised as a buffer state because Russia conceded that it was beyond its sphere of influence. Even in the convention of 1907, which came into force without the formal consent of the ruler of Afghanistan, and which generated Afghan fears that the two imperial powers might one day partition the country between themselves, Afghanistan was not recognised as a buffer state. It retained its "independence" within the British sphere of imperial influence; Britain promised not to interfere in its internal affairs, nor to tamper with its territorial integrity; Russia was given the right only to have "local contacts" with Afghans across the border; for substantial business with Afghanistan, the Czar had to use the good offices of Great Britain.[2]

Afghanistan succeeded to some extent to ease out of the British sphere of influence only after World War I. The process began with the coming of Amanullah to the throne in Kabul, with his declaration that Afghanistan was no one's puppet, but a fully independent, sovereign state. His demand that this status of Afghanistan be formally recognised by the British government and the Viceroy of India was rejected by both. But support came immediately from a newly-born state: the Soviet Union. Lenin recognised Afghanistan as a sovereign independent state and received a friendly communication from Amanullah. In less than a month, the British declared their third war against Afghanistan. Nearly 350,000 British troops, equipped with aircraft, heavy artillery and armoured cars, were opposed by a rabble of 50,000 Afghan soldiers. Even then victory eluded the British. The shortest of the three Anglo-Afghan wars did not last more than 30 days. The armistice signed on June 3 led to a peace treaty on August 8, but in neither did the British government formally recognise Afghanistan as a sovereign independent state. Afghanistan, however, signed a treaty of friendship with the Soviet Union on 28 February 1921. Lenin, in a letter to Amanullah, observed that the treaty gave "formal consolidation to the friendship and mutual sympathy between Afghanistan and Russia which have grown and strengthened in the first past two years." Both countries, Lenin added, "prize their independence; they want independence and freedom for themselves and for all the nations of the East. . . . There are no issues between Afghanistan and Russia likely to lead to differences, or even cast a shadow on Russo-Afghan friendship."[3] Following this agreement, Afghanistan concluded treaties with Turkey, Iran, France and Italy. These treaties led at last to an Anglo-Afghan treaty in which Britain renounced control of Kabul's external relations.

This brief outline of Afghanistan's career as a nation and a country is of some relevance to the events of 1979-80. Whether or not history actually repeats itself, the human mind sees the present with lenses borrowed from the past, indeed summons capsuled myths and memories of the past to simplify the confusions of the present. This it did about Afghanistan in 1980 also. Statesmen and analysts, confronted with the Soviet military intervention in Afghanistan, harked back to the reconstructed accounts of the 19th century cleavages and collisions to find out how these were handled by diplomacy in an era when war was the conduct of diplomacy by other means. The captive spell of the past often blurred the vastly different realities of the present. British policy towards Afghanistan had been shaped on the twin anvil of the southward drive of Russian empire and the turbulent character of the Afghan tribesmen. Russophobia dominated the psyche of the India-based knights of the British empire. Because both Britain and Russia sought to advance their respective influence, if not control, over Iran and Afghanistan, each tried to follow a comprehensive foreign policy strategy for the whole southwestern region of Asia. In 1979-80 also, this region, its strategic importance enhanced a hundredfold in a world vastly different from what it used to be when Britannia ruled the waves, turned into a flashpoint of the cleavages and conflicts of two global powers, leaders of two rival world systems. The USSR, however, was seen by statesmen and analysts as the 1980 avatar of the 19th century Russia pushing inexorably towards the warm waters of the Persian Gulf. And the Afghan of the last decades of the 20th century was seen as a double of the 19th century tribal whom even the might of the British could not break.

The labelling of Afghanistan as a "buffer" state was another dive into the past to reclaim a conceptual tool that had served the British well although it had no legal sanction. Nevertheless, the Soviets were accused in 1980 of having violated a buffer state with their military intervention.

Soviet influence in Afghanistan began in 1919 when Lenin, in a prompt response to Amanullah's request for arms, made his famous pronouncement: "The Workers' and Peasants' Government is inclined to grant such assistance on the widest scale to the Afghan nation, and, what is more, to repair the injustice done by the former government of the Russian Czars by adjusting the Soviet-Afghan frontier so as to add to the territory of Afghanistan at the expense of Russia." Lenin, then, chose Afghanistan to be one of the first countries to project his unique contribution to Marxist strategic thinking on world politics: the "natural ally" relationship between the Bolshevik revolution and the national liberation movement in the colonial and semicolonial countries of the East. Over time, the ideological thrust of Leninism in Afghanistan flowed into the real political imperatives of Soviet foreign policy. Stalin, in his secret negotiations with Hitler before the German invasion of the Soviet Union, asked for an agreement which would recognise "the area south of Batum and Baku in the general direction of the Persian Gulf" as "the focal point of the aspirations of the Soviet Union." Stalin's successors adopted Afghanistan, in the words of a knowledgeable American scholar, as a sort of "economic Korea" —"a testing ground on which to determine whether or not simple economic penetration could enable the USSR to shape the recipient nations' social and political institutions, and on which to gauge the economic responses of the West—particularly in the United States— just as Korea had constituted an arena for testing the military responses and perseverance of the US and its allies."[4] Since 1953, when

Lt-General Mohammed Daoud Khan seized power in Kabul in a bloodless coup and became Prime Minister, the Soviets have poured into Afghanistan more economic and military aid than any other external power. Afghanistan also received economic assistance from the United States. For well over a decade great power competition in that country evolved into de facto, if not de jure, cooperation—the United States helped the Afghans to build roads from south to north and the USSR from north to south.

Soviet aid did help in Afghanistan's economic development but could not bring about its political evolution from feudal monarchy to a representative democratic polity. In fact, the political history of Afghanistan since the thirties, particularly since the fifties, is one of an unequal struggle between the concentrated power of the monarchy and a group of urban intellectuals pressing for representative rule. In the urban areas, a Leftist movement sprouted gingerly over the years and acquired a Marxist orientation, but it received little patronage or encouragement from the Soviet Union. The two prominent Marxist groups to emerge in the political life of Afghanistan were the Khalq (Masses) and Parcham (Flag), so called after the publications they spoused during the 1930s. The leader of the Khalq faction was Nur Mohammed Taraki, and of the Parcham faction, Babrak Karmal. Both opposed the rule of Daoud, the Khalq more trenchantly than the Parcham. The two factions united in July 1977 to form the People's Democratic Party of Afghanistan (PDPA). Before they could build their organisation as a strong rallying point of the anti-monarchy urban educated class in Afghanistan, even before they could come to grip with the rush of political change, the coalition found itself catapulted to power as a result of the "revolution" or Leftist coup d'etat of 27 April 1978.[5]

It was brought about by a series of accidents and took almost everyone by surprise including the Soviet government. Mohammed Daoud had used the Parcham faction for several years to give his regime a popular flavour. In the seventies, however, he was working with the late Shah Mohammed Reza Pahlavi of Iran and the government of Pakistan to diminish Afghanistan's dependencies on the Soviet Union. In 1977-78, Mohammed Daoud turned against the Afghan Left and imprisoned several hundred Leftists including some of the Khalq and Parcham leaders. The events which precipitated the Leftist takeover began with bloodshed on April 27 after Mir Akbar Khyber, a popular Leftist theoretician, was found murdered in Kabul.

On 19 April, 15,000 mourners paraded the streets and marched past the American embassy shouting anti-US slogans. Alarmed, the government of Mohammed Daoud arrested the ranking leaders of the Left. But Hafizullah Amin, "strongman" of the Khalq, contacted military cadres sympathetic to the Left, among whom he had already built a nucleus of support. A plan was hurriedly drawn up. The coup or the revolution was launched on the morning of April 27 as Daoud's cabinet assembled to consider the fate of the arrested leaders. In 24 hours the Republic of Afghanistan that Daoud had declared in 1973 was shattered; he and some 30 members of his family were killed; and the Democratic Republic of Afghanistan (DRA) was proclaimed with Nur Mohammed Taraki as Chairman of the Afghan Revolutionary Council and Prime Minister. The Soviet Union welcomed the new government and was the first to offer it diplomatic recognition, but there is little evidence that it had any hand in the dramatic change.

Leaders of the new regime insisted that they were not communists and that their policies would be based on Afghan nationalism, respect for Islam, economic and social justice, nonalignment in foreign affairs and respect for all international agreements signed by the previous governments. The Revolutionary Council began to govern with decrees and regulations. It appointed a 21-member cabinet of relatively young people,[6] conferred equal rights on women, regularised dowry and marriage expenses, forbade forced marriages, introduced land reforms which laid stress on private ownership of land though within established limits, and abolished usury in the countryside. The land reforms avoided rural collectivisation. The applied Marxism of the new Afghan regime "appeared to be a mixture of idealist Maoist localisation of power and of the Yugoslav style individual ownership within cooperatives."[7] Even these moderately radical measures alienated the powerful mullahs of Afghanistan, created a sizeable armed insurgency against the regime and led to the exodus of several hundred thousand Afghans to Pakistan.

The regime might have been able to face the mullahs' challenge if the Marxist coalition did not split within months of the takeover. Before the DRA regime could consolidate itself, the Khalq and the Parcham factions fell out and Babrak Karmal, together with most other non-Khalq members of the cabinet and the Revolutionary Council, were "exiled" to ambassadorships. Karmal himself was appointed ambassador to Czechoslovakia; he soon left his post but still remained in exile in Eastern Europe until December 1979. The expulsion of the Parcham faction from the Revolutionary Council and the cabinet did not bring about a cohesive Khalq regime, but led to a rapidly escalating power struggle between Taraki and Amin. On 28 March 1979, Hafizullah Amin became Prime Minister as well as foreign minister in a new 18-man cabinet announced by Taraki who was still president of the Revolutionary Council, secretary-general of the PDPA and supreme commander of the armed forces. Amin adopted a hardline policy towards the mullahs alienating them still further, and with them the bulk of Afghanistan's rural population. In September 1979 the conflict between Taraki and Amin exploded. Each tried to eliminate the other. Amin emerged victorious. It was announced that Taraki had resigned because of ill health (and some weeks later that he had died of an "incurable illness"). Amin took over as chairman of the Revolutionary Council and of the Supreme Defence Council. By November Amin purged almost all the prominent leaders of the original April 1978 takeover and concentrated all levers of powers in his own hands and in the hands of a small group of people carefully selected by himself. "In intellect, ability and determination the extrovert Amin was undoubtedly a more formidable figure than the rather naive Taraki. But his uncompromising pursuit of the party's unpopular policies made his regime dependent on ruthless coercion and awakened opposition more widespread than that which had already developed against the Taraki regime."[8]

After the April 1978 revolution Soviet-Afghan relations became closer than ever before. The Soviet leadership made a departure from past practice in promptly recognising the PDPA regime as a revolutionary one, worthy of ideological adoption. The USSR and Afghanistan signed a number of treaties including a treaty of friendship and goodneighbourliness in December 1978. The number of Soviet civil and military advisers increased from about 3,000 before the revolution to about 4,500 in early 1979. Large sums were made available for economic development, new military equipment was supplied including T-62 tanks, MiG-21 fighters and Mi-24 helicopter gunships. Unconfirmed reports said that Soviet pilots were flying combat missions and military advisers were employed at company level.

It appears that from the spring of 1979, that is, as soon as the Marxist coalition in Afghanistan began to crack and an intense power struggle developed in the Revolutionary Council, the Soviet government began to press for a more cautious and less radical socio-economic programme and a policy of conciliation of the opposition and formation of a broadbased government. The Soviet Union also demanded a greater say in the formulation of policies and programmes of the Afghan government in return for economic and military support. Probably under Russian pressure, the Afghan Revolutionary Council abandoned in July 1979 the land reforms programme and declared itself in favour of a more broadly-based government. Amin opposed the retreat. His victory over Taraki strained relations between the PDPA regime and Moscow. According to the London-based International Institute of Strategic Studies, "Faced with an apparent choice between withdrawing from Afghanistan, with an inevitable loss of prestige, and supporting a man whose policies she believed to be unworkable, the USSR maintained her support but at the same time prepared to overthrow Amin and to install a more cooperative leadership in Kabul."[9] A steady buildup of Soviet presence in Afghanistan was visible since the autumn of 1979. It must have taken the Soviets "at least four months" to plan the military intervention that occurred late December,[10] which means that they were getting ready to intervene immediately after Amin removed Taraki from the leadership of the Revolutionary Council and PDPA government, and placed himself in the driver's seat. On the night of December 27, all telephone connections went dead in Kabul after an explosion at the central telecommunication station. This was the signal of the start of the Soviet military operation. Soviet troops took over the radio and television station, the presidential palace and the Darulaman palace where Amin had taken up residence only a few days before. Whatever resistance Afghan troops offered was quickly put down. Simultaneously, Soviet troops poured from across the border at three points, heading for Kabul in the centre of the country, and then fanning out to the Pakistan border and to Herat in the northwest. On December 28, Kabul radio broadcast a speech by Babrak Karmal announcing that Amin had been deposed and that he had taken over as Prime Minister. Karmal, however, was seen in Kabul only on the night of January 1 when he addressed the nation on television. By January 5, there were at least 50,000 heavily armed Soviet troops in Afghanistan maintaining control over the main roads and the main cities. Most of them were reservists recently called up from the Turkmenistan, Uzbekistan and other border republics; many of them spoke the same languages as the Afghans. By the end of the month, the Soviets had 70,000 to 80,000 combat troops deployed in Afghanistan. There were six divisions of them—three in the west, near the Iranian border, and three facing Pakistan in the north and east, with elements in Kandahar and in Kabul. By early February, the Afghan army was reduced to less than half of its original strength by defection and desertion. With the exception of the air force, what was left could no longer be regarded as an effective fighting force. The survival of the Marxist regime as well as Afghanistan's security from external attack became the sole responsibility of the Soviet Union.[11]

Soviet Version

The Soviets gave a somewhat different version of the turn of events in Afghanistan since the April 1978 revolution. The following paragraphs from a journalistic report printed in the June 1980 issue of *International Affairs* are worth quoting for both what it said happened in Afghanistan and what it said did not happen. Readers should note that this authoritative Soviet version did not accuse Hafizullah Amin of directly plotting with foreign powers to throw Soviet advisers out of Afghanistan as Anwar Sadat of Egypt did in 1976. With the April revolution (the report by A. Demchenko said):

> Afghanistan entered a period of change it had never known before. A radical agrarian reform was proclaimed to do away with the domination of landowners in the countryside. A campaign was launched against illiteracy: in five years' time all Afghans would be able to read and write. Plans for industrial and transport development were expanded and a decree was approved on women's emancipation. The implementation of these reforms was boosted by the invigoration of political and social activities. The PDPA increased its ranks, its organisations were founded in all 28 provinces and in a number of big enterprises and in higher educational establishments. Women's and youth leagues were formed, the trade unions once again legalised, were strengthened and new newspapers and magazines began to come out. However, a few months after the Revolution difficulties arose in governing the country. It became obvious that several reforms (including the agrarian changes) had been premature and that most of the people were

not ready for them. Pressure and administrative injunction had a negative effect on the country, stepping up to a large extent the opposition to the democratic regime, especially on the part of the clergy, village and tribal chiefs who had been apprehensive about many of the revolutionary changes. The situation was further exacerbated in September 1979 when Amin virtually instigated a state coup. On his direct orders, Taraki, the DRA's first President, was removed from all his posts and later killed.

Amin's regime unleashed a massive campaign of repressions, chiefly against the intelligentsia and the clergy. Reforms were essentially replaced by revolutionary verbiage. Even the anti-illiteracy campaign was cut short. Surrounding himself with a clique of loyal and ruthless followers, wielding specious slogans, Amin discredited progressive ideas and undermined the people's hopes for the future, thereby playing into the hands of the imperialists and the Afghan reactionaries.

Documents that have become accessible show the huge scope of foreign interference in Afghan affairs. Saboteurs, arms and subversive literature were smuggled into the country from China and Pakistan. The imperialists and their henchmen actually unleashed an undeclared war against revolutionary Afghanistan.

With the situation inside the country and on its borders taking a sharp turn for the worse, the opposition to Amin from among the progressive PDPA elements rallied its forces. On December 27, 1979, Amin's regime was deposed. Babrak Karmal became head of the Revolutionary Council and the Afghan government. In his first public address, he said that the country's new leadership "will continue to develop the cause of the great April Revolution" and rectify past miscalculations. During this change of power a limited contingent of Soviet armed forces was brought into Afghanistan at the request of the Afghan leadership. Imperialist, especially US, propaganda immediately raised a hulla-balloo around the matter, presenting it as nothing less than "Soviet invasion" of the DRA. It goes without saying that Washington and other Western capitals are well aware that there has been no "intervention" in Afghanistan as such. Its leadership had applied to the Soviet government for military aid under the Soviet-Afghan Treaty of Friendship, Good-Neighbourliness and Cooperation signed in December 1978. In view of the growing foreign imperialist intervention threatening Afghanistan's independence, the request had been repeated several times.[12]

INDIAN REPORTS

Under Babrak Karmal's leadership, the politbureau of the PDPA was reconstituted with seven members, all of whom held ranking positions either in the party or in the cabinet after the April revolution, but had been purged by Amin. Most of the 57 members of the reconstituted Revolutionary Council and all the 36 members of the PDPA central committee also claimed impeccable revolutionary credentials. Both the Revolutionary Council and the cabinet included some non-party members—a gesture to broadbase the regime. The new government moved quickly to contribute a "broad national front comprising different segments of the population." It repeatedly proclaimed its intention to respect Islam and the mullahs and promised smooth relations between the regime and the clergy.*

In January-February 1980, two Indian journalists visited Afghanistan to have a close look at the situation there. Their reports were more or less identical. Kuldip Nayar, of the *Indian Express*,[13] found Karmal's stock with the people to be very low—his government was taken as "Moscow's instrument" and he was himself referred to as *watan farosh*, one who sells his country. "It is openly said that the government would fall within a few minutes if it were not for the presence of Russian soldiers," Nayar reported. J.D. Singh, of the *Times of India*,[14] noticed a decline in the popular base of Babrak Karmal who used to be more popular with the communist rank and file than Amin. Singh reported that Karmal had restored the old coalition, giving his own Parcham group 60 per cent and the *Khalq* group 40 per cent of the ministerial offices. Karmal initiated efforts to broaden the popular base of the DPDA, and might have done better if he were not looked upon by his people as a "Soviet puppet." The government made it clear on the one hand that the threat of external aggression against Afghanistan had increased and therefore Soviet troops would continue to be there as long as necessary; on the other hand, it tried to persuade the outside world that Russians did not interfere with the work of the government. The Afghan minister for information and culture, Abdul Majid Sarbuland, for example,

---

*For the regime's political and economic actions, see Chapter Five.

told reporters early February that there were only four Soviet advisers in his ministry and "none of them has a hand in policy-making."

Kuldip Nayar found every Afghan airport to be under Russian control. So was each of the 28 provincial capitals. The Russians manned the two main highways, guarded all key buildings in cities. The 10 divisions of the Afghan army was disarmed immediately after the installation of the new regime; nearly one half of them had been rearmed after scrutinising the credentials of the soldiers. Moscow had plans to modernise this force, equipping it with the latest weapons. "Every ministry," Nayar added, "has a set of Soviet advisers. The ministry of interior has the maximum number; they are said to be engaged in reorganising the police and intelligence services."

J.D. Singh saw "not a single Soviet soldier" at the Kabul airport, only a few Russian helicopters and military trucks. Nor did he find any Russian soldier in the city bazars. "Generally speaking, the Soviets kept a low profile in Kabul and the soldiers one met face to face later were never rude. In the light of stories of looting, arson and rape one had heard about occupation forces in other parts of the world, the Soviets were a well-behaved lot—perhaps for fear of summary execution or a lifelong spell in Siberia."[15]

The Afghan Rebels

All revolutions produce its rebels and its refugees, and the Afghan revolution was no exception. Indeed, as Soviet analysts freely acknowledged, the "miscalculations" and "excesses" of Hafizullah Amin swelled the ranks of the opponents of the Marxist regime. At the time of the Soviet military intervention, about 400,000 Afghan refugees had crossed over to Pakistan, and nearly one-half of them were reportedly armed. Reports said that strong armed insurgency against the regime raged in 14 of the 28 provinces, and that outside the main cities and towns, the writ of the regime was shallow. As noted, Soviet troops fanned out to the threatened provinces immediately after December 27, and by January 5, brought the main insurgencies under temporary control.

The Afghan refugees inevitably created a complex political problem and an abrasive international controversy. The Soviets accused Pakistan, China, the United States, Iran and Egypt of aiding and abetting the insurgents; to Moscow, this was nothing short of a menacing foreign intervention in Afghan affairs with the goal of drowning the fledgling Marxist regime in a sea of anger, hatred and blood. The Soviets as well as the Karmal regime in Kabul rejected the Pakistani claim that half-a-million (one million by June) Afghan refugees had assembled on Pakistani territory; according to Moscow, the great bulk of this humanity was the nomad tribes of Afghanistan (three million in number) who move freely across the border to graze their cattle. Moscow was convinced that the Afghan counterrevolutionaries were being fed arms and weapons by external powers, and this prevented Kabul from honourably rehabilitating those of the insurgents who might elect to return home and live as peaceful citizens.[16]

There was no doubt that the Afghan rebels did receive assistance from Pakistan, the United States, China, Iran and Egypt. Early January, *Counterspy*, an American journal, disclosed that the rebels were getting help from the CIA and China. "US intelligence agents are highly active in the Afghan-Pakistan border as a cover for the Drug Enforcement Agency and the US Asian Fund Organisation." A Chinese air force commander, it claimed, had visited the border in the spring of 1979 and camps to train Afghan rebels were set up in Xianjiang province adjacent to Afghanistan. The *Washington Post* reported on February 15 that the CIA had opened a secret supply line to funnel small arms and anti-tank weapons across the Pakistan border to the Afghan rebels. Confirming the report, US officials told the *New York Times* the next day that infantry weapons, largely of Soviet design, were being supplied to Afghan insurgents since mid-January. Reports that China and Iran supplied arms and weapons to the Afghan rebels were confirmed by West European military officials.[17]

According to Soviet sources, Chinese-backed Afghan rebels established themselves in May and June 1978, immediately after the Marxist takeover in Kabul, in Badakshan, a narrow sliver of territory separating the USSR from Pakistan. Chinese-run supply and training centres were set up in north Pakistan with one major base located in the Chitral region, 320 kms northeast of Kabul. Supplies bound for Afghan rebels came along the Karakoram highway which follows the Silk Road from Xianjiang to Islamabad over 4,200-metre high mountains. Pakistan opened at least 20 training centres in the Peshawar region south of the Khyber Pass. At these centres, Afghan rebels were trained in command and control techniques, in handling electronically controlled weapons, and in communications.[18] A Soviet delegate told a meeting of the UN Human Rights Commission in Geneva that the US and China had trained 15,000 Afghan "terrorists" at 30 special bases and 50 support bases in Afghanistan. "If there had been no outside interference in the internal affairs of Afghanistan, the Afghan government would not have had to ask the Soviet Union for assistance," he maintained.[19]

Even if the bulk of the military aid the Afghan rebels were getting came from the US and China, the Soviets fastened their *angst* on Pakistan whose rulers, Moscow's spokesmen repeatedly claimed, had turned Pakistan to an advance base for the operation of the Carter doctrine. The Soviet newsweekly, *New Times*, said early February that the leaders of Pakistan had assumed an unsavoury and dangerous role and denial of involvement in anti-Afghan activities by Pakistani spokesmen could not be taken seriously. "Any government bears responsibility for everything done in its territory. More so, when officers of Pakistan army, of which Gen. Zia is commander-in-chief, have been sent to the camps of anti-Afghan rebels. More so, when counterrevolutionaries using the banner of Islam as a cover-up, are allowed use of two big radio stations in Peshawar and Quetta and are given assistance in the preparation of anti-Afghan printed matter."[20]

In January-February, there was considerable speculation in the world press that Soviet troops operating in Afghanistan might enter Pakistan in "hot pursuit" of the Afghan rebels, and this might lead to engagements between Russian and Pakistani troops. The rebel factor received a big political boost when President Carter's national security assistant, Zbigniew K. Brzezinski, and the Chinese Foreign Minister, Huang Hua, visited Afghan refugee camps along the border and spoke in inflamatory language. The rebels were able to keep the flames of insurgency burning through the winter, spring and summer of 1980, making the Soviet military presence in Afghanistan expensive as well as bruising, and delaying stabilisation and legitimacy of the Marxist regime in Kabul. It became clear in the autumn that the USSR would have to live with the insurgency in Afghanistan for some more time. It also became clear that the rebels had lost their *political* future. World support for them was waning.[21]

The main weakness of the rebels lay in their disunity. Selig Harrison reported in the columns of the *New York Times* that there were between 40 and 160 different armed insurgent groups balkanised throughout Afghanistan.[22] "Too many rebel leaders envision themselves as Afghanistan's emerging Ayatollah, and they have been unwilling to allow the practical benefits of coordination to cloud their views." Insurgent disunity remained intact in spite of anti-Soviet demonstrations in Peshawar in late February. Pushtoon rebels lived up to their centuries-old tradition of fractiousness. "The most stubborn and cohesive rebel groups are operating in North and Central Afghanistan. By far the fiercest rebellion has taken place in the northern provinces of Takhar and Badakshan where ethnic Turkomans and Tajiks were on the verge of taking over provincial capitals before Soviet troops poured across the Oxus river." Harrison added that in terms of longevity and tenacity, the Hazari tribes of central Afghanistan were rated among the most coordinated and effective. The best known and most discredited of the insurgent groups were those with rear bases in Peshawar. Most of these groups wanted to turn Afghanistan into an orthodox Islamic state. The largest and most fundamentalist of them was Hezbe-i-Islami, the Islamic Party of Afghanistan. It was headed by a former engineering student at Kabul university named Gulsuddin Hekmatyar "whose piety is manifested in a facial expression that foreigners have never seen creased with a smile. His fighters have recently taken to carrying Super-8 movie cameras to battle to supply the world with visual evidence of their exploits. Back in Peshawar various committees turn out daily mimiographed communiques on 'battle reports' and disagreements with other rebel groups."

During the Islamic foreign ministers' conference in Islamabad in January, Salem Azzam, secretary-general of the Islamic Conference of Europe, flew into Peshawar and in 48 hours got the leaders of six groups to agree to unite under something called "The Islamic Alliance for the Liberation of Afghanistan." They were given until March 1 to turn verbal promises into concrete coordination—and promised millions of dollars in Islamic aid, if they succeeded. But even before their news conference at Flashmans Hotel in Rawalpindi was over, the leaders were disagreeing with one another. One of the six faction leaders was not even there. He sent a deputy, saying that he had more important things to do. At the May session of the Islamic conference in Islamabad, the "Alliance" was given participant status. But all attempts on the part of the rebel groups' international patrons to bring them together and set up an "Afghan government-in-exile" proved to be fruitless. Indeed the fragmentation of the rebels and their contention for the "laurels" and "rewards" of armed resistance to the Kabul regime made them increasingly vulnerable to Moscow's punishments and blandishments.

The rebels, however, were recognised as a political actor by the Islamic Conference. The three-member committee appointed at the second session to explore ways and means of a settlement of the Afghan question insisted that the rebels be recognised as a party to the crisis and therefore to its settlement, a demand which both Kabul and Moscow rejected outright. It became evident in the summer that the demand was losing its edge,[23] even though the insurgency within Afghanistan continued throughout 1980.

A Pakistani Parallel

There was a limit beyond which Pakistan could not back the demand, nor give active support to the Afghan rebels. The Afghan refugees are for Pakistan a potential problem of great magnitude. They are encamped in Pakistan's softest political terrain, where resentment against the military regime is deep-rooted and pervasive among the Baluchis and Pathans. The rulers of Pakistan had particular reason to be worried about the Baluchi nationalist leaders' linkages with the USSR; the Baluchis had fought a four-year-long bloody guerrilla warfare with the Pakistani army in the seventies, inflicting severe losses and themselves suffering heavily. They might take to arms once again, this time with Soviet-Afghan active assistance. The London correspondent of the *Hindustan Times* asked in early January a question which disturbed not only the rulers of Pakistan but also their international allies and friends. The question was framed thus: "Supposing, just supposing that the new, relatively flexible Afghan president, Babrak Karmal, is able, in due course, as the Islamic fundamentalist wave begins to wane, to divert the attention of these tribal elements, who are not political animals exactly as we might know the breed in India and elsewhere, but thrive on the right kind of slogans, to renewed demands for some kind of Pakhtoonistan, even as reports keep coming in of disaffection in Iranian as well as Pakistani Baluchistan?"[24]

The Baluchi problem took a somewhat menacing turn for the Pakistani rulers within 30 days of the Soviet military move into Afghanistan. *The Guardian,* of London, reported that hundreds of Baluchi guerrillas, trained and equipped in Afghanistan, had taken position to storm into Pakistan's western province of Baluchistan. They had crossed into Afghanistan in 1973-77 when the Pakistani army stamped out the Baluchi insurgency.[25]

For over a decade rulers of Pakistan and Iran have viewed with grave concern nationalist stirrings among the Baluchi population inhabiting a contiguous area spawning the two neighbouring countries. Some 60 per cent of the 2.3 million people who live in the Pakistani province of Baluchistan, are of Baluch origin. The Baluchis of Iran number 2.5 million. Baluchistan, a vast, scarcely populated desert region split between Afghanistan, Pakistan and Iran, can any time emerge as a geopolitical factor in Southwestern Asia if the Soviets decide to support the concept (and demand) of a sovereign Baluchi state. The late Mohammed Reza Pahlavi of Iran considered this to be a distinct possibility and publicly committed himself to come to the defence of Pakistan in the event of a Baluchi uprising. He did place helicopter gunships at the disposal of Prime Minister Zulfikar Ali Bhutto to put down the 1975-77 Baluchi insurgency.

Baluchistan is paradoxically a leftist stronghold though its political leaders are big landlords. The majority of leaders have been made pro-Soviet by the persistent refusal of the Pakistani rulers to satisfy their political aspirations. Younger Baluchi leaders have a Marxist orientation. One of the avowed Marxists is Akbar Khan Bukti, hereditary leader of the 100,000-strong Bukti tribe. It is a well organised group, staunchly pro-Soviet and most amenable to Soviet influence. Another is a 4,000-strong contingent of the Marri tribe that fled to Afghanistan during the 1973-77 rebellion. One Baluchi guerrilla leader was reported to have told *The Guardian* that they were convinced that the Pakistani army could not fight a second successful war against the Baluchi insurgents. "Fifty per cent of officers are engaged in administering martial law. The moment Zia goes to war, he will be toppled by other army officers, who want Mercedez cars, not tanks."[26]

Strong sentiments against the ruling junta also prevailed among the Pushtu-speaking Pathans of the Northwest Frontier Province of Pakistan. Their revered 90-year-old leader, Badshah Khan, widely respected in the subcontinent as the Frontier Gandhi, lived in Kabul and unequivocally welcomed the Soviet intervention. His son, Wali Khan, is a sworn enemy of the military regime headed by Gen. Zia. Reports said that Ajmal Khan, a former leader of the outlawed National Awami Party, had raised a militant guerrilla force with Pushtuns in Afghanistan and would be readily available for action against Pakistan[27] (see Chapter Five).

The Baluchi-Pakhtoon factor manipulated by the Soviets acted from the beginning of the Afghan crisis as an element restraining Pakistan as well as its allies, the United States and China, from using the Afghan insurgents more effectively or venturously in their geostrategic conflict with the USSR. What Washington and Peking feared most was a second dismemberment of Pakistan as a result of another national liberation war waged, with Soviet help, by another large deprived and suppressed nationality of that country. The *Washington Post* reported in February that Baluchi leaders treated with "deep distrust" the US move to arm Pakistan, and were determined to extract "a political and economic price if they were to support the military regime in Islamabad." If the price were not paid, the Baluchis might "take Soviet help in furthering long-suppressed goals of regional autonomy or independence." In that event, American arms flowing into Pakistan would wind up being used against the Baluchis. A concerted effort to arm Afghan rebels would probably entail a retaliatory Soviet "subversion campaign" in Baluchistan. "The US dilemma is compounded by widespread opposition to Pakistan's military ruler, generally regarded as the most unpopular leader in the country's 33-year history as an independent nation."[28]

The foregoing account suggests that the Soviet decision to intervene in Afghanistan was motivated primarily by the perilous situation in which the fledgling Marxist regime in Kabul found itself in December 1979. Under Hafizullah Amin the revolution was being polpotised—debauched into genocidal terror as in Kampuchea under Pol Pot. It was not only that the insurgency could not be put down without Soviet military help. Amin could not be removed and the revolution saved without Soviet troops directly backing a coup by Babrak Karmal. The CPSU politbureau, then, resolved to rescue a fraternal regime outside the East European block, but still adjacent to the Soviet border.

In executing this resolve, the politbureau certainly took into account the overall strategic scenario existing in southwestern Asia including the Persian Gulf. The Soviets knew that the intervention in Afghanistan would act as a catalyst and produce far-reaching chain reactions; that its impact on Pakistan and Iran would be profound. The politbureau planted the flag of Soviet power in one of the most unstable geostrategic areas on the planet, releasing chemistries of corrosive change, the end result of which would be visible only at a remove of time.

CHAPTER THREE

The Theory of Linkage

> Whose large style
> Agrees not with the leanness of his purse.
> *King Henry VI*, Part II, 1, i, 112

Was the Soviet intervention in Afghanistan *sui generis*—a class by itself—or was it a response to a series of provocations by the United States? This was probably the most searing question raised by the Soviet action; from answers to it stemmed the various actors' response to the intervention. We have seen how answers differed not only from nation to nation but also within the various nations. The Soviet Union, of course, stuck stubbornly to its claim that it had merely responded to a series of provocations from the United States affecting the entire spectrum of superpower relationship, and, more specifically, to US, Pakistani and Chinese intervention against the Afghan revolution. At the other end, President Carter held on to his "quantum jump" theory, labelling the Afghan intervention as a *new* Soviet offensive to threaten the jugular of the western world. The majority of Americans shared Carter's view, but a strong dissident minority came from all walks of life—government, the mass media, the universities, business, even the military. West European governments were torn between rejecting the Soviet explanation of the intervention and accepting the Carter administration's interpretation of it; on the whole, they struck a middle or "nonaligned" posture, indicating that they were less than certain about what it really meant. In India, Indira Gandhi believed that the Soviet explanation was valid, but it did not justify a prolonged Russian military presence in Afghanistan. Many third world nations shared the Carter administration's view. Some did not. The third world elites too were similarly split.

Clearly, nations saw Soviet global power differently. They also reacted differently to a dramatic assertion of that power.

Indeed for both Washington and Moscow, the Afghan crisis was the culmination of a series of provocations slugged by one to the other over a period of four to five years. For the United States, Afghanistan was a daring climax of Soviet military intervention through proxy powers in third world conflicts through the seventies, a direct assault on the global balance of power. For the Soviets, the US response to their perfectly legitimate and entirely defensive action in Afghanistan was the culmination of a series of invasions against detente, noisy herald of an off-season cold war.

What were the provocations from the one that so burnt the other? The Soviet provocation was two-fold. First, vigorously outspending the United States over a period of 15 years—when America was consumed by the wasting war in Vietnam—the USSR caught up with, perhaps even edged ahead of, its adversary in strategic nuclear power. Secondly, it also proclaimed its arrival on the world scene as a global power, with a seven-ocean blue-water navy, military capability to intervene in "local conflicts" far away from the borders of the USSR, and a demonstrated political will to use this capability as a selective tool of Soviet foreign policy. Under the impact of these two colossal events, the personality of the USSR as a world power profoundly changed. It posed an unprecedented challenge to the United States. As Henry Kissinger put it, "Little in our historical experience prepared us for dealing with an adversary of comparable strength on a permanent basis. We had never needed to confront nations sharply opposed to us for more than brief periods of great exertions."[1] For 20 years the United States had dealt the Soviet Union as the *junior* superpower. Even in 1967 Zbigniew Brzezinski could claim that the US "is today the only effective global military power in the world"; Moscow had indeed the nuclear deterrent, but it was "insufficient to make the Soviet Union a global power." Faced with a showdown, the Soviets "didn't dare to respond even in an area of its regional predominance—in Berlin. It has no military capacity to fight in Cuba, or in Vietnam, or to protect its interests in the Congo."[2]

This great global preeminence of the United States was stolen by the Soviet Union in the decade of the seventies. In jeopardy were the worldwide "security perimeters" erected by the United States since the fifties, the strategic and military doctrines nourished in the snug security of superior power, the basic concepts and designs of US foreign policy.

To make it worse, the Soviet challenge hit a United States bruised and wounded by a series of economic, political and military blows, and caught in the coils of anguished social change that had a direct bearing on its role as a world power. For America, the decade of seventies was erected on the smouldering wreckage of the sixties threatening the loss of a way of life. The decade itself turned out to be more revolutionary than any since World War II, one of the bleakest for American foreign policy and one of the stormiest for its domestic politics. It went down in American history as a decade of run-away oil prices, Watergate, two bouts of double-digit inflation meshed with two major recessions in seven years, military defeat in Vietnam, and climaxing all these debacles, the fall of the Shah of Iran, Washington's most steadfast ally in the third world. Within the United States, the Me Decade (as the seventies were named by social critic Tom Wolfe) generated an obsessive self-regard and an aggressive narcissism. Most Americans—in the universities and the mass media, in government and business and in public life—came to believe that the old order was dying, if it had not already died. High unemployment, continuing fall in productivity, far-reaching demographic changes, decline of public regard for Authority as manifested in government, political institutions and political personalities combined together to crack the ramparts of optimism of the American capitalism, and set the limits of the American Dream. Thoughtful Americans gazed upon the planet with Splengerian gloom. The Club of Rome warned of a worldwide limit of growth. Economist Robert Heilbroner predicted disintegration of social systems in a world getting rapidly denuded of resource, Wasily Leontief, of Harvard, gave the industrialised world a life-lease of 20 years before its primary energy resources were exhausted. Patrick Moynihan pleaded that the US assume the role of leader of minority opposition in a disorderly and disobedient United Nations.

Soviet parity in strategic power, Soviet capability to wield a global foreign policy, and the binds on American power provided the backdrop to the efforts of Nixon and Kissinger to erect detente as the infrastructure of world politics in "an era of negotiations." For, as Kissinger observed, "The problem of our age is how to manage the emergence of the Soviet Union as a superpower," a problem that "will confront any American president no matter who he is."[3] As Kissinger was reflecting on global change in 1975, for the benefit of a group of journalists, before his eyes lay the demonstrated Soviet ability to help the MPLA in Angola with arms and weapons and a

Cuban expeditionary force win the civil war against forces backed by South Africa and gingerly by the United States and establish a pro-USSR regime in strategic southern Africa.

"We must draw the Soviet Union into relationships which are at once concrete and practical and we must create the maximum incentives for a moderate Soviet course," mused Kissinger, explaining the thrust and the objective of Nixon's foreign policy of coexistence. The US had no choice, for "with the Soviet Union as an emerging superpower, we are doomed to coexistence."[4] The changed power relationship called for a new balance of power. Kissinger was ready to concede a balance of strategic power based on parity; on the gospel of parity stood the slow-moving SALT process. But the real trouble lurked in the "gray areas" of the third world where the United States was neither in a position to preserve the western predominance (as it had all these years) nor in a mood to yield to Moscow's sustained pressures. To get over the problem, Kissinger crafted his "linkage" theory which, in one form or another, has remained till 1981 the principal US concept of a new relationship with the Soviet Union. Kissinger offered Moscow institutionalised strategic parity—the SALT treaties—but demanded Soviet "restraint" in the third world. The Basic Principles of US-Soviet relations, proclaimed at 1972 Moscow summit, laid down that the two powers "will always exercise restraint in their mutual relations" and agreed that "efforts (by one) to obtain unilateral advantages at the expense of the other, directly or indirectly, are inconsistent with the objectives of detente." Kissinger explained the linkage theory in some details in his memoirs:

> In our view, linkage existed in two forms: first, when a diplomat deliberately links two separate objectives in a negotiation, using one as leverage on the other; or by virtue of reality, because in an interdependent world the actions of a major power are inevitably related and have consequences beyond the issue or region immediately concerned. . . .
>
> The new administration sometimes resorted to linkage in the first sense. . . . But in the far more important sense, linkage was a reality, not a decision. Displays of American importence in one part of the world, such as Asia or Africa, would inevitably erode our credibility in other parts of the world, such as the Middle East . . . We saw linkage, in short, as synonymous with an overall strategic and geopolitical view.[5]

Jimmy Carter shied away from Kissinger's balance of power strategic thinking labelling it "too cynical" a game of power politics bereft of idealistic objectives. With Brzezinski its main architect, Carter's foreign policy started with allocating a relatively low priority to the relationship with the USSR; his first summit with Brezhnev came in the summer of 1979, nearly three years after his election. From the thirteenth floor of Columbia University's imposing International Affairs building, Brzezinski had sniped at Kissinger's balance-of-power strategy as yielding too much to the Soviets for too little, and had opposed the opening of a large portfolio of relationship in Moscow. As Carter's principal foreign policy strategist, he separated SALT from the rest of the superpower relationship. Brzezinski's position was that while the US would be willing to pursue the SALT process in its own interest, on the broad front of relations with the USSR it must remain assertively ready to compete, even confront; it would build cooperation only on the basis of demonstrated reciprocity. "We are willing to widen the scope of cooperation as far as the Soviet Union is prepared to go along with us, but we will compete as assertively as Soviet actions require."[6]

Brzezinski's policy of assertive competition was, in effect, a mirror US version of Soviet foreign policy strategic thinking. The Soviets rejected the linkage theory. In Soviet thinking, detente stemmed not from subjective sentiments of peace and goodwill among nations, but from the objective reality of decline of capitalist, and rise of socialist, power. The "battle of ideas" and the national liberation struggles could not be sacrificed at the altar of detente; if anything, detente accelerated both ideological polarisation and the struggles of the third world for political, economic and social emancipation.[7] Brzezinski took on the Soviets on their own strategic concept. His argument was that the Soviet acquisition of strategic parity made the SALT process imperative. But SALT could not be linked with anything else including trade, technology, credits; nor could there be an acceptance without challenge of expanded Soviet influence in the third world through the use of Moscow's global military power.[8]

The pursuit of the policy of assertive competition with the USSR, however, raised immediate problems for the United States. As the ruling elite got over the traumas of Vietnam and Watergate, it woke up to the strategic parity acquired by Moscow and the Soviet gains in Africa. It began to demand that the US fill the "strategic gap" and restore the lost favourable strategic balance of power. Thus, even within the indulgent boundaries of SALT-II, a vertical strategic arms race was triggered, and, once this happened, the SALT process itself got clogged. Doctrines of limited nuclear war were promoted in both camps, noisily in America, quietly in the Soviet Union. Assertive competition in the third world called for a new doctrine of direct US military involvement in third world conflicts, an adequate and effective interventionist force and capability to deploy it in distant areas with the utmost speed and adequate supplies. The size of the American navy had to be substantially increased. In short, there had to be a massive buildup in peacetime of American military strength, strategic, conventional and interventionist, for the first time since the sixties, in a very different world and with severe limitations on resource. To catch up with the rate of Soviet military spending—the Rand Corporation estimated that Moscow had outspent Washington on defence by $ 100 billion in the decade of the seventies—the US had to devote a much larger slice of the resource cake to military buildup and even then remain uncertain if it could get in step with its adversary. For, most American strategic analysts believed that the trends in the military balance were running against the United States. For instance, in strategic missiles, while the US had just begun in 1979 to deploy a new submarine-launched rocket, the Trident, Moscow was installing three new land-based systems and two new sea-launched weapons. Without SALT-II, Moscow would deploy five new types of land-based missiles during the eighties, and triple the number of warheads carried by its existing missile forces. In conventional arms, the Soviet Union was producing three times as many tanks as the US, almost twice as many combat aircraft and an equal number of naval vessels. In the past, Moscow's edge in conventional arms was believed to be offset by American weapons' superior performance. Most US experts expected this technological lead to narrow and, in some areas, vanish in the eighties. The *New York Times* concluded in January 1980 that the military balance between the US and the USSR "cannot probably be redressed before the end of the decade, if then." With America's present military-industrial capability, "seven to nine years must pass before a weapons system goes to the services. Also, it cannot be assumed that the Soviet Union will fail to maintain its advantages in such fields as theatre nuclear weapons."[9]

US foreign policy has to perform simultaneously on three fronts of assertive competition: confrontation with the USSR, regional conflicts in the third world, and global issues that include new economic forces and problems. The US has also to distinguish between its available power, which remains enormous, its usable power, which can be severely limited, and the *effective* power it can deploy in third world conflict situations.[10] The American predicament is all the greater in the eighties, because while its dependence on the raw materials and markets of the third world has increased enormously, its political clout has decreased sharply. From the economic standpoint, the era of self-sufficiency is now behind the United States. Apart from oil, there are 15 minerals and other raw materials which must be imported to keep the wheels of American industry moving in peace or war. West Asian oil, and African copper and chrome are militarily vital imports which could be denied the United States by leftward swings in producing countries. To maintain the flow of essential raw materials in times of war, or even in a clime of assertive competition with the USSR, calls for increasing allocations for more sea control ships and surveillance aircraft and for expanded research and development in anti-submarine warfare. In peace time, the United States exports 37 per cent of its manufactured goods to the third world, more than to *all* of Europe. Farm products of one-fourth of the entire acreage cultivated in the US are exported to the developing nations. About 1.2 million American jobs are directly dependent on exports to the third world.[11]

The clout once enjoyed by the United States in the third world symbolised America's status as the world's Number One power. The sharp decrease in that clout in the seventies makes the policy of assertive competition with the USSR difficult to operate. After World War II, the United States stood astride the rubble of the developed world. Now, 35 years later, it stands astride the poverty of the developing world, no longer recognised as *the* leader of the non-communist nations.

Profound changes have occurred in the developing societies in the last 20 years. The elites of these nations—royal families, landed aristocracies, urban middle classes reared in the image of the West, mandarin generals—to whom the colonial powers transferred power in the first round of decolonisation—have lost their power and ability to rule their increasingly turbulent peoples. Where they are still in power, they preside over shaky unstable regimes kept together by brute military force. The disorders wrought by revolutions, rebellions, protest movements on the one hand and by oppression, exploitation and injustice on the other create conditions in which assertive competition between the two superpowers can only act as a further destabilising factor.

Assertive competition with the Soviet Union in the third world is made difficult for the United States by American preference for 'moderate" elements which are often a euphimism for those who can be depended upon to preserve the status quo or permit only gradual incremental change. Also because of US identification with personalities rather than social trends and processes. Even the strongest personalities in feeble societies often turn out to be straw men. A major flaw in the strategy of assertive competition is the weak links in America's chain of friends and clients. As Stanley Hoffman observed in 1978: "Several on whom we could count either as allies against Soviet influence, or elements of stability in regional conflicts or supporters of some of our positions on global issues, are plagued by domestic insecurity, political strife, economic inefficiency, corruption or oppression. Our concern for order, plus our fear of losing our allies' confidence, should we fail to support a friend in trouble, have repeatedly led us to tie ourselves far too tightly to dubious regimes whose strength was only apparent."[12]

Brzezinski's assertive competition with the Soviet Union was at first based on Trilateralism—unity of purpose and resources among the advanced industrialised nations, the US, Western Europe and Japan. It became clear in the course of implementation of the policy of assertive competition that the US could not depend on its friends and allies not only in the third world but even in Western Europe. The West European governments had lost their appetite for cold war; Afghanistan showed that they were reluctant to back Carter's confrontation with Moscow over a piece of real estate not vital for their own wellbeing.

In the third world, the US had operated its containment strategy during the cold war through a chain of alliances. In the "era of negotiations" Nixon transferred to these allies the larger portion of the task of defending themselves. With the result that, as Paul N. Wranke pointed out in 1980, the US administration did not appear to have precise ideas of defence issues in the "gray areas." Since 1969 the basic measure of adequacy of US armed forces had been the ability to fight "$1\frac{1}{2}$ wars"—a "major" war in Europe and a "minor" war elsewhere at the same time. If in reality, the US lacked this capability, it did not matter very much because the Soviets lacked it even more. The situation in the eighties is entirely different. Authoritative American estimates of Moscow's military capability differ, but there is broad agreement among analysts that the Russians can, and are ready to, fight "1½ wars" simultaneously.[13] Since the late seventies, US analysts started debating which of the two superpowers had acquired a larger and more effective interventionist punch. A CIA secret study in 1977 concluded that though the Soviets had three times as many airborne troops as the United States, its paratroopers had only about half as much airlift capacity at comparable ranges. Moreover, the Soviet amphibian landing fleet was only a seventh as large as that of the US, and "unlike a US Marine Corps force, which is designed to sustain itself in combat for 30 to 45 days, a Soviet naval infantry force would have to be reinforced within four to five days." Moscow also had limited in-fight refueling capability, and their ability to sustain an intense, long-term conflict like Vietnam at long range remained untested.[14] The balance, however, seemed to be changing in Moscow's favour. *Newsweek* reported in June 1978 that the Soviets' arsenal gave them "a new ability to project their military power to distant corners of the globe, *as the US had done for decades.*"[15]

A year and a half later, in February 1980, the *New York Times* reported that the Soviets, without reducing the large force stationed in Eastern Europe, had tripled the size of their forces in the Far East. They were developing naval and other capabilities that should permit them to operate simultaneously in several parts of the world. The decision to face Soviet forces directly in the third world would call for a radical shift in US strategic policy, requiring a large increase in military capability and an equally large and durable political clout in key third world countries and regions. The *Times* analysis maintained that in the spring of 1980 it would take about a month for the US to move a fully equipped army division of 15,000 men to the Persian Gulf; with the Rapid Deployment Force in full shape, the US should be able to send 1,10,000 troops there in three weeks or less in the mid-eighties. The new ships, aircraft and military equipment for transporting the existing Marines and army forces would cost more than $ 10 billion. The RDF, however, would go only part of the way towards blocking Soviet military drives in the developing world. To keep a permanent naval presence in the Indian Ocean, the size of the American fleet would have to be increased. New commitments to defend third world allies would entail large increases in military and economic aid. Both had substantially decreased over the last 20 years —US security aid to allies by 20 per cent, while, among the 17 major industrialised nations, the US stood 13th in the percentage of GNP devoted to development assistance to third world nations.[16]

The Carter Administration, as noted, rejected Kissinger's linkage theory, but as soon as it began to move early 1978 towards sowing up the SALT-II treaty with Moscow, it made detente, or whatever was left of it, hostage to Soviet "conduct" in the third world. In March, the Carter Administration got a clear vision of the "scope" of the Soviet-Cuban involvement in Ethiopia, although the Russians had sent in the 1977 winter 200 transport planes and a fleet of ships to deliver 17,000 Cuban troops and $ 1 billion worth of arms to the Ethiopian revolutionary regime.[17] In April 1978 came the Marxist takeover in Afghanistan, amidst an ascending populist challenge to the rule of the Shah of Iran. In May, when rebels from Katanga "invaded" Zaire, the Carter Administration instantly perceived a Cuban-Soviet role behind the threat to the bankrupt regime of Mobutu, which was saved by paratroopers rushed by France. Both Cuba and the USSR strongly denied involvement in the Zaire civil war, but the denials were rejected by the US Government. The Carter Administration now put Moscow's "global challenge" on top of its foreign policy agenda. A *Washington Post* report, which an angry Jimmy Carter quickly denied but which the newspaper's executive editor insisted was correct, disclosed that the President had put the SALT negotiations on the back burner.[18] Brzezinski affirmed that the Soviets had violated "what was once called the code of detente"; differences between him and Secretary of State Cyrus Vance surfaced; the foreign policy making elite broke up into mutually opposing fragments, some calling for "bite and backbone" into foreign policy, others counselling patience and caution. Carter attended the NATO summit of June 1978 armed with a classified study predicting that, despite severe domestic problems, the Soviets would be able to sustain their military buildup at a constant rate in the coming decade, and urged the alliance leaders to accept a 15-year programme, the US contributing a little more than half the cost, designed to boost NATO's mobility and firepower and set up a new integrated communication and command system.[19]

It became clear that a SALT-II treaty, signed in 1978, would not pass the Senate that year. The US mass media wondered if a new cold war had not actually broken out. In any case, a new arms race between the two global powers received the green signal and the two were visibly moving towards a period of confrontation. The gravitational pull of confrontation was now unmistakably in the third world.

By the end of 1978, contours of the new confrontation revealed themselves in what Brzezinski called the "arc of crisis," which he defined as "a number of countries that have different internal causes of instability but cumulatively are facing widespread regional imbalances."[20] Henry Kissinger, returning to the diplomatic circuit from his book-writing chores, met with French President Valery Giscard d'Estaing, West German Chancellor Helmut Schmidt and British Prime Minister James Callaghan, and warned with apocalyptic finality: "Russia has engaged in a massive buildup of its military forces which, if projected into the 80s and unmatched by the West, is bound to create a grave political weakness. This, in turn, is bound to be translated into political benefits for the Soviets. Either the Soviet buildup has to be stopped or we have to build up our own armed forces."[21]

The hitherto clashing foreign policy tactical lines of Kissinger and Brzezinski seemed to have substantially narrowed. Both agreed that Moscow would "project" its military power in the arc of crisis. Both prescribed matching US military strength and will to use that strength to hold the Soviets at bay. But neither knew how to compensate for the weakness of local regimes friendly towards the US. Kissinger preferred to promote moderate forces in the third world avoiding radicalism of the left as well as the right. Brzezinski was willing to indulge even left radicalism if this would help the US dam Soviet influence. In Rhodesia (Zimbabwe, when it became a sovereign state in 1980), the Carter Administration abandoned the middle-of-the-road Kissinger plan and leaned towards the guerrillas fighting the white regime headed by Ian Smith. In Afghanistan, the Administration did not cut off economic aid from the Marxist regime till the kidnapping and killing of the US ambassador, Adolph Dubs, in February 1979. Even in Iran, the Carter Administration tried in the last weeks of 1978 to come to terms with the forces determined to topple the regime of Mohammad Reza Pahlavi.[22] British and American diplomats and military advisers cautioned the beleaguered Shah against crushing the aroused masses with military force. According to the Shah, the moderation they advised led to his capitulation.

The fall of the Shah ended the regime that used to protect the giant oil tankers passing through the Persian Gulf to the United States, Europe, Israel and Japan; kept vigil on "radical" Iraq, treaty bound with the USSR, as well as on local radicalism and Soviet communism. It also meant the loss of 5 per cent of America's total oil import— 920,000 bbls. a day from Iran alone. It meant the loss of $ 10 billion worth of arms and weapons sold to the Shah in less than a decade, and $ 2 billion worth of annual exports in food, construction materials and services. It meant the displacement of 45,000 Americans who had found lucrative military or civilian jobs in Iran in 1977-78 on behalf of the US government, or corporations or other private interests. It threatened $ 700 million of US investments. Above all, it eliminated the only strong and reliable "proxy" power the United States had been left with in the third world, and it jolted—more severely than Hanoi's victory in Vietnam—the credibility of the US as defender of personalities and regimes tied to it in alliances or treaties. In the wake of the anti-American Islamic upsurge in Iran, US relations with almost the entire Islamic world came under a menacing cloud, obliging Washington to reduce American presence in as many as 11 Muslim countries stretching from Turkey to Bangladesh.

"The biggest foreign policy debacle for the United States in a generation was the collapse of the government and of the Shah of Iran without support or even understanding by the US of what was involved," cried out Kissinger whose own contribution to the "loss" of Iran was not negligible.[23] The Carter administration's failure to protect the Shah ended the brief period of shared thinking by Kissinger and Brzezinski.

1979 turned out to be a probably the stormiest year for American foreign policy. Carter's popularity nose-dived with the fall of the Shah; his leadership qualities were seriously questioned both by Americans and West Europeans. He became all the more vulnerable because of the approaching presidential election year. A majority of the foreign policy decision making elite, within and outside the US government, came to the conclusion that the most effective answer to the twin challenge of Soviet global power and regime instabilities in the arc (or arcs) of crises was a rapid enhancement of America's own global military power. Kissinger observed in an interview with *Newsweek* that "basic Soviet strategy is to achieve a maximum degree of influence (in the Gulf and southern Africa) and the gradual reduction of our own world position." US inaction in one conflict area after another would shake world confidence in American leadership, and the Soviet Union "will certainly press to the limits of its geopolitical strength. That is its nature as a great power and as a Communist power,"[24]

The Carter Administration, as if to compensate for the "loss" of Iran, moved early 1979 to cement America's fledgling friendship with the People's Republic of China. The "triumphant" US tour of the PRC "strong man", Vice-Premier Deng Hsiaoping, conjured up prospects of a US-China-Japan alliance to contain Soviet power. In the arc of crisis, Brzezinski proposed the erection of a "protection umbrella" over North Africa, the Middle East and Southwest Asia, on the foundation of visible American military power and "signed understandings" with several governments, at the very least, with Egypt, Jordan and Israel, and an American military shield that would stretch as far west as Morocco.[25]

The United States immediately put into operation an ambitious programme of military buildup in the northwestern Indian Ocean, and, by the end of the year, when the youth cohort of Ayatollah Rohulla Khomeini seized the American embassy in Tehran and took some 60 hostages, protesting the admission of the deposed Shah to a New York hospital and demanding his extradition to Iran for "trial," the National Security Council started looking for military bases in the Middle East and the Indian Ocean littoral. Early 1979, persistent American prodding persuaded a majority of the NATO allies, including Western Germany, to agree, in principle, to deploy in the next few years some 600 Pershing and Cruise missiles in West Europe. These medium-range missiles could strike at any point of the European part of the USSR. NATO claimed that these missiles were designed to deter 200 Soviet Backfires already installed and aimed at Western Europe, but Moscow looked upon the decision as a serious provocation for a new round of nuclear arms race. In the autumn, the "little Cuban crisis" created by the US charge—later virtually withdrawn by Carter himself—that the Soviets had assembled a combat brigade in Cuba killed all chances of the SALT-II treaty receiving Senate advise and consent in 1979. The treaty had been concluded in the preceding summer at the Carter-Brezhnev summit in Vienna. Everyone knew that if it did not receive Senate approval before the year expired, it would get coiled with the overheated politics of American presidential election and might become its first casualty. In January 1980, Carter, realising that the Soviet intervention in Afghanistan had planted the kiss of death on the treaty, used it as a tool of reprisal, and asked the Senate to put the accord in deep freeze. With Carter's defeat in the presidential election died

SALT-II. The president-elect, Ronald Reagan, pledged to bury SALT-II but work for SALT-III—a treaty that would provide for "real nuclear disarmament."

During the "little Cuban crisis" Henry Kissinger put forward a tougher linkage theory than he had advanced when he was Secretary of State. Testifying before the Senate Foreign Relations Committee, he said that he would approve of the SALT-II treaty only if it formally committed the Soviets to behave in the third world. He recommended that

> The Senate should attach to its instrument of advise and consent an expression of the following principles:
> That the absence of political restraint (on the part of the Soviet Union) will seriously jeopardise continuation of the SALT process.
> That the Senate understands this to include Soviet supply or encouragement of intervention by proxy military forces; the use of Soviet forces on the territory of its allies such as Cuba to free Cuban forces to fight in Africa; the support, financing or encouragement by any member of the Warsaw Pact of groups and activities seeking to undermine governments friendly to the United States; or the exacerbation of regional conflicts.
> That the Administration be required to submit an annual report to the Senate on the degree to which the Soviet Union is living up to these criteria.
> That the Senate vote every two years its judgment whether the Soviet Union has lived up to these criteria. If the judgment is negative, the Senate should then vote whether whatever SALT negotiations are taking place should be continued.[26]

The contradiction between strategic parity and mutual assertive competition in vital third world regions strained the US concept of linkage. "Linkage" was motivated by the imperative to preserve Western, and therefore largely American, predominance in these regions. The threat to predominance came in 1979 not from the Soviet Union, but from the strident Islamic nationalism of the revolutionary regime in Iran which flourished on obstreperous anti-Americanism. Faced with the grim prospect of losing its entrenched leverage in the oil-rich Persian Gulf region, the United States embarked on a series of measures the Soviets regarded as provocative particularly because these measures were justified in part as steps to contain Soviet expansionism.

As soon as the hostage crisis broke out, American military planners went to work so that US military forces could respond swiftly to the President's order if he chose to intervene with force. The crisis made the Carter administration to seriously consider whether "spreading political turbulence and Soviet advance in the Persian Gulf require new American responsibility in the region."[27] Carter announced his plan to increase the 1981 military budget by more than 10 per cent and ordered the quick assembling of the Rapid Deployment Force for use in future crises in the developing world. Brzezinski explained around mid-December that RDF would be "designed to protect Western oil supplies in the Middle East" and "will give us the capacity to respond quickly, effectively and perhaps preemptively in those parts of the world where our vital interests might be engaged and where there are no permanently stationed American forces."[28] Illustrating probable contingencies, officials anticipated that Egypt might ask for an American presence if it were threatened with a Libyan invasion; sparsely populated Saudi Arabia might want help if it were invaded by "well-armed Iraqis" or "hordes of Iranians"; Thai rulers might seek an American presence if Vietnam forces moved beyond Cambodia.[29]

A secret Defence Department report on the military situation in the Persian Gulf region took measure of Soviet military power but skirted around the factor of regional political turbulence. It examined the capacity of the United States to respond to a number of potential contingencies including a Soviet attack on Iran, an attempt by Moscow to bomb major oil facilities in the Gulf and a Soviet submarine campaign against Western oil tankers in the Indian Ocean. Written before the Soviet intervention in Afghanistan, the report listed large forces available to the Kremlin in the Northern Caucasia, Trans-Caucasia and Turkistan military districts: 23 mechanised divisions consisting of about 200,000 men, 70 tactical fighters including 35 advance Fencer fighter-bombers, 193 long-range bombers, 103 naval bombers, and about 10 submarines. The Soviet forces located opposite Iran were not as well equipped as the Soviet units in Eastern Europe, but the Iranians would not be able to contribute effectively to their own defence. It would take the United States about 30 days to get 20,000 troops and four tactical fighter squadrons—about 72 aircraft—to Iran. The only opportunity for stopping a Soviet thrust would be to impede Soviet forces in the rugged terrain along the Soviet border and in the mountanis to the Southeast. "Unless the mountains can be exploited, or substantial assistance can be obtained from allies, the Soviets will surely prevail easily because of their large advantage over us in ground forces." Therefore, "to prevail in an Iranian scenario we might have to threaten or make use of tactical nuclear weapons." However, the US should be able to deal with other threats in the region particularly any attempt to disrupt oil shipments in tankers leaving the Gulf. "Until recently it was widely believed that the Soviets could close the sealanes rather easily through mining and through attacks by submarines and aircraft. However, our analysis indicates that Soviet submarines would have severe problems because of the long distances between the region and their home bases in the Northern Pacific and in the White Sea in the Western Soviet Union." The report estimated that in 30 days Soviet submarines and bombers could sink about 30 per cent of the 550 loaded oil tankers in the sealanes leading from the Gulf. But after a month or so the war would turn to US favour once the submarine warfare planes and fighter inceptors were flown quickly into the region.

In making this assessment, however, the report assumed that the United States could make full use of naval bases in such countries as Oman and Djibouti. It also said that it would be an ominous development if the Russians built major regional port facilities for resupplying submarines in the area. "Our ability to deny the Soviets a submarine resupply sanctuary near the Cape of Good Hope will depend on cooperation from South Africa."[30]

The Pentagon report reached three grave conclusions. First, the Persian Gulf was the most likely flash point for confrontation between the United States and the Soviet Union. Secondly, if Moscow took control of Gulf oil, it would "destroy NATO and the American-Japanese alliance without recourse to war by the Soviets." Thirdly, Moscow might be tempted to exploit the political turmoil in Iran to change the world balance of power.[31]

The Carter administration saw the Soviet intervention in Afghanistan in the context of the convulsive change in Iran, and came to the immediate conclusion that the intervention was a "strategic challenge," not a local one. Brzezinski's thesis separating the SALT process from assertive diplomacy in the third world now stood thoroughly discredited. Brzezinski himself made it clear in March 1980 that what the US was seeking was *more* than a strategic balance;

it sought to improve its position "in the *geostrategic* balance with the Soviet Union." Explaining how this could be done, he said, "We have to be able to project our power credibly, and to make it clear to all concerned that American power exists, that it could be used, and that our decision-makers will not shrink from using American power when either our vital interests or the vital interests of our friends are jeopardised."

In Brzezinski's perception, "historical turbulence" in an era of "genuinely profound change" and global dimensions of Soviet military power combined together to mount a new geostrategic challenge to the United States. The challenge called for a new military doctrine since the current US military doctrine was largely based on the thinking of the 1960s, "When we could afford to disregard Soviet concepts of nuclear conflict because we could afford to ignore Soviet capabilities." Brzezinski said he had been urging the national security bureaucracy for a year to find substantive answers to three fundamental questions: "One, what are the requirements of stable deterrance at all levels in the likely conditions of the 1980s? Two, what are the requirements of effective bargaining during crises under the likely conditions of the 1980s? Three, what are the requirements of effective and politically focussed conflict management under the conditions of the 1980s?"

One of the answers to these fundamental questions, remarked Brzezinski, was the position taken by Carter's defence secretary, Harold Brown, on the question of nuclear war. The United States must be able to "respond to nuclear threats in a flexible manner." A "flexible" nuclear war policy would permit not only the use of tactical weapons in theatre warfare but also "limited nuclear war". Brzezinski was still for the linkage theory, which he saw mainly as a frame of bargaining, which, in effect, it was. He would replant direct US military presence in the vital third world regions, be ready to use military power to defend vital US and allied interests and craft a new military doctrine that would provide for "limited" nuclear war and use of tactical weapons in conventional engagements. He would do all this not to provoke the Soviet Union to an apocalyptic collision, but to be able to bargain with the adversary from a strong, credible position. Then alone could there be real linkage between strategic parity and a mutual standoff in the gray areas.

Ronald Reagan, who had a landslide victory over Jimmy Carter in the US presidential poll on 4 November 1980, had not put together the strategic position of his administration at the time of writing. In an interview shortly before the election, however, Reagan said that he, too, supported the theory of linkage. Judging from his campaign articulations and the views expressed by his close associates, it seems clear that the Reagan administration's interpretation of linkage would mirror Brzezinski's. The difference would be that while Carter's vacillations between "toughness" and "softness" stood in the way of implementing the strategic designs of his hawkish national security adviser, the Reagan administration would have few qualms in adopting them to shape its own bargaining posture.[32]

The quantum jump in Soviet military power, then, threatens to bring about fundamental change in world politics. How powerful is the Soviet Union really? What are the binds on Soviet power?

CHAPTER FOUR

The USSR: Emergent Global Power

> Hannibal ad portas.
> *Latin saying.*

To a three-day international conference on human rights and world politics held in Berlin towards the end of April 1979 came a single Soviet participant, a professor of international law from Moscow. He was the conference's great listener, contributing exactly 200 words to three days of animated debate. But he would open up at breakfast table at the posh Kempinski Hotel not far from Adenauerplatz. He was not unaware of the Soviet Union's economic and managerial problems, of its technology lag, and its dependencies on the outside world for foodgrains. But the professor was quietly confident of his country's future, and was intensely patriotic. "For 60 years, the Soviet Union has been the grand obsession of the capitalist world," he told the writer one morning. "They have done everything to keep us down, to ensure that we fall apart. But we have not only *not* fallen apart, we have finally arrived. The Soviet Union today is the world's number one power. They don't admit it, but they know it. They just cannot accept it. But they will, I tell you. By the end of the century, they will have no way of not accepting the reality."

The identity of the Soviet professor is not important; he is not a well-known academic. What is important is that he represents the great bulk of Soviet intellectuals one happens to meet so often in so many places these days, and also the great bulk of the Soviet people. The USSR has hundreds of problems. But these weigh far more with Western elites than with the Soviet people. The great majority of Russians are intensely proud of what their motherland has achieved; world recognition as the true peer of the United States in global military power. To be sure, they want more of the good things of life, but are quietly confident that their lot will be better in the years to come. They respect the political system which has transformed the

USSR to a superpower in six decades, and they will not chafe at making sacrifices to further enhance its strength. A Soviet journalist at the United States in New York put the rationale to the writer in the autumn of 1979: "More than anything else, Russia wants peace, for we lost 20 million people in the Great Patriotic War. We want peace also because in peace alone can our political and social evolution proceed without serious distortion and hindrance. And we know that peace depends on the defensive strength of the Soviet state and the Socialist System." He paused to take an aggressive puff at his State Express cigarette, and added, "Whatever the Americans may say and write about the Soviet Union, we have maintained a stabler balance between guns and butter than any of the capitalist countries. We have not made the USSR the world's number one power depriving the Soviet citizen of the fruits of his labour. Inspite of all our problems and shortages, the average Soviet citizen is better fed, clothed, schooled, and health-cared today than he was in 1970. Can you say this of the United States?"

What startled the writer was that twice in 1979 he should hear two Soviet citizens affirm with cool confidence that the USSR was the world's "number one power." As a student of Soviet-third world relations, he was acquainted with the claim made in the most authoritative Soviet documents of the seventies, like Brezhnev's reports at the 24th and 25th CPSU congresses, that the world balance of forces had shifted "decisively" in favour of the socialist system. He also noted that Soviet analysts no longer identified the United States as *the* leader of the capitalist system, but merely as *one* of the leading capitalist states.[1] But this was the first time he heard two Soviet intellectuals matter-of-factly describe the USSR as the leading world power.

The Soviet self-image has indeed taken a profound boost in the decade of the seventies.

The non-communist world's preceptions of the USSR, however, are shaped more by the United States than by the Soviet Union. Americans have more information about the Soviet Union than any other country, and American images of the USSR are carried by electronic wire services to the entire third world. These images are crafted with a blend of information, knowledge, pride, prejudice, rivalry and wishes. Americans are confounded by the fact that a nation which cannot make good quality shoes and falter with automobiles, should equal or even edge ahead of the United States in the sophistication and deadliness of strategic weaponry. It bewilders Americans that the

Soviet people should tolerate endless lines for meat or cheese and even at times go without bread but not rise in rebellion against a regime that chains them down to perpetual shortages. Americans do not understand how the Soviet Union, with its ubiquitous bureaucracy which discourages enterprise and muffles innovation, its maddening inefficiencies and the long catalogue of social ills and economic lags, could still quietly accumulate so much military power and exhibit so much stability in one of the most turbulent periods of world history. They do not understand why the Soviet system does not burst at its Islamic seams when so much Islamic anger and resentment is hurled at the United States. Americans see no ideological sparks in the minds and brains of Soviet decision makers and perceive the 16 million members of the CPSU (9 per cent of the Soviet population) as nothing but a new class of privileged exploiters; they cannot therefore comprehend why the USSR should have so much clout in so many countries in the third world. Americans see the Soviet Union mainly as the keeper of the Gulag and the Lubianka; they just cannot stomach the sight of the USSR being hailed as liberator.[2]

The Soviet Union has indeed dominated the mind of the 20th century more than any other political phenomenon; at the century's ebb, it is even more of a paradox than ever. It occupies 15 per cent of the earth's land surface and a heterogenous, far-flung swathe of humanity—262.4 million people, made up of over 100 ethnic groups, speaking as many languages. Its gross national product (GNP) of $ 1.4 trillion is second only to that of the United States ($ 2.4 trillion). It produces more steel, pig iron and cement than any other country, and is second in the production of aluminium and gold. Its farmers produce more barley, cotton fibre, wheat, oats, rye, sugar and honey than any other land; its huge petroleum reserves are second only to Saudi Arabia's, and, unlike the United States, it is self-sufficient in energy. By numerous indexes—electrification, physicians and nurses per capita, teacher-to-pupil ratio, cinema houses, newspaper readership, books published each year, leisure enjoyed by its citizens, the USSR ranks among the advanced countries of the world, and *is still advancing*.[3] Yet on the scale of combined social and economic indicators, it ranks 17th, after countries like Sweden, Australia and Iceland. The Soviet economic system bristles with bottlenecks, inefficiencies, waste and duplications, but *it works*, and is slowly and painfully getting better. The Soviets must import millions of tons of grain from the non-Communist world to feed their cattle population, if they were to maintain the steady improvement in the meat intake of their citizens. But the efforts to improve Soviet agriculture continue with increasing earnestness; only the pessimist would assert that the efforts cannot succeed.[4] The Soviet economy is smothered by rigid central planning, bureaucratic concentration of power and managerial and technological gaps, creating reasonable doubt if the USSR can ever be an economic superpower. At the same time, the economy has continued to grow, albeit slowly, in recent years in contrast with the no-growth or minus-growth economies of the advanced capitalist countries. In spite of chronic shortages of consumer goods and other hardships, the Soviet citizen is visibly better off today than he was ten years ago, and he looks at the future with hope, which cannot be said of the citizens of the leading capitalist states. Despite the liberal provisions of the 1977 constitution, the USSR still denies several political rights to its people, but here too the Soviet citizen is better off in 1980 than he was in 1970. He may not organise open opposition to the regime, but he is permitted a modest degree of dissent. He is not terrorised as he used to be in the Stalin years. The average Soviet citizen may appear to be socially apathetic and politically submissive, but the truth is that he does not currently feel suppressed, nor groans that the system is immune to change or that his voice is not heard and responded to. The few thousand "dissidents" with their underground bulletins and books, clandestine meetings and sporadic actions may feed grist to anti-Soviet propaganda in the West but within the USSR they have little impact. Any foreign visitor to the Soviet Union knows that Russians today are no blind worshippers of their rulers and are willing to articulate grievances. But there are no paroxysms of self-denunciation, self-doubt and self-flagellation among Soviet citizens.[5] One can legitimately doubt if the Soviet Union is the utopia the Bolshevik revolution promised in 1917. One cannot deny that the CPSU has built a modern leviathan in an astonishingly short period of time on the ruins of a largely feudal empire that was trailing far behind Britain and France in the industrial revolution.

The image of the Soviet Union straining against its chains is a deeply-cherished myth in Western Europe and the United States. It is self-fulfilling and self-perpetuating; indeed the stability of the Soviet system seems to strengthen the myth and prolong its life. There are still many people who refuse to accept the USSR as a legitimate state, who hate and disapprove of the Soviet system on moral or other ground. The multi-billion dollar Soviet studies industry in the US and

Western Europe closely and constantly watch the Soviet system for the minutest chink; never before in history have so many people for so long a time predicted so many dooms with so much passion and with so little verity. The West knows an awesome lot about the Soviet Union. It still does not seem to understand the Soviet Union very well.

Among the doom theories currently in vogue, two may be mentioned. Several Western specialists on the Soviet Union predicted in 1980 that Islamic fundamentalism would subvert the nearly 43 million Muslims living in the Asiatic republics of the USSR. Both Carter and Brzezinski tried to incite Islamic passions against the Soviets during the Afghan crisis. However, not only was there no ripple of unrest among the Muslims of the Soviet Union, no Muslim mob seized a Soviet embassy anywhere in the Islamic world, though here and there small groups assembled near Soviet missions to protest the intervention in Afghanistan.[6] The other theory, also cherished by many, is that the USSR is heading towards a cataclysmic ethnic conflict between the Russian and Asiatic elements of its population when, around the turn of the century, the Russian element, now 52.4 per cent of the population, loses its numerical majority. The demographic doom may or may not come; in any case, it is not coming in the next two or three decades because the impact of the demographic change will take time to be felt on political command and control. The Soviet nationality policy has not delivered all that it promised. But it has woven several disparate nationalities in different stages of social and economic development into a single sovereign state, and this state has survived for 63 years without any major ethnic or subnational convulsions. The Soviet system, despite its hierarchies and its resistance to change, has not been unadoptive; large numbers of Asiatics have been promoted to the mainstream of Soviet life, even if the masses have preserved their cultural and national identities. In the long haul of time, the relatively backward and underprivileged Asiatic nationalities will demand their legitimate share of power and comforts all through the Soviet system. But one cannot be dogmatically certain that the system will break down under that pressure. In any case, it is foolhardy to fashion national responses to the Soviet Union in 1980 on the hope that the USSR will burst at its Asiatic seams in 1925!

The world, then, has to accept the great paradox that the Soviet state which has caused, directly or indirectly, so much convulsion in this century of revolutionary change has itself proved to be one of the most stable political societies. The Stalinist purges and terror of course removed real and imaginary agents of protest or challenge. But terror has not been used as a strategic instrument of regime stability for 27 years. The system has absorbed considerable change in the three decades after Stalin. The process of change continues. Indeed, the Soviet system stood the trauma of de-Stalinisation much more calmly than China seems to be standing the trauma of de-Maoisation.

Steady progress in stability has been the hallmark of the 16 years of the regime that took over from Khruschev in 1964. It has proved to be one of the longest in contemporary history and certainly one of the most fruitful. These 16 years have made the USSR, if not the world's leading power, at least an equal of the United States; have brought about a continuum of social progress in a climate of peace and order; have kept internal and external conflicts under control; and have contributed to the maintenance of world peace. The remarkable achievements of the Brezhnev period are acknowledged even by some of the Soviet experts in the United States. According to Sewryn Bialer, of Columbia University, the sixties and seventies have been "a very benign period in Soviet history. It is quite possible that future historians will say this was the greatest, the best period in their history."[7] The success is all the more impressive when seen in the context of the political and economic convulsions that rocked most of the advanced capitalist nations and many countries in the third world, including China, during this period.

The widely acclaimed achievements of the ruling team has to a large extent blocked leadership change in the USSR, though this cannot be held up much longer. True, the Soviet system has not so far built a credible mechanism for peaceful political succession, and "power struggle" is likely to characterise each transition from one stable leadership to another. However, even the dourest critic of Soviet affairs no longer expects succession to lead to a crisis of the system.[8] The USSR is the world's worst case of gerontocracy, the average age of the 11 members of the CPSU politbureau being 70. But a massive leadership change across the board is looming over the next 10 years. More important than who succeeds Brezhnev and Kosygin for what interim period before a stable team of new leaders take command of Soviet affairs is the near certainty that before the end of the eighties, officials holding 5,000 to 6,000 top jobs will yield to younger people, must of whom started their careers after the death of Stalin. Jerry Hough, of Duke University, who maintains the most comprehensive profiles of the upcoming Soviet elite, finds the younger generation to be better and more formally educated, better informed, more exposed to the outside world, more assertive, more conscious of the might and power of the USSR, more oriented to problem-solving and more managerially inclined.[9]

It is the military might and power of the USSR that has made the most profound difference to the global balance of power. Devoting 11 per cent to 13 per cent of GNP to defence, and maintaining a steady annual 5 per cent increase in defence expenditure over the last 15 years, the Soviets have equalised, if not surpassed, the strategic might of the United States, acquired a stable edge in conventional forces and built up an interventionist capability and a full-fledged blue water navy that impart its military power a truly global reach.[10] The 3.6 million strong armed forces of the USSR are nearly twice the size of those of the United States, and second only to China's 4.4 million. The Soviets spend only 30 per cent of their defence budget on personnel as against 53.4 per cent by the US; each Soviet young man of 18 is compulsorily drafted for military service, while the US was forced to end conscription as a result of youth protests against the Vietnam draft. Draft dodging in the USSR is rare, and only 12 per cent of Soviet males are given exemption for various reasons. The backbone of the Soviet military is its 400,000 commissioned and one million non-commissioned officers, whose training equals the best in the world. Military leadership is provided by the 48 marshals and fleet admirals, some of whom are among the world's most outstanding strategic thinkers and planners.[11]

In the last decade, the Soviet Union passed the US in the production of most categories of modern weapons. It has 50,000 tanks against America's 10,000; 4,350 war-planes (US: 4,164); and 523 major warships against America's 260. During the seventies, the Soviet tank force has grown by 35 per cent, artillery by 40 per cent, fixed wing tactical aircraft by 20 per cent. The Soviets deploy every week on an average one new medium-range SS-20 mobile missile system with three warheads. Twenty new ships are delivered to the Soviet navy each year against 12 for the US in 1979. The United States is believed to still maintain an edge in high technology weapons like guided anti-tank missiles and in ability to deploy forces rapidly into distant areas with aircraft carriers. The technology gap, however, is narrowing fast.[12]

Strategic weapons consume only a small portion of the military budget of the superpowers (only 7 per cent for the US), but they set the tone for what goes on in the world. The Soviets have wiped out American superiority in strategic weaponry in the course of the past decade. In megatonnage, a measure of the sheer destructive force of nuclear arsenal, the Soviets lead the US 7,836 vs. 3,253. The Soviets deploy 1,400 landbased intercontinental ballistic missiles against 1,054 by the US; have 950 submarine missile launching tubes against America's 656. In five years, the Soviets should be able to completely close the current American lead in strategic nuclear warheads: 9,200 vs. 5,000. The US will still remain ahead in manned strategic bombers, but the aircraft providing this lead are mostly the aging B-52s, some dating back to the fifties. Soviet strategic buildup and modernisation will soon neutralise the US Minuteman ICBMs subjecting them to surprise attacks.[13]

The USSR is catching up fast with the sophistication and deadliness of the most advance US warplanes—the F-15 Eagle, A-10 Thunderbolt, and F-16. Moscow's is no longer a primarily defensive air force. In the 70s, it has deployed a family of tactical aircraft—Su-17 Fitter C, MiG-23 Flogger B, MiG-27 Flogger D, and Su-19 Fencer—that have greater range and payload than the aircraft they are replacing, as well as much improved avionics. Many are nuclear-capable and have considerable ability to penetrate at low level. In sheer quantity, the Soviets have a big lead over the US—turning out 1,159 fighters a year against America's 500, and exporting 25 per cent of the output to the Warsaw Pact members (the US sells 30 per cent of its production to other nations).

The most spectacular growth of Soviet military power has occurred on the oceans. Two decades ago, the USSR did not have anything more than a coastal navy. Today 1,769 vessels constitute a full-fledged blue-water fleet, though a substantial number are overdue for replacement and can only be used for coastal operations. If the 458-ship US navy (declining from 955 two decades ago) has still a greater punch, this is because of the 13 mammoth aircraft carriers (one more in the offing), and the high technology of the American surface ships and submarines. However, the Soviets have been placing emphasis on new amphibious shipping, carriers (two operational, another launched), and attack submarines. There are reports that they are building their first large deck aircraft carriers and that a nuclear-powered cruiser of over 20,000 tons was fitting out in the Baltic in 1979.

The Brezhnev regime has used the fast growing military might of the USSR as an instrument of a global foreign policy—though on a far smaller scale than the United States has used its own since World War II.[14] The regime has not been reluctant to turn the predicament of the West into opportunities—in the Middle East, Indochina and southern Africa; but the projection of power, until Afghanistan, was more or less within the recognised parameters of detente. The United States could not reasonably object to the substantial military assistance the Soviets extended to its allies in the Middle East before, during and after the 1973 Arab-Israeli war, nor to India during the Bangladesh war of December 1971, nor to Hanoi in the last years of the Vietnam War. The fact that at the turn of the seventies, the Soviets could intervene, albeit indirectly, in three far-flung local conflicts in Asia simultaneously, each at a considerable geopolitical remove from the Russian borders, each intervention reaping a surfeit of foreign policy success, did not go unnoticed, but no one made a big noise about it. Then came, in rapid succession, the Cuban-Soviet intervention in Angola and Ethiopia. That relatively small contingents of Cuban forces 10,000 to 20,000 strong—armed, equipped, and transported by the USSR could help African Marxists gain and hold power in one country after another was a stunning experience for the United States and the West, especially because of the vulnerability of their political and economic positions in several key African states.*

The Soviets have suffered major setbacks in the third world in the seventies—losing Egypt and Somalia to the West, and forfeiting considerable clout in Iraq.[15] Nevertheless, Soviet success has been impressive and seen in conjunction with the reverses suffered by the United States, have perhaps more than compensated the setbacks. With eight third world nations the Soviets have concluded long-term treaties of peace

---

*"The Afghanistan operation has obviously given the Soviet Union practice in her mobilization procedures. It has no doubt provided experience for those officers and men involved in the planning and execution of the operation itself. It has been apparent that a force designed and prepared for a war on European lines took time to adjust to low-intensity conflict, and some lack of flexibility and understanding of the problems involved have been noted. Reports clearly indicate that the Soviet Union has placed great reliance on the armed helicopter for dealing with insurgency, and greater use of this system may be expected."—*Military Balance 1980-81*, London, IISS, p. 5.

and friendship; each treaty carries its own precise or imprecise security commitment. These friends of the USSR belong to the Middle East, South Asia, Southeast Asia, Africa and Latin America and cover a wide range of political colours—from India with its capitalist mode of development to Vietnam and Cuba which are full-fledged communist-ruled nations. Located in crucial geostrategic regions, these friends of Moscow are, individually and collectively, conduits of the Soviets' global influence. Some of them—Cuba and Vietnam—act as viable surrogates or "proxies" of the USSR. The regimes with socialist orientation—Ethiopia, South Yemen and Angola—defend Soviet actions and policies and promote Moscow's global interests which, they believe, protect their own national and regional interests. The "gray" allies—India, Iraq and Syria—are problematic; they stay along with the USSR more to defend and promote their own national and regional interests than the global interests of the USSR. Often the two sets of interests tend to converge. Sometime they do not. In India's case, the regional strategic divides mingle with global strategic alignments to lend durability to India's linkages with the Soviet Union. So is the case with Syria. But the Soviets lost Egypt as a friend when Anwar Sadat decided to desert Moscow for Washington and their relations with Iraq are less than warm in 1980. However, outside these treaty-bound friends, the Soviets enjoy various degrees of clout with a number of radical regimes, whose ruling elites derive military, economic and political support from Moscow for the interests and causes they elect to champion. In this category fall countries like Algeria and Libya in North Africa and shadow regimes like the Palestine Liberation Organisation in the Middle East.[16]

The alliance relationship between the USSR and third world countries is highly dynamic and often responds to changes in the local, regional and global political and strategic alignments. They also consume resource that is badly needed for the development of the Soviet Union itself and of its East European allies. Vietnam probably costs the USSR $ 3 million a day and Cuba $ 2 million. The Soviets appear to be capable of paying the wages of power. The bill, at any rate, is far below the $ 20 billion the United States spends annually in the post-Vietnam period to defend its interests in Asia alone. Stray Western press reports notwithstanding, there is no credible evidence that the Soviet people resent the expending of resource to shore up influence abroad as long as returns are handsome and visible and losses do not hurt.

Indeed what the friends do for the USSR is of no less political and military value than what Moscow does for them. Cuba has been of considerable help to the USSR to erect the Marxist regime in South Yemen and to bring much of southern Africa within the shadow of Moscow's global power. The Soviets could not have despatched their own interventionist forces to Angola and Ethiopia without igniting a major world crisis, perhaps a war. But Russian-equipped Cuban troops transported in Soviet ships and aircraft did not violate legitimate international conduct in an age distinguished by breakdown of conventional diplomatic norms. Vietnam, with the world's third largest armed force of more than 2.6 million men, plays a major role in the military containment of China. The Soviets have helped Hanoi double its regular army in a single year since the Sino-Vietnamese war of February 1979; in return, 250,000 to 300,000 fully armed battle-ready Vietnamese soldiers are now massed along the border with China, making it extremely expensive and risky for Peking to undertake a second Chinese invasion of Vietnam or intervene with force in Kampuchea. Vietnam, Laos and Kampuchea are effective transmission belts for Soviet influence in Southeast Asia. The military might of Vietnam, the strongest in the region, mirrors for the elites of the Southeast Asian nations the power of the USSR. ASEAN images of Soviet power are shaped by Hanoi's military performance—against China, in Kampuchea, on the Indochinese borders with Thailand, and more specifically by the MiG-21 interceptors, SS-22 swing-wing fighters, radar and anti-submarine systems, frigates and submarines, anti-aircraft weapons and air-to-air missiles and the 6,000 Soviet advisers who train the Vietnamese in the use of modern weapons. The Chinese see Vietnam's military power as an awesome extended manifestation of menacing Soviet might.

The might of the USSR has had two opposite effects on the failed Sino-Soviet relationship. It has frightened the Chinese to court the US, Japan and the West. It has also restrained Chinese intransigence. Using the stick and carrot simultaneously and exploiting internal contradictions and conflicts in China as well as contradictions between China and the US, Brezhnev has been able to keep the "China Question" under control. Peking's verbal attacks on the USSR may become shriller and shriller. Its diplomatic exertions have sought to reinforce resistance to Soviet power among Europeans, Africans, Iranians, Afghans and Pakistanis. But the reach of China's ability to hurt the

USSR has been found to be limited. This has cautioned the Chinese leaders not to provoke Moscow to a clash of arms. While the war of attrition shows no clear sign of abating, both leaderships keep channels of communication open. They have even sat down intermittently to discuss the pervasive differences and disputes.

The latest round of discussions was broken off by the Chinese protesting the Soviet intervention in Afghanistan. The Sino-Soviet relationship, however, was not markedly worse in 1980 than it had been in 1979. In each country, the Party leadership was divided on what to do with and about the schism. In the CPSU, Kosygin probably would have gone further than Brezhnev to mollify Mao and Chou En-lai: it was he, not Brezhnev, who conducted summit level negotiations with China at critical times of the Brezhnev-Kosygin period. Brezhnev probably took a centrist position on relations with China and received support from both hawks and doves. Similarly, in China after Mao, there are factions that would prefer to make up with Moscow. In domestic policy, the post-Mao leadership has gradually gone back to the 1950s, when relations with the Soviets were overly friendly. In foreign policy, however, the Chinese still pursue the Maoist line of strident anti-Sovietism. The contradiction between Chinese domestic and foreign policies cannot last long; perhaps foreign policy will gradually fall in step with domestic policy as the decade rolls on. It seems possible that the leadership that takes over firmly in the USSR after the passing of the Brezhnev regime would decide to go a step further than Brezhnev to make it up with China. Similarly, the CPC leadership after the passing of Deng Hsiaoping may open up to the Soviet Union. In short, the possibility of a Sino-Soviet rapprochment lurks in the corridors of the decade. It may be hastened by US effort to forge a grand Pacific coalition with China and Japan. The Soviets have not played their China card yet. Nor has China its Soviet card, though Deng himself warned the US President-elect, Ronald Reagan, darkly in December 1980 that if his administration reversed the Carter policy to diplomatically "unperson" Taiwan, China might proceed to "improve its relations with the Soviet Union."[17]

The Soviet Union is not only a global power on its own right, it is also leader of the Socialist System—a group of communist and fellow-travelling countries spanning four continents. While the Warsaw Pact is the military plinth of the system, the Council for Mutual Economic Assistance (CMEA) is its economic spine. CMEA has now ten full members—the Soviet Union, the German Democratic Republic, Poland, Hungary, Bulgaria, Czechoslovakia, Rumania, Mongolia, Cuba and Vietnam. Yugoslavia and North Korea are associate members, while Laos, South Yemen, Iraq, Ethiopia and Angola attend its deliberations as "observers", to which category of nations, Afghanistan and Kampuchea are certain to be added in the near future. CMEA, then, is a transcontinental system of Soviet-led economic cooperation; its full members alone account for over 440 million people, more than 10 per cent of mankind and produce about a third of the world's industrial, and a fifth of its agricultural, output.[18]

This spatially world-spanning Socialist System joins together fullfledged communist nations tied to the Soviet Union in the Warsaw Pact and third world nations ruled by communist parties or socialist-oriented national-democratic fronts, with security ties with Moscow but not belonging to the Warsaw Pact. The second cluster of nations are therefore entitled to be recognised as nonaligned. In Soviet perception, the Marxist-ruled group of nonaligned states form the vanguard of the nonaligned movement. This group, consisting of Cuba, Vietnam, Yemen, Afghanistan, Angola, Ethiopia, Mozambique, Laos, Kampuchea, Mongolia and North Korea (nations that have gone through what a former principal aide to Indira Gandhi has termed "revolutionary decolonisation") illustrates the Leninist concept of "natural alliance" between the Socialist System and the national liberation movement. The Soviets expect their treaty-bound allies—those that are not ruled by Marxists but pursue radical domestic and/or foreign policies - to work with the vanguard group. Brezhnev, for instance, remarked during his visit to New Delhi in December 1980, "Recently, I happened to read some words written in India to the effect that at present friendship between the Soviet Union and India constitutes an important element of the powerful solidarity front of socialist and nonaligned countries, a front which stands in opposition to the aggressive forces of imperialism and restrains their actions aimed against peace and independence of peoples. And this is particularly important today, when the international climate on the planet has grown considerably colder."[19] The socialist-nonaligned solidarity front is a theoretical concept, an operational hypothesis and a major short-to-long-term objective of Soviet foreign policy. The concept stems basically from the Marxist-Leninist interpretation of the historical process of change, and is the central conceptual tool for the CPSU's analysis of the third world's evolving relations with the first world of industrial capitalism and the second world of Marxist socialism.

In the current epoch of "deepening crises" of capitalism, the concept of solidarity or natural alliance between socialism and national liberation operates at two levels of tension and conflict, to which a third level has been added by the schism between the Soviet Union and China. The first level of tension and conflict—between national liberation movements and imperialism—has worked out handsomely to the advantage of the USSR. The second level of tension and conflict is primarily internal, between the conservative, and often reactionary, ruling elements in third world countries and the broad masses of deprived, exploited and oppressed people. In the seventies, Soviet analysts identified increasing polarisation of haves and havenots in the third world, and came to the broad conclusion that the focus of tension and conflict in many of these nations were tending to gravitate to the domestic fields. Once the analyses received approval of the topmost CPSU leadership, the Soviets moved swiftly to test it in the field. Foreign policy resource, including military aid, was now placed selectively at the disposal of movements or elements straining to set up "regimes of socialist orientation," that is, Marxist regimes whose first task would be to bring about "democratic revolutions" in their respective societies, applying the CPSU's "national-democratic" model for each society's transition to socialism. Maoist attempt to wean away some of the radical elements in the national liberation zone added a third dimension to the conflict. In Vietnam, Angola and Mozambique the Soviets succeeded in besting China, but in Zimbabwe, Moscow backed the horse which only came second in the race for power following the end of white racist rule.[20]

Since the mid-fifties the Soviets have operated the natural ally foreign policy strategy at all the three levels of tension and conflict in the third world: the nationalist-vs.-imperialist level, the progressive-vs.-reactionary internal level, and the Maoist "deviation" level. Success has come more easily and in abundance when the Soviets have gone to the help of nationalist regimes defending their land or wealth or independence or pride from imperialist encroachment. When the first two levels of conflict have meshed to create the process of revolutionary decolonisation, the Soviets have found it possible to intervene on behalf of revolutionary forces. The harvest has been more handsome. Since the seventies, however, internal conflicts in third world nations have tended to mesh with interstate conflicts, making intervention a complex and often difficult choice. The Soviets could not offer substantial military assistance to the Marxist-military regime in Ethiopia without alienating neighbouring Somalia because there was no clear-cut demarcation between internal Ethiopian conflict and inter-state Ethiopian-Somalian conflict. The Soviets therefore had to choose between Ethiopia and Somalia, and chose the former inspite of the considerable investment they had made in Somali friendship. The choice in Angola was far easier; indeed it was made so for Moscow by South African intervention on behalf of the forces opposing the MPLA. For years, the nonaligned summit had called on all nonaligned countries to extend all the help they could to the national liberation struggle in Angola. When the Soviets made it possible for Cuba to send an expeditionary force to Angola, they could count on broad third world support because the MPLA had for years fought the Portuguese imperialists and were, on the morrow of independence, fighting the forces of South Africa. Afghanistan, however, was a very different matter. The Soviet intervention was aimed at securing a Marxist regime that had divided the Afghan people into two warring camps. The Soviet explanation was that the Kabul regime had been threatened by external intervention—by the US, Pakistan, Iran, China and other countries. The Soviet intervention, then, was meant to counter an international intervention against the Marxist regime in Afghanistan. The explanation itself showed how complex and difficult the operation of the natural ally policy was getting with the passage of time.[21] The Soviet intervention in Afghanistan was condemned by the vast majority of third world nations at the United Nations in January and December 1980. Brezhnev's statement in Delhi, cited above, betrayed Soviet fear that the intervention would be censured by the foreign ministers of nonaligned nations scheduled to meet in the Indian capital in February 1981.

Afghanistan marked an important stage in Soviet-third world relations because it brought Moscow to a direct confrontation with the United States. This was a development of considerable importance. In most of the third world conflicts since the fifties, the Soviets supported national liberation forces locked in various norms of struggle with colonial-imperial powers of Europe—Britain, France, Belgium and Portugal. The US stood by its European allies, not without a sense of guilt; it even opposed Britain and France during the Suez crisis. In the Congo crisis of the early sixties, the US confronted the Soviets from behind the screen of the United Nations. The UN won, and it was visibly a US victory. The Vietnam war became tragically an American war: the Soviets gave substantial help to North Vietnam but never came to a face-to-face confrontation with the US. On the contrary, both President Johnson and President Nixon sought and received Soviet help to negotiate with Hanoi. The Soviet gains in southern Africa occurred when the US was caught in the trauma of Vietnam.

The Soviets intervened in Afghanistan when the Carter administration had already adopted a policy of "assertive competition" with the USSR in the third world. The US perceived the Soviet lurch into Afghanistan as a move to outflank Iran, and as part of a Russian grand design to gain control of the Persian Gulf sealanes through which Arab and Iranian oil must flow to Western Europe, Japan and the United States. Carter's response to Afghanistan, as we have noted, was to threaten the USSR with a second cold war.

Direct confrontation between two global powers locked in assertive competition is an entirely new development in world politics. It has induced analysts in the Soviet Union to look closely at the vulnerabilities of the US as a world power, as it has induced American analysts to look for every chink in the armour of their adversary. The Soviets do not minimise American power; indeed they have great respect for the might of their rival. However, taking all the pluses and minuses of the current international situation into account, Soviet analysts seem to believe that the USSR can take on the US in the new confrontation. The oft-repeated Soviet pronouncement that makes this belief clear is that the US tried the strategy of confrontation and containment before, when American power was much greater and the Soviet Union was considerably weaker. It did not work. It therefore cannot work in a period when US power has diminished, Soviet power has increased, and the US is no longer the unquestioned leader of the Western world. Soviet analysts are convinced that an arms race would hurt America sooner and harder than it would hurt the USSR, and that Washington would find its European allies reluctant to bear additional defence burdens when the West European economies are facing mounting unemployment and deepening recession. In Soviet foreign policy strategic thinking, the detachment of Western Europe from the United States—a stable trend, though not yet a stable process—has acquired perhaps the utmost importance. The Soviets expect the American foreign policy elite to divide on a new cold war as soon as its deleterous effects on the economy begin to be felt; more than that, they expect the Western nations to divide. Soviet analysts expect assertive American military presence in strategic third world regions to generate polarisations within and between the local nations, creating opportunities for Moscow to make foreign policy use of national and regional instabilities.[22]

At the same time, the Soviets have no intention to provoke the US to the point of a head-on collision. The intervention in Afghanistan will not be followed up with intervention in Iran or Iraq. Another intervention in the third world must wait till the time and the correlation of forces are seen to be distinctly favourable. On the other hand, there will be no knuckling down under the threat of American power. Toughness will be laced with sweet reasonableness. There will be a worldwide "peace offensive." Without giving in to American pressure, the Soviets will bend over backwards to reopen the dialogues that they hope will reopen the road to detente. "As for the Soviet Union, our approach remains one of principle," affirmed Brezhnev in December 1980, five weeks before the inauguration of Ronald Reagan as US president. "We are always prepared to discuss any issue in a spirit of realism and to take into account the legitimate rights and interests of others."[23]

What Brezhnev left unsaid but wanted to be universally understood was that the Soviet Union too expected others to take into account its legitimate rights and interests. Having achieved equality in military power, the Soviets now want to be recognised as an equal partner in the settlement of major conflicts and in the management of the global order. This message the Russians have been signalling to the world for quite some time.* An unidentified Soviet official told *Time* magazine in the summer of 1980, "You (the United States) assign to yourself a global role and to us a very limited, regional sphere of influence. Well, you'll have to get over that notion. It's outdated and unjust. We too are now a global power, and we have the right to compete with you on a global scale. That is only fair if we are truly your equals."[24] This sentiment was echoed by a scholar at the Moscow's Institute for the Study of the USA and Canada: "The problem with you Americans is that you can't bring yourselves to live with us now that we've finally corrected the imbalance. All this talk

---

*This was the keynote of Brezhnev's speech at the 26th Congress of the CPSU held in Moscow early March 1981.

about 'Soviet threat' in your country is nothing more than disguised nostalgia for what you regard as the good old days when you had a monopoly or at least superiority of power."[25]

The Soviet leaders probably welcome the current confrontation with the United States. If they can manage it adroitly, they will wrest from their adversary recognition of the USSR as its co-equal and this recognition may generate genuine cooperation to preserve world peace. The diplomacy of confrontation management will not be easy; it will demand the best of the CPSU leadership. Above all, it will require a fine blending of toughness and softness, and an ability to turn inter-Allied differences into opportunities without appearing blatantly to be doing so. It will also need cohesion and unity at home and within the bloc. Soviet policy-makers derive comfort from their knowledge that the adversary they face in the 80s is in no better shape than their own nation, that there are too many binds on American power, that the US stands lonely and forlorn in the universe of nations, that it is psychologically incapable of a war of attrition, and that it cannot remain unresponsive to gestures of friendliness.

The Soviets reject the linkage concept of Henry Kissinger—they do not perceive detente as a converge of the world capitalist and socialist systems. But they have their own concept of linkage. Soviet international relations theorists see the world to be bipolar in the vital strategic relationship; the planet's survival depends on the ability of the two superpowers to keep their nuclear weapons leashed. This is the great linkage between the two powers. The future of the USSR, indeed of Marxism-Leninism, lies in world peace, in the prevention of nuclear war. The Soviets have not expanded so much resource and made such massive sacrifices for such a long period to acquire global military power in order to perish in a nuclear war. The CPSU believes that it can wage peace much more effectively in the 1980s than it could in the 1950s and 1960s. They have the weight of contemporary Western wisdom on their side. "In our time, the art of war is identified with the art of preventing war," observes Raymond Aron. And Henry Kissinger declared when he was at the centre of American foreign policy-making, "The challenge of our time is to reconcile the reality of competition with the imperative of coexistence."

CHAPTER FIVE

Moscow: Diplomacy of Intervention

> We go in to gain a little patch of ground
> That has in it no profit but the name.
> *Hamlet*, IV, iv, 18

The Soviets, all available evidence suggest, had nothing to do with the April revolution in Afghanistan. A high-ranking Soviet official in Moscow told Louis Dupree, an American sociologist, not long before the event: "If there is one country in the developing world we would like not to try scientific socialism at this point of time, it is Afghanistan."[1] However, when the revolution did take place and the Khalq-Parcham coalition took over in Kabul, the Soviets lost no time to recognise the Marxist regime. For months, Moscow advised moderation and impressed upon the leaders of the regime the necessity to rally broad sections of the working people behind its social and economic programmes. Between April and December 1978, the Soviets concluded 29 different aid agreements with the Marxist regime headed by Noor Mohammed Taraki, but the total financial commitment did not exceed $ 104 million. In contrast, aid pledged by the West during this period totalled $ 121 million, half of the amount offered by the World Bank.[2] US aid was cut off only after the killing by four armed terrorists, apparently from the ultra-left *Setem-i-Meli*, of the American ambassador, Adolph Dubs, in February 1979. By that time, however, the Soviets had taken the crucial decision to "adopt" the April revolution: crucial because Moscow must have known from the beginning the tenuous social base of the Afghan Marxists and the deep-rooted factional and personalitywise divisions that characterised the relatively small, predominantly urban Afghan left movement since the 1940s and 1950s. We have no knowledge of the debates the Afghan revolution generated in the CPSU leadership. It is moot to ask if the CPSU leaders did not realise from the beginning, and particularly after the Taraki-

Amin rivalry surfaced in the spring of 1979, that the Afghan revolution was doomed to collapse unless it were propped up by strong Soviet backing including military support. The regime faced anticipated resistance within two months of its inauguration but with increasing tensions among its leaders; efforts by Soviet representatives to keep the two major communist factions united proved to be increasingly fruitless. By the end of 1978 Moscow apparently braced itself to play the role of the revolution's protector. The number of Soviet military advisers increased to 1,000 in December from about 350 in April, and nearly doubled to 2,000 in June 1979. In July, the first Soviet combat unit was deployed in Afghanistan when an airborne battalion of 400 men was moved to the Bagram airport near Kabul. Two strong Soviet military delegations visited Afghanistan. Military cooperation was formalised in December 1978 by the Soviet-Afghan friendship treaty. Signing the treaty with Taraki, amidst a fanfare of Kremlin splendour, Brezhnev declared that the accord "will not only provide the foundation for the further strengthening of Soviet-Afghan friendship, but will also serve the interests of peace and security in Asia and, thereby, all over the world." A Soviet analyst observed that the treaty became necessary because the earlier Afghan-Soviet accords of 1921 and 1931 did not reflect the "qualitative changes" that had visited the relationship since the April revolution. The treaty was erected on a strong spine of defence collaboration. Article 4 laid down that the two parties would consult each other and undertake, by mutual consent, appropriate measures to ensure their mutual security, independence and territorial integrity.[3]

The decision to intervene was taken probably in September after Amin had overthrown and killed Taraki, purged a large number of Parcham leaders and cadres and still totally failed to contain the insurgency which controlled at least one half of Afghanistan's 28 provinces. Even Kabul was threatened. *Pravda* reported *after* the intervention that in the autumn of 1979 "the fiery ring of counterrevolution backed actively from abroad became tighter and tighter around the capital."[4] On December 25 Soviet troops began to land in Kabul and other places.

Moscow's diplomacy of intervention showed impressive imprints of sophistication—somewhat surprising because Moscow did not previously intervene in any conflict outside the geographical frontiers of the Soviet bloc. The first impressive element was its astonishing massiveness, and the stunning impact it had on a surprised world. The fact that Foreign Minister Andre Gromyko was now a full-fledged member of the CPSU politbureau helped in orchestration of the military and diplomatic aspects of the intervention. Brezhnev affirmed later that the Soviet leadership had pondered "all" short- and long-term implications of the intervention before taking the final decision, meaning that the action was taken only after the pro and con were taken fully into account. For the first week or so, the emphasis was on perfect execution of the military operation. The terse announcement of December 27 stressed the intervention's legitimacy as well as objectives. Legitimacy rested on the Soviet-Afghan friendship treaty. The request for military help came from the "political leadership" of the April revolution rather than from the government then existing in Kabul. The objectives were to "defend the gains of the April revolution" and to prevent the imperialist powers from converting a "neighbourly country with a border of great length into a bridgehead for preparation of imperialist aggression against the Soviet State."[5]

The focus of Soviet diplomacy in the wake of the intervention was *not* the United States, but Pakistan, Syria, India and Iran in the region in which Soviet military power was so awesomely projected, and France, Western Germany and other NATO members that were more perturbed than enthused by Carter's belligerent response to the Russian action. The first capital visited by Gromyko was Damascus, the second, New Delhi. The diplomatic offensive against Pakistan was conducted at three simultaneous levels: military pressure on the border, raising the grim prospect of Soviet troops penetrating Pakistani territory in hot pursuit of retreating insurgents; direct diplomatic pressure by Moscow; and diplomatic-realpolitical pressure by the Marxist regime in Kabul. Syria's help was sought to counter US efforts to arouse Islamic nationalism against the USSR. India was accorded top priority because Moscow needed India's benign neutrality if it could not obtain India's political support. France and West Germany became major targets of Soviet diplomacy because of their refusal to toe the US line. If detente could be shown as divisible, it would be easier to isolate the US from its allies and many of its clients and expose it as a lone bugler of cold war and confrontation.

When Soviet diplomacy took on the United States, the focus of Moscow's attack was Carter's lurch for dominant American globalism. The burden of Moscow's carefully orchestrated articulations was that the US was turning Nelson's blind eye on the changes that had occurred to the global balance; that it had determined to take the world back to the wasted epoch of cold war; and that this exercise in muscle-flexing would fail because the USSR had emerged as an equal of America and could not be cowed down by threats of military superiority. Thus in its first reaction to Carter's State of the Union report asserting "vital US interests" in the Persian Gulf region, Moscow objected that the president should have "arbitrarily proclaimed the areas of the Persian Gulf which lies thousands of miles away from American shores, a sphere of US vital interest. The absurdity of Washington claims is an axiom which needs no proof." The purpose was "to keep the dominant position of American monopolies in the region." The "only outside threat" to the Gulf region, a *Tass* despatch dated January 5 added, came from the US, which had concentrated the biggest ever armada of naval forces in the region thus effectively blocking the Persian Gulf. *Tass* called Carter's reprisals against the Soviet Union "an unfriendly action . . . drawn from the cold war arsenal."[6]

Pravda asserted on February 2 that Moscow had no designs on West Asian oil and no intention of pushing through to the warm water ports on the Indian Ocean. In an authoritative commentary, *Pravda* said that Carter had made "a new claim" to American world supremacy.

> What is meant by the U.S. leading role is Washington's intention to dictate its orders in any region to any state . . . to use any means, including arms, to resist national liberation and revolutionary and progressive movements. Unceremoniously, the US government proclaims various areas of the world as spheres of American vital interests. In the process, the tendency to advance these spheres directly to the borders of the Soviet Union is manifesting itself with growing clarity for some time already. The impression is that an attempt is being made to carry us out of the eighth decade of the 20th century back to the end of the 19th century . . . . The strategists in Washington are counting mostly on strength as the principal means of attaining world hegemony. At no time since the peak of the cold war has the cult of brute force been professed so openly.

Pravda went on to say that Carter's report revealed that the US aimed at disrupting the existing approximate parity of forces between the superpowers and at achieving American military superiority. "Absurd inventions about the USSR and, in particular, about Soviet policy in respect of Iran and Afghanistan hold a considerable place in the presidential message. By means of these inventions Washington tries to 'substantiate' its belligerent programme, to cover up the fact that the ruling circles of the US started the implementation of their unprecedented programme of militarisation at least three years ago and if there were no Afghanistan, they would have certainly found some other false pretext. It is the United States and not the Soviet Union that has continued to speak to Iran in the language of diktat, that is most unceremoniously interfering in the affairs of that country. In its calumny against Afghanistan and Soviet policy in connection with the Afghan events, the US government is breaking all records."

Reiterating that the Soviets had only responded to requests for help by the "legitimate leadership of Afghanistan," *Pravda* for the first time spelled out the condition for the withdrawal of Soviet troops. "As soon as the imperialist interference has ceased, the causes which made the Soviet assistance necessary will no longer exist." *Pravda* pointedly accused the Carter Administration of replacing detente with a new policy of confrontation. "Thus everything has been turned upside down: it is exactly Washington that manifests itself as an unreliable and non-serious partner, which arbitrarily violates concluded agreements and universally accepted norms of inter-state relations."[7] And, finally, it reminded the US that the time had changed, confrontation wouldn't work any longer. "If the White House has an intention to somehow influence the Soviet Union and its foreign policy, that is a hopeless thing. Such attempts failed in the past and will suffer a fiasco this time as well." *Pravda* implied that Carter's new cold war was dictated not so much by the Soviet intervention in Afghanistan as by the exigencies of election politics. "The present US government is trying to divert the American attention from the obvious setbacks in the field of domestic policy and a number of failures in foreign policy. For this purpose, a militarist-chauvinistic psychosis is being stirred up in the USA. Acting as the initiator of a new flareup of jingoism, the White House is hoping to win the backing of the most reactionary circles."[8]

Earlier, Gromyko went to Damascus for three days' intense talks with the leaders of Syria and PLO evidently seeking their support to counter US efforts to make the Soviet intervention in Afghanistan a major target of Islamic attack. In a formal speech at Damascus on January 28, the Soviet foreign minister described the US as "the worst enemy of Islam and the third world nations." He mocked Washington's attempt to confuse Muslims about the issues really at stake in Afghanistan, which were not Islam, but the Afghan people's right to protect their revolution. How could America pretend to champion the interests of Islamic nations when it went on protecting Israel and Israeli occupation of Islamic lands and holy places? Gromyko asked.[9]

The most authoritative statement on the Soviet position on Afghanistan came from Brezhnev himself on February 22. By that time the American campaign against the Russian intervention had peaked and the contradictions between the US and its European allies and Middle Eastern and Southwest and South Asian clients stood more or less exposed. Brezhnev's long interview with *Pravda* was addressed mainly to Washington and its allies.

"It has become obvious," said Brezhnev, "that the present leadership of the United States is pursuing a line of undermining detente and aggravating the international situation. It is trying to dictate its will to the socialist states and other countries." He accused Carter of using Afghanistan as a "convenient pretext" for unleashing a cold war. Carter and the people around him knew very well that there "has not been and is no Russian intervention in Afghanistan." The USSR acted on the basis of the Soviet-Afghan treaty of friendship. "Three consecutive Afghan governments pressingly asked us for assistance in defending their country from the invasion from outside by forces of counterrevolution." That intervention, directed by the US and China, had created a serious threat to the Afghan revolution and also to the security of the Soviet Union's southern border. "The White House also knows that the USSR will withdraw its military contingents from Afghanistan as soon as the reasons that caused their presence there disappeared and the Afghan government decides that their presence is no longer necessary." Brezhnev maintained that while the United States "loudly demands" the withdrawal of Soviet troops, it was, in fact, doing everything "to put off this possibility by building up its interference in the affairs of Afghanistan." "I want to state very definitely that we will be ready to commence the withdrawal of our troops as soon as all forms of outside interference directed against the government and the people of Afghanistan are fully terminated. Let the US together with the neighbours of Afghanistan guarantee this and then the need of Soviet military assistance will cease to exist."

Brezhnev then pointed his gun on Carter himself. "The anti-Soviet hysteria is needed not only for somebody riding the creast of this wave to win the presidential elections in the autumn. The main thing is that the US has decided to create a network of its military bases in the Indian Ocean, in countries of the Near and Middle East, in countries of Africa. The United States would like to subordinate these countries to its hegemony, to pump out unimpeded their natural wealth, and, in the process, to use their territories in its strategic plans against the world of socialism and the popular liberation forces. This is the crux of the matter."

Claiming that the allies of the US would not go along with Washington, Brezhnev said that Western Europe and Japan "will not so easily renounce detente for the sake of the American plans of world domination. On our part, we continue to stand for the development of peaceful cooperation with these along all lines including, *incidentally*, with the United States. The people in Washington like to speak about the need to ensure the safety of the routes along which oil is delivered to the United States. This can be understood to some extent. But can this really be achieved by turning the area of communications into a power keg? It is clear that the result will be the reverse."

Brezhnev's concluding words were a firm assertion of Soviet power. "Nobody will intimidate the Soviet Union. Our strength and possibilities are tremendous. We and our allies will be able to stand up for ourselves and rebuff any hostile sallies and nobody will succeed in provoking us."[10]

Tougher statements followed from Kosygin and the Soviet Defence Minister, Ustinov. Russia would not brook any "violation of the existing equilibrium of forces in the world to the detriment of its security," affirmed Kosygin in an election speech. "Imperialist plans to turn Afghanistan into an outpost of reaction on the southern borders of the Soviet Union have suffered a failure. The Iran and Afghanistan crises were the outcome of the non-recognition by the US and its supporters of the new realities which have emerged in the world. Their attempts to stop the world liberation process are the true cause of the current tense international situation."[11] Ustinov accused the US and China of turning Pakistan into a military base for aggression against the countries of the region. The creation of numerous military bases close to the Soviet borders and the socialist countries and an unrestricted arms race formed the basis of American policy of brinkmanship.[12] To this awesome array of authoritative Soviet voices *Pravda* added its own:

> The Soviet Union will not remain passive in the face of actions against our security. Everything will be taken into account and nothing will be left without a response, be it establishment of military bases, deployment of new American nuclear missiles near the Soviet frontiers or attempts to instigate the states lying near the Soviet Union to take unfriendly acts towards the USSR.[13]

The *Pravda* article came a day after *Tass* carried a new warning to Washington saying that the SALT-II treaty could enter into force only after it was ratified officially by both sides. The Carter Administration had pledged to carry out the treaty's limitations on strategic weapons as if the pact were in force as long as the Soviets did the same. *Tass* stopped short of saying that Moscow would not abide by the treaty's terms. "Who will believe in the sincerity of Washington?" *Tass* asked.[14]

The Soviets reacted sharply against the lifting of US embargo on arms transfers to Pakistan and even more sharply to Carter's bid to enlist Pakistan's cooperation to operate his doctrine of containment of Soviet power. Direct pressure upon Pakistan by Moscow took largely the form of threatening invectives. The Soviets sought the help of Cuba and India to dissuade Pakistan from aligning with the US, and the help of Syria, South Yemen, Algeria, Libya and PLO to mollify the Islamic conference's anger at Moscow's intervention in Afghanistan.* The Babrak Karmal government in Kabul, operating a parallel level of diplomacy, dangled before Pakistan the carrot of goodneighbourly relations as well as the stick of stirring up rebellions among the Baluchis and Pakhtoons, thereby threatening Pakistan with civil war and possible dismemberment for the second time in 10 years.

Typical of Soviet attacks in Pakistan was *Pravda's* accusation on February 13 that Islamabad was carrying out a policy of aggression

---

*For details, see the next chapter.

against Afghanistan and that Gen. Zia was turning his country into "the principal base" for the external interventionist forces. Pakistan was moreover strengthening its border detachments and moving regular troops into combat positions along the Afghan border.

"All this bears witness to the fact that Pakistan does not intend to stop its aggressive policy directed against Afghanistan and is making its territory available for the realisation in the region of the aggressive plans of the US and its allies."[15]

New Times said two days earlier that Pakistani leaders had assumed an "unsavoury and dangerous role"; their denial of involvement in anti-Afghan activities could not be taken seriously. "Any government bears responsibility for everything done in its territory. More so, when officers of Pakistani army of which Gen. Zia is commander-in-chief, have been sent to camps of anti-Afghan rebels. More so, when counter-revolutionaries using the banner of Islam as a coverup are allowed use of two big radio stations in Peshawar and Quetta and are given assistance in the preparation of anti-Afghan printed matter."

Adding the weight of its own voice to these serious charges, *Izvestia* observed, "Pakistan is the first country to which the so-called Carter Doctrine is being applied. . . . Nobody threatens Pakistan. At any rate, not Afghanistan, because aggression is not being waged against Pakistan from Afghan territory but the other way round. Now, thanks to the American aid, weapons will be even more readily available. It is precisely the unpopularity of the military dictatorship that brings about instability in Pakistan. Pakistan is advancing to the foreground of military activity in the region because the Islamabad regime had long been maintaining close political and military contacts with Washington and Peking simultaneously. Experience shows that the arming of reactionary Pakistan military has always led to wars in the region and to an increasingly brutal suppression of the struggle of the Pakistani people themselves for freedom, democratic and social progress."[16]

The Soviets took particular care to mollify the leader of Iran's Islamic revolution, the Ayatollah Ruholla Khomeini. Brezhnev sent a warm message to him on the first anniversary of the revolution, reiterating Soviet opposition to "any aggression against countries of the Third World, particularly Islamic lands in this region."[17] The Soviet ambassador to Iran, Vladimir Vinogradov, called on the Iranian Foreign Minister to assure him that Moscow had no "ambitions" in Iran. These diplomatic efforts did not bring desired results; the Iranian leaders strongly resented the Soviet action in Afghanistan and were clearly apprehensive of Soviet ability to intervene in Iran if Moscow decided to do so. Khomeini asked Moscow not to use force against Islamic countries if it wanted to have friendly relations with Iran, and he pledged support to the Afghan insurgents, declaring that Iran would fight "intruders from the east."[18] Iran's President, Bani Sadr, announced that he would allow volunteers to fight in Afghanistan. No Iranian, however, came forward.[19] Iran's Foreign Minister, Mostafa Charnan, said on January 20 that the Soviet intervention in Afghanistan posed serious dangers to Iran's southeast border provinces of Sistan and Baluchistan. "Soviet troops are 30 kms from the Iranian border; naturally, their presence in Afghanistan poses a serious danger. We cannot accept this danger." He was concerned that the Soviet Union might one day invoke the 1921 Friendship and Cooperation Treaty with Iran which gives it right to intervene militarily if Iran were to be used as a base for military operation against it. The provisional government of Bazarghan revoked the treaty in November 1979 but the Foreign Minister said that this was a unilateral move not reciprocated by the Soviet Union. "The 1921 Treaty has only been suspended unilaterally by us. So we might face the same consequences as Afghanistan."[20]

Iran's Islamic revolutionary regime had good reasons to take an anti-Soviet position. Khomeini and his ardently Islamic followers were as strongly opposed to, and afraid of, US domination as Russian. Their Islamic sentiments made them particularly resentful of the Soviet military move into Afghanistan. They had not the slightest intention of responding to Moscow's blandishments lest this might be used by Carter as an excuse for military action against Iran. And finally, they were not sure that the Soviets would not, at the appropriate time and in appropriate circumstances, try to bring Iran within their expanding sphere of influence.

These apprehensions were not entirely groundless, for Soviet reaction to the American hostage crisis had been ambiguous. Moscow supported Washington's call for the release of the hostages both at the United Nations and outside. In a broadcast beamed to Iran from a radio station in the southern Soviet Union in the middle of November 1979, the Soviet Union called for the release of the hostages, but, earlier, the same station said that the taking of the hostages by revolutionary Iranian youth was "understandable."[21] East

Germany, on the other hand, expressed its full support in November for the students holding the hostages.[22]

In its first comment on the hostage issue, *Pravda* supported Iran in its war of attrition with the United States. The US, said *Pravda* commentator Alexei Petrov, was trying to "blackmail Iran by massing forces on its frontiers" instead of extraditing the Shah. US naval manoeuvres around the Gulf were "a gross violation of international legal norms." Petrov did concede that the seizure of the hostage was not in keeping with the international convention on the respect of diplomatic privileges and immunity. But he added that "this act cannot be taken out of the overall context of US-Iranian relations." He warned against "outside interference in Iran's internal affairs by anyone, in any form, under any pretext."[23]

The pro-Soviet Tudeh (Communist) Party of Iran followed the Khomeini line on all but the most insignificant points. According to the *International Herald Tribune*, its deferential support for the Ayatollah made Tudeh "a part of the post-revolutionary Iranian political establishment."[24] Tudeh leaders brought flowers to the students holding the American hostages, were received in government offices in Tehran and even in the Qum by representatives of Khomeini himself. In the constitutional referendum, Tudeh was the only left party to urge a yes vote. But the complaint policies of Tudeh mellowed Khomeini's attitude towards the USSR only for a short period *before* the Russian intervention in Afghanistan. The Iranian revolutionary government suspended anti-Soviet press campaigns and played down Moscow's support for the American move at the Security Council to secure the release of the hostages.

Iran's attitude towards the Soviet Union hardened after the Afghan intervention and went on hardening through 1980. The revolutionary regime terminated a $ 3 billion 20-year agreement the Shah had concluded with the USSR in 1975, under which a 1,000-mile pipeline was being constructed to supply 13.4 billion cubic foot of Iranian natural gas every year for consumption in West Germany and Austria. Iran was piping the gas to the Soviet Union for domestic consumption: the Soviets, in turn, were piping an equal amount of its own gas to West Germany and Austria. In the summer of 1980, rumours that Islamic youth cohorts were about to lay seige on the Soviet embassy in Tehran drew forth a stern warning from the Kremlin. Iranian suspicions that the rebellious Kurds were receiving aid from the Soviets through Tudeh brought relations with Moscow to a new low in August. The Iranian Foreign Minister, Sadegh Ghotbzadeh, fired off an angry letter to Moscow, describing the Soviet leadership as "no less satanic than the USA." At Iran's demand, the Soviets had to reduce the personnel at their Tehran embassy and close down a number of consulates.

The Soviets, however, appeared to take the pinpricks of Tehran in their stride, with the tolerance of one who knew that things would change for the better in the undistant future. Soviet articulations continued to support the Iranian revolution ignoring its Islamic excesses. The target of Soviet attack was not Khomeini or the anti-Soviet government in Tehran. It was the United States. The Kremlin dismissed Ghotbzadeh's blistering letter as a buffalo scatters flies with a casual flourish of its tail. In listing the major international issues which demanded the urgent attention of all peaceloving people, a Soviet analyst remarked in August that "the tension around Iran would be eased at once if Washington observed the generally recognised standards of international law instead of merely lecturing others on this score and renounced its tactics of crude pressure on a country and a region which the White House has arbitrarily proclaimed a 'sphere of US vital interests'."[25]

KABUL'S DIPLOMACY

The Marxist regime in Kabul launched its own political-diplomatic efforts within two weeks of the Soviet intervention with the three-fold objective of earning popular support, making a dent in the anti-Soviet Islamic front perked up by Pakistan and others and preventing India and Pakistan from working together to oppose the Soviet military presence in Afghanistan. Its first major foreign policy statement was issued on January 11 after five days of intense talks between the regime's leaders and a special envoy sent to Kabul by the Indian prime minister for an on-the-spot study of the situation created by the Soviet intervention. It was a remarkably soft-worded statement. Kabul, it declared, wished to solve all problems with Pakistan through peaceful and amicable negotiations without resorting to force if Pakistan reciprocated similarly and adopted a more responsible attitude towards Afghanistan. The Afghan government, it added, favoured continuing its "all-sided efforts of maintaining friendly relations with all peaceloving countries, particularly neighbours like the USSR,

India, Pakistan and Iran." The limited contingents of Soviet forces would be withdrawn as soon as the cause which necessitated the request for such military assistance ceased to exist under a credible guarantee.[26]

The Karmal regime went out of its way to cultivate India's goodwill. In a personal letter to Indira Gandhi, Karmal assured the Indian Prime Minister of Afghanistan's continued adherence to the policy of nonalignment, and said that he had been forced to ask for Soviet military help as a result of American, Chinese and Pakistani intervention in Afghanistan's internal affairs. A similar message went out to the Ayatollah Rohulla Khomeini. Towards the end of January, Kabul's Foreign Minister, Shah Mohammad Dost, welcomed India's efforts to "defuse" the crisis. Six of the seven members of the politbureau of the ruling party attended a dinner hosted by the Indian ambassador to celebrate the anniversary of the Indian republic. Babrak sent in an apology for his inability to attend, but took the first opportunity to have a 75-minute meeting with the ambassador, Dr J.S. Teja. Dost invited two Indian reporters to a special press conference in the foreign office. Answering questions, he made serious allegations against China and Pakistan of helping the Afghan "counterrevolutionaries" with arms and weapons, and stressed that, on its own part, Kabul would not interfere in the neighbouring countries' internal affairs. The presence of Soviet troops would not inhibit Kabul's nonalignment, Dost claimed, and cited the example of several nonaligned African countries that had foreign troops on their respective territories.[27]

In February, however, the Afghan regime's attitude towards Pakistan hardened as Pakistan began to negotiate seriously for a large package of American military and economic aid. Interviewed by *The Times*, of London, Karmal affirmed that Afghanistan needed Soviet forces for "peace and protection." The Americans, Pakistanis and Chinese had stitched up a "joint plan" to "attack Afghanistan on January 6." It was foiled by the timely arrival of Soviet troops. "Ten days later, it would have been too late." The Soviet forces would stay as long as the danger of external attack remained. They would withdraw only when "proper conditions are created including the elimination of all signs of aggression against us." Karmal said that he was not opposed to a "regional initiative" which might guarantee the security of Afghanistan as well as its neighbours. But he did not wish to see Gen. Zia or the United States involved in that initiative. He would rather join hands with the Soviet Union and India to forge a regional security framework. Karmal also denied that he was transported by the Russians to Kabul with the first units of airborne troops. Months before the arrival of Soviet forces, he had returned to Kabul from Czechoslovakia, Karmal claimed. "I was working underground in Kabul with my comrades."[28]

On March 5 an Afghan representative at the United Nations made a blistering attack on Pakistan accusing it of interfering in Afghan internal affairs by arming and instigating the insurgents to launch guerrilla warfare. He said Pakistan was a tool of imperialism raising a multimillion-dollar army with the help of the United States and China.[29] Two days later, Karmal told a Lebanese newspaper that experts from America, China and Pakistan had readied 63,000 guerrillas to invade Afghanistan and execute its partition. The invading force was based in 50 camps in Pakistani territory close to Afghanistan's south-eastern border. The bulk of the guerrilla force was to cross overland and the rest was to be parachuted to carry out the conspiracy. Kabul and central Afghanistan were to come under active control of US operatives to prop up the regime of Hafizullah Amin.[30]

The Afghan cabinet met at the beginning of March to discuss the issue of Soviet military presence. The meeting adopted a resolution saying that the Russians would "definitely remain in free and independent Afghanistan until such time as all indications, intrigues and designs of the reactionary forces of the region and expansionist and warmongering imperialists against the national independence, sovereignty, territorial integrity and security of our country are completely, positively and absolutely uprooted and wiped out for ever."[31] The rhetoric reflected both the might and power of the USSR and the weakness of the revolutionary regime.

Exactly a month later, Moscow and Kabul concluded and ratified an agreement governing the "temporary stay" of a "limited contingent" of Soviet troops on Afghan territory. *Tass* reported that the treaty was concluded during the recent visit to Moscow of a highpowered Afghan cabinet mission and had already been ratified by the appropriate bodies of the two countries. The terms of the treaty remained undisclosed, but Indian press reports from Kabul said that it underplayed the theme of withdrawal of Soviet forces. "In fact, during the last few weeks, the media have proclaimed that the Soviet presence is being welcomed by the people of Afghanistan. The Afghans are no longer told as to when the Russians would leave. One result of this appears to be confusion in the ranks of the government as to how to approach this problem. It is widely believed that the Afghan government would like a definite move by the Soviet Union to thin down its presence, instead of legalising it." The reports suggested that the Minister of Communication, Mr Watanjar, who is an important member of both the government and the party, did not agree to legalisation of Soviet military presence.[32]

A More Liberal Regime

The Karmal government also hastened to correct the excesses of Hafizullah Amin and to make the regime more broadbased and liberal. Thousands of political prisoners were released in Kabul and the provincial capitals. Karmal assured Amnesty International that no political prisoners would be tortured or killed and that they would be tried in open courts. He said that AI's observers were welcome to visit Afghanistan at any time. He also widened the political base of his government by inducting into the cabinet and the administration men of different political shades. In all more than 40 politicians, diplomats, technocrats and civil servants were rehabilitated, many of them for the first time since April 1978. More than 100 senior appointments were made, many of the appointees were identified as "rightists", known personally to Karmal who had been a member of parliament before the April revolution.

The government also set out reorganising the Afghan armed forces with Soviet help. Reports said that the men in arms were carefully screened and only the politically reliable were retained; the others were dismissed. Since April 1978 defections reportedly had reduced the army from 80,000 to 40,000. The Karmal regime was not worried about the small size of the army as long as it was politically reliable. Officers began to be sent to the USSR for special speedy training. The People's Democratic Party paid special attention to political training of old and new recruits. In the summer, compulsory military training was introduced for all able-bodied men between 20 and 50, but the draft was not rigorously enforced because it was far from popular.

In April the Revolutionary Council proclaimed a new Afghan constitution. Its official name was Fundamental Principles of the Democratic Republic of Afghanistan. If defined the rights and duties of citizens as well as the functions of the national and provincial executive and judicial agencies. The constitution guaranteed the "democratic rights" of Afghans, including the right to peacefully assemble and demonstrate. No one could be arrested except with a warrant; no one could be tortured in prison; trials of political prisoners must be open to the public and each accused had the right to self-defence. Freedom to profess and practise Islam was also guaranteed. Article 5 of the Fundamental Principles said: "Respect and defence of the holy religion of Islam are ensured in the Democratic Republic of Afghanistan. All Moslems are guaranteed and ensured complete freedom in the performance of Islamic religious rites." The same freedom was guaranteed to people of other faiths also. At the same time, the government was determined not to allow religion to be "turned into a weapon of anti-popular propaganda."

The new constitution ensured equal rights of women as well as "genuine equality" of all big and small nationalities and tribes in Afghanistan, providing them with equal opportunities in the development of their languages, traditions, literature and culture. It forbade discrimination on national, linguistic, racial or tribal grounds. A special status was conferred on the "numerous Pathan tribes inhabiting southern and southwestern Afghanistan." The government would 'go on building its relations with them on the basis of trust, peace and cooperation."

The constitution provided for a mixed economy, committing the government to encourage, protect and preserve "different forms of ownership." The economy and productive forces were to be developed through "planned, dynamic and mutually complementary cooperation between the public, mixed and private sectors." The public sector would extend chiefly to the production of capital goods, power development and transport. The main concern of the private sector was to manufacture traditional handicraft goods, operate the service industry, and run small and medium-size shops. The state would provide retailers with goods. Private businessmen wishing to take part in building industries or public catering and service establishments or in setting up transport companies would get credit, tax privileges and legal protection. Private ownership of land would remain untouched except in the case of big landlords and there would be no collectivisation of agriculture The economic thrust of the constitution was clearly aimed at assuring Afghanistan's one million small traders and entrepreneurs and the great bulk of its peasants that their interests were safe and secure in Marxist-ruled Afghanistan.[33]

The constitution came into force on April 15, seven weeks after a week-long demonstration of popular resentment at the presence of Soviet troops in Afghanistan. The demonstration paralysed life in Kabul and several provincial capitals, reportedly "stunning" the revolutionary leadership no less than the Soviets. It began as a general strike in Kabul on February 21, backed by almost 95 per cent of the traders and developed into mass "civil disobedience." There were reports of sporadic fighting between Afghan government troops and rebels. Soviet troops kept to their barracks, leaving the Afghan soldiers and police to persuade shopowners not to close their shops. Thousands of Afghans demonstrated against the presence of Soviet troops in Afghanistan.[34]

Kuldip Nayar, noted Indian journalist, who was in Kabul early February, believed that the "uprising" had been "blown out of proportions" by Western and Pakistani media. It was doomed to be short-lived, Nayar said, because there was no way the protesters could get outside help. The city was surrounded by Soviet troops who also controlled the Kabul airport. Nayar guessed that the protest was an act of desperation by Kabul citizens who had been mocked by Afghans of several provinces for their "cowardly" submission to the Soviet military presence.[35]

If the demonstrations in Kabul were to be credited to one or the other of the rebel groups operating within or outside Afghanistan, they were pregnant with lessons for the Soviets as well as the Marxist regime of Babrak Karmal. The first lesson was that the revolution and the massive Soviet military presence had alienated not only the traditional elements of Afghan society—landed peasants and the clergy-dominated rural masses—but also the urban trader, businessman, small entrepreneur and fledgling educated middle class. Two lessons that were derived from the first were that the regime had to capture the wavelength of the mass of urban-rural population without going back on the essentials of a Marxist revolution, and that the first diplomatic gestures had to be made towards an eventual withdrawal of the Russian forces. Both Moscow and Kabul must have realised how complex and enormously difficult was the task before them. The April revolution, with a proper renewal and right kind of leadership, might still win over, gradually and over time, the mass of the working people of Afghanistan. But the ubiquitous Soviet military presence stood as an emotional barrier between the revolution and the people, distorting the latter's perceptions of the former. Yet so tenuous was the popular base of the Karmal regime and so potentially, if not actually, strong were the resistance forces that the Soviets, by pulling out their troops, could only send the regime to its doom.

The immediate Soviet-Kabul response to the February demonstrations was a mixture of political concessions and military firmness. The Revolutionary Council hastened to draw up and promulgate the Fundamental Principles of the Revolution, already outlined. At the same time, military operations against the rebels were rapidly revived up. Moscow and Kabul also jointly stepped up their propaganda campaign against foreign intervention in Afghanistan. The knowledgeable New Delhi correspondent of *The Hindu* reported that Moscow perceived the "hidden hand" of the US and Pakistan behind the "uprising" in Kabul: a provocation to the Soviets to use force against the civilian population.[36] *Tass* confirmed this perception when it affirmed that the disturbances "were no protest but a plot that was planned outside Afghan territory. Afghan sovereignty and independence continues to face a serious threat from Pakistan."[37] The Voice of America reported that Soviet armoured vehicles took position on the Afghan side of the border with Pakistan with a view to "completely seal" the frontier;[38] going a step further, reports from London suggested that Soviet troops were poised to retaliate against Afghan rebel camps located on Pakistani territory.[39]

Soviet forces intensified their operations against the rebel groups soon after the Kabul protests, and their spring offensive did subdue the insurgency to a considerable extent. The military offensive was coupled with a "peace offensive" (discussed later in this volume) which succeeded in broadly stabilising the external political ambience of the Russian intervention in Afghanistan. Pakistan claimed to have stopped extending military help to the rebels; Soviet troops never crossed the border into Pakistan in pursuit of insurgents. A certain amount of American, Chinese and Arab help continued to flow to the different resistance groups, but the volume was not overly disturbing to the Russians. Yet the insurgency continued to simmer, and occasionally there were major clashes. It was no easy task for an objective analyst to separate grains of facts from an abundance of chaff of hearsays, rumours, and doctored reports mostly emanating from Afghan refugee sources in Pakistan or from travellers returning from Afghanistan. The Soviets themselves admitted the continued existence of "bandit groups" aided and abetted by the US, China and Pakistan, though verbal attacks on Pakistan tapered off after May. But it was not unexpected of the Soviets to highlight continued insurgent activity as long as Moscow resolved to keep its troops in Afghanistan. Western and Pakistani reports spoke of frequent desertions from the Afghan army, an upsurge of guerrilla activity close to Kabul and several provincial capitals in June, the killing of school children by Afghan troops. More ominous were reports of another factional showdown in the Revolutionary Council, the purging and arrest of the interior minister, Lt-Col. Syed Mohammed Gulbzoi, followed by a purge of more Khalq members of the Council of Ministers, and the shooting down of two ministers. Some of these reports were false; the veracity of others remained unconfirmed. Indian analysts even talked about an attempted coup against Karmal.

Revolutions have the habit of eating up their own children; the Afghan revolution's appetite for the blood of revolutionaries was both a cause and a result of its weakness. Karmal, however, exuded self-confidence in mid-1980. Towards the end of June he announced plans to build a "broad national front" of all democratic forces in Afghan society; he also bitterly attacked Pakistan, among others, for goading Muslims to kill Muslims in Afghanistan, thus confirming the existence of significant volumes of insurgency. But then he, too, needed some insurgency to keep Soviet forces in Afghanistan. Soviet troops would not leave as long as "the slightest remainders of foreign aggression and intervention" remained, Karmal told a West German journal.[40] Interviewed by the sympathetic *L'Humanite*, the French Communist Party daily, Karmal claimed that Afghanistan was "more democratic" in July 1980 than at any time in its history, and that his government had done for its people in six months more than the previous governments could do in six years.[41]

The Afghan Defence Minister, Mohammed Rafi, visiting Moscow in July, claimed that the remaining "detachments" of "bandits and saboteurs" had been isolated, though they still destroyed roads and bridges, making it necessary to place Kabul under night curfew.[42] Reports in the Soviet press said that Afghan peasants had returned to cultivation with the advent of spring. It seemed that in July, the Soviets had the overall insurgency situation under control, but many of the tribal chiefs continued to remain hostile to the Karmal regime and could still rally significant rural following. The world was getting slowly reconciled to a Marxist-ruled Afghanistan led by Babrak Karmal. In July, Inder Malhotra, one of the ablest Indian journalists, dismissed as "absurd" the charge that Karmal was a Soviet puppet, and affirmed that the Afghan leader "is no less a patriot than any other Afghan, though circumstances have placed him in an unenviable position."[43] A few weeks earlier, a Press Trust of India correspondent found Kabul "free from troubles and worries" contrary to notions abroad; but tensions did exist in the provinces.[44]

Some American analysts still believed that the Soviets reached a "military deadlock" in Afghanistan: they could hang on as long as they wished but could not win. Some Indian analysts were "surprised" that the resistance should survive so long and make itself felt against the far superior armoury of Soviet troops. Most observers agreed that Afghanistan could not be Moscow's Vietnam, although some American reports did suggest that the "heavy casualties" taken by the Soviets had begun to tell on the morale of Russians.[45]

It became clear that the rebels had lost the war in Afghanistan even if they could still do well in a few hit-and-run battles. The Russians had no previous experience of guerrilla war: they gained some in Afghanistan. They were also able to battle-test some of their latest weapons and military techniques. No Kabul regime in history ruled over an entirely peaceful Afghanistan. The temper of the Afghan and the terrain of the land make gunshots part of his life's day-to-day sound of music! There was little doubt that the Soviets would eventually "win" in Afghanistan. But the victory would cost them dearly. Not so much in terms of resource, which they could bear, as in terms of popularity in the third world. To move into a third world country with troops in support of a Marxist regime that cannot stand on its own feet is not the same thing as extending military help to a government fighting imperialism and colonialism. This was the lesson the Soviets learnt in Afghanistan more concretely than anywhere else. But as the world's emergent communist global power, the USSR is apparently bracing itself for loss in popularity if it can gain by altering the balance of power in vital geostrategic regions in favour of the Socialist System.

The Soviet diplomacy of intervention, however, showed a high degree of sophistication in dealing with the different major actors in the Afghan drama. The intervention itself, as noted, was quick and conclusive; the Soviets stood firmly by a friend, seeking to create a worldwide impression of the credibility of Moscow's commitments.[46] The political effort in Afghanistan was to help the Karmal regime broaden its popular base and reach out to the people. The Soviets issued dark verbal threats to Pakistan, warning its rulers that the country's territorial integrity almost waited on the pleasure of the Kremlin. The warning derived a measure of credibility from the closeness of Soviet military might to the Pakistan border and Soviet patronage of the restive Baluchi population. However, no Soviet soldier crossed into Pakistan. The political effort was to build and nourish a pro-Soviet constituency in Pakistan, and this effort, as we note later in this volume, was rewarded with some success. Although Iran too extended some help to the Afghan rebels, and the insurgency remained for a long time more effective in the provinces close to the Iranian border than in those close to the Pakistani border, the Kremlin kept its anger for Iran muted, though not totally unarticulated. The Soviets adroitly separated their differences with India on the question of troops withdrawal from the "time-tested" Indo-Soviet friendship, and went a long way to please India in other fields. The CPSU sent Gromyko to New Delhi in February 1980 and in December, Brezhnev himself made a four-day visit to show how highly was India regarded in the Kremlin. Brezhnev's visit did not resolve differences on the question of withdrawing Soviet troops, but he and Mrs Gandhi approved several agreements including one under which India would get one-third of its entire crude import from the USSR by 1985. The 1980-85 trade agreement, also signed during the visit, promised to make the Soviet Union once again India's largest single trade partner.

Of no less significance was the five-point proposal placed by Brezhnev to members of the Indian parliament for a comprehensive settlement of the crises building up in the Persian Gulf. Leaving the details of the proposal to be taken up in the next chapter, we may note here that by making a diplomatic announcement of great import while on a visit to New Delhi, Brezhnev appeared to recognise India as the major power in the intermeshing Persian Gulf-South Asian region. This helped balming the wound inflicted on the Indian mind by Brezhnev's refusal to withdraw Soviet troops from Afghanistan except on terms and conditions laid down already by Moscow and Kabul. Brezhnev perhaps also wanted to restrict the US role to a Persian Gulf settlement; the US, in his plan, was only one of several powers who were required to come to an agreement.* This attempt

---

*At the 26 CPSU Congress Brezhnev offered to link Afghanistan to his Persian Gulf Peace plan, thus proposing, in effect, a neutral zone in Southern Asia comprising the Gulf countries, Pakistan and Afghanistan.

to highlight the role of the local powers in a new order in the Persian Gulf agreed with the Soviet diplomatic effort to boost the role of the West European powers in European security and cooperation. The main thrust of Soviet diplomacy, then, was to try to persuade America's allies in Europe and the Persian Gulf that their best interests no longer coincided with the "vital interests" of the United States, and that they could trust the USSR as a responsible global power to respect their legitimate interests. Soviet diplomacy now rode on proven Soviet military power rather than on rhetorical missiles as it used to do in the past.

CHAPTER SIX

India: Diplomacy of "Crisis Defusion"

Every cloud engenders not a storm.
Henry VI, V, iii, 13

No international incident spurted as much diplomatic enterprise in New Delhi as did the Soviet military intervention in Afghanistan. Never before in the history of Indian diplomacy was there so much groping for ideas and directions. Never before was India's foreign policy an act of sterner choice.

The crucial choice was made by Indira Gandhi, as noted in Chapter One, on January 12, even before she took over as Prime Minister after the stunning victory of her party in the just concluded parliamentary election. Under her instruction, the Indian envoy at the United Nations, Brajesh Mishra, in a speech that reportedly took many governments by surprise, made the following points: (1) the Soviets sent troops to Afghanistan on December 26 at the request of the Afghan government; (2) while India was against the presence of foreign troops and bases in any country, it had no reason to disbelieve a friendly country like the Soviet Union when it said that it would withdraw troops from Afghanistan when asked to do so by the government in Kabul; (3) India hoped that the Soviet Union would not violate the independence of Afghanistan and would not keep troops in that country a day longer than necessary; and (4) India was gravely concerned over the response of the United States, China, Pakistan and others to the Soviet action; the arming and training of Afghan rebels and encouragement given to subversive activities in Afghanistan amounted to external interference in Afghan affairs; building bases, pumping arms to small and medium countries, and expanding naval activities in the Indian Ocean might lead to intensification of the cold war and threaten the peace and security of the region. These activities "pose a threat even to our own nation."[1] The Indian envoy was speaking in the debate on a 17-nation resolution urging immediate withdrawal of foreign troops from Afghanistan. In the voting on the resolution, which was carried with a two-thirds majority, India abstained.

Thus, the inaugural foreign policy action of Mrs Gandhi's Congress-I government was one of clear and incisive choice. In a fresh outbreak of great power rivalries over pieces of real estate in South Asia, Mrs Gandhi chose to remain with the Soviet Union. It was not that no other option was available to her. She could condemn the Soviet intervention and join the United States, China and Pakistan in a concerted effort to contain Soviet influence from extending to the interlinked geostrategic regions of the Persian Gulf and South Asia.

She could plough an independent diplomatic furrow together with likeminded Asian countries to bring pressure simultaneously on the Soviets to withdraw their forces or reduce them substantially and on the United States, China and Pakistan not to use the insurgency as an instrument of interference in the internal affairs of Afghanistan.

She could fasten Indian diplomacy on persuading Pakistan not to act as a proxy of the US and China but to work with India, Nepal and Bangladesh to protect the independence and integrity of the region and reduce the Soviet military presence in Afghanistan.

She must have weighed each of these options before deciding that India's regional and national interests would be safer if she stayed with a time-tested friend in an ambience of polarisation of the major powers. To be sure, Mrs Gandhi did not support the Soviet armed presence in Afghanistan, as she made clear on January 16. But she (1) made it clear that the Soviets did act on the request of the government existing in Afghanistan prior to the first big airlifts (a point that was made also in the *New York Times* but was kept deliberately ambiguous by the caretaker regime of Charan Singh)[2]; (2) trusted the Soviet assurance that the troops would be withdrawn as soon as Afghanistan asked for it; (3) perceived more danger to India's own security in the concerted cold-warish responses of the United States and China to the Soviet action; (4) gave advance notice to Pakistan, China and the rest of the world that any Sino-American move to arm Pakistan and destabilise the region would compel India to renew its strategic collaboration with the USSR; and (5) by abstaining from voting in the UN General Assembly, kept some distance from Moscow so that India could work patiently—unilaterally or in conjunction with other nations—to ensure at least a sizeable Soviet withdrawal from Afghanistan at the earliest possible time.

Foreign diplomats and correspondents in New Delhi were surprised by the finality of Mrs Gandhi's decision. Many of them wondered if she had not acted in haste, without adequate information of what had actually happened and was still happening and whether a certain ambivalence on her part would not have induced the Soviets to reduce their involvement in Afghanistan. "What was the great urgency of siding with the Soviets even before she actually took over as prime minister?" the author was asked by an editor of a well-known London weekly. "Even if the moral aspects of the issue were dismissed, why doesn't India understand how the United States, China and Pakistan feel about the Soviet move but only wish that she be understood by these three countries?" was the question of an anguished American reporter.

The "finality" of Mrs Gandhi's choice, however, related only to the strategic divide in South Asia. The divide was (and is) between Pakistan and India. It got meshed with the global strategic divide since the early fifties when Pakistan became a cold war ally of the United States. The Pakistan-US military linkage produced the Indo-Soviet non-military linkage in the mid-fifties. The Indo-Soviet linkage acquired military import only after the India-China border war of 1962. Since the 1972 Sino-US diplomatic breakthrough, India had been apprehending the forging of an axis of Pakistan, China and the United States. Even if the axis were formed primarily to contain the Soviet Union, it would be perceived by Indians as a threat to India's legitimate stature and interests in South Asia. The Indian image of this kind of an emerging axis produced the Indo-Soviet treaty in August 1971.[3] Any joint Sino-US effort to prop up Pakistan as an operational base against the USSR could only fortify the Indo-Soviet strategic linkage.

By making this quite clear to everyone concerned, Mrs Gandhi believed she made an immediate contribution to stability in the region. Any ambiguity on her part would have seriously destabilised the strategic relationship which had stood India in good stead in the past and was expected to pay dividends in the future. In no conceivable circumstance could India line up with Pakistan, China and the United States against the Soviet Union; this would have gone against the grain of India's foreign policy since independence. Any measured censure of the Soviet action in Afghanistan could only have cost India a valued and tested friendship, without compensation from any other quarter. Isolation would have increased Soviet intransigence;

India would have no occasion to influence Moscow's thinking and action as a friend. American arms would have flown to Pakistan in large quantities; the Chinese would have trained the Afghan rebels; the Soviets, with the help of Afghan government, would have determined to destabilise Pakistan; Pakistan would conduct its nuclear explosion. . . . What would India have gained in such a baroque scenario?[4]

These were the thought currents behind the crucial choice Indira Gandhi made in the second week of Soviet military movement into Afghanistan. She did not seek the advice of the heads of the foreign office bureaucracy who, she suspected, had succumbed to the Janata regime's "genuine nonalignment," a camouflage, as far as she was concerned, for moving closer to the United States. She took counsel with a few of her old-time foreign policy aides. Contrary to the claim of some Indian analysts that by taking some distance from the Soviet position later, Mrs Gandhi virtually conceded that her first decision was a mistake, the prime minister did not resile from her basic stand. In fact, she kept to her own, and her father's, tradition. In 1968 she "non-opposed" and "non-deplored" the Soviet intervention in Czechoslovakia (as Jawaharlal Nehru had done in 1956 when the Soviets intervened in Hungary), without supporting Moscow's action and without giving up her right to express private misgiving and disapproval.

Indeed, the objectives of India's diplomacy with regard to the Afghan crisis were determined by three fundamental premises in Mrs Gandhi's foreign policy strategic thinking: (1) the Soviet intervention, though unfortunate and regrettable, was essentially a defensive move to secure the Afghan revolution and defeat US-sponsored efforts to destabilise the international situation; (2) for India, far more dangerous than Soviet military presence in Afghanistan would be the rearming of Pakistan by the US and China and the conversion of Pakistan into a cold war base; and (3) in a new cold war confrontation in which the United States, China and Pakistan joined forces to contain the USSR, India's national and regional interests dictated the pursuit of a single policy: to try to defuse confrontation in the South Asian region by keeping close to the USSR without completely identifying India with Soviet policies and actions.

The massive Indian diplomatic enterprise of January-June 1980 was tuned to this strategic thinking. It was conceptualised as diplomacy of defusing the crisis, revealing both its tactics and objectives.

A proud, imperial political actor, one who could legitimately claim to have elevated India to the status of the dominant regional power as a result of its military victory over Pakistan in 1971, Indira Gandhi chafed under the cavalier manner in which both Moscow and Washington treated India in regard to the Afghan issue. The Soviets did not care to inform India of their intervention until 25,000 troops had already moved into Afghanistan. Carter did not consult India before responding to the Soviet action by offering substantial military aid to Pakistan and sending his defence secretary, Harold Brown, to Peking to solicit Chinese help in the rearming of Pakistan. Both superpowers made it clear that when their own interests were at stake, they cared little for the sensitivities of medium powers not committed to their respective alignments. Mrs Gandhi came to the conclusion that India must act primarily to defend and promote its own interests. Foreign office officials later explained to the author that by choosing to invoke India's core relationship with the Soviet Union in an ambience of a renewed regional conflict, Mrs Gandhi sought to prevent a consolidation of the Sino-US alliance in this region. The very "finality" of Mrs Gandhi's choice had a sobering impact on strategic decision-makers in several capitals. It opened several channels of diplomatic dialogue—between India and Pakistan, between India and the United States, and between Pakistan and the Soviet Union. The "finality" of India's decision to stay with the USSR, then, did not close the possibility of a regional initiative. It opened this possibility.

"Two Different Threats"

In the first week of Mrs Gandhi's return to power, the US and Soviet ambassadors called at the Foreign office separately in what an Indian daily called "a new form of competitive diplomacy."[5] The official briefings on the diplomats' conversations revealed the contours of Mrs Gandhi's strategic thinking. The Soviet ambassador was told that the sooner Moscow pulled out its forces from Afghanistan, the better would it be for "all concerned"; reversely, the longer the troops stayed, the more difficult would it be to extricate them from the quagmire. This was the principal line of India's reasoning with Moscow through the spring and summer. The US ambassador was told that the Carter initiative to promote a security framework in South Asia was unacceptable to India; it could only escalate local tensions and conflicts. In vain did the ambassador try to reassure the Indian government that the proposed arms transfers to Pakistan were designed to improve the "general security environment" in the region rather than the military muscle of Pakistan. The US case was made worse by a clumsy dangling of carrots. The envoy expressed US readiness to meet India's defence requirements "in specific spheres" without imposing any preconditions and offered to discuss how to ensure early despatch of two pending shipments of American nuclear fuel for the Tarapore plant.[6] The unconcealed attempt to offer incentives for Indian acquiescence to the rearming of Pakistan was construed in the foreign office as a sign of American weakness in the region.

From India's point of view, Carter's diplomatic operations lacked finesse and ignored New Delhi's sensibilities from beginning to end. Carter sent his national security assistant, Brzezinski, and deputy secretary of state, Warren Christopher, to Pakistan, but picked up only a special envoy in the person of Clark Clifford to repair to New Delhi. The simultaneous dispatch of two unequal missions exhibited to Indians the relative importance India and Pakistan enjoyed in Carter's schema of response to the Soviet intervention in Afghanistan. It was only predictable, then, that Clifford's talks with Mrs Gandhi and Narasimha Rao should prove to be barren. As the *Indian Express* put it, they showed how totally different were US and Indian perceptions of the "mounting problems of South Asia and their cure."[7] With Clifford still to see the minister of external affairs, Mrs Gandhi made a statement on Afghanistan in the Lok Sabha which more or less endorsed the Soviet explanation of the reasons of their intervention. Clifford was said to have been "somewhat taken aback" by the sharpness of her criticism of US policies and action.[8] Clifford's 75-minute meeting with Mrs Gandhi on January 31 only confirmed that Washington and New Delhi were "concerned with different threats." Clifford's focus was on the Soviet intervention which "compelled" the US to offer military aid to Pakistan and take other counterveiling measures. The Indian focus was on the danger US arms aid to Pakistan would pose to the subcontinent. Clifford did not embellish Indian images of the US by affirming at a news conference that any further move by the Soviet Union to "reach out" to the Persian Gulf "will mean war."[9] He left New Delhi leaving behind him impressions of a President who had given up the path of detente and chosen the path of confrontation, even war.[10] Indians were dismayed by the performance of the Brzezinski mission in Pakistan and somewhat heartened by the strong criticism of Carter's proposal to rearm Pakistan in the United States itself.* The most lethal blow to Carter's Pakistan initiative came from Henry Kissinger, famous for his pro-Pakistan tilt in the Bangladesh crisis of 1971. Kissinger observed on January 22 that it was extremely unlikely that the Soviets would attack Pakistan and warned that the real threat would develop if the Soviet Union and India cooperated. "We must of course do our best to prevent this from happening. But the greatest danger is that India may seek, with Soviet cooperation, to dismember its neighbour by splitting Baluchistan and the Northwest Frontier Province and by occupying (Pakistan-occupied) Kashmir. Both India and the Soviet Union would then be surrounded by weak client states. A serious policy must deal with that contingency." Kissinger's own prescription was the stationing of airborne units in Pakistan "for an interim period."[11] Clifford had already given ominous hints of US military advisers being posted indefinitely in Pakistan to ensure that American arms were not used against India.[12]

The Kissinger statement, despite a prompt denial by the Administration that a decision had been taken to station troops and aircraft in Pakistan, widened the gap between Washington and New Delhi. On February 3, *The Hindu* came out with an evidently officially inspired account of what the United States had already planned to do to bolster Pakistan's military strength. The report said that apart from reequipping some of the existing Pakistani formations to improve their mobility, fire power and communications, the US plan for rearming Pakistan included the raising of at least five new Divisions over the next two years to double the deployment along the Afghan border without reducing its present strength on the Indian front. The US strategy was to build up Pakistan's military strength on the Afghan border to a point when Pakistan could absorb the first shock of a Soviet attack until the US air and naval forces stepped in to stem the advance. US policy was to avoid commital of its own ground troops as far as possible either for the defence of the Persian Gulf or Pakistan. The US continued to base its overall strategy to deter a Soviet attack on its backup nuclear power and the capacity of its naval and air forces to confront the Soviet Union.

---

*See the following chapter.

The US was therefore giving higher priority to reorganisation and expansion of the Pakistan army than its air force, the report continued. It was taking upon itself the responsibility for not only reequipping the existing formations with the latest weapons but also finding money on a long term basis to meet the support costs of the new divisions that were to be raised. The US was seeking participation in the programme of western allies and Saudi Arabia.

Pakistani army experts were reported to be of the view that the Soviet threat through Afghanistan could be met by deploying five Divisions, equipping them with the latest weapons and building a network of land communications along the Northwest Frontier and Baluchistan. They were particularly worried about vulnerability in the politically volatile Baluchistan with no road or rail system worth the name except in the Quetta region. The rest of the border with its low hills and greety terrain was ideal for a surprise thrust by Soviet units equipped with light tanks and armoured personnel carriers and self-propelled artillery, not to speak of the helicopter gunships and the MiG fighter bombers backing them.[13]

INDIAN INITIATIVES

The Indian government, then, was convinced that the US, with Chinese assistance, was planning to add substantially to Pakistan's military capability. It regarded this possibility with the utmost concern because the added Pakistani muscle would alter the balance of power in South Asia, seriously eroding India's regional supremacy.[14] The concern gathered an added edge when it became clear that Pakistan was in no mood to abandon its nuclear development programme, nor did Carter any longer regard Islamabad's nuclear ambitions to be a barrier to the flow of US military aid. In the last week of January, official sources disclosed that India had made it clear to Washington that it would regard as an "unfriendly act" the attempt to arm Pakistan whether this was done by the United States singly or in conjunction with China. If the US decided to ignore India's sentiments, it would be doing so "at the grave risk of increasing New Delhi's dependence on the Soviet Union for defence requirements to meet the situation."[15]

The Government's policy received the broad approval of parliament. Right wing opposition members were of course more critical of Moscow than of Washington and there was some demand that India got hold of its own China card for use against the USSR.[16] Some members asked for a stronger position on the question of withdrawal of Soviet troops from Afghanistan. Both Mrs Gandhi and Narasimha Rao assured members that they opposed foreign intervention and, particularly, prolonged presence of foreign troops in any country and that diplomatic efforts to persuade Moscow to pull out of Afghanistan as soon as possible were continuing. At the same time, India was not ready to condemn the Soviet action. "We do not believe in condemnation," Mrs Gandhi said in the Lok Sabha on January 30. What happened in Afghanistan was that country's internal affair. The Soviets had told her that even Hafizullah Amin had asked for military help. Mrs Gandhi chided those who criticised the Soviet action for didn't they remain "surprisingly silent" when Chinese troops had marched into Vietnam in February 1979?[17] A few days earlier, she affirmed to men and women of her own party in parliament, "We are neither pro-Russia nor pro-America. We are only pro-India."[18] In numerous interviews given to foreign journalists, Mrs Gandhi persistently defended the Soviet justification of their Afghan intervention. The crisis in international relations, she repeatedly made clear, did not begin with Soviet troops moving into Afghanistan, but with US efforts to recreate the cold war since the outbreak of the Iranian revolution.[19] Supplementing Mrs Gandhi's efforts, the three points that Rao stressed most in parliament were that India's stand did not mean support for the Soviet intervention; that in India's perception, the rearming of Pakistan by the US and China, and the extension of great power confrontation to South Asia were more destabilising for the whole area and for each of its members than what had happened in the Hindu Kush; and that the main thrust of India's diplomacy was to defuse the crisis and dam the confrontation.[20]

Between January and April, more than 30 foreign dignitaries came to New Delhi mainly to discuss the Afghan developments with Mrs Gandhi. They came from all continents, representing great, medium and small powers, governments of all political colours, belonging to all existing alignments and groupings. The prominent among them were the UN Secretary-General, the Presidents of France and Austria, the Foreign Ministers of the USSR, Britain, Italy and Rumania, the Prime Minister of Vietnam and the Foreign Ministers of Cuba and Algeria, and the leader of the Palestine Liberation Organisation (PLO). Altogether 130 hours of conversations took place in Delhi between Mrs Gandhi and her foreign minister on the one hand and the visiting statesmen on the other. At the same time, Indian diplomats travelled to the capitals of all neighbouring countries and farther off to Washington, London, Moscow, Paris, Bonn, Tokyo and Peking to project the diplomacy of crisis defusion. The United States did not send a cabinet officer to New Delhi, but Rao did talk to the Secretary of State, Cyrus Vance, in Washington. India's personal diplomacy was capped with Mrs Gandhi's meeting with Gen. Zia-ul-Huq, the Chinese Prime Minister, Hua Guofeng and Leonid Brezhnev in Salisbury and Belgrade. It became clear in the midst of this diplomacy in a crowded region that India's principal targets were the Soviet Union and Pakistan; at a slight remove, the United States demanded a great deal of attention because India saw the Carter White House as the main carpenter of the coming crisis. It also became clear that in its diplomacy of defusing the crisis, India received encouragement and help not from its traditional friends but from the middle-of-the-road powers of Europe—France, Western Germany, Rumania and Poland. India became a member of an international constituency which did not wish to throw away the gains of detente, which opposed extreme reactions to the Soviet action, and which persevered to lift the cold war and defuse the superpower confrontation.

The Indian foreign policy establishment has always expected the country to play a major role in world affairs and a dominant role in regional affairs. The convulsions caused by the Soviet intervention in Afghanistan stirred the foreign policy elite to great expectations. The foreign minister, Rao, who had no previous experience of handling international affairs, and whose appointment coincided with a major world crisis vitally affecting India's interests, was easily tempted to cater to the elite hopes. In his maiden statements in parliament, he crafted the mistique of Indian "initiatives." He would, however, throw on it only the smallest trickle of light and keep himself confined to such tantalising sentences as: "The Government has kept its diplomatic initiative intact, and we are going to make full and effective use of it."

Journalists rushed in where the minister refused to tread. In one of the first journalistic curtain-raisers on the Indian "initiative," *The Hindu*'s G.K. Reddy reported that in the sphere of foreign relations, the government intended to do all that was possible to mobilise opinion against the growing dangers of great power involvement in the region. "It is thinking of an Indian initiative to bring the neighbouring countries and the interested powers together to defuse the deepening crisis and foster better understanding amongst them. The proposed diplomatic move will take some time to take shape but preliminary consultations with the concerned countries will be initiated soon."[21]

Four days later, Reddy revealed that the Government was considering whether it should confine its current exchanges to bilateral talks with other countries in the region or take the initiative in convening a conference of the foreign ministers of these countries to discuss what could be done to avert the danger of big power rivalries in the region. "One of the suggestions is that India should invite Pakistan, Iran, Afghanistan, Nepal, Bangladesh, Sri Lanka and even Burma to such a conference if these countries were willing to take part."[22]

The fortunes of the Indian initiative flickered and flinched until, like the Cheshire cat in Alice's Wonderland, it disappeared altogether leaving its smile to analysts and commentators as a reward for hard work.

A Bridge to Pakistan

The UN Secretary-General, Kurt Waldheim, helped Indira Gandhi build a tenuous bridge to Pakistan. Having gone to Islamabad to seek Gen. Zia's help to get the American hostages in Iran released, Waldheim took the opportunity to discuss Afghanistan also. His talks with Mrs Gandhi on January 23 satisfied Waldheim that India was trying privately to persuade Moscow at least to thin out its military presence in Afghanistan. Waldheim later informed Mrs Gandhi that Gen. Zia would be delighted to open a dialogue with India.[23] Mrs Gandhi chose the foreign secretary, Ram Sathe, to undertake a probing mission to Pakistan. Sathe arrived in Islamabad on February 5 when the air was still nippy with the hot flavour of an on-coming US-Pakistan-China alliance. He was ready for a frosty reception, and was pleasantly surprised to get a warm one. A 100-minute palaver with his Pakistani counterpart broke the ice; a courtesy call on Zia developed to a full-fledged diplomatic session lasting an hour. The two neighbours' perceptions of the crisis remained widely apart, but there were subtle nuances of pressure at work, gently pushing the closed door to strategic cooperation slightly ajar. The Brzezinski mission made it clear to Zia that without India's tacit approval the proposed US-Pakistani compact would not stand; it would fall down if India took a hostile view and lurched to further cement its military relationship with Moscow, Gen. Zia and his aides therefore took considerable pains to convince Sathe that the military help Pakistan was seeking from the US must not cause India any concern; on the contrary, India should be pleased that Pakistan was taking on the Soviet giant, thereby making a solid contribution to the security and stability of the region. The message Sathe conveyed from Indira Gandhi was a mixture of sympathy and admonishment spiced with an instruction on the politics of great power confrontation. India, Sathe told Zia and his aides, shared Pakistan's anxiety about superpower military involvement in the region, and realised that Pakistan needed to augment its defence. Pakistan had nothing to fear from India in the context of the events in Afghanistan—an opaque assurance that India had no intention of taking advantage of Pakistan's predicament. However, Pakistan's understanding of the nature of the crisis was wrong. What was building up in South Asia was a great power confrontation. This confrontation had a logic of its own; it cared little for the interests and sensibilities of small and medium powers. The confrontation would undermine stability and development in the entire region. Pakistan and India must act together to defuse it. There should be no big flow of arms and weaponry to the region from the arsenals of the major powers, nor should any country do anything which might add to tension and confrontation.

The discussion on bilateral issues was marked by a restoration of both countries' commitment to the Simla Agreement which, both said, provided a suitable framework to establish a cooperative relationship.[24]

On February 6, Gen. Zia was in an expansive mood when he talked to a group of Indian reporters. He had already spoken to Mrs Gandhi on the telephone in the morning and he said he was much encouraged by a letter from Mrs Gandhi he had received through the Indian foreign secretary. Zia said that there should be an Indian initiative to secure the independence of Afghanistan. As a "big country and as the most important regional power in the area," India should assert its position and influence with the Soviet Union to get the Russian troops withdrawn from Afghanistan. And he favoured the raising of a peace-keeping mission consisting of India, Pakistan and Iran to facilitate withdrawal of Soviet troops from Afghanistan and to give the people of Afghanistan an opportunity to decide their future, although, according to Sathe, this issue was not discussed at all during his talks in Islamabad.

The Afghan issue, Gen. Zia said, was not a regional issue but a global one. A superpower had overrun a neighbouring state, disturbing the equilibrium in the region. A buffer state had been vanquished in next to no time. It was the responsibility of the world community to come to its rescue. India must not speak in the language in which the Russian ambassador might be speaking. "Look at China. The moment world opinion went against it, it took less than three weeks to vacate Vietnam. To my mind, the Russians will not vacate Afghanistan immediately though they may eventually."

Gen. Zia painted a scenario of the Gulf region which mirrored American visions. After Soviet intervention, he said, Afghanistan had become a "big red wedge." The question was whether the wedge moved west to Iran or east to Pakistan. If it moved west, the entire Gulf would be overrun. Either way the prospects were grim. He was certain that the Soviets had larger geopolitical designs. Otherwise, the presence of 80,000 Russian troops in a rugged barren country devoid of any mineral or natural resources did not make sense. The Soviet presence in Afghanistan was as much a threat to Pakistan as it was to India. More in pain than in anger Zia agreed with a reporter that Pakistan perceived Indira Gandhi to be "pro-Soviet."[25]

Before leaving Pakistan, Sathe told newsmen that India was not against Pakistan getting military help from the United States but this "should not contribute to tensions in the subcontinent." His Pakistani counterpart was more candid. He said, "Pakistan and India have different perceptions regarding the situation which has developed as a result of Soviet invasion of Afghanistan."[26]

Two interesting sidelines to the first round of Indo-Pakistan talks on the Soviet intervention in Afghanistan were quite revealing. The first was the disclosure made by Gen. Zia that India had struck a $ 2.6 billion arms purchase deal with the USSR. He had received the information from US official sources. The report of the deal was denied in New Delhi. It was, however, confirmed several weeks later that agreements had been concluded for the purchase of $ 1.6 billion (Rs 1300 crore) worth of arms from the USSR over a period of 15 years.[27] The second was that Pakistani officials let the Indians know that the diplomatic channel between Islamabad and Moscow was quite active and that messages were being frequently exchanged.

In the weeks that followed, ranking officials of the Indian foreign office were sent to Colombo, Kathmandu and Dacca. The results of these diplomatic forays were summed up by G.K. Reddy in *The*

Hindu of February 11. The diplomatic soundings, he wrote, did not "hold out much hope of any joint initiative for exerting collective pressures on the superpowers to desist from further involvement in the internal affairs of the region." Although India did not expect a common regional stand on the Afghanistan crisis to emerge from its diplomatic endeavours, it was at least keen on creating a better awareness among the neighbouring countries of the inherent dangers of a much bigger crisis before long if nothing was done to discourage the developing confrontation between the superpowers. But unfortunately none of these countries was inclined to see the two developments in the same light as India did. India continued to maintain that the Soviet action in Afghanistan should not be viewed in isolation since "it is not the cause but a consequence of the deepening superpower rivalries in the region." India was also of the view that the best way of persuading Moscow to withdraw its forces was not by arming Pakistan but by promoting greater stability in the area with the support of the regional states concerned. "The result is that no common denominator of understanding is emerging from the differing approaches of these countries even for the limited purpose of counselling the Soviet Union to pull out of Afghanistan or cautioning the US against the dangers of arming Pakistan. The Indian contention that these two inseparable components of the same crisis cannot be tackled compartmentally but have to be dealt with concommitantly as parts of one and the same problem is not making much impression on them. The sad part of it all is that not a single Asian country has gone the whole hog with India over issues like Kampuchea and Afghanistan because many of them seem to imagine that India invariably tends to give the benefit of doubt to the Soviet Union. The fact that the initial Indian reaction is often quite different from its subsequent policy positions has not also helped to generate confidence among the neighbouring countries about its readiness to apply the same standards in all such situations."[28]

TALKS WITH MOSCOW: "THE MOST VITAL LINK"

Now came India's most important diplomatic engagement of the Afghan season: talks between Indira Gandhi and Andre Gromyko in New Delhi. Brisk diplomatic exchanges between New Delhi and Moscow had been going on since mid-January; the Gromyko visit was arranged at the Kremlin's initiative.[29] Both the Indian government and the press were fully aware of the visit's importance. It would make or mar India's diplomatic initiatives. The visit would provide "the most vital link in India's process of consultations," observed the *Times of India*.[30] Evidently reporters were signalled by the foreign office to play down India's quest for a regional framework to settle the Afghan crisis. India's talks with a large number of governments had had only one aim: defusion of tension, affirmed the *Times of India*'s diplomatic correspondent. "It has no regional plan of its own to resolve the crisis."[31] The *Indian Express* echoed that the foreign office discounted "the theory that India is trying to evolve a regional initiative on the Afghan question."[32] The initiative could wait, now that Gromyko was coming.

On the eve of Gromyko's visit, the Soviets dropped hints that they might be willing to withdraw their troops from Afghanistan in the near future in case the United States and China were prepared to take steps to reduce tension in the area. The Soviet ambassador in Tokyo was quoted as saying, "Much depends on the US and China. The present situation can end in the near future unless the two countries try to escalate it."[33] A few days earlier, an official of the Indian foreign affairs ministry, S.K. Singh, who had been an ambassador to Kabul, went to the Afghan capital on a special mission and had talks with Karmal as well as foreign minister Dost. Following Singh's visit, the Afghan government issued a statement saying that the Soviet forces in Afghanistan would be withdrawn as soon as the cause which "necessitated the request for such military assistance" ceased to exist under "a credible guarantee." This was construed in New Delhi as an improvement on Afghanistan's earlier stand, reaffirmed by Karmal himself early February, that it was neither necessary nor possible to fix a time limit for the withdrawal of Soviet forces. "They are here to consolidate the gains of our revolution, protect our land and secure peace in the region. As long as there is danger from outside, the Russians will stay," Karmal had declared.[34]

The Hindu found in Karmal's mellower statement "the promise of a reasonable settlement that could lead to the withdrawal of the Soviet forces." Reflecting hopes entertained in the foreign office, the paper's New Delhi correspondent said that Babrak's statement contained some hopeful elements for future discussions with neighbouring countries either bilaterally or collectively for providing credible guarantees to the new regime of non-interference in the internal affairs of Afghanistan. New Delhi apparently believed that the Kabul government was prepared to engage in discussions with Pakistan in order to find a mutually acceptable solution. "The Indian policy is to encourage a direct dialogue between the two neighbouring countries with or without its own participation." The report said the talks with Gromyko would take place against this general background with India neither supporting nor condemning the Soviet action but calling for an early withdrawal of at least the bulk of Russian troops to remove the "justification for US attempts to arm Pakistan." The report then sprung a surprise which none took very seriously at that time. "The US, too, is not insisting on an immediate rollback of the Soviet troops from Afghanistan, but only on ensuring that Moscow would not try to do elsewhere what it did in this buffer state. The focus therefore is not on the Soviet presence in Afghanistan but on the danger of a similar thing happening in Iran or Pakistan."[35]

In the clear cool morning of February 12, Gromyko landed at the Palam airport on his 16th visit to the Indian capital. The same day he had a hour-long meeting with Narasimha Rao, followed by a three-hour discussion with Mrs Gandhi and a half-hour meeting in which none but Gromyko and Mrs Gandhi were present. Very little information was officially given out about the first round of talks. But news reporters were unanimous in speculating that the first meetings were devoted to the statement of mutual positions. *The Hindu* correspondent said that at the private meeting, both Mrs Gandhi and Gromyko "talked candidly of what could be done to defuse the crisis, whether Moscow was prepared to start reducing soon at least a part of its massive military buildup in Afghanistan."[36]

On February 13, Gromyko and Rao met for two hours. *The Hindu* reported that no agreed proposals emerged which could be put across to the US, China and Pakistan with any reasonable hope of acceptance. The Indian and Soviet officials were working until late in the night to produce an agreed draft statement highlighting the near proximity or close identity of views and reaffirming the desire on both sides for closer relations. But the Soviet draft was not acceptable to India since the formulation on Afghanistan did not clearly spell out its stand on inviolability of frontiers and non-interference in the internal affairs of other nations. "It became quite evident at the end of these talks that unless a way could be found for dovetailing the regional concerns of India with the global considerations of the Soviet Union, it was going to be extremely difficult to persuade Moscow to make the first move for defusing the Afghan situation."[37]

The political correspondent of *Indian Express* reported that the talk had failed to throw up a solution to the Afghan situation. India wanted the Soviet Union to withdraw its troops from Afghanistan so that the tension in India's neighbourhood was defused. Gromyko gave no indication of a time-frame for Soviet withdrawal. "This is the first time in 25 years that the two countries have clearly differed on a major international question although the two delegations are still making efforts to arrive at a coordinated view of the strategic threat to the region." The Indian government failed to convince Moscow that it must withdraw troops from Afghanistan as part of Soviet contribution to normalising the situation in the region. Gromyko, on the other hand, failed to convince India entirely on the Soviet Union's military intervention in Afghanistan.[38]

The *Hindustan Times* reported that the talks broke off rather prematurely without any agreement over the steps needed to contain the situation from further deterioration. The Indian side seemingly repeated its viewpoint that both superpowers should steer clear of the South Asian region and argued that the Soviets come to an "understanding with the US." The reciprocal basis of the understanding could be the pulling out of Soviet troops and non-transfer of US arms to Pakistan.[39] According to the *Times of India*, the Indian side made it clear to Gromyko that the initiative to help develop a regional response to the Afghan crisis outside the parameters of superpower confrontation could not get off the ground without some positive response from the Soviet Union.[40]

On the 14th morning, Gromyko delayed his departure by two hours and had a 40-minute discussion with Mrs Gandhi in the presence of Rao and Nikolai Firyubin. A joint statement issued at the end of the talks did not mention Afghanistan at all, not to speak of a time-table for the withdrawal of Soviet troops. It only said that "the developments in the region and around it" were reviewed "in an atmosphere of mutual trust and cordiality." Also reviewed were bilateral relations in the perspective of the long and traditional friendship between India and the Soviet Union and in the spirit of the Indo-Soviet treaty.[41]

In two formal speeches during his visit to Delhi, Mr Gromyko strongly attacked Pakistan for collaborating with the United States and China to destabilise Afghanistan. At a dinner hosted by Rao,

Gromyko said, "Pakistan would get nothing if it went along the path followed by the US and China. Pakistan's interests would imply good and friendly relations with all the neighbouring countries." His defence of the Soviet intervention was unusually tough. It was absurd and dishonourable for the imperialists to suggest that the Soviet action in Afghanistan started the present crisis or that it was a prelude to further aggressive designs. They could not but know that Afghanistan "would defend its independence" with its might and that the Soviet Union would respond to its request for help. He said the United States was determined to "convert Pakistan into a hot bed of tension and a springboard for further escalation of aggression against Afghanistan."[42] Again, at a dinner he himself hosted for the Indian External Affairs Minister, Gromyko warned Pakistan and its leaders to weigh "which political path for it will be better—the path of peace and goodneighbourly relations or the path of tension and hostility with neighbouring countries. If Pakistan wants to live in friendship with Afghanistan it should cease intrusions into Afghan territory and this cessation should be effective and guaranteed." He said that the Afghan government wished to normalise its relations with Pakistan "for ensuring that the border between these two states were the border of peace, friendship and cooperation." Unfortunately, Pakistan did not reciprocate. "The USSR was and is ready to develop relations with Pakistan in the political, trade, economic and other spheres, provided Pakistan also wants it and follows the course of peace and relaxation of international tension. Here again we did not get any response of readiness to act in the same direction. Thus the leadership of Pakistan has spoilt, though in different degrees, its relations with a number of states at the same time. We do not think this is a wise policy."[43]

The instant journalistic measurements of the talks between Gromyko and Indira Gandhi did not get their real depth, nor size.[44] Neither got from the other all that he or she asked for; neither was completely disappointed. Mrs Gandhi pressed very hard for one or more of the following: (1) an immediate token withdrawal of Soviet troops from Afghanistan; (2) a public pledge that the bulk of the troops would be withdrawn within a specific period of time; (3) a statement affirming Soviet adherence to nonintervention in internal affairs of other countries and inviolability of the territory of sovereign nations; and (4) Soviet contribution to the creation of a regional security system without both superpowers—the contribution being in the form of pulling out of troops from Afghanistan and a declaration of approval, in principle, of a regional system autonomous of the great powers. Gromyko refused to make any one of these gestures. In the new confrontation with America, manufactured entirely by President Carter, the USSR would not be the first to blink. Pakistan and the United States must first stop interfering in Afghan affairs before the Soviets could make any concrete move about troops pullout. Gromyko made it clear that the Soviets had every right to rush military help to friendly regimes in dire distress; this was no intervention, and was no third party's business.

The Gromyko visit was a new experience for India. The Soviets were deeply offended by Carter's handling of the entire situation. They were convinced that the US was bent upon bringing the cold war back. The remarkable thing was Gromyko's assertion of Soviet power. It was clear that in the new confrontation with the US, the Soviets were determined to operate from a position of equal strength. The terrain—not only Afghanistan, but the entire Southwestern region—was far more slippery for the Americans than for the Russians. Gromyko left a clear impression on Mrs Gandhi that Soviet diplomacy was active on two fronts. At the superpower front, Moscow would deal directly with the United States, or through America's allies like West Germany. The objective was to salvage detente. At the regional level, the main target of Soviet diplomacy was Pakistan. Moscow was determined to soften up Pakistan's attitude to the Marxist regime in Kabul. In this, any help India could render was highly welcome. But Moscow was not depending on India. It had its own channels open to Pakistan. It had its allies in the Islamic group of nations. It had a solid knot of loyal supporters in the nonaligned group. Gromyko's message to India was crisp, precise and unambiguous. "Please don't ask us to do something we can't do," he, in effect, told the Prime Minister. "We appreciate India's friendship and realise its value. We do not want that Afghanistan should come as a cloud over this friendship. Afghanistan is a neighbour of the USSR, and a close ally. We cannot leave Afghanistan to the imperialists. We are not in that country for ever. But when and how we withdraw our troops depends on what Pakistan and the United States choose to do. We shall be pleased if you could help Pakistan and the US realise this. As far as Indo-Soviet relations are concerned, it is our firm desire to strengthen them still further. The defeat of the imperialist designs about Afghanistan will, in our view, improve the stability and security of the entire South Asian region, including India."

The message was taken by Mrs Gandhi. New nuances now embellished India's diplomacy of crisis defusion. The prime minister told reporters on February 20 that she had been assured by the Soviet Union that it would withdraw its troops from Afghanistan if Pakistan stopped training and sending guerrillas for raids. She indicated that the focus of Indian diplomacy was not on the withdrawal of Russian troops but on the stopping of American arms transfers to Pakistan.[45]

Indian officials repeatedly denied during Gromyko's presence in New Delhi that the question of Indian arms purchases from the USSR figured at all in the talks. However, the letter that Mrs Gandhi received from Brezhnev through Gromyko carried enough hints that the Soviets would be sympathetic to India's expanding defence requirements in view of the American-sponsored arms race in the region. Differences over Afghanistan were not allowed to impair the bilateral relationship in the least. *The Hindu* correctly reported that the Afghan factor was being "isolated step by step from the mainstream of Indo-Soviet relations so that the two countries can agree to disagree on this issue without impairing their wide-ranging cooperation . . . ." India "understands" why the Soviets moved into Afghanistan; it realised that Soviet troops withdrawal "can only be part of a wider accord between the superpowers."[46] This understanding and realisation on India's part made the visit of I.V. Arkhipov, Soviet deputy premier, to New Delhi late February handsomely fruitful for further expansion of bilateral relations.[47]

SOUNDINGS IN WASHINGTON

Meanwhile, Soviet diplomacy kept zeroing in on Pakistan. Russian diplomats had informal exchanges with Pakistani diplomats at several world capitals, including Washington and London. By the end of February, there were signs that the two governments had reached the rudiments of an understanding. Moscow assured Pakistan that it had no wish to violate the Durand Line. Soviet troops operating in Afghanistan scrupulously refrained from crossing the border in pursuit of the Afghan rebels. The Soviet ambassador, a frequent caller at the Pakistani foreign office, made it repeatedly clear that the only way to avoid a "bigger conflict" was to arrive at "some understanding" with the regime in Kabul, which Moscow would "defend at any cost." On Pakistan's side, Zia did not remove a single division of troops from the Indian border to Pakistan's border with Afghanistan. Apparently he now saw the Soviet presence in Afghanistan as a political rather than a military problem.[48]

The change in Gen. Zia-ul-Huq's perception fuelled India's Pakistan initiative. *The Hindu* reported that encouraged by Gen. Zia's "gradual disengagement from his earlier confrontationist posture," New Delhi asked whether he would be willing to discuss the "entire Indo-Pakistan relationship" with a special envoy of Mrs. Gandhi like Sardar Swaran Singh, for many years a senior member of successive Congress cabinets.[49]

But before sending a special envoy to Islamabad, Indira Gandhi decided to carry her diplomacy of crisis defusion to Washington. In this too, reports said, she was encouraged by Gromyko himself as well as by signal beamed from the US capital. In India's perception, neither superpower was now "itching for a showdown"; both were "equally keen" on keeping their differences "within manageable limits."[50] Mrs Gandhi thought that it was worth exploring with the US and the UK possibilities of a direct Pakistan-Afghanistan understanding on the basis of which Soviet troops could be withdrawn from Afghanistan and the Karmal regime left in peace. India had already apprised almost all governments in the Persian Gulf region of the results of Gromyko's visit to New Delhi, and reports said that these governments were impressed that India was not pursuing an "avowedly pro-Moscow stand."[51] There was evidence that the talks with the Soviet Foreign Minister created contrary pulls of thinking in the Indian foreign office. One pull was for working out an understanding with Pakistan as a prelude to a wider understanding among the USSR, the US, Afghanistan, Pakistan and India. The other pull was to work with the West European powers to narrow the divide between the USSR and the US, the hypothesis being that once the superpowers arrived at an understanding on the basics of normalising the situation, an accord between Pakistan and Afghanistan could not be far behind.[52]

The man who was sent in the last week of February to sound officials in Washington was Eric Gonsalves, one of the three secretaries in the foreign affairs ministry, a suave, matter-of-fact diplomat with a long stint at the Indian embassy in the US capital. He also took London and Ottawa in his stride. In Washington, Gonsalves met with Brzezinski, Clark Clifford, Warren Christopher and other officials, as well as Senators Charles Percy and John Glenn. He gave the Administration officials a gist of Mrs Gandhi's conversation with Gromyko and probed, but could not find, a meeting of Soviet and American perceptions of the Afghan situation. Nevertheless, Gonsalves did see a change in the American attitude towards the crisis; the US was now seeking a diplomatic rather than a military settlement. He was assured by US officials that the Administration had not taken any major decision about arms transfer to Pakistan. In London, Gonsalves found the British foreign secretary, Carrington, canvassing the concept of a "neutralised" Afghanistan, with tacit American backing. Gonsalves returned to New Delhi with the reassuring impression that the Afghan crisis had peaked; it could now only de-escalate. The diplomatic stalemate could not last for ever. Early March, the Indian foreign office sighted indications that the Soviet Union and the US were "edging towards a direct dialogue on Afghanistan, instead of relying on other countries to bring them together."[53]

When Gonsalves was in Washington, *The Hindu* carried a report which, if it were not entirely speculative, showed that there was at least a strand of foreign policy strategic thinking in the Indian foreign office that sought a "balanced relationship" with the two superpowers. The report stressed the strains visiting India's relations with the USSR. "For the first time, India and the Soviet Union are faced with a conflict of interests as well as a divergence of ideas on Afghanistan. The main thrust of Indian diplomacy is now directed towards persuading Moscow to pull back its forces, if possible, or else isolating the Afghan factor from the Indo-Soviet relationship in a manner that the two countries can continue to differ on this issue without prejudice to their wide-ranging cooperation in other spheres. It poses a challenge and also provides on opportunity to India to take a fresh look at the character and content of its treaty relationship primarily from the point of view of its own enlightened self-interest and stability in the region.

"Although the Indian government has been equally critical of US actions, the Soviet Union is not impressed by this equivocal approach since Moscow expects India to measure its responses to the Afghan imbroglio to meet the requirements of the Indo-Soviet bilateral relations."

The report added that India's on-going diplomatic initiative aimed at not only defusing the Afghan crisis but also regaining a certain measure of flexibility in developing a "balanced relationship with the two superpowers without identifying itself too closely with either of them."

"The intention is not to dilute the existing relationship with the Soviet Union but not let this become an impediment to the development of equally beneficial links with the United States. Though the Carter Administration has not been happy with the tardy Indian reaction to the Soviet intervention in Afghanistan, it has been quite appreciative of how this country has been resisting the Soviet pressures to take a more sympathetic attitude.

"There are some in Delhi who in the name of greater pragmatism are not looking upon the Soviet action as an unmitigated evil because they are inclined to believe that its very presence on the other side of the Khyber Pass will have a sobering influence in Pakistan. The argument runs that no matter how far the US and China go in arming Pakistan, it will have to think several times before embarking on any fresh military adventure against India with the Soviet troops breathing down their necks from Afghanistan. The advocates of this strategic doctrine go a step further in proferring the theory that China too will be careful not to commit its troops to any course of action in conjunction with Pakistan that would bring them into confrontation with the Soviet forces in Afghanistan. The arm-chair strategists engaged in this inverted thinking do not seem to realise that whatever its deterrent value in narrow Indo-Pakistan terms, the very presence of the Soviet army in Afghanistan would give Moscow additional leverage in exercising further pressures and extending its influence to the subcontinent irrespective of what the US does or does not do to forestall it.

"The India dream of insulating this area from superpower rivalries bristles with dilemmas of many imponderable factors involved in it. It is both conceivable and possible for India to steer a middle course between the US and the Soviet Union while seeking mutually beneficial, bilateral relations with both of them.

"But its not going to be easy to disengage itself from its far reaching commitments with the Soviet Union without the promise of some consistency in the US dealings with the countries of the region. It should not be difficult for India to keep up its present level of relationship with the Soviet Union without prejudice to its policy of normalisation with China or better understanding with the United

States. A sine qua non for the pursuit of this dual policy is closer links with all the neighbouring countries including Pakistan.⁵⁴

A Cuban Interlude

The results of diplomatic probings in Washington added to India's dilemmas. India had succeeded in blockading the US-Pakistan arms deal. When Gonsalves was in Washington, the deal had not fallen through, but had run into severe difficulties. India wanted to move a little closer to the US position about the basics of normalising the Afghan situation, but was aware that the Soviets would neither make a token withdrawal nor announce a time-table for military pullout without adequate reciprocal gestures from the United States. What, in the circumstances, should be the next step in India's diplomatic enterprise? Kuldip Nayar ventured that India would now move towards convening a Geneva-type conference of countries "directly interested" in the Afghan crisis: he offered a pretty long list that included the USSR, the US and Britain, Afghanistan, Pakistan, India, Iran and Saudi Arabia—with China a "perhaps" candidate.⁵⁵ Within three days, G.K. Reddy shot down Nayar's report with transparent briefings from the foreign office.⁵⁶ Clearly, different people in the foreign policy decision-making setup were thinking differently. Then, in the first week of April, came the announcement of the Soviet-Afghan treaty formalising the presence of Russian troops in Afghanistan.⁵⁷ It had a freezing effect on India's diplomatic efforts.⁵⁸ How could India move to the next step of its diplomacy if the Soviets were not willing to discuss proposals for troop withdrawal?

The dilemma did not resolve as a result of Mrs Gandhi's conversations with leaders of the two leading Communist members of the nonaligned group of nations, Prime Minister Pham Van Dong, of Vietnam, and the Foreign Minister of Cuba, Isidoro Malemiera Peoli. If anything, it got worse. Indo-Vietnamese relations have been particularly cordial; India is a major aid-giver to Vietnam, whose stability and strength is regarded by Indians as important to contain Chinese power. The talks between Dong and Indira Gandhi were held in a "cordial and warm" atmosphere. But the two differed on Afghanistan and the difference was candidly admitted by the visiting Prime Minister. The concrete point of difference was the timing and modality of Soviet troops withdrawal. Mrs Gandhi failed to coax Dong to join her even privately in pressing Moscow to pull out some troops and set a time limit for complete withdrawal. She was indeed asking Dong to ask Brezhnev to do in Afghanistan what Vietnam was itself refusing to do in Kampuchea! Naturally, Dong gave his unqualified support to the Soviet stand. The Afghan issue, however, was not allowed to cloud the growth of bilateral Indo-Vietnamese relations.[59] The visit of the Cuban Foreign Minister proved to be an irritant. New Delhi was surprised when it first learnt that Isidoro Malmeira was hopping between Moscow, Islamabad and Kabul. Inquiries made by the Indian embassy in Moscow as to whether the Cuban diplomatic intervention was mounted on Castro's personal initiative or at the request of the Soviet Union did not elicit clear information. In any case, officials in New Delhi viewed this intervention with distaste; they had little wish to concede to Cuba the role of a peacemaker in South Asia. Cuba had blocked a debate on Afghanistan at the nonaligned group at the UN, with Indian support—a debate could only divide the group into predictable factions. Even at the 12-member working group of the nonaligned at the UN, three shades of views on Afghanistan surfaced early March—those who condemned the Soviet intervention, those who justified it, and those who did not wish to see the group split on this account. When Isidoro Malmeira "unexpectedly" arrived in Kabul on March 25 and soon later earned the distinction of being the first senior official from a pro-Soviet country to visit Pakistan since the Soviet intervention in Afghanistan, an agonising question creased foreheads in the Indian foreign office: Is Moscow trying to take the wind out of the sails of India's crisis-defusing diplomacy?

Mrs Gandhi treated Isidoro Malmeira to one of those monosyllabic sessions for which she is famous. They met on April 8, after the Cuban Foreign Minister had spent 75 minutes with Narasimha Rao. Malmeira did the talking; Mrs Gandhi only asked a few questions. It seemed clear, however, that Cuba was trying to bring Gen. Zia and Babrak Karmal together at Havana or anywhere else; Castro himself in a communication to Mrs Gandhi asked for her help to realise this shared objective. Indians were relieved when Gen. Zia turned down the Cuban proposal. They also noted with some relief that Nikolai Firyubin, the deputy Soviet foreign minister who has specialised in South and Southeast Asian affairs, made no mention of the Cuban effort when he had an unscheduled meeting with Ram Sathe a few hours after Malmeira had his frosty session with Mrs Gandhi.[60]

SECOND MISSION TO PAKISTAN

A significant aspect of the Cuban interlude was that it was initiated *after* the Pakistani decision not to go in for American military aid as offered by the Carter Administration. Perhaps Moscow thought that the breakdown of the arms negotiations would make Pakistan more receptive to a "proxy" diplomatic overture. Pakistan's rejection of the Cuban initiative coincided with an opening towards India: Gen. Zia told New Delhi that he would be delighted to receive a special envoy of Mrs Gandhi. So Sardar Swaran Singh arrived in Islamabad on April 10, a full month and five days after Pakistan's final rejection of the Carter package, billowing like a ship of goodwill, with a white flag of amity and goodneighbourliness fluttering from its mast. On the eve of his departure from Delhi, the Indian press saw "a far greater degree of closeness in the Indian and Pakistani approaches (to the situation created by Soviet intervention in Afghanistan) now than there has been so far." Formal articulations during Swaran Singh's visit exuded warmth, if not cordiality. Singh said he did not bring any specific proposals in his portfolio, but came only to discuss with Pakistan's leaders "anything" which would ease the crisis and confrontation in the region. India had the friendliest feelings for Pakistan. It wanted a break with the past. For peace and stability in the region, it was essential that the two neighbours narrowed down their differences. The Pakistan foreign minister, Aga Shahi, reciprocated by saying that Pakistan looked forward to a goodneighbourly and tension-free relationship with India.[61]

At their meetings lasting for five hours in two days, Swaran Singh, Agha Shahi and Zia-ul-Huq ploughed deep into the conflict-ridden soil of India-Pakistan relations. Singh found the military ruler of Pakistan surprisingly relaxed about Afghanistan, the border more peaceful than ever before since April 1978. Zia had practically ceased fuelling the Afghan insurgency. He was still stubbornly resisting Soviet pressure to meet with Babrak Karmal which would amount to recognizing the Marxist regime in Kabul. In any case, he was now looking at the Afghan crisis not through American eyes, but through the eyes of the Islamic conference. He had worked out a live-and-let-live relationship with the Soviets. Having rejected American military aid, he was no longer under strong pressure from Washington or Moscow. Gen. Zia did not need India to defuse the crisis. He had defused it himself for his own country.

The talks between Swaran Singh and Zia-ul-Huq therefore skirted around the complex and difficult question of building strategic bridges and narrowing, if not closing, the traditional strategic divide in South Asia. Zia renewed his proposal for mutual force reduction, conceding, for the first time, that India's defence commitment was far larger than Pakistan's, but arguing, in the same breath, that Pakistan's commitment had also increased, with Soviet forces stationed in Afghanistan perhaps for several years. The talks ended without concrete results, but with a bagful of goodneighbourly effervescence. Before returning to New Delhi, Singh told reporters that differences on Afghanistan had narrowed as a result of his visit, that India wished to seek Pakistan's cooperation to promote peace and security in the region and would look forward to a visit by Agha Shahi to pursue the discussions further.[62] This visit was mooted for May, but actually took place in July. It proved largely barren, as we shall see in a moment. By that time the Indian government had decided that it could not accept the Pakistani proposal that field commanders of the two sides meet to discuss possibilities of mutual force reduction. However, one substantial, though intangible, gain of the Swaran Singh mission to Islamabad was a reasonably friendly meeting between Gen. Zia-ul-Huq and Indira Gandhi at Salisbury. Gen. Zia offered to have a UN supervisory group stationed in Pakistan, drawn from countries like India, to ensure that Afghan rebels were not armed, trained and sent across the border to carry on guerrilla war. This offer was transmitted by New Delhi to Moscow.[63] For the Soviet reaction, Mrs Gandhi had to wait till her meeting with Leonid Brezhnev in Belgrade on May 8.

Moscow Once Again

This meeting, lasting a mere 45 minutes, half of which time was consumed in interpretation, could hardly be an occasion for serious, detailed discussion; at least in "news value" it was overshadowed by Mrs Gandhi's first-ever meeting, the next day, with the Chinese Prime Minister and Chairman of the Chinese Communist Party, Hua Guofeng. Afghanistan was not discussed at all except in tandem; Brezhnev and Mrs Gandhi rapidly surveyed the larger issue of world peace and the easing of tension in the South Asian region. A certain pressure had been building up for convening a nonaligned meet to discuss the new cold war between the US and the USSR and its manifestation in

Afghanistan. Brezhnev appeared to be in favour of the nonaligned nations playing the role of crisis defusion, and he welcomed whatever India could do in that direction. He repeated the Soviet perceptions of the current crisis—how it had been deliberately manufactured by the United States, and pointed to the US muscle-flexing in the Gulf region, at Iran, in Western Europe and, particularly, in the Indian Ocean. Mrs Gandhi observed that the prolonged presence of Soviet troops in Afghanistan was being used by interested powers to confuse, divide and weaken the nonaligned movement; it was therefore causing considerable worry to Asian-African nations. Brezhnev shared these nations' concern, said he too was anxious to ease the situation in Afghanistan. This could be done only through a political settlement, which was blocked by Pakistan's refusal to discuss the issue with the Afghan regime. Brezhnev suggested that India, as a nonaligned neighbour of both, try to arrange a Tashkent-type meeting between Gen. Zia and Babrak Karmal, not to mediate in the dispute, but to help them come to an understanding, as Kosygin brought Lal Bahadur Shastri and F.M. Ayub Khan together at Tashkent after the 1965 India-Pakistan war. True to the form and content of Moscow's India policy since the fifties, Brezhnev was ready to offer India a specific prestige-and-influence-wielding role in the region, something the United States was still unable, or unwilling, to match. Brezhnev did not raise Indira Gandhi's coming meeting with Hua Guofeng, but did mention the extremely negative role China was playing in the Afghan crisis. Mrs Gandhi volunteered the assurance that India would not improve its relations with China or any other country at the cost of its friendship with the Soviet Union.[64] From the Soviet point of view therefore the meeting was a success, and it was so described by *Tass*. The Indian press played up Mrs Gandhi's references to the problems created for the nonaligned nations by the prolonged presence of Soviet forces in Afghanistan.[65] Mrs Gandhi herself, however, stated on her return to New Delhi that Brezhnev was not happy to keep troops in Afghanistan and was keen on pulling them out. He only wanted the creation of a situation which would make this possible.[66]

The Afghan government offered to work out a political solution through bilateral or trilateral talks with Pakistan and Iran. If Pakistan and Iran pledged that they would not support the Afghan rebels, and if their pledges were underwritten by the United States and the Soviet Union, this, a Kabul announcement said, would pave the way for withdrawal of Soviet troops. The proposal was released just on the eve of the second meeting of Foreign Ministers of Islamic countries at Islamabad since February.[67] Mrs Gandhi chose the occasion to extend a helping hand to Afghanistan. She sent Ram Sathe to Kabul on May 16, the day the Islamic conference began its deliberations. Sathe's mission was to probe the technology of the Afghan peace move, to find out if Karmal had anything more to offer, like inviting some of the opposition elements to join his government. But the main thrust of the visit was to emphasise India's support for tripartite talks —among Afghanistan, Pakistan and Iran—or for the convening of a larger forum; it was meant to be a rebuff to the Islamic meet.[68] At that meet, six radical countries—Algeria, Iraq, South Yemen, Libya, Syria and the PLO—a formidable minority—fought a dogged frontal as well as rearguard action to blockade an extremist Islamic approach to the Afghan crisis. They failed to persuade the conference to hear Karmal, but succeeded in influencing the conference's search for a solution of the crisis. The conference set up a three-member committee, headed by the Foreign Minister of Pakistan and including the Foreign Minister of Iran, to explore all possible ways of a political settlement, including talks with the Soviet Union. New Delhi took an optimistic view of the Islamic conference's decision. Sathe who spent three days in Kabul talking with Karmal and Foreign Minister Dost, and looking closely at different aspects of the situation, claimed on his return to New Delhi that the Afghan problem was "nearer to a solution."[69]

To bring it nearer still, Narasimha Rao went to Moscow on June 3 in an atmosphere of "considerable optimism." Ripples of personal diplomacy blurred the lines of the new cold war—the Brezhnev-Gandhi meeting at Belgrade, Brezhnev's much publicised meeting with President Valery d'Estaing, of France, in Warsaw, the first meeting between Gromyko and the new US Secretary of State, Edmund Muskie, in Vienna. Also, Brezhnev's offer, in the course of a speech welcoming the South Yemeni president at the Kremlin, "to negotiate a deadline for the beginning of the withdrawal of the Soviet troops from the Afghan territory" and "appropriate international guarantees of ending and nonresumption of all forms of outside interference" in Afghan affairs. This statement of Brezhnev was interpreted in New Delhi as a relaxation of the earlier Soviet position that the pulling out of Russian troops was contingent on a political settlement between Kabul, Islamabad and Tehran, guaranteed by Washington and

Moscow.[70]

Indian diplomatic reporters said that in his talks in Moscow, Rao would try to work out the framework of a "negotiating process," an ambition that was cushioned on the assumption that India's analysis and interpretation of Soviet diplomatic moves was correct. The talks proved that it was not. Rao and Gromyko spent six hours together in three sessions, the third a "restricted" one. Rao had also a 75-minute session with Brezhnev, at which Gromyko was also present. Gromyko was assisted by Firyubin and M.S. Kapitsa, noted China expert in the Soviet foreign office. For India, the crucial matter was the situation created by prolonged Soviet military presence in Afghanistan; for the USSR, Afghanistan was only one of the several symptoms of a new cold war let loose by the United States with Chinese help and cooperation. The talks between Rao and Gromyko began rather badly, each side reiterating its known position in rigid language; later, the gap was "narrowed down." Rao himself disclosed that he and Gromyko had scrutinised the various peace proposals mooted by different parties to put together the framework of a political settlement. He realised that the optimism he had allowed himself was premature. The Soviets were in no mood to accept the Islamic Conference framework for talks among Afghanistan, Pakistan and Iran. It was sculpted to deny the Kabul regime the legitimacy it must have. Iran and Pakistan therefore must sit down with Aghanistan at the negotiating table as equals and thrash out the agreed frame of an accord; this would then be guaranteed by the Soviets and the US. If India wished to help, it should bring whatever pressure it could on Pakistan to talk to Afghanistan. In Soviet perspective, the Afghan crisis was meshed with the worsening Sino-Soviet relationship; India could not close its eyes on the role Peking was playing to aggravate international and regional tensions. Both Gromyko and Brezhnev took pains to explain how the United States and China were pushing the world to the brink of conflict and war, and how it was the foremost duty of all peaceloving nations to defeat the imperialist offensive. Gromyko allowed that Indian diplomacy had achieved positive results. India could even work for a "mini-Geneva-type" conference with only those countries which had not taken sides in the Afghan crisis to hammer out the basics of a political solution that would be acceptable to the Soviet Union, Afghanistan, the United States "and others."

Bilateral relations between India and the USSR prospered as a result of the June meetings in Moscow. The final details of the agreement for $1.6 billion worth of arms sale to India were worked out. The Soviets agreed to step up their contribution to India's development, especially in on-shore prospecting for oil. On Afghanistan, however, there was no meeting ground. In fact, the total absence of Afghanistan from the joint communique released on the talks and the omission of Rao's references to Afghanistan in reports of his formal statements printed in the Moscow press indicated that India's nagging pressure for withdrawal of troops from Afghanistan was more than a temporary irritant. The Soviets were now attacking the Afghan problem simultaneously at two levels, *without* Indian help. At the superpower level, the Gromyko-Muskie meeting faintly signalled a thaw, for which the Soviets must wait till the US presidential election was over; if the superpowers could manage to limp back to the cracked and deeply rent terrain of detente, an understanding on Afghanistan would not remain beyond their grasp. At the regional level, the Soviets did not expect Pakistani resistance to direct negotiations with Afghanistan to survive many months. Rao returned from Moscow with the sobering feeling that India's ability to influence Soviet action with regard to Afghanistan was very limited. He had his ample compensation, however. In his own words: "This issue had not allowed even the slightest clouding of our bilateral relations. These have indeed grown from strength to strength during the last five months."[71]

In a statement to the Lok Sabha on June 17, Rao outlined the Indo-Soviet differences on Afghanistan with some candour. The Afghan proposals had set a mechanism for negotiations from which the Soviets were unwilling to depart. Direct contacts must first be established between Afghanistan and Pakistan, and between Afghanistan and Iran. Only when this had happened "could other countries think of participation in the working out of a guaranteed solution." The Soviets had left India in no doubt about their readiness to pull out of Afghanistan once a political settlement was reached. But withdrawal must be accompanied by international guarantees of noninterference in Afghan affairs.

However, reports coming out of Afghanistan during the past few months, even after they are discounted for the inevitable interested propaganda element, do seem to suggest that in view of the situation there the hope that Soviet assistance to Afghanistan could indeed remain limited in time, as originally intended, is not very strong.

This is naturally a matter of concern to India as indeed to the others who seek a reduction of tension and a peaceful solution to the problems of the region. It is time for us to ask ourselves the question whether the Soviet troops meant for assistance in Afghanistan have not become, or are not likely to become, a pretext for those who wish to create further instability in that country.

Our fear is that beyond a reasonable time frame this could well come to pass and this is why we urge that a stage has come when ways and means, other than military, should be devised to bring about a solution to the problem while this is still within the range of possibility. The emergence of a political solution in Afghanistan has, therefore, acquired an urgency greater than ever before.[72]

When within a week of this statement, Moscow announced that it was withdrawing, with the consent of Kabul, "some army units whose stay in Afghanistan is not necessary at present," neither the Indian government nor the press was impressed.[73] The government kept its silence; the press showed its skepticism. The wind of India's diplomacy gave out too soon forcing Rao to cobble things up as best as he could. He now plugged himself to the task of bringing Kabul, Tehran and Islamabad together. An aide of Babrak Karmal made two undisclosed visits to New Delhi in July. Rao himself met with the foreign ministers of Pakistan and Afghanistan separately in New York, carrying messages from one to the other. He thought he had almost brought about a meeting of the two in New York. But the deposed Shah of Iran died in Cairo, and the Pakistani foreign minister, Agha Shahi, had to hurriedly return to Islamabad. Rao himself returned to New Delhi somewhat disappointed, but still "cautiously optimistic" that a dialogue between Afghanistan and Pakistan would start off before long.[74]

The dialogue did not start till August 1981. It became clear during the Pakistan Foreign Minister, Aga Shahi's visit to New Delhi in July 1980 that Gen. Zia-ul-Huq had taken firm refugee in the Islamic conference and was in no mood to indulge India to play the role of an honest broker between Pakistan and Afghanistan. The USSR, too, clung stubbornly to its own terms for restoration of normal conditions in Afghanistan. As autumn turned the leaves of trees to dusty gray, the Afghan crisis took leave of the front pages of the world press and tended to become non-news. The war between Iran and Iraq shifted the focus of crisis back to the Persian Gulf. With a great difference, however; for both superpowers maintained an appearance of studious neutrality in a war in which both were vitally interested. In October, Babrak Karmal paid a swaggering visit to Moscow, giving the lie to a spate of rumours that he was on his way out, if this had not already happened; Brezhnev treated him to the most lavish Russian hospitality; the end-result of the visit was a firm Soviet commitment to his regime, and a resolute reiteration of the Soviet position that Russian troops would stay in Afghanistan until Pakistan and Iran worked out, together with Kabul, agreed arrangements facilitating their withdrawal.

When Brezhnev visited New Delhi in December, five weeks before Ronald Reagan's inauguration, there was much speculation in the Indian press that he might come closer to the Indian position on the question of withdrawal of Soviet troops from Afghanistan. Mrs Gandhi, however, entertained no such hope. In her long conversations with Brezhnev, Mrs Gandhi argued the case for withdrawal, only to make the Soviet leader reiterate his own stand with unshakable firmness. The ball was in the court of Pakistan, said Brezhnev; as soon as Pakistan had made up with Afghanistan, the Soviets should be able to pull out their forces. *He did not mention Iran.* Brezhnev blamed the United States and China for the sharp deterioration in international relations, but his language was mild, not vituperative. Brezhnev put forward a five-point peace proposal for the conflict-torn Persian Gulf region, a foliage of formulas that chilled Washington but created ripples of interest in many countries in the third world and Western Europe. According to the Brezhnev plan, no nation is to set up foreign military bases in the Gulf area and on the adjacent islands, nor deploy nuclear or any other weapon of mass destruction; no one must use or threaten to use force against the countries of the Persian Gulf area, nor interfere in the internal affairs of the regional nations; no one must raise obstacles or pose threats to normal trade exchanges and to the use of sealanes linking the states of the region with other countries of the world; all nations are to respect the nonaligned status chosen by the countries of the Persian Gulf, and none must draw them to military groups with the participation of nuclear powers; and all nations must respect the sovereign right of the states of the area to their natural resources.

The Brezhnev plan was interpreted by some in India as a "revised version" of the earlier Soviet concept of Asian collective security.

Brezhnev's proposals left enough room for a regional security system without the participation of the nuclear powers; at the same time, it gave the United States, China, Japan, the Soviet Union and, implicitly, Western Europe the role of approver of such a security system, if not its formal guarantor.

The 2,500-word communique issued on the Brezhnev-Gandhi talks showed that the Soviet Union and India had shared perceptions of most of the world problems of the eighties, including East-West relations, nuclear arms control, and the naval arms race in the Indian Ocean. Their approach to these and other problems were identical. They still differed on the issue of continuing Soviet military presence in Afghanistan. But Afghanistan was not even mentioned in the communique, which probably meant that Mrs Gandhi no longer saw this problem as an issue of great international concern. In any case, Pakistan's refusal to work with India or the USSR and Gen. Zia's stubborn decision to anchor his foreign policy on the Islamic conference robbed India of its desired role as South Asia's peace-keeper and security provider, and blunted the edge of India's pressure on the Soviet Union to withdraw its armed forces from Afghanistan.

India's diplomacy of crisis defusion was not entirely unsuccessful. Its success was seen more in Pakistan than in India, however. The Indian elite wished to see India succeed in persuading the Soviet friend to pull out its troops from Afghanistan. But the Indian diplomacy's principal objective was to prevent a major US effort to rearm Pakistan with the active help of China. That objective was achieved at least for the time being. It was achieved because neither the Carter administration nor Gen. Zia-ul-Huq wished to see India and the Soviet Union getting closer to counterveil a revived military alliance between Rawalpindi and Washington. If the world found out that India did not really have great clout in the Kremlin, it just could not be helped. The Soviets had done a lot to build India up as the dominant power in South Asia, and if in 1980 they had to clip India's regional power wings, that, too, could not be helped. As the year drew to its end, tensions once again visited the India-Pakistan relationship, and with Ronald Reagan about to take the seat in the Oval Office in the White House, and a wasting war raging between Iraq and Iran for nearly three months, Mrs Gandhi thought it wiser to make India's friendship with the USSR stronger. She therefore joined Leonid Brezhnev in December to "declare their firm intention, in accordance with the treaty of peace, friendship and cooperation between India and the USSR, to continue strengthening and deepening Indo-Soviet friendly and mutually beneficial cooperation in the interest of the peoples of the two countries and the cause of international peace and security."[75]

CHAPTER SEVEN

Pakistan: Diplomacy of Survival

> Which is the side that I must go withal?
> I am with both; each army hath a hand;
> And in their rage, I having hold of both,
> They whirl asunder and dismember me.
> *King John*, III, i, 326

If there is any country that has reaped a happy harvest in the crisis following the Soviet intervention in Afghanistan, it is the Islamic Republic of Pakistan. The military regime installed by Gen. Zia-ul-Huq after deposing the charismatic elected Prime Minister Zulfikar Ali Bhutto in July 1977, stood forlorn and pallid in December 1979. For two years it had failed to coax the oil-rich Arab and Gulf nations to extend generous aid to Pakistan. Now its exchequer was near-empty, and it was about to default on debt-servicing. It faced a widening gap between imports and exports and was facing a straining shortage of grain since 1977. Politically, its stock was low in the entire world as a result of the hanging of Bhutto in the summer of 1979. Gen. Zia's own stock in the United States was the lowest for any head of government of Pakistan. His broken promises to hold election, the oppressive measures with which he chose to keep his people subdued, his muzzling of the press, and, above all, his determination to acquire Pakistani capability to explode a nuclear device—no different from making nuclear bombs—led to the suspension of direct US economic and military aid to Pakistan. Gen. Zia-ul-Huq was presiding in December 1979 over a country torn by internal dissensions, a nation threatened with domestic explosions, and a people seething with resentment and frustrations. He was in power because the military stood firmly behind its own regime and the opposition groups were too divided and confused to mount an organised challenge. The only party which could, the Pakistan People's Party founded by Bhutto, had been systematically emasculated by the junta.

A Summer of Opportunities

The winter of Zia-ul-Huq's discontent turned into a summer of oportunities with the movement of Soviet troops into Afghanistan. For two years Gen. Zia had been asking the United States, Iran, Saudi Arabia and other countries for money and weapons to halt the spread of Soviet influence from the Durand Line to the Arabian Sea. None except China took him seriously. Reports said that when the Chinese Vice-Premier, Keng Piao, visited Pakistan in 1978, the deposed king of Afghanistan, Zahir Shah, who had been living in Rome for the past four years, secretly arrived in that country and stayed for a few days at Abbotabad, 40 miles west of the Pakistani capital. Also reportedly present was a special emissary from Iran. If there was a conspiracy to restore the Afghan monarchy, nothing came out of it because it could draw no international support, probably because of the steadily mounting populist upsurge in Iran against the regime of the Shah. Gen. Zia, however, had kept another option open. He took Pakistan out of CENTO, and got India's help to be admitted to the Belgrade conference of nonaligned foreign ministers as a guest. With the feather of nonalignment in his turban, Gen. Zia visited Kabul in September 1978, had "friendly" talks with Noor Mohammad Taraki and invited the Afghan Marxist leader to pay a return visit to Pakistan. Pakistan and Kabul, however, failed to work out agreed norms of goodneighbourliness. Afghanistan raised the controversial issues of Baluchi and Pakhtoon self-determination at the 1978 session of the US General Assembly. The old geopolitical tensions between Pakistan and Afghanistan were renewed, with the difference that there was now in Kabul a Marxist regime potentially more capable of exploiting the divisions and discontents in Pakistan's two most sensitive minority ethnic provinces, Baluchistan and the NWFP.

Afghans had started crossing over to Pakistan since the summer of 1978. Many of them were armed. The Pakistani junta started extending in 1978 small-scale help to Afghans conducting hit-and-run guerrilla warfare inside Afghanistan. As the number of refugees swelled, insurgency based on Pakistan also increased, and by September 1979, when the Soviet leadership probably took the first crucial steps towards the decision to intervene, there were as many as 30 rebel camps operating on Pakistan territory. The number of Afghan refugees swelled to half a million. Gen. Zia had no doubt succeeded in enlisting significant international support to the Afghan rebels. Hafizullah

Amin told the *New York Times* in September 1979 that the Afghan insurgency was being fomented by "reactionary circles in Pakistan and Afghanistan."[1] As noted, the Soviets held Pakistan to be one of the authors of an international "plot" to seduce Amin to repeat a Sadat by asking the USSR to withdraw all of its advisers from Afghanistan. If this allegation had any truth in it, Gen. Zia made himself acceptable to a number of governments in the last quarter of 1979 by spearheading a collective effort to rid Afghanistan of Soviet influence, if not of Marxist rule. But several of these governments, notably the United States, did not forgive him for sending Bhutto to the gallows and for harbouring "illegitimate" nuclear ambitions.

The perfumes of Arabia that sweetened Gen. Zia-ul-Huq's hands and prompted America to grasp them blew in with the planeloads of Soviet forces landing in Kabul on 27 December, 1979. Gen. Zia at once realised that his moment in history had arrived: he saw himself cast in a role none else was there to play after the exit of Mohammad Reza Pahlavi of Iran: a surrogate of the United States in Southwest Asia *and* an Islamic bulwark against the rising tide of Soviet power and influence. Zia therefore began with playing two cards—his American card and his Islamic card—simultaneously: there was, for a while, the exciting prospect of both cards working out excellently. He offered to make Pakistan the frontier of the "free world" in the southern flank of the Soviet Union, but demanded a price that took many Americans aback and outraged India: a new treaty executed with the advice and consent of the US Senate, committing America to the defence of Pakistan; a multibillion dollar package of military and economic aid; and non-interference with his nuclear power development programme. While hurried negotiations to bridge the chilling divide between what Gen. Zia asked for and what the Carter Administration was willing to offer proceeded, the Pakistani leader kept his Islamic option open. At the same time, he kept a low-key line of communication with the USSR alive and active.

The First Islamic Meet

The thorn on Gen. Zia-ul-Huq's side was not Afghanistan, but India. He realised from the beginning that India had the ability to plant the kiss of death on his negotiations with the United States. No US Administration would commit America to the physical defence of Pakistan against a common front forged by the USSR and India. Gen.

Zia therefore took the dourest view of the Indian stand on the Soviet intervention and turned away from India's diplomacy of crisis defusion. He also realised that each opportunity also meant a new dilemma for a country not cushioned on its own strength and its own stamina. The United States from the beginning of the Soviet intervention sought to enlist Chinese cooperation in the arming of Pakistan and the Afghan rebels. This pleased Gen. Zia and at the same time increased his predicament. His first important foreign visitor in the new year was the Chinese Foreign Minister, Huang Hua, who toured an Afghan refugee camp on the Pakistan-Afghanistan border and promised China's help to Pakistan. Aga Shahi who took Huang Hua to the rebel camp and had intense discussions with him lasting for two days was at pains to discount reports of an emerging Washington-Peking-Islamabad axis. He was very critical of Indira Gandhi's "negative and far-from-reassuring" attitude to Pakistan's need for US military aid, and he told reporters that Huang had made it clear that China's capacity to supply arms to Pakistan was "limited."[2]

Gen. Zia's first diplomatic triumph was the special session of the Foreign Ministers of 37 Islamic countries held at Islamabad from January 27. He was now not only the prodigal son returned to the Islamic fold, but also a rallying point of anti-Soviet forces in the so-called Islamic world. Addressing the Foreign Ministers in the heavily guarded Pakistan National Assembly Hall, General Zia exhorted the Islamic world to join hands not only to make the Soviet Union withdraw its troops from Afghanistan, but also "to consider ways and means for the collective defence of the Islamic Umma (brotherhood) rather than the defence of individual countries."

The Soviet armed intervention in Afghanistan, he said, was entirely contrary to the established and fundamental norms of international relations. "It is the first instance since World War II when a superpower has made a sovereign and independent Muslim country the target of its attack. We view this development with the utmost apprehension, because unless this trend to subjugate small countries through the use of force is arrested in time, world peace and the independent existence of small countries will be endangered. In plain words, if this precedent is allowed to perpetuate itself then what has happened in Afghanistan today could happen in another country tomorrow."[3] The stridently anti-Soviet resolution adopted by the Islamic Conference, its decision to deny the Kabul regime a hearing and a seat and hear leaders of the Afghan insurgents, its demand for complete and unconditional withdrawal of Soviet troops from Afghanistan and its resolve to render all possible help to the rebels were heart-lifting victories for Gen. Zia-ul-Huq.

Kuldip Nayar, an Indian journalist who attended the Islamic Foreign Ministers' Conference, had his doubts about the actual, concrete results of their resolutions. "It is not yet known," he reported, "how far the Islamic countries are willing to back up their words of support to Pakistan with money and armaments. Islamabad is expecting a bounty and has employed all its resources and energy to make the conference a success."[4]

Three days after the conference, General Zia gave a long interview to Kuldip Nayar who got the impression that the Pakistani leader's attitude on Indo-Pakistan relations had "hardened since I met him last about a year ago." General Zia did not favour a no-war-pact with India nor did he wish to join with India to sculpt a regional approach to the Afghanistan crisis. "It is for the Muslim countries to get together to defend the sovereignty of a Muslim country, not only of Pakistan but of the entire Islamic world." General Zia exuded more self-confidence than before and looked as if the recent happenings in Afghanistan had entrenched him internally and earned him international legitimacy. "He is conscious of the fact that his importance has suddenly gone up." He was quite obviously flattered by the announcement that no less a man than Zbigniew Brzezinski was coming to Rawalpindi to talk to him. He was critical of the statements made by Indira Gandhi on the Afghan crisis, which he thought were contradictory, but he said he was looking forward to the visit of the Indian Foreign Secretary, Ram Sathe.[5]

The Zbig Session

On February 2 and 3 General Zia and his colleagues were engaged in intense discussions with Brzezinski and other members of his team on Pakistan-US cooperation for the containment of Soviet power in South Asia. Reports said that there was no agreement on two important points: the size of the US aid to Pakistan and the structure of US-Pakistan security relationship. General Zia had earlier rejected as "peanuts" the US offer of $400 million in military and economic assistance. Brzezinski told reporters that the $400 million was "only a beginning of the American response to the threat posed" by Soviet troops in Afghanistan; he hoped that other countries would also indicate what they wished to countribute to Pakistan's defence and economic strength. Gen. Zia asked for a formal military treaty between Pakistan and the United States while Brzezinski held that the United States "is committed to safeguarding Pakistan in terms of the 1959 (Mutual Security) agreement against the (Soviet) danger from the North." Brzezinski told reporters that US aid to Pakistan had been "finalised," but consultations would continue between the two governments and other countries interested in the long-term security of the region. "Our aim is to enhance the security of both (Pakistan and India) largely because Afghanistan has gone as a buffer. It has been transformed into an offensive wage."[6]

Gen. Zia shared Brzezinski's geostrategic perception of the Soviet move into Afghanistan, but he was not exactly itching for a clash of arms with Soviet forces stationed quite close to Pakistan's borders. At one of his several meetings with the Russian ambassador in Islamabad, Zia alluded to the danger of Soviet attack across the border on Afghan rebel camps. The ambassador coolly replied without batting an eyelid that this was quite possible.[7] Zia's fears were turned into anxiety by Brzezinski's offer, before arriving in Islamabad for talks, to post American troops on the Pakistan-Afghan border to take care of Soviet forces crossing the frontier in hot pursuit of rebel elements. Zia took up this issue with Carter's national security assistant. After seeing Brzezinski off at the airport, Agha Shahi told reporters that the proposed military cooperation agreement between Pakistan and the US would not apply to any "hit and run" operation along the Pakistan-Afghan border. "We do not think it necessary to invoke the 1959 agreement with the US in the event of violation of Pakistan's territory on the pretext of hot pursuit."[8]

His talks with Brzezinski made Gen. Zia more aware of the Indian shadow on a compact between Pakistan and the United States. The Indian Foreign Secretary, Ram Sathe, was coming to Islamabad. On the eve of his arrival, the Press Trust of India found the climate in the Pakistan capital for talks with India not "as bleak or disappointing" as it used to be even a little while before. There were "positive elements" in Pakistan which India could exploit, including a considerable body of public opinion, articulated more in living rooms or across coffee tables than in the columns of the press, that Pakistan could be defended only on a "subcontinental basis," that is, on the basis of cooperation between Pakistan and India.[9]

Sathe's visit, we have already seen, helped Gen. Zia get a clearer view of the main thrusts of India's diplomacy of crisis defusion. The principal thrust was to prevent largescale arming of Pakistan by the US. While this negated what Pakistan was trying hard to get, Zia himself was interested in a partial defusion of the crisis, if only to avoid physical clashes between Soviet troops and Afghan rebels on Pakistani territory. So, talking to a group of Indian and Pakistani reporters at Rawalpindi on February 6, before Ram Sathe's return to New Delhi, Gen. Zia said, "We are prepared to join our Indian friends in any initiative that would help defuse the present situation." When a correspondent asked if some kind of a neutral body could be set up to police the borders of Afghanistan, he exclaimed, "It is an excellent idea!"[10] Later, in an informal chat with Indian reporters in his dining room, Gen. Zia, elaborating the point, remarked that a peace-keeping force consisting of contingents from India, Pakistan and Iran could oversee the borders of Afghanistan. This would also help encourage Afghan refugees now in Pakistan to return home without any fear of persecution. The peace-keeping force could look after the affairs of Afghanistan, "but let the Russians first withdraw." This force could also ensure that there were no forays into Afghan territory. He then returned to his theme of expanding Soviet power. With the help of a map he showed how Soviet influence was growing in the region. Not only Pakistan but India, too, faced great danger to its security. The security of the entire region, including Iran, the Gulf, and even Saudi Arabia, was in jeopardy. "It is not a regional matter. It is now a global problem. Russia is a superpower and to any action or reaction of a superpower there must be a global response."[11]

Sathe returned to Delhi from Islamabad on February 7 and told reporters that though India and Pakistan continued to view the Afghan problem from diametrically opposite directions, they at least shared a common concern that unless the crisis was defused soon, it could pose a serious threat to peace and security in the entire region. Otherwise there was no meeting ground between the Indian view that the Soviet intervention was not the cause but a consequence of big power rivalries in the area and the Pakistani contention that in either case it posed a grave threat to its own security which could be met only with the assistance of other powers like the US.[12] *The Hindu* reported that Sathe's talks in Islamabad made it clear that Pakistan was prepared to go more than half the way in meeting the Soviet demand that the territory of Pakistan not be used by other powers to arm or incite the Afghan refugees to carry on their fight. Pakistan's condition was that the Soviets must pull out from Afghanistan. Zia, however, made no concrete proposal to India embodying his concept of a regional peace-keeping force. His cordiality for the visiting Indian official was interpreted in New Delhi as an effort to reassure the US that there was no danger of an India-Pakistan conflict in the wake of the Afghan crisis even if the two were unable to agree on the nature of the threat posed by Soviet action.[13]

The rest of February was consumed by a hectic, often confused, quest for an accord with the United States. Gen. Zia knew what he wanted from Washington, but knew not what he could give in return. He kept his line of communication open to Moscow, exchanging messages, but making no significant conciliatory signals. Everything was getting so complex! He should have been pleased at the lack of agreement on Afghanistan between Indira Gandhi and Andre Gromyko. His Foreign Minister, Aga Shahi, described Gromyko's pronouncements in New Delhi to be "entirely negative"[14] What worried Gen. Zia was Gromyko's strong and bitter attacks on Pakistan, signalling a harder Soviet stance, and he feared that Indira Gandhi might decide that discretion was the better part of nonalignment and move closer to Moscow despite her much publicised differences with the Soviets on the issue of troops withdrawal.[15] To add to the confusion of the situation, Moscow itself sent feelers to Pakistan in February for a bilateral understanding, trading the withdrawal of a "meaningful number" of troops from Afghanistan for a Pakistani pledge not to extend aid to the rebels. Gen. Zia said he could not start off a dialogue with Moscow "for the present"; he confirmed that certain proposals had come from Moscow to which he would give his reply "in due course of time."[16]

Meanwhile, Pakistan faced a grave economic crisis, having failed so far to reap any major financial benefit from becoming a centre of attraction since the Soviet intervention in Afghanistan. According to the newspaper, *The Muslim*, the donor countries and the World Bank showed no willingness to meet Pakistan's repeated requests to reschedule repayment of 75 per cent of its outstanding borrowings. The newspaper said Pakistan could not possibly raise $ 1 billion by June to service its foreign debts. Pakistan was "surprised" at the attitude of donor countries, especially the US, which during the two months following the Afghan crisis, had been giving Pakistan plenty of verbal assurances but had done little to meet its needs. The donor countries were opposing rescheduling of Pakistan's loans on the ground that as Pakistan could not put its economy on a healthy footing even after three rescheduling facilities in 1970 and 1971 for one year each and then in 1972 for four years, another rescheduling was not going to help in any way.[17]

ZIA REJECTS US AID

Pakistan's negotiations with the United States ran into heavy weather in the last week of February when it became clear that none of the donor countries was willing to invest large sums in Pakistan's ability to check the expansion of Soviet influence and power and that, in the absence of its allies contributing generously, the US alone was not prepared to raise its initial contribution to more than the stipulated figure of $ 400 million in two years.[18] The *New York Times* reported that Pakistan's foreign policy initiatives "have boiled down to waiting anxiously for Saudi Arabia to say how much help it can offer." Pakistan reportedly wanted a total military and economic aid package of $ 2 billion a year over a 5-year period from all sources. So far the only firm promises of contributions, apart from the American offer, had been from Japan and Britain. Japan offered $ 128 million, twice last year's aid. Britain promised $ 38 million. The French reportedly offered nothing. China had for the last decade provided the bulk of Pakistan's heavy military imports as grants. But "there have been indications that China, committed to its own modernisation, would be obliged now to seek payment for some of its military deliveries." Giving reasons for the poor commitments of aid, the *Times* said that Gen. Zia's military regime "is unpopular with reports of dissent and dissatisfaction in many sectors. There is a latent but perceptible secessionist feeling in Baluchistan." The ruling military junta was divided on military linkages with the US. One section believed that US and Pakistani interests were now converging. This section wanted a relationship with the US "as the North Vietnamese have with the Soviet Union." But even these elements found Washington's signals to Pakistan to be conflicting.[19] Zia himself was bitterly disappointed with the price the US was willing to pay for Pakistan's cooperation. He told a German news magazine that $ 200 million of US aid would not meet Pakistan's requirements but would make Pakistan an enemy of the Soviet Union. What Pakistan needed was ten times that amount. Pakistan would prefer the US to either reaffirm its 1959 agreement or turn it into a proper treaty. About Pakistan's nuclear programme, Zia said, "I shall try to get it, no matter whether openly or secretly, for this is the only way to meet Pakistan's future energy needs."[20]

It was reported on the last day of February that US military aid for Pakistan had been placed on an indefinite hold amidst growing indications that Pakistan "is not interested." A week later, Aga Shahi announced the rejection of the American aid package. He confirmed that Washington had been officially told that Pakistan was not interested in the $ 400 million aid offer.

> Acceptance of the US offer would have detracted from, rather than enhanced, our security. Also, we could not ignore the fact that the US sensitivity to Indian reactions appeared to be determining the size and nature of the aid package. The Soviet Union too has made its relationship with Pakistan conditional on the nature of Pakistan's relations with its two neighbours, India and Afghanistan, with both of whom Moscow had treaties of friendship. We shall remain persistent in our search for a relationship of trust and confidence with that great power and we do not view the future with pessimism.

Pakistan, Agha Shahi said, was prepared to participate in any process, bilateral or international, for a guarantee by the superpowers of the independence, neutrality and nonaligned status of Afghanistan after the withdrawal of the Soviet armed forces. Any guarantee on Pakistan's part would necessitate reciprocal Afghan recognition of the international frontier and a commitment to non-interference in Pakistan's internal affairs. Pakistan had specifically dissociated itself from any US initiative to introduce relevant legislation on the aid package in Congress. "It is a matter of history that a provision in the 1959 agreement for assistance to Pakistan remained inoperative in the 1971 conflict between Pakistan and India." Shahi also hinted that one reason for rejecting the US package was American insistence that Pakistan *limit* its nuclear development plans for the duration of the aid programme. He said economic aid and Congressional affirmation of the 1959 agreement were "inseparably linked to Pakistan's acceptance of the military supplies deal." Pakistan must primarily rely on its own strength and also on material and moral support from Islamic and nonaligned nations "as well as the time-tested friendship of China."[21]

Accommodation With Moscow

On the day of Agha Shahi's breath-taking announcement, a Soviet drive into Afghanistan's Kunar province brought a regiment of Russian troops "within a stone's throw" of the Pakistani border.[22]

Rejection of US military aid was Gen. Zia's main response to the diplomatic proposals and military pressure emanating from Moscow. He was now anxious to reassure the USSR that the Afghan insurgencies were not being fuelled by Pakistan. A report from Islamabad closely following the rejection of US aid, said that Pakistan had offered three alternatives to satisfy Moscow and Kabul that it was not feeding the insurgency. Zia himself announced at a convention of municipal councillors that if Moscow and Kabul did not believe the Pakistani denials, any international body could verify the fact or Afghanistan could seal its borders with Pakistan. The third alternative was an international peace force to be stationed in Afghanistan to see that no foreign power interfered in its internal affairs. Pakistan would put no conditions on the composition of the peace force. It could be drawn from the Muslim countries or nonaligned countries or be raised by the UN.[23]

Major US newspapers agreed that Zia was now seeking some accommodation with the Soviets because of his alarm at the possibility of hot pursuit, his fear of complications with India, the Islamic world and the third world, and his perception of the inadequacy of the aid amount. There was in the American press an understanding of Zia's predicament but little credence in his anti-Soviet intentions. The *Washington Post* said that if Zia made Pakistan the American surrogate in Southwest Asia, he would expose the smouldering protest movement of the Baluchis to Soviet encouragement. The real Soviet threat to Pakistan was not of a direct invasion but of "meddling" in its ethnic discontents. Zia was evidently anxious to buy some insurance against such meddling. Confirming this assessment himself, Gen. Zia told a news conference on March 25 that "all doors for a dialogue with Moscow must remain open." Answering a question whether approaches had been made by either side, Zia affirmed, "In international affairs there is never the last word. Our options must remain open and we will do what is good for Pakistan."[24]

Among the developments Gen. Zia regarded as definitely *not* good for Pakistan was the growth, for the first time, of a strong and expanding pro-Soviet constituency in the country as well as among

Pakistanis living in England. This constituency's strongest base was the Baluchis. It was spreading to the cadres and supporters of the suppressed Pakistan People's Party and had already enlisted its ranking leaders. Bhutto's wife and daughter, both politically important, came out openly in favour of Pakistan's friendship with the USSR, while his London-educated son made several trips to Kabul. Among Pakistanis living in England, a strong minority was propagating the view that friendship with Moscow was essential for Pakistan's social progress and for the restoration of representative government.* The latter sentiment, strange as it might sound to Americans, was fortified by consistent US support for military rule in Pakistan. Intelligence reports reaching New Delhi suggested that in the middle and junior ranks of the officers of the Pakistani armed forces, there were factions that would heed to Moscow if only because neither the US nor China had given Pakistan a fair price for its friendship.[25]

Even faint contours of Soviet-Pakistan friendship raised eyebrows among Indians who have been always apprehensive that Pakistan might one day ease India out of its special relationship with the Soviet Union. In the spring of 1980, the bargaining that took place between Moscow and Islamabad, and, more particularly, the initiative taken by Cuba to bring Pakistan and Afghanistan together appeared to trigger a brief diplomatic competition between the USSR and India for influence on Pakistan. Soviet diplomacy sought to bring about an understanding between Afghanistan, Pakistan and Iran with or without India's help. India viewed its own exclusion or isolation from such a development with extreme disfavour. It would not only diminish India's stature as the region's leading power; worse, it might divert Soviet foreign policy resource to an area of greater strategic importance to the USSR as the emergent global power. India therefore activated its own diplomacy, sending a special envoy of Indira Gandhi for comprehensive talks with Zia and Agha Shahi.[26]

But Zia had no intention to go beyond a limited understanding with the Soviet Union with the limited purpose of ensuring the peace of Pakistan's frontier with Afghanistan. This achieved, he rejected walking the political terrain with the USSR. He received proposals from Brezhnev early May for a political settlement of the Afghan crisis and he took the proposals with him when he visited Peking and discussed them with the Chinese leaders. He stubbornly resisted Soviet induce-

---

*For details, see Chapter Nine.

ments to negotiate directly with Kabul until Russian troops were pulled out from Afghanistan. Talks with the United States for economic aid continued. In May, it became clear that without closing any of his options completely, Gen. Zia-ul-Huq decided to lean primarily on his Islamic option to get maximum advantages from the Afghan crisis.[27]

ISLAMIC OPTION

When Foreign Ministers of 40 Islamic countries assembled once again in Islamabad for a six-day session in May, with Afghanistan as the "first and foremost problem" before it, according to its two specially appointed official spokesmen, the air no longer smelt of confrontation. Several peace initiatives had blossomed, some of which we have noted in the previous chapter, and all of which receive further analyses in Chapter 9. The agenda of the May session was almost evenly balanced *against* the two superpowers, though the media coverage gave more prominence to the Afghan crisis in view of its topicality. On the Afghan crisis, the Foreign Ministers, most of them still highly critical of Moscow, were on the look out for an acceptable settlement, a perceptible change from their outraged, confrontationist mood in January. Five delegations—those of the PLO, Algeria, South Yemen, Iraq and Syria—fought doggedly for a mellower attitude to the Soviet intervention in Afghanistan, and though they failed to get Kabul readmitted to the Islamic conference, they succeeded in keeping the Afghan rebels out and in considerably toning down the attack on the USSR in the resolution adopted on Afghanistan. The resolution itself called for a political solution, the first step being withdrawal of Soviet troops. It accepted, in principle, the concept of negotiations between Afghanistan, Pakistan and Iran. It set up a three-member committee, as noted, with the Foreign Ministers of Pakistan and Iran and the Moroccan Secretary-General of the Islamic conference, to hold informal talks with Babrak Karmal. The three members of the committee, however, betrayed somewhat different attitudes towards Moscow. The Iranian Foreign Minister, Sadegh Ghotbzadeh, who had included representatives of Afghan insurgent groups as members of his own delegation, affirmed that the rebels must be "part of any solution." He also said that the committee would go to Moscow if invited: "We won't take the initiative." Habib Chatty, of Morocco, explained the setting up of the committee thus: "We have decided on an initiative to resolve the Afghan issue politically by contacting the Afghan people and the Afghan regime without recognising it as a government." The mellowest stance was Agha Shahi's, who was to chair the committee. He said members of the committee would go to several capitals including Moscow and could have contact with the Karmal government. It was a "great forward step" towards finding a political solution of the crisis, he believed. The Foreign Minister of Saudi Arabia, Prince Saud-al-Faisal, without whose approval the conference could not have taken the "forward step," remarked that the committee would test the "will of the Soviet Union. If it wants to get out of Afghanistan, the Islamic countries have shown they are willing to cooperate."[28]

The May session of the Islamic Foreign Ministers spent as much time grappling with the Afghan question as it did with the worsening relationship between Israel and the Arabs and the continued crisis in US-Iranian relations. The PLO delegates warned the ministers not to make "too much" of the Soviet intervention in Afghanistan; it would only weaken the Arabs' ability to fight for a national home for Palestinians. The Foreign Minister of Iran accused both superpowers of harbouring parallel aggressive designs against the Persian Gulf and Arabia. Gen. Zia put himself more or less on the same wavelength. The two superpowers had the same tendency to interfere "constantly" in other nations' affairs, he said in his speech—a tissue of pan-Islamic sentiments almost impossible to break down to concrete policies or actions. No foreign power can be allowed to impose its own ideology on our peoples against their wishes. It is for this reason that we vehemently oppose the Soviet military presence in Afghanistan. We also oppose the presence of US naval forces which have been deployed in a threatening posture in the vicinity of Iran." The conference bestowed on Gen. Zia the cosmetic honour of drafting a "collective security plan" for the Islamic countries. Zia was more pleased with his appointment as the spokesman of the Islamic conference at the 1980 session at the UN General Assembly.[29]

The author learnt later from sources in Pakistan that in closed sessions, Gen. Zia did not hesitate to vent his frustrations about the paltriness of aid he had received from the Islamic nations. The aid promised in January had not come in except for a modest amount from Saudi Arabia. His moderation on the Soviet Union led to the conclusion, during the week the conference was in session, of a long-term agreement with Libya for military, economic and scientific-technological cooperation.

Gen. Zia used the Islamic forum to make a casual reference to the Kashmir dispute between Pakistan and India, an act on his part that confused and infuriated Indians. The Indian foreign office was baffled by the ambiguity of Zia's attitude towards India; he seemed to be trying to be soft and tough at the same time. The Indian foreign office, as noted, was heartened by the decision of the Islamic conference to initiate informal discussions with "all groups" involved in the Afghan crisis including the Marxist regime in Kabul; Indira Gandhi sent Ram Sathe to Kabul to see if India could help bring Afghanistan and Pakistan together. Weeks passed. No contact took place between the three-man committee set up by the Islamic Foreign Ministers and the regime in Kabul. The Soviets would not invite the committee to Moscow as long as it refused to meet Babrak Karmal on an equal footing. Meanwhile, even bilateral Indo-Pakistan relations refused to take off, and Indians blamed Gen. Zia for stalling. The Indian foreign office felt that Zia was just not anxious to "give the kind of positive push which alone can help clear the air between the two countries."[30]

In June, the Islamic committee unfolded its diplomatic portfolio. Agha Shahi visited Vienna and conferred with the Austrian Chancellor, Bruno Kreisky, and Bucharest where he met the Rumanian President, Nicolai Ceausescu. Shahi was actually probing for an opening to Moscow which had attacked Pakistan for rejecting the latest Afghan proposal for direct negotiations. In mid-June the Islamic panel invited the Kabul regime as well as the major Afghan rebel groups to send representatives to Geneva. Some of the rebel groups did. Kabul did not respond. Toward the end of June, Shahi met the chief Soviet delegate at the UN and proposed talks with Kabul within the framework of the Islamic conference resolution. A few days earlier, he had met leaders of insurgent groups at Mont Pelerin, Switzerland. The Soviets did not relent from their position that Pakistan and Iran must work out an accord with Afghanistan to enable Moscow to start pulling out its troops.[31]

ON THE BACKTRACK

The ides of July brought Agha Shahi to New Delhi, and Indians were surprised to notice a remarkable change in Pakistan's diplomatic posture. In six and a half months, Zia's Pakistan became a bornagain regime, snatching international recognition from the jaws of conflict and confrontation. Agha Shahi was no longer Foreign Minister of a regime shaken to its roots by competing superpower pressures to influence its conduct. Pakistan was still a weak and derelict regime, torn by internal dissensions, threatened more from within than from without. But in the seventh month of the Afghan crisis, Gen. Zia appeared to have found his moorings in the Islamic platform, and was not prepared to question whether the platform would survive the next storm in international politics. He had coaxed out of the crisis a status for Pakistan it could never have acquired otherwise. This he had done by keeping his distance from both superpowers, with a moderate tilt towards the United States. But he had taken care to keep the Soviets in good humour by stopping the funneling of aid to Afghan insurgents. Sooner or later, he would have to recognise the Marxist regime in Kabul; he could not antagonise it for ever, especially when it brought the bulk of the Afghan people under its effective rule and addressed itself more confidently to the task of national reconstruction. But that was some time yet, perhaps longer than even the pessimists allowed. The Soviets were trapped between the rugged "fingers" of the Hindu Kush and would not begin a major withdrawal of their troops for quite some more time. Agha Shahi was therefore in no hurry to go beyond the framework of the Islamic conference resolution to seek contacts with Kabul. He could wait.

His talks with Indian leaders focussed more on bilateral relations than on Afghanistan. On the latter issue, he merely narrated to Indira Gandhi and Narasimha Rao what the Islamic panel had done to seek contacts with Kabul and Moscow, and, also, how it had drawn a blank. He was not prepared to go outside the terms of the resolution of the Islamic conference; in fact, he could not; he was only the panel's Chairman. Nor was Pakistan on its own separate initiative at that time seeking any contact with Kabul. India was welcome to use its influence to propel Babrak Karmal or his representative to face the Islamic panel. As for an Indian effort to bring Pakistan and Afghanistan together outside the Islamic panel framework, no, thank you very much, it wasn't necessary.

In interviews with journalists and informal chats with others, Agha Shahi said that Pakistan had considered several options—American, Soviet, even Indian—before fastening on the Islamic one.[32]

On the bilateral front, Agha Shahi asked for serious modification of Indian strategic thinking with regard to Pakistan as a precondition for better political and even economic relations. He repeated the proposal that field commanders of the two countries meet to determine if there were scope for agreed mutual force reduction taking into account the changed defence needs of both. He also repeated that South Asia be turned into a nuclear free zone, and assured his hosts that Pakistan's nuclear development programme aimed at nothing more than India's. He reiterated Pakistan's adherence to nonalignment and its sincere wish to live in peace and friendship with all of its neighbours, especially India; but he betrayed no readiness to accelerate the pace of improvement in India-Pakistan relations.

The visit dismayed the Indian foreign policy decision-making elite. The Indian press judged it a failure; one report said that Indira Gandhi faulted her Foreign Minister for mishandling it. What galled Indians was that Gen. Zia's Pakistan should have emerged shipshape from the traumas of the Afghan crisis. He was no longer looking for a survival kit. He had found his Helican to water his horses.

What the author wrote in July 1980 in a commentary on Agha Shahi's visit bears to be quoted:

The blunt truth is that the Soviet military intervention in Afghanistan has not brought India and Pakistan together in search of common security and shared stability. India's defusion-of-the-crisis diplomacy probably prevented the direct rearming of Pakistan by the United States. This is not something which endeared India to General Zia. If India were able to persuade the Soviet Union to start the process of withdrawal of Soviet troops from Afghanistan, it could exercise some leverage on Pakistan to negotiate a common security strategy for the subcontinent and South Asia.

India's mild disapproval of prolonged Soviet military presence in Afghanistan has not only not lowered Indo-Soviet friendship, it has not even prevented a substantial $ 1.6 billion new arms deal between the two friendly nations. India, then, has not been able to offer Pakistan a regional security and stability strategy which would diminish India's own "special relationship" with the Soviet Union. Nor has Pakistan shown the slightest inclination to move away from its own "special relationship" with China, the United States and the Islamic world to forge new strategic linkages with India. In short, the Soviet military intervention in Afghanistan has not released fluids of friendship in South Asia. If anything, it has sharpened the traditional strategic divisions of the region or at least reinfored them.[33]

Once the improvised silver-plating of the India-Pakistan relationship began to wear off, the coarse metal which it is made of started to bare its ugliness. The outbreak of Hindu-Muslim riots in several Indian towns in the summer of 1980 was utilised by Gen. Zia to restore Pakistan's claim to oversee the welfare of 80 million Indian Muslims. India paid back in kind. The Indian government lodged a diplomatic protest while responsible Indians alleged that Pakistan had a hand in the riots. When, in August, the Indian ambassador to Pakistan paid a courtesy call on the widow and the daughter of Zulfikar Ali Bhutto and spent over an hour with them, the *Pakistan Times*, owned by the government, attacked India for "interfering" in Pakistan's internal affairs. The melancholy incidents persuaded *The Hindu* to observe:

> Once again the Indo-Pakistan syndrome is producing multiple symptoms of a much deeper malaise that is threatening to put the clock back to the pre-partition days. After the Soviet intervention in Afghanistan, President Zia-ul-Huq made some reassuring noises about the need for better understanding between the two neighbouring countries in the larger interests of peace and stability in the subcontinent. But he is back at the old game of India-baiting and has started to talk darkly of Indian ill will towards Pakistan. The martial law regime is propagating the kind of animosity that could place the two countries on a collision course again.[34]

Discerning Pakistanis, however, realised that Gen. Zia was building Pakistan's future on ninepins. His regime stood totally isolated from the people. There was not a single applause when Zia rose to address a large assembly at the Pakistan national day parade. He was heard in silence. When he finished speaking, only three people applauded.[35] Several Pakistani intellectuals told the author that it was "foolish" to think that the obelisk of Islam could sustain modern statecraft except for a short while when big upheavals distorted combatant realities. Not many Pakistanis believe that Saudi Arabia, with its poor industrial and technological base and its poorer arms backup, could satisfy Pakistan's economic and defence needs for more than a short period. Things could get very bleak for Pakistan if Saudi-US relations slumped under the strain of Israel-Palestinian differences. In any case, as a Pakistani strategic expert mused, "it is absolutely necessary for Pakistan to find working relationships with its neighbours, who, acting in collusion, can once again dismember Pakistan." He added, after a pause, "Like it or not, the Soviet Union is a next door neighbour, after what has happened to Afghanistan. This is the supreme reality that Pakistan's external and even internal policies must reckon, and I cannot say that this has happened yet."

Gen. Zia's diplomacy bought a lease of life for himself and his military regime. It remained doubtful if it ensured the survival of Pakistan through a convulsive decade.

CHAPTER EIGHT

China: Diplomacy of Insecurity

> He is come to open
> The purple testament of bleeding war.
> *Richard III*, III, iii, 93

No power takes a more alarmed view of the ascending military might of the Soviet Union than does the People's Republic of China. Mao Zedong was the first among world statesmen to perceive the USSR as the emerging global power and also to see American power, and the American will to use power, declining. Henry Kissinger has recorded that in their conversations with Richard Nixon and his national security adviser early 1972, Mao Zedong and Zou Enlai focussed single-mindedly on the world balance of power, which, in their perception, was changing in favour of the USSR. At those epochal meetings, the Soviet Union was Mao's principal security concern. The primary problem in world politics, Zou Enlai told Kissinger, echoing the Helmsman's concern, was how to maintain the global balance of power in the face of Soviet expansionism, the latest manifestation of which Peking had noticed in South Asia—in the Soviet-backed Indian intervention in the Bangladesh war. The cooperation with the US that Mao was seeking was not to gain "small" benefits, like the return of Tawain to the PRC, but to hold Soviet power in check. He was certain that Soviet expansionism would lead to war, and war was the cataclysm China feared most, for it might mean the end of Mao's revolution. "This world is not tranquil," Mao's shattered hulk emitted with pain, "and a storm—the wind and rain—is coming. And at the approach of the wind and rain the swallows are busy. . . . It is possible to postpone the arrival of the wind and rain, but it is difficult to obstruct the coming."[1]

Through the decade of the seventies, Chinese fear of Soviet power continued to expand, turning into near-panic when Vietnam "invaded" Kampuchea with a surfeit of Soviet support, and the USSR itself "invaded" Afghanistan. Panic stirred up pride, and China embarked

China: Diplomacy of Insecurity   161

upon its tardy and self-defeating "educational war" against Vietnam early 1979; the failure to "teach Hanoi the necessary lesson" sharpened, even distorted, China's visions of Soviet power. Even in 1972, Mao and Zou, in their talks with Nixon, failed to stress a community of interest between China and Vietnam; their strongest argument for rapid American withdrawal from Vietnam was that the US was spending its vitality as a power in a wrong, wasting war.² When, almost immediately after its victory, Hanoi elected to hitch the Vietnamese wagon to the Soviet star, Vietnam became, in Chinese perception, the Soviet Union's advance base in Southeast Asia. China's proven inability to dislodge Vietnam from Kampuchea and to prevent Hanoi (and therefore the Soviet Union) from bringing the entire Indochinese peninsula under its own influence, further fanned Peking's fear of Soviet power. Finally, when the Soviets intervened in Afghanistan, the Chinese saw a new threat building up to Xingiang, home of their nuclear power complex, as well as to the logistical infrastructure of their close relations with Pakistan. The latter threat was regarded as darker; it was a potential bodyblow to China's geopolitical presence in the Karakoram-Gilgit-Hindu Kush region, built with considerable diplomatic and financial investment over a period of 25 years.³ The twin thrusts of Soviet power—in Southeast and South Asia—aggravated the Chinese psychosis of "encirclement" by its powerful and hostile communist neighbour. Thus, the world's two giant communist nations was each chained to its own hubris of encirclement: the Soviet Union by the United States and its allies, China by the USSR and its clients. For China, the feeling of encirclement acted like an exciton adding energy to the molecules of foreign policy.

In the years after the death of Mao Zedong and Zou Enlai, China has been going through a painful process of de-Maofication; the process reached a certain culmination in 1980 when Hua Guofeng yielded the prime ministership to Zhao Ziyang, supposed to be a close associate of the strongman of the post-Mao period, Deng Xiaoping. Half-a-dozen aging deputy prime ministers also stepped down making room for younger "radical pragmatists". In the realm of foreign policy, however, furtive attempts to downgrade the cold war with the USSR perished in the flames of Soviet gun powder in Afghanistan. Talks aimed at a "substantive" improvement in Sino-Soviet state relations, resumed in June 1980 after a lapse of years, were abruptly broken off by China immediately after the Soviets intervened.⁴

In the 60s, visions of Soviet peril persuaded Mao to sculpt a foreign policy that saw the world equally threatened by the two superpowers and that sought to mobilise the "intermediate zone" —the family of medium and small powers—against the giants. As the USSR attained strategic parity with the US, and acquired a blue-water navy with the advent of the seventies, Mao concluded that of the two superpowers, the new one—the USSR—was more dangerous. Now, in the wake of the Vietnamese intervention in Kampuchea and Soviet intervention in Afghanistan, Mao's successors took the most apocalyptic view of the USSR. The last vestiges of ideology in the Maoist world-view were dredged out. For Mao's successors, the world in 1980 stood polarised and divided between the Soviet Union and its clients *versus the rest*. So menacing was China's image of Soviet power, so grossly distorted out of proportion, that the Chinese leaders came to the conclusion that they must build a worldwide anti-Soviet front with all kinds of assorted regimes including the most oppressive (like Argentina and Chile), the most unpopular (like Pakistan), the most corrupt (like Zaire) and the most reactionary (like Saudi Arabia). Primarily, China sought protection from war in a restoration of America's global military leadership. It ploughed patiently and noisily for an alliance binding China, Japan and the United States in an anti-Soviet axis; it moved to normalise relations with India hoping that this would make India less dependent on the Soviet Union; it pledged assistance to Thailand in the event of a Vietnamese "invasion."

NERVOUS CHILD OF FEAR

To a very large extent, the They-Us polarisation of Peking's world view stemmed from the Soviet-backed April 1978 revolution in Afghanistan and the simultaneous consolidation of Soviet influence in Vietnam. In three months of the summer of 1978, Chinese officials visited 25 countries in an unprecedented rattling of Peking's diplomatic sabre against the USSR. The diplomatic offensive was led by prime minister Hua Guofeng himself. He visited Rumania, Yugoslavia and Iran, attacking "hegemonism" in each capital, and making the Balkans, in the words of *Pravda*, "an object of hostile intrigues." Hua's most dramatic performance was a dance of the hora with a ring of colourfully costumed Rumanian belles in the Victory Square of Bucharest. Deng Xiaoping toured ASEAN capitals mainly to warn the Southeast Asian nations of the threat to their security and stability coming from Soviet-backed Vietnam. In separate junkets, politbureau member Keng Piao went to Jamaica, Guyana and Trinidad-Tobago to stir up anti-Cuban feelings. Foreign Minister Huang Hua arrived in Zaire in a show of solidarity with Mobutu in the wake of rumours that Cuba was behind a Katangan rebellion which he crushed with the help of an invited expeditionary force from France. Deputy prime minister Ku Mu hopped from Paris to Geneva to Copenhagen to Bonn reinforcing China's five-year trade agreement with EEC concluded in April 1977. PLA deputy chief of staff, Chang Ai-ping, visited Sweden and Italy. Former foreign minister Chi Peng-fei went to Ryadh on a probing mission, while Oman agreed to establish diplomatic relations with Peking.

In June 1978 China capped its biggest diplomatic reward: the peace treaty with Japan with its "anti-hegemony" clause which, however, the Japanese foreign minister made clear in the Diet the two countries would interpret differently. In October, Deng Xiaoping made a triumphant tour of Japan with a 40-man entourage, deporting himself like a consummate diplomat in his talks with government leaders as well as the leading figures of the *zakai* and Japan Inc. Deng broadcast the Chinese belief that "hegemonism" was pushing the world into war; for peace the planet needed a strong American military presence in the Pacific and the security treaty between Japan and the US.[5]

The stridency of Deng's anti-Sovietism was derived to a large extent from the revolutionary turmoil in Iran threatening the regime of Shah Mohammad Reza Palhavi, America's most powerful surrogate in the Persian Gulf region. In six months the regime fell and the Shah was a homeless exile. No country was more shaken than China by the inability of the United States to defend a true and trusted ally.

As the Khomeini regime began in Iran in February 1979, Deng Xiaoping accomplished a tour de force in the United States, bringing out what Michael Oksenberg, a leading China scholar, called "the take-off of Sino-American relations."[6] Deng's introduction to Washington life was a roast-beef dinner at the Georgetown home of Zbigniew Brzezinski whom he had met in Peking about a year before. His talks with Jimmy Carter were described by the President as "very cordial and harmonious." Deng was sought after with equal eagerness by Congressmen, Senators, business tycoons and television cameramen. Deng maintained a strong anti-Soviet posture throughout the visit, virtually pleaded for a US-China-Japan-Third World alliance against the USSR, and publicly notified his hosts and the world that China would have to teach "some necessary lesson" to Vietnam—the "Cubans of Asia."[7]

While the rewards of Hua Guofeng's diplomatic forays into the Balkans remained intangible, Deng collected an impressive array of economic, commercial, technological and strategic gains in Tokyo and Washington. However, in Tokyo, Deng could not persuade the Japanese government to abandon its "omni-directional" foreign policy which included substantial economic and inconsequential political relations with the Soviet Union. Nor did he find the United States quite ready in February 1979 to fold up its policy of "even-handed" relations with the Soviet Union and China. Just before Deng arrived in the United States, Carter had promised that he would be "cautious in not trying to have an unbalanced relationship (with) China and the Soviet Union." Detente and SALT still stood as a formidable barrier between the Chinese world-view and the foreign policy priorities of the United States and its European allies. Hua Guofeng made a second trip to Europe in November 1979, even as Sino-Soviet talks were proceeding gingerly in Moscow; he visited London, Paris, Bonn and Rome, voicing China's "deep concern" about what was going on in Afghanistan, and emphasising that Vietnam's ambitions in Southeast Asia coincided with the Soviet Union's "drive towards the Pacific." Next month brought the Japanese Prime Minister, Masayoshi Ohira, to China, further cementing Sino-Japanese friendship which, however, like the burgeoning relationship between China and the US, still remained bereft of visible strategic content.[8]

"Fundamental Breakthrough"

The Soviet intervention in Afghanistan brought about what Brzezinski called "the fundamental breakthrough in Sino-American relations." The US-Soviet detente was in ruins; the SALT-II treaty was frozen. When Carter despatched his defence secretary, Harold Brown, to Peking in January 1980, he signalled to Moscow that the period of "even-handed" or "balanced" relationship with the Soviets and China was over and the US was now tilting towards the latter. Brown initiated talks for military cooperation, a process that could make only slow progress after wearing out obstacles and inhibitions on both sides, no less psychological than political. The tilt began with giving China the most favoured nation status in trade, and substantial Exim Bank credits, both denied to the USSR. It moved slowly to acquire a strategic character.

Harold Brown was introduced in January to China's military weakness: its best military aircraft was a copy of the Soviet MiG-21. The first step towards adding to China's military muscle was taken during Premier Hua Guofeng's official visit to Japan in May 1980. It was a historic event, the first ever by the head of a Chinese government to Japan in the millennia-old history of Sino-Japanese relations. Hua's rhetoric was stridently anti-Soviet, causing some embarrassment to his Japanese hosts, but the talks between the two prime ministers laid the foundation of a long-term Sino-Japanese friendship supplementing either country's relations with the United States, and thus creating great potentials for bilateral cooperation in specific areas of defence and foreign policy. The Soviet factor, with its American counterpoint, finally brought the two Pacific powers together over the long haul of half-a-century's conflicting ambitions and attitudes.[9]

Hua Guofeng's highly rewarding visit to Tokyo was closely followed up by Peking with a no less fruitful visit to Washington by Geng Biao, a deputy prime minister. During the visit, the United States announced its decision to sell to China air defence radar, helicopters and transport planes, components of an early warning radar system, long-distance communications equipment and equipment to test jet engines. American companies were permitted to build electronic and helicopter plants in China. Harold Brown announced that the US would be prepared to sell to China dual-use civilian technology which it would not consider selling to the USSR. The "strange sort of partnership" that was born in 1972, and which, in Kissinger's words, was "all the more effectual for never being formalised," was still a long remove from a military alliance. But the ground was now laid for limited military cooperation for specific shared objectives. Geng Biao left no doubt about what the main objective was from the Chinese point of view. The Soviet and Vietnamese military presence in Afghanistan and Kampuchea, he affirmed, were "global issues ... actions of a long-premeditated strategic offensive," and warned, "Since they represent a strategic challenge, they call for a strategic response."[10]

The quest for a common strategic response continued through 1980, though progress was more rhetorical than real, the fledgling relationship too sensitive to absorb the shockwaves emanating from the numerous contradictions built into it. The relationship had been brought to a "new level of political intimacy" during Vice-President Walter Mondale's visit to Peking in August 1979. Mondale had assured his Chinese hosts that the United States was determined to attain full military preparedness and maintain its global presence, adding in the same breath, "A strong and secure and modernising China is also in the American interest in the decade ahead."[11] The political intimacy was elevated to the level of "essential strategic agreement" when Hua Guofeng and Jimmy Carter met in Tokyo on July 10. After their 75-minute conference, the President's press secretary told reporters, "There is essential agreement between the United States and the People's Republic of China with regard to strategic perspectives and particularly as they relate to the Soviet invasion of Afghanistan and the invasion of Cambodia by Soviet-backed Vietnamese." Japan did not take part in the talks. But a spokesman of the Japanese foreign office volunteered that the conference "demonstrated the strengthening of solidarity among Japan, China and the United States."[12]

IMAGES VS. REALITIES

A good deal of the solidarity, however, was necessarily optical, designed to craft technicolour images much larger than realities. The objective was to frighten Soviet foreign policy decision-makers to restrain themselves in the vital peripheries. It was not clear in 1980 that the technology of building optical illusions as inputs of the new cold war actually worked. The Soviets reacted with shrill invectives to each Chinese step towards political cordiality and strategic understanding with the United States and Japan. At the same time, they were persistently arguing with those among the Chinese leadership who might be in a listening mood that the future of communist China could not lie in the embrace of monopolist Japan and imperialist United States. The Soviets had exposed the weaknesses of China convincingly at least thrice in less than 10 years: neither during the Bangladesh war, nor in its military and geopolitical conflict with Vietnam, nor, once again, in the face of Moscow's intervention in Afghanistan could China's military-diplomatic resources sustain an effective major-power role. The Soviets knew—like everyone else—that numerous dilemmas inhibited the construction of a Chinese foreign policy that would not look purely opportunistic, an offspring of convenience, but would convince the world that China was a revolutionary, if also anti-Soviet, major power. The foreign policy dilemmas got inextricably meshed with the dilemmas and confusions of burying Maoism without hurting the images of the Great Helmsman too much, with the pervasive power struggles between "radical pragmatists" and Maoists, and with the agonising dilemmas residing in the ambitious programme of Four Modernisations.

Soviet analysts relied on the "changed realities" of the international situation to defuse a trilateral Pacific alliance binding China, Japan and the United States, and on Moscow's ability to coax foreign policy gains from these realities. Japan, they believed, could not risk provoking the USSR beyond a tolerable limit, not only because of the trade and economic relations already existing between the two, but also because it could hardly afford to see China emerge as the dominant Pacific power at the end of the century. The United States, in Soviet view, could not turn its back for all time on strategic arms limitation and control; once the SALT process was revived, detente with a small 'd' could not possibly be far behind. For some years, the projected tripartite alliance would be strained by China's weaknesses and fed by China's potentialities. China's attraction for the US and Japan lay primarily in its vast domestic market. But apart from China's limited ability to pay for the goods and services it needs, to open or not to open that market widely to foreign penetration, in Soviet view, might tear the Chinese leadership apart. Also, the enormity of the price China was asking must sober prospective buyers of Chinese friendship. The Chinese were asking for the scrapping of SALT, burial of detente, a dizzy altitude of military buildup whipping the planet to a frenzy of nuclear and conventional rearmament, and a global united front against the USSR. The last concept, Soviet analysts maintain, is so weirdly out of tune with international realities, so wishfully oblivious of the temper of nations that it hardly merits serious analysis. The Chinese leaders may need the frightening image of an awesome enemy to galvanise their people, but international credibility of their images of the USSR is weakened by their extravagance of tone and colour.[13]

So riddled is the Chinese scene with ifs and buts that it is difficult to exclude abrupt foreign policy turns from the realm of probability. Mao's successors have carried his anti-Sovietism to extravagant limits; but they also initiated a formal quest for ways and means to normalise Sino-Soviet state relations. Deng, during his visit to the United States, assured Americans that Sino-Soviet relations would never return to the level of the friendship of the 1950s; he did not, however, rule out a certain level of improvement. For some years

America's China scholars have been expecting the relationship to thaw. Professor A. Doak Barnett, of the Brookings Institute, interviewed by an Indian editor in June 1979, expected a movement towards normalisation to begin "in the not too distant future." Deng, he hazarded, wished to defuse the crisis. The relationship, in fact, worsened in view of the Soviet intervention in Afghanistan, but there is no guarantee that it will not change course once the leadership issues in China are more or less stably resolved.[14] Generational changes in the governmental leadership of both the Soviet Union and China are in the offing. The Brezhnev-Kosygin team, we have noted, has proved to be more circumspect than Khruschev in handling relations with China. But it has not been able to play a China card of its own. The team's successors may well elect to design and play Moscow's own China card and they may find the new leaders of China responsive. If the prospects of a Sino-Japanese-American alliance is too frightening for the USSR, the prospect of a real Sino-Soviet rapproachment should be no less frightening for the United States. The Soviets, however, will have to lighten China's fear of encirclement, which in 1980 they were clearly in no mood to attempt.

Linkage with Pakistan

Much of China's diplomatic industry was employed to break out of, or disrupt, the encirclement. It worked at two levels: at the major power level (noted in the foregoing pages), and at the local level, which was broken into several geographical parts, each connected with the other. To thwart the southern arc of the ring of encirclement, Peking cultivated the ASEAN group and Burma, all of the six countries being covered by no less a man than Deng himself in diplomatic forays in 1978-80. In southwestern Asia, the Chinese leaders relied on Pakistan to make Afghanistan as heavy and prolonged a burden on Soviet shoulders as it could be made, funneling arms and weapons at the same time to Afghan rebel groups. In the latter task, the Chinese probably were the first external power to come forward. They had a geographical advantage to begin with: they could extend aid to insurgents operating in the north-eastern provinces of Afghanistan using the mountain passes cutting through the narrow neck of land connecting Afghanistan with Xinjiang; and they could funnel aid to rebel groups operating from Pakistani territory as well as in Afghan provinces close to the Pakistani border. Unknown quantities of aid were being funneled to the rebels months before the Soviet intervention; the quantity was certainly stepped up after the Soviets moved in. The Chinese foreign minister, Huang Hua, was the first foreign dignitary to visit Islamabad after the Soviet intervention; his talks with Gen. Zia-ul-Huq and Agha Shahi covered, as already noted, not only Chinese aid to Pakistan and the Afghan rebels but in greater depth, the "global strategic response" to the Soviet challenge. In a symbolic gesture of support to the Afghan rebels, Huang visited an insurgent camp located on Pakistani territory, and assured the Afghans that their cause enjoyed international backing—a gesture that was repeated with a touch of dramatic bathos by Zbigniew Brzezinski early February. The Sino-Pakistani talks disclosed shared strategic perceptions of the Soviet lurch into Afghanistan; both countries saw it as part of a grand design to bring the Persian Gulf region under Soviet influence; both felt threatened by the disappearance of the Afghan "buffer". However, even at that early stage of the Afghan incident, chinks were visible in the Sino-Pakistan united front against the Soviets. Huang urged Gen. Zia to accept the American aid package, but demurred in committing definite Chinese contribution to the arming of Pakistan. China had rushed certain quantities of arms through the Karakoram highway immediately after the Soviet intervention in Afghanistan. China's capacity to supply arms was limited, Huang Hua told the Pakistani leader. He had another piece of chilling news to transmit. China had given Pakistan $ 6 billion worth of military aid since 1966, most of it free of cost. But it was no longer in a position to gift arms; Pakistan would have to pay for future supplies, though on very liberal credit terms. Gen. Zia, on his own part, was reluctant to provoke the Soviets beyond a certain point. He was willing to accept the American aid provided the United States was prepared to go beyond cosmetic commitments to Pakistan's integrity, security and defence.

A reliable source disclosed to the author that Huang Hua advised the Pakistani leader to try to resolve the strategic differences between Pakistan and India, arguing that as long as India remained tied to the USSR and Pakistan to the US and China, the balance of forces in the South Asian region would remain overwhelmingly in favour of the Soviet Union. The source said that Gen. Zia's decision to open diplomatic negotiations with India was prompted by advice he received from China rather than from the United States.[15]

The Sino-Pakistani united front against the Soviets in Afghanistan carried some political weight though it had no visible deterring impact on the Soviets. When Zia found it necessary or useful to take a hard line on Moscow, he invoked Pakistan's Chinese as well as Islamic, rather than American, connection. His boldest affront to the Soviet Union came early May when he took with him to Peking a set of peace proposals he had received from Brezhnev and discussed them with Hua Guofeng and Deng Xiaoping. Zia thus recognised China to be a legitimate partner in a settlement of the Afghan crisis. Gen. Zia's perception of the Soviet threat mirrored those of the Chinese leaders. With the Soviet move into Afghanistan, he told *Xinhua*, "Pakistan is threatened, Iran is encircled. It is an outflanking movement against China as well. It is a threat to the sealanes of the entire supplies of oil to Western Europe and Japan. . . ." Zia apparently exchanged views with his Chinese hosts on how the forthcoming conference of Islamic foreign ministers was likely to respond to the Moscow-Kabul peace initiatives. The Soviet media blamed Zia's anti-Russian outbursts in Peking on Chinese blandishments and threats rather on the Pakistani leader himself. "The Chinese side has succeeded in intimidating the Pakistani visitor with notorious 'Soviet menace' verbiage," reported *Tass*. They had also offered him "nuclear partnership", it added, suggesting that a Pakistani nuclear device could be exploded on Chinese territory. The *Tass* report remainded Zia of the political weakness of his regime and warned him that it was in Pakistan's interest to remain "independent and neutral."[16]

Gen. Zia also reported to the Chinese leaders on the talks he had had a few weeks before with Indira Gandhi at Salisbury, and the two sides no doubt discussed the Indian role since the Soviet move into Afghanistan. In his formal speeches, Gen. Zia made ritualistic references to the Kashmir issue, knowing well how this would irritate, even infuriate, Indians.[17] The Chinese leaders, however, studiously refrained from mentioning Kashmir in their formal articulations, and ordered the Peking media to ignore Zia's reference to that issue. This probably indicated that the Chinese leaders and Gen. Zia differed on how to yoke India's diplomatic effort to a regional initiative to press for withdrawal of Soviet troops from Afghanistan. However, the Chinese gesture, happening for the first time since 1960, during the visit by a Pakistani head of state to Peking, pleased Indians. It was symbolic of the new diplomacy of goodneighbourliness China was seeking to project to India, hoping that India would reciprocate, which India did for some time and then suddenly faltered.

OPENING TO INDIA

Sino-Indian relations started improving in 1976 when Indira Gandhi sent an ambassador to the Indian embassy in Peking and China immediately reciprocated. The ice that had accumulated since 1962 started thawing in the fringes. The process was quickened when Janata came to power with its "genuine" nonalignment, which, in essence, meant building a balance of relationship with the Soviet Union and the United States. The demand for normalisation of relations with China received support from assorted segments of the Indian foreign policy elite—from the "American lobby," which included almost all constituents of the Janata coalition, from splintered groups of Maoists, and from the Communist Party of India-Marxist (CPI-M) which captured power in the eastern states of West Bengal and Tripura in the 1978 election. Only the pro-Soviet CPI stood firmly against any visible warming up of Sino-Indian relations; Mrs Gandhi and her followers had no appetite for the Janata style of improving relations with China. She would do it her own way, choosing her own time and modalities.

The Chinese themselves blocked a breakthrough in Sino-Indian relations. Janata's foreign minister, Atal Behari Vajpayee, once a fiery opponent of the Chinese connection, made a journey to Peking early 1979, but the Chinese launched their "educational war" against Vietnam even while he was their guest, without giving him an inkling of it. Outraged, Prime Minister Morarji Desai asked Vajpayee to return to India at once cutting off the wagging tail of the visit. Whatever had been gained in the direction of normalising Sino-Indian relations was drowned in a flood of Indian indignation and anger at the Chinese invasion of Vietnam and the cavalier manner in which Peking treated the visiting foreign minister.

If Janata's effort to reduce India's dependencies on the USSR and downplay India's peace and friendship treaty with the USSR stirred Peking to warm up to its southern neighbour, the return of Indira Gandhi to power in January 1980, with her well-known preference for close Indo-Soviet ties, chilled Chinese bosoms. Especially after Mrs Gandhi's virtual endorsement of the reasons given by the Soviets for their intervention in Afghanistan and her refusal to join the chorus of condemnation of the Soviet action. Mrs Gandhi, however, hastened to open a window on China, probably to show the Soviets that she was far from a client. The Indian President while inaugurating the newly elected Lok Sabha, declared India's readiness to "discuss all issues with China including the boundary question in search of a peaceful solution based on equality." The Chinese were prompt to return the gesture. The Indian diplomatic community in Peking was agreeably surprised when the Chinese People's Committee for Friendship with Foreign Countries, headed by Wan Ping Nan, a senior member of the CPC central committee, celebrated India's Republic Day at a special function. Even more delectable was the presence of Huang Hua at a dinner given at the Indian embassy to celebrate the anniversary—the first presence since 1962 of the Chinese foreign minister at this annual occasion. The Indian foreign office continued to receive mollifying messages that China was not getting too deeply involved in the American design to transform Pakistan into a forward base of the Carter doctrine; that China did not step up its own arms supplies to Pakistan after the initial shipments through the Karakoram highway immediately after the Soviet move into Afghanistan; that Peking was not playing its Pakistani card too hard, but was observing restraint in intervening in the new crisis in South Asia.[18] In March a statement in the Lok Sabha by Narasimha Rao went a step further from the presidential gesture of January. Replying to a question put in by a Marxist member, the foreign minister said India was willing to discuss all issues with China including the border issue in quest of a peaceful and *equitable* solution. If he chose his words deliberately, Rao implied that India might not exactly spit upon a quid pro quo.[19]

The next act in the slow-moving complex drama opened at Salisbury where Indira Gandhi had a 30-minute meeting with Huang Hua. They agreed that talks to normalise Sino-Indian relations should be comprehensive, covering the border issue as well, and that "problems of the past" should not be allowed to block prospects of the future. Huang offered to return Vajpayee's visit, and Mrs Gandhi remarked that she would be delighted to see him in New Delhi.[20] The Salisbury meeting opened India's Chinese window a little wider. G.K. Reddy reported in *The Hindu* that India was no longer "averse to the idea of consulting China at some point" of its diplomatic initiatives to defuse the Afghan crisis, although so far China was about the only country which India did *not* consult with. Reddy disclosed that a "section of opinion" in New Delhi held that since there could be no settlement of the Afghan crisis without American consent, and since the United States would not approve of any solution that the Chinese might find totally unacceptable, it was only proper that India tried to enlist Peking's support for any concrete proposals it might come up with. "So it is argued there is no harm in discussing all aspects of this problem with China to assess how far Beijing (Peking) would be prepared to go to recognise the geopolitical interests of the Soviet Union in Afghanistan to make a wider settlement possible for insulating South Asia from a superpower confrontation."[21]

This strand of Indian foreign policy strategic thinking in the spring of 1980 implied that some of the policy-makers in New Delhi believed that China could be persuaded to recognise some Soviet geopolitical interest in Afghanistan. They seemed to cherish two rather exalted ambitions: to bring about some sort of a Sino-Soviet understanding about Afghanistan and to recognise China as a legitimate party to an overall settlement of the Afghan crisis.

The Gandhi-Huang meeting at Salisbury was followed in less than a month by a meeting in Belgrade on May 8 between the Prime Ministers of China and India, the first Sino-Indian summit since Zhou Enlai's glacial reception in New Delhi in April 1960. Reports said that the Belgrade summit took place at Mrs Gandhi's initiative; it was carefully scheduled for the morning *after* her meeting with Leonid Brezhnev, and it was shorter than her session with the Soviet leader by a few minutes. In less than half-an-hour, the two Prime Ministers could only skirt around several major issues, of which Afghanistan was one, but not the most important. Hua focussed on improving bilateral relations, pleading that both sides "put aside past differences." The two leaders agreed that Huang Hua should visit India before the end of 1980 to initiate comprehensive negotiations for all-round improvement in Sino-Indian relations.[22] Close on the heels of Mrs Gandhi's return to India, Eric Gonsalves, foreign secretary in charge of East Asian affairs, was sent to Peking to sow up Huang's visit which was scheduled for October, the exact date to be announced later.[23]

At this stage some resistance built up within the Indian Government as well as outside to quickening the pace of normalising relations with China. The foreign policy elite was split: powerful individuals and groups cautioned the government against moving too fast. At a meeting of the parliamentary consultative committee of the external affairs ministry in May a "consensus" emerged that India should normalise its relations with China "with great circumspection and caution."[24] The minister for foreign affairs assured the members on two accounts: "normalisation of relations with China will not be at the cost of our tested friendship with the Soviet Union"; and that the pro-Vietnamese government in Kampuchea, headed by Heng Semrin, would be recognised soon.[25]

The same assurances Mrs Gandhi had given firmly to Brezhnev in Belgrade: the Soviet leader reportedly left the subject of China well alone except obliquely speaking of a "US-China collusion" against the USSR. Apart from the Soviet snarl, contradictions in the objectives sought by India and China came to the surface. Inder Malhotra pointed out that the Chinese were attempting

> to improve relations with India, promote, if possible, an understanding between this country and Pakistan and at the same time retain the special position in Pakistan that they have so far enjoyed. These objectives are not quite consistent. But the pursuit of diverse and even contradictory objectives in a complex, confused and confusing international situation is nothing new.
>
> For its part India wants a rapprochement with both China and Pakistan without in any way impairing its excellent bilateral relations with the Soviet Union, especially the Soviet underpinning of Indian security, which have remained unaffected by the fairly strong differences of opinion between New Delhi and Moscow over Afghanistan.[26]

As Indians debated whether diplomacy should trot or gallop towards normalisation of relations with China, the Chinese end of the game was picked up by Deng Xiaoping himself. Imparting an unexpected verisimilitude to the on-coming negotiations, Deng offered India a "package deal" to settle the border dispute, a give-and-take on the basis of the existing lines of actual control, China recognising the McMahon Line in the eastern sector of the border, and India accepting the status quo in the western sector.[27] The "package" was not new; it had been offered by Zhou Enlai to India ten years ago. What was new was the changed Indian attitude. In 1960, Nehru did not have the courage to accept Zhou's offer which was rejected by all of his cabinet colleagues except V.K. Krishna Menon. In 1980, the Indian foreign minister told the Lok Sabha that India would 'respond' to Deng's package. "We welcome the prospect of the eastern sector being settled without any particular difficulty," Rao told the House.

"It may be that ways other than the package solution suggested by the Chinese Government could prove more effective. In any event, I am sure, the House will agree that we should proceed forward meaningfully while also keeping our best interests in mind."[28]

What tantalised Indians was the silhoutte of a new Chinese geopolitical stance on South Asia. Pakistan was too infirm and rankling a basket to put all the Chinese eggs in; it would be in Chinese interest to narrow, if not bridge, the strategic divides in the subcontinent, which the Soviets were in a better position to exploit to their advantage than the United States. For 20 years Peking kept up its "principled" tilt towards Pakistan; the result was adding cement and concrete to the Indo-Soviet linkage. Now, in the summer of 1980, commenting at length on Indian affairs for the first time in years, the *People's Daily* gave glimpses of new Chinese strategic thinking. Normalisation of Sino-Indian relations, it said, would "undoubtedly exercise a positive influence" on international politics in view of the "serious situation" that had developed in South Asia. The assertive expansion of Soviet power, then, gave Sino-Indian goodneighbourliness a "positive content" and therefore a certain priority for Chinese foreign policy which it lacked in the last two decades or more. The only "fundamental" problem between the two countries, the *People's Daily* added, was the frontier problem. Its solution would contribute enormously to the stability of the entire region. But the border dispute had mingled with the larger and deeper India-Pakistan divide; Deng, in his interview with the Indian journalist, indicated a new Chinese geopolitical stance that was bound to please Indians. He reversed China's "principled" position on the Kashmir issue. Hitherto the Chinese unfailingly supported the Kashmiri people's right to self-determination, and backed Pakistan against India in the dispute. Now, China believed that "This is a problem between India and Pakistan and should be settled amicably."[29]

China experts in the Indian foreign policy establishment poured over Deng's interview and the *People's Daily* commentary with magnifying glasses, trying to read between and behind the lines. Two questions thrust themselves from the dense print: Was Deng signalling a message to Moscow by his offer of a package deal to India to settle the border on the basis of the status quo? And, how did the welcome Chinese emphasis on peace and stability in the region relate to China's support for a confrontation between the superpowers in the interlinking regions of the Persian Gulf and South Asia? The two questions gave birth to two lines of interpretation: one was that Deng was trying to adopt the South Asian strategy of Mohammad Reza Pahlavi of Iran who believed that the best way to reduce Soviet influence in the region was to bring the regional powers closer to one another; in this interpretation, Indian effort to defuse a superpower confrontation in South Asia appealed to the Chinese leaders because it meant *limiting* Soviet influence. The other was that by offering a status quo package to India, Peking was signalling to Moscow that China might offer a similar package to the Soviet Union if Moscow recognised the existence of a border dispute and made a few concessions to the Chinese position.

The two lines of thinking converged on one point of agreement: *the weakness of China*. The potentials of power of the Chinese People's Republic were no doubt great; China might as well make considerable headway in the coming two decades on the road to modernisation. But at the turn of the 1980s, China was a weak and torn power, frightened to its bones by the Soviet Union, unable to discover a safe and stable cushion of security in the American embrace,[30] trapped in the searing schizophrenia of burying Maoist social engineering while keeping untarnished the populist images of Mao and intact the paradox that the Leader's Thought was immaculate, only his actions were wrong. China, in any case, was passing through what looked like a long period of painful, perhaps convulsive, change, which lent an awesome air of uncertainty to Chinese policies, foreign as well as domestic. Could the process of de-Maofication at home go hand in hand with dei-Maofication in foreign policy? What longevity could be attributed to the improvisations of a 76-year-old man in a great hurry to change the course of the Chinese ship of a state in a weather as fair as it is foul? These were some of the questions that tormented Indian foreign policy strategic thinkers. To them an alliance among China, Japan and the United States is potentially as injurious to India's interests as the leading South Asian power as a restoration of Sino-Soviet friendship. To either eventuality, Indians would prefer the present alignment in the region, which enables India—as it did in 1980—to prevent largescale arming of Pakistan by the US and China. Realpolitik, then, would emit from Indian lips words and sentiments in favour of Sino-Indian rapproachement, but would not prod diplomacy to limber up for that goal.

To the backdrop of this kind of thinking, the Indian government, announced somewhat suddenly its diplomatic recognition of the Heng Semrin regime in Kampuchea. The timing of the decision rather than the decision itself, which was a-coming for months, stunned the diligent diggers of the tunnel of Sino-Indian goodneighbourliness. It certainly took the wind out of the sail of China's diplomatic demarches to India at least for the time being. The Chinese media deplored the Indian action as "exceptionally regrettable." Its first casualty was the visit of Huang Hua to New Delhi fixed for October 1980. It was indefinitely postponed; reports from Peking indicated that it would not take place until early 1981.[31]

It was clear in the summer of 1980 that South Asia had more or less absorbed the shock of the Soviet military thrust into Afghanistan; China and the United States did not. The Soviet action did not destabilise prevailing power alignments in the region. Pakistan did not feel threatened enough to rush to the embrace of India. Nor did India feel threatened enough to seek alternative linkages. The intervention brought China and the United States closer to one another, but the form and content of the linkage remained uncertain. The tremors of the Afghan event threw open an India window in Peking and a China window in New Delhi.[32] Both windows let in whiffs of fresh air, but not strong enough to blow off the accumulated cobwebs of mistrust and suspicions of 20 years. Indians remained divided and doubtful about the value of Chinese friendship if the price to pay for it was a loosening of Soviet commitment to India's development and security. The outcome of Brezhnev's visit to Delhi could not lift Chinese hearts. As the Afghan crisis took leave of the front page of world news and television prime time and mingled with the fluids of conflicts that criss-cross the pages of contemporary history, Chinese foreign policy makers were somewhat bent under the perplexing uncertainties of the planet's affairs. They were not sure that the Reagan administration would not strike a mortal blow at the Sino-American friendship by resurrecting the Two China concept. They regarded Western Europe's growing independence of the US with unhidden gloom. They did not know if they should play their Soviet card.[33] To make their dilemmas worse, the "power struggle" among the Chinese leadership remained unconclusive, and recovery from the wounds of the Cultural Revolution was painfully slow.

There were, however, some silver linings too. Neither China nor India turned its back on normalisation. The Chinese leaders seemed to have come to the conclusion that India-Pakistan amity was essential if South Asia were to be relieved of the towering presence of competing global powers. A Chinese analyst wrote in *Peking Review* in January 1981: "The necessity does exist for these two subcontinental nations to stand together or, in other words, to unite and cooperate, and the need today is more pressing than ever."[34]

CHAPTER NINE

Towards Denouement

> Time's glory is to calm contending kings.
> *The Rape of Lucrece*, 1, 939

So highly charged is the voltage of international politics in the nuclear age that it cannot take a doubler for more then a while. A crisis peaks with awesome velocity; than the dividers begin to work; the fever climbs down; the fatigued contenders look forlorn and a little foolish as they count their gains and losses. The wheel never turns exactly the full circle. But every actor tries to pretend that though a great deal happened, nothing really changed very much.

The crisis created by the Soviet military intervention in Afghanistan peaked in January and stayed there for a couple of months, meshing unavoidably with the more dramatic and serious crisis generated by the collapse of Iran as a surrogate of the United States in the "vital periphery" of the Persian Gulf. The "peace process" started even in February but picked up momentum only in May. By that time, Afghanistan paid a heavy price in blood and agony for the April revolution and the civil war; the Soviet Union was so bloodied in the rugged terrain that *Pravda* gave out a gasp of frustration: "stuggle against the bandits is no easy matter;"[1] The Carter administration lost its secretary of state,[2] some more credibility as leader of the "free world", and quite a bit of the cold war andrenalin that had gushed through its veins in the maiden weeks of 1980.[3]

From May onwards, the "struggle for peace"—a Soviet phrase quite applicable to the Afghan case—proceeded gingerly, and often noisily—at four different levels. At the superpower level, the three-and-a-half-hour meeting between Andre Gromyko and the newly appointed secretary of state, Edmund Muskie, on May 16 in Vienna's Hofsburg Palace not only signalled the beginning of the end of Cold War II, but actually went over concrete proposals for a political settlement. The two sets of proposals were, of course, diametrically opposed to one another, but they set off a process of tough and tortuous negotiations at the summit of the international order, and made Afghanistan part of the quarry with which the superpowers must rebuild the shattered mosaic of coexistence.[4] At the local level, the Marxist regime in Kabul was trying, with Moscow's full backing, to seduce Pakistan and Iran to work out the arithmetic of a political settlement that would guarantee the security of the frontiers of each of the three troubled, insecure states and provide the sine qua non for gradual withdrawal of Soviet troops. Into the jagged arteries of the two parallel peace efforts, four governments were trying to inject momentum from two different levels. France, Western Germany and Britain were deploying their separate diplomatic resource to bring the superpowers together to a political settlement. India, at the other end, was using its diplomatic skills to persuade the Kabul regime to broaden its political base, nudge Pakistan and Iran to negotiate directly with Kabul and convince Moscow that it was in its own interest to withdraw its forces from Afghanistan as soon as possible. The four different streams of the peace "struggle" mingled, reluctantly but unavoidably, during the 1980 session of the UN General Assembly. A political settlement was still quite a distance off when the session ended, but, like all coming events, it was casting its first coy shadows as the first anniversary of the Soviet landing in Afghanistan drew near.

Even in September, the local scenario changed significantly in favour of the Soviet Union in Afghanistan. *The Times*, of London, reported, "The loose alliance of Afghan resistance groups with headquarters in Peshawar has all but crumbled." Resistance was still going on in Afghanistan, but the rebels were split into as many as 60 groups, often quarrelling, even fighting, among themselves. "A guerrilla group wanting to cross another tribal area will have to negotiate or even pay toll . . . There is a romantic image of the Afghan tribesman . . . but there is also another aspect. The tradition of banditry is well established in Afghanistan and it is difficult to draw a line between acts of war and acts of brigandage."[5]

In Pakistan, reported the *International Herald Tribune*, armed clashes had started breaking out between Afghan refugees and Baluchis in Baluchistan province and tension build between the Afghans and the Pathans of the Nortwest Frontier Province because "it has become clear to the Pakistanis that the refugees will not be able to return to Soviet-occupied Afghanistan any time soon."[6] The over 1 million

Afghan refugees located on Pakistani territory, many of them armed, and all of them fed on promises of international help to enable their return to a "liberated" Afghanistan, could turn against the regime of Gen. Zia ul-Huq—a grim eventuality some had foreseen even at the beginning of the Afghan crisis.[7]

In a third related development, the Islamic regime in Tehran and the Islamic military regime in Islamabad fell out on the issue of Pakistan's growing military ties with Saudi Arabia, which the Ayatollah Rohulla Khomeini and his followers regarded as a malefic connection. Things came to such a pass that the Ayatollah exhorted the Shia segment of the Pakistani population to "overthrow" the military rule of Gen. Zia ul-Huq. All these three developments somewhat eased the political position of the Babrak Karmal regime in Kabul and the military position of the Soviet Union in Afghanistan. The insurgency was still far from flushed out. However, people visiting Afghanistan in the autumn of 1980 found that disciplined organised resistance spread over large areas in the interior provinces no longer existed, and that external aid to the rebels had largely dried up.[8] The Marxist regime seemed to be slowly gaining self-confidence. A high-powered team of Soviet military officers was in Afghanistan in September. The general expectation in Kabul was that the team would work out plans for withdrawing a second batch of Soviet troops in the new year, the first batch of some 10,000 plus over 100 tanks having been withdrawn in June. The Soviets could take on the remnants of the rebel forces with a smaller army, trained and equipped in the past eight months in guerrilla warfare and schooled in the peculiar terrain of the Hindu Kush.[9]

No one ever doubted Moscow's ability to put down the Afghan insurgency. Doubts, however, lingered about the cost. In January-February, it was even hoped in certain quarters in the United States that Afghanistan would turn out to be Moscow's Vietnam. The idea behind funnelling international assistance to the insurgents was to make the Soviets' Afghan expedition as prolonged and politically and militarily as expensive as possible. Estimates of what the expedition had cost and might still cost the Soviet Union differed in the autumn of 1980, but the exhaustion of the will of nations to confront the USSR in Afghanistan shifted the emphasis to a political settlement.

POLITICAL SETTLEMENT

Here, too, the Soviet position was less equivocal than the United States'. The Soviets had left no doubt in anyone's mind about the reasons of their intervention. They moved into Afghanistan with 80,000-85,000 troops in order to save the Marxist regime, defend a Marxist-ruled Afghanistan from external intervention and to secure the southern flank of the Soviet Union. Afghanistan had long been in the Soviet sphere of influence; no Afghan government could possibly survive with an anti-Soviet posture. Now, instead of a friendly non-aligned Afghanistan, Moscow wanted a secure, internationally-recognised pro-Soviet Marxist nonaligned Afghanistan—like Cuba and Vietnam. Nothing less would satisfy the Soviet Union or be acceptable to it. The United States' political stand moved between January and May from an extreme anti-Soviet to a middle-moderate position.

The Soviet "peace offensive" was launched in May at two levels: (1) at the global level by Moscow itself and (2) at regional level by the Afghan government with full backing of the Soviet Union.

Moscow put forward a 3-point peace proposal covering super-power relations, relationship between NATO and the Warsaw Pact and Southwest and South Asia. The three main elements were: (1) A top level meeting of the leaders of states of all the regions of the world to focus on the task of removing hotbeds of international tension and preventing war. (2) A long list of proposals on arms control including a freeze on the size of all military forces in Europe; a ban on all nuclear testing; negotiations to limit the deployment of medium range nuclear missiles in Europe and ratification of the SALT-II treaty. (3) A formula for settling the Afghanistan crisis providing for withdrawal of Soviet troops from Afghanistan, if, Iran, Pakistan and the United States would stop aiding the Afghan rebels.[10]

The third proposal was elaborated by the Afghan government. Kabul called for bilateral discussions between Afghanistan and Pakistan and between Afghanistan and Iran. These talks should lead to concrete steps to prevent "foreign intervention in Afghan affairs"; the prevention of use of Pakistan and Iran territory for the purpose of aggression; and for non-intervention in each other's internal affairs. While the talks were in progress all hostile activities against the Afghan government must stop. Once agreement was reached among the three countries, talks could begin on the withdrawal of Soviet forces and on superpower assurances on non-intervention in Afghanistan's internal affairs. These were the proposals that Gromyko put up to Muskie in Vienna.

Before the Soviets formulated their peace package, the British government had proposed, and the EEC endorsed, a plan to solve the Afghan crisis on the basis of (1) internationally guaranteed neutrality of Afghanistan; (2) withdrawal of Soviet troops; (3) cessation of external help to the Afghan rebels; and (4) return of the Afghan refugees to Afghanistan. The proposals were supported by President Carter but were rejected by the Soviet Union and cold-shouldered by nonaligned countries like India, Yugoslavia and Algeria.

A third proposal for the solution of the Afghan crisis came from the Austrian Chancellor, Bruno Kreisky. He suggested (1) restoration of Afghanistan's nonaligned status as a fully independent buffer state following withdrawal of Soviet troops and (2) freedom of choice for Afghanistan to determine its relations with the big powers. This proposal remained a non-starter.[11]

At the Islamic foreign ministers' conference at Islamabad in May, the secretary general, Habib Chatti, of Tunisia, in his report demanded: (1) total and unconditional Soviet withdrawal from Afghanistan: (2) return of the Afghan refugees to their homes; and (3) the right of the Afghan people to elect their own government. These demands, however, were not formulated into concrete proposals for a settlement of the Afghan crisis.

In his talks with Mrs Gandhi at Salisbury, the Pakistan President, Gen. Zia proposed the stationing of an international supervisory force with units drawn from countries like India to oversee the cessation of the channeling of military aid to Afghan rebels through Pakistan territory, once the Soviets had withdrawn their troops from Afghanistan.

The Bangladesh President, Ziaur Rehman, proposed on May 20 a summit conference of six South Asian countries—India, Pakistan, Bhutan, Bangladesh, Nepal and Sri Lanka—to promote regional cooperation. The proposal had no direct bearing on Afghanistan. It was lukewarmly received in New Delhi and Islamabad.

Concept of Neutrality

The concept of a "neutral" Afghanistan merits reflection.

In the third week of February 1980, the British government came out with a proposal to confer on Afghanistan an internationally guaranteed status of neutrality roughly on the Austrian model. The British foreign secretary, Lord Carrington, told a news conference in London that if the Soviet intervention in Afghanistan had been prompted by fears of the USSR's own security, then "a neutral Afghanistan overcomes this difficulty and enables the Soviet Union to withdraw on a perfectly respectable basis." He implied that a neutral independent Afghanistan free of outside interference could attract the support of the third world, particularly, the Islamic countries.[12]

The foreign ministers of the EEC meeting in Rome in the third week of February endorsed the British neutrality plan which was also approved by the US Secretary of State, Cyrus Vance, who was visiting the European capitals to rally America's allies behind US policy to contain Soviet power in the "arc of crisis". President Carter in a message to an ailing President Tito expressed America's willingness to join other countries, including the Soviet Union, to guarantee Afghanistan's neutrality if the Soviets withdrew from Afghanistan. The neutrality concept was also supported by Gen. Zia ul-Huq of Pakistan.

For a while there was a certain amount of optimism in London that the neutrality concept might start diplomatic efforts rolling for a settlement of the Aghan crisis. There was a great deal of speculation about India's reaction; analysts hovered between hope and despair when they tried to anticipate New Delhi's response. It was suggested at one stage that if the reaction of India and several other nonaligned countries were positive, the British government would send out a special envoy for more concrete diplomatic probings.[13]

Although the first Soviet reaction to the neutrality concept was negative—*Tass* questioned the EEC's right to determine the status of a sovereign nation like Afghanistan[14]—Whitehall was not easily discouraged. Reports suggested that the *Tass* comment was not to be taken as Moscow's last word. A flicker of hope was lighted when the *Evening News* printed an informal message from a Soviet source suggesting that Moscow might even accept the stationing of UN troops in Afghanistan provided an Afghan government to be "freely elected" would not be anti-Soviet. The message which was attributed to Victor Louis, Moscow's well-known trouble-shooter, suggested that Carrington continue with his efforts to institute further negotiations between the Soviet Union and the West.[15] The optimism, however, died soon. By February 27 it was clear that the proposal seeking a neutral status for Afghanistan was a mere trial balloon. It found no favour with India, Yugoslavia and Algeria. This became evident in the course of discussions the Yugoslav and Algerian foreign ministers had separately with Indian officials in New Delhi. The political correspondent of the *Indian Express* reported that these three major nonaligned nations believed that what Afghanistan needed was not neutrality in the technical sense of the term but the safeguarding of its independence and nonalignment. "From nonaligned nations like India the word 'neutrality' and what it connotes in international affairs is not evoking an enthusiastic response."[16] A spokesman of the Indian External Affairs Ministry said on February 27 that India and other likeminded nonaligned nations wished that the independence of Afghanistan be preserved at all cost and that its status should not be converted into one of "technical neutrality."[17]

Undaunted by the negative reaction of the three nonaligned powers, Britain formally presented the neutrality proposal to the Soviet ambassador in London on February 28. A similar proposal was also made by Rumania.

The neutrality concept was shot down by the USSR in March. It was dismissed in the columns of the *New Times* as "unworthy of discussion." The weekly said that the plan "merely distracts attention from the undeclared war which the henchmen of imperialist circles are waging in Afghanistan." It was an attempt to avoid giving a clearcut reply to the Soviet proposal contained in Brezhnev's statement of February 22.[18] From now own, the Soviets became highly sensitive to any Western proposal that questioned legitimacy of its presence and influence in Afghanistan.

The Soviet position became a lot more clear during the Moscow visit of the Afghan foreign minister, Shah Mohammed Dost. Hosting a luncheon for the Afghan minister, Gromyko said that "search for political ways to settle questions relating to Afghanistan could only be welcome. At the same time, it should be clear that no attempts to settle the affairs of the Afghan people behind their back, no plans affecting the sovereignty of the Afghan state or ignoring the lawful government and failing to guarantee Afghanistan against outside interference in its internal affairs will have any success."[19] The *Hindustan Times* correspondent in London reported in the middle of March: "Any consideration at this stage of the pros and cons of an Afghan neutrality conference would seem premature. The neutrality suggestion is still an idea and has to be developed yet into a full-fledged proposal."[20]

The transient career of the concept of a neutral Afghanistan showed how the same political phrase has come to acquire different meanings in different parts of the world. The British excavated the phrase from the archives of the Anglo-Afghan wars; it was, for Britain, a late 20th century incarnation of the buffer state of a bygone era of power politics. The Austrian parallel was a miscue from the beginning. The neutrality of Austria was not designed by the four allies of World War II. The treaty providing for the withdrawal of allied forces from Austria is silent on neutralisation. After the treaty was concluded, the Austrian parliament *itself* adopted a constitutional law declaring the country's perpetual neutrality: "Austria will not join any military alliance and will not permit the establishment of any foreign military bases on her territory." Austria communicated the law to all states with which it had diplomatic relations and asked them to recognise its perpetual neutrality as defined in the law.[21]

Britain and the United States meant by a neutral or neutralised Afghanistan a land from which all Soviet troops were withdrawn unconditionally, where the Soviets had no military bases or installations and which was governed by a government freely elected by the people. This government would declare itself nonaligned and neutral and its status would be guaranteed by the world community. The Soviets understood by neutral Afghanistan a land freed of intervention by outside powers, which would be ruled by the Marxist regime proclaimed in April 1978 (individuals could come and go but the revolution must stay). This regime must remain friendly towards the USSR which would guarantee its security together with the United States. It would not have a military pact with the Soviet Union but only a treaty of friendship. It would be a nonaligned state, fully sovereign and independent. From this kind of a neutral Afghanistan, the Soviets would withdraw all their troops.

DIALECTICS OF PEACE

Since Afghanistan provided the first occasion for direct Soviet military intervention in a third world country, how Moscow proceeded to defuse the crisis and bring about a denouement to their liking is of interest to students of international politics, especially those who look closely at the style of Soviet diplomacy. Peace, in Marxist-

Leninist analysis, is a dialectical process; it is not made of the milk of compassion that courses in human bosoms; it is dictated by political and social realities, national as well as international. Peace, then, is not the opposite of war; the two are part and parcel of the larger dynamics of international change. The Soviet intervention itself was an act in "defence of peace."[22] It took place in an area where geography and the correlation of forces overwhelmingly favoured the USSR. If it still stirred an avalanche of anger and protest it was because the capitalist-imperialist powers possessed enormous capability to create worldwide confusion about Soviet intentions. But the sound and fury of the protest did not perturb the Soviet leaders too much; from the beginning they appeared to be quietly confident that they could defend peace from the "aggressive designs of the enemies of progress and detente." This confidence was cushioned on their understanding of the contradictions within the opposite camp and among the regional nations directly affected by the intervention. Soviet foreign policy decision-makers proceeded from the assumption that their action in Afghanistan would divide rather than unite the Western powers to a common line of counterattack, and that it would sharpen rather than narrow the strategic divisions in South Asia.

Soviet diplomacy from the beginning sought to exploit the contradictions between the United States and Western Europe on the one hand and among the regional nations on the other. Soviet diplomacy found a strong ally in the "peace axis" formed even in January by France and India, with which West Germany linked its own crisis-defusing efforts a little later, less openly but perhaps more effectively. This transcontinental "peace axis" neutralised the China card of the United States, and stole the thunder of Carter's cold war. The Soviet foreign office regarded every peace initiative emanating from Western Europe as a nail in the coffin of Cold War II. When Britain launched the balloon of Afghan neutrality, the Soviets made sympathetic noises and took a full month to shoot it down. They contrasted their own readiness to ease tensions and strengthen detente in Europe with Carter's penchant for a new nuclear arms race and cited the unilateral withdrawal of 20,000 troops from the German Democratic Republic as a convincing earnest of their intentions. Their handling of the regional powers showed a high degree of sophistication. They did not allow their differences with India on the issue of troops withdrawal to cloud the Indo-Soviet relationship which expanded rather than shrunk in 1980. Where the Soviets went wrong was in their underestimation of the impact of their Afghan action on the American resolve to step up US military power and in their failure to gauge the size and stamina of the Afghan insurgency. It is doubtful if the Soviet intervention galvanised the Afghans into a nation of resisters and gave them a new nationalist identity. But it certainly did not endear the USSR to the broad mass of Afghans. The smallness and weaknesses of the Marxist movement in Afghanistan deprived the Soviets of the advantage of an effective ideologically oriented working-and-middle-class constituency which could have acted as political broker between Moscow and the Afghan masses.

The Soviets' main difficulty, then, resided within Afghanistan rather than in the wrath of Jimmy Carter or the effervescence of Islamic indignation. The brute fact that the Marxist regime in Kabul could not survive the pull-out of Russian troops hardened the Soviet position on withdrawal and at the same time triggered a search for ways and means to make withdrawal possible. The Soviets could withdraw only if the rest of the world helped the Marxist regime in Kabul to survive.

The "peace offensive" was designed as a ways-and-means instrument. Each initiative was launched with an eye for timing and surprise; as a frontal, flanking or rearguard operation. The first peace package offering terms and technology of a political settlement was released, as noted, on the eve of the second meeting of foreign ministers of Islamic nations in Islamabad in May. It was carefully aimed both at the United States and the Islamic neighbours of Afghanistan. The ersatz olive branch was received by the world with cynicism and suspicion; it failed to evoke much response even in India. But it did impress West Europeans as the "first real indication that the Soviet Union seemed prepared to consider a political settlement linked to a withdrawal of Russian troops."[23] It made it easier for Edmund Muskie to meet Gromyko in Vienna.

Muskie's Dignified Bend

The meeting itself implied a bending of the American stand, executed with dignified stiffness. The two foreign ministers did not talk confrontation. In very different rhetoric that gave out glints of steel, they were looking for a way out of confrontation. No firm steps in the reversing of direction could be taken before the inauguration of the next US presidency in January 1981. But the necessary groundwork must begin at once in preparation for a Carter second term or a Reagan White House. Muskie had been brought from the Senate to the seventh floor at Foggy Bottom to tame Zbigniew Brzezinski; he must be quick to use the leverage he enjoyed with Carter if he were to be the president's principal adviser on foreign policy.[24] While Muskie and Gromyko traded the expected polemics, they also set in motion a channel of "continuing dialogue", with the Soviet ambassador in Washington, Anatoli Dobrynin, feeding it from the Russian end.[25] The Soviets moved to add a little muscle to Muskie's diplomacy even while relishing the pressure they could put on Carter through the French president and the West German chancellor. Muskie did not enjoy the sight of Giscard d'Estaing meeting with Brezhnev in Warsaw just two days after his own session with Gromyko.[26] But he could, if he wished to, count as the first fruit of his meeting with his Soviet counterpart Brezhnev's June 22 announcement that "some army units" were being immediately pulled out from Afghanistan. In four days Washington received indications that the Russians went ahead with their pulling out 108 tanks, anti-aircraft missile units and possibly many battlefield rockets.[27] It was disclosed at this stage that the Carter Administration had offered the Soviets more flexible terms for a political settlement of the Afghan crisis. An unidentified "senior official" travelling in the plane that was taking Carter to the funeral of Tito in Belgrade, told reporters, "We recognise that the Soviet Union has a legitimate security interest in Afghanistan not being transformed into an anti-Soviet outpost of some sort. We are prepared whenever the moment is right to enter into arrangements designed to make sure that this is stable, that this is not a threat to anybody, particularly the Soviets, who have to be reassured that if they leave, Afghanistan doesn't become an outpost either for Western or American or any other anti-Soviet political-military orientation."[28] Though Carter himself in his public pronouncements raised the question of public acceptability of a pro-Soviet regime in Kabul—which brought forth an immediate Soviet growl—US officials left little doubt that the United States would finally acquiesce in a Marxist government cosmetically broadbased to make it look different from the one formed on the heels of the Soviet intervention.[29]

Carter was aware, according to these officials, that the "necessary ingredients for a full removal of Soviet troops may include assurance that a mass slaughter of pro-Soviet elements would be prevented and that an anti-Soviet government would not emerge."[30] This sounded like a veiled offer even to recognise the need to keep a certain number of Soviet troops in Afghanistan for some time to stabilise the political settlement that might emerge from international negotiations going on simultaneously at multiple levels.

These negotiations will no doubt be long and tortuous, with their ups and downs, punctuated, as they meander, by considerable posturing and manoeuvring, attended by a good deal of verbal invectives. Afghanistan is not a simple issue that can be seen in black or white. It is part and parcel of the highly convoluted superpower relationship at the turn of the 1980s. The Soviets will not loosen their grip of Afghanistan, but they will probably be willing to give some satisfaction to the United States if they can get back detente or another incarnation of it. In the 1980s, the Soviets have other alternatives—working with the West Europeans for a separate detente, making it up with China. But neither is nearly as attractive or rewarding as detente with the United States. Not only because what the leading capitalist power can offer by way of rewards, but also because the West Europeans wouldn't walk far on the road of a divided detente if this meant seriously alienating the United States and because the US could make things more difficult for the USSR in Eastern Europe, even within the Soviet state than any other power or combination of powers. The Soviet leaders therefore made Afghanistan one of the chips in the hard bargaining that lay ahead with the US. In his talks with Giscard d'Estaing and Helmut Schimdt, Brezhnev spoke of nuclear arms control in Europe, the SALT process and Afghanistan in the same breath. When Brezhnev, at his July meeting in Moscow with the West German chancellor, accepted the Western position on the terms for opening negotiations to limit missile deployment in Europe, he expected Carter or his successor in the White House to show a better appreciation of the Soviet stake in Afghanistan.

In an interesting display of unofficial diplomacy, the Soviets invited Leslie H. Gelb, of the *New York Times*, to visit their country in June and Kremlin officials told him the Soviet side of the story, playing the "totally aggrieved party," having done nothing to deserve the unleashing of Carter's cold war. Soviet officials bared to Gelb the layout of their peace diplomacy. They wanted to fasten on "atmospherics" first. "They said they would start by withdrawing some troops from Afghanistan and by accepting the Western position on the terms for starting negotiations on missiles in Europe, and they have done this. In return, they want Carter to tone down his anti-Soviet rhetoric and make a full-faith effort to rally the country to support the Strategic Arms Treaty. If all this happens, "other good things could follow," they hinted. This long-range signalling process has begun already. Gelb concluded his report on the mood of the Soviet Union with these words:

> The Soviet Union—facing some large-scale economic and political problems that do not have ready solutions, and with vast untapped military power—probably presents a greater challenge to the world than ever before. That was demonstrated in its decision to invade Afghanistan, and in what it saw as the decision to stay there for a long time. But I did come away from my conversations in the Soviet Union with the feeling that Soviet leaders, having acted against Afghanistan, are now in a generally reactive mood. I sensed that they expect us to increase military spending and to be more competitive, but that beyond a certain point they will react accordingly. Neither we, nor they, will give up very much, but the choice is basically ours about how far the competition will go in the next few years.[31]

Will the Soviets assure the United States that there will be no more Afghanistans if detente were restored to its Nixonian glory? Will they accept Kissinger's linkage concept after all, and agree to show restraint in the vital peripheries in return for the economic and political rewards of detente? Is the darkly ominous wind blowing in Poland and Rumania enough reason for the Soviets to prefer another long spell of political stability and economic reconstruction to a further demonstration of their global power in the grey zones of the planet?

In rhetoric, the Soviets will not compromise on the ideological front. They will stick to their position that detente does not rule out ideological competition or the international class war, but makes its waging easier and less expensive. In practice, however, they may well refrain from another direct military intervention in third world conflicts for quite a long time. After all, Afghanistans do not happen every year. They have already notified the world of what they can do if developments in Iran or Turkey threaten the security and stability of the southern flank of the Soviet state. Every international actor, big or small, will take into account the sobering fact of Soviet power while dealing with crisis situations in regions adjacent to the USSR. Meanwhile, the CPSU may well decide that the states with socialist orientation which have sprouted in strategically important regions of Asia and Africa be consolidated and stabilised before the time comes to use military power to deliver another natural ally from the wounds of a civil war or a national liberation struggle.

Whether the next intervention will be necessary will, to be sure, not depend on the Soviets alone. The necessity to intervene will diminish if the United States recognises the USSR as an equal global power and tries to make accommodation. Specifically, if the United States activates the Geneva conference mechanism for a political settlement of the Arab-Israeli conflict, there will hardly be an occasion for Moscow's direct or proxy intervention in Middle Eastern conflicts. Similarly, the Soviets would expect to be accepted as a legitimate power to determine war and peace in the Persian Gulf region where they command overwhelming military advantage, have acquired a certain political clout and which is close to their frontiers. In short, what the Soviets are labouring for is a series of helsinkies locking them with other actors on the basis of equality to control and manage conflicts, promote cooperation, engineer change. This is confirmed by Brezhnev's peace proposal for the Gulf region to which he has, for all practical purposes, linked Afghanistan. The Soviet peace offensive will surely gather greater momentum in 1982; the 26th CPSU Congress in February appropriately adopt a five-year plank of "peace and strength." The intervention in Afghanistan was an extreme demonstration of Soviet power. The CPSU will now watch how the rest of the world perceives the power of the USSR, how the various international actors react to it, how the international system adjusts itself to it. The peace offensive will try to help the world's adjustment.

Zeroing in on Pakistan

Meanwhile, Soviet peace diplomacy zeroed in on Pakistan as the US was getting ready for the inauguration of the Reagan administration. Apart from the possibility that Reagan might offer to the Pakistani military regime what Carter had refused in January 1980, the Soviets had also their eyes on two coming international meetings, the Islamic summit at Taif, Mecca, in January 1981 and the nonaligned foreign ministers' conference in New Delhi in February, in both of which Moscow was vitally interested. Early January, the Soviet charge d'affaires in Islamabad told Agha Shahi that Afghanistan was ready to open a dialogue with Pakistan without any pre-condition in the presence of a representative to be appointed by the US Secretary-General. In a series of follow-up conversations between the Pakistan ambassador in Moscow and the Soviet foreign office, the Soviet-Afghan position became clearer. Afghanistan would not quibble about whether in sitting down with Babrak Karmal or his representative at the conference table Pakistan labelled him as representing the Afghan government or the ruling party of Afghanistan. In other words, Pakistan would not have to even implicitly recognise the Karmal regime while starting talks for a political settlement. However, the Soviet Union and Afghanistan would not agree to hold talks in terms of the resolution on Afghanistan adopted by the UN General Assembly in November 1980 because both had rejected that resolution. Pakistan was also told that talks should begin bilaterally if Iran were unwilling to join, and that Pakistan must not insist on a trilateral forum.[32]

The proposal was put out by Kabul Radio. Apparently, both Moscow and Kabul kept India fully informed, if they did not consult with the Indian government.[33] The Soviet-Afghan diplomatic initiative activated Pakistani diplomacy also. Reports suggested that the military junta was once again divided on the issue of reconstructing the American connection. Some of the military leaders preferred to wait for what concrete offer might come from the Reagan administration before embarking on the less exciting road to a political settlement. Agha Shahi himself was probably in favour of venturing on the diplomatic road. He told the writer in February that American policy with regard to Pakistan had changed so many times in the 15 years that it was difficult to predict what Reagan might come up with; in any case, he did not visualise a relationship with the US that might infringe on Pakistan's non-alignment. General Zia ul-Huq probably stood somewhere in between his foreign minister and more hawkish brother generals.[34]

Gen. Zia surprised the diplomatic community in Islamabad by turning up at a function at the Soviet embassy to celebrate the anniversary of the October revolution. Diplomatic exchanges were then going on between Islamabad and Moscow on the question of starting a dialogue between Afghanistan and Pakistan. Towards the end of December, Shahi went to Peking and presumably consulted the Chinese leaders about the Soviet proposals. Returning to Islamabad, he announced on January 3 that "favourable conditions" had arisen for a political settlement of the Afghan crisis; he formally asked the

UN Secretary-General to name his personal representative in whose presence, though not through his mediation, the talks were to be held.[35] Suddenly, however, certain "difficulties" propped up in mid-January. Pakistani sources blamed Moscow, but actually, it was Pakistan that backtracked, insisting that Iran, too, must join the talks from the very beginning. Iran's absence from the Islamic summit resulted in the adoption of a resolution on Afghanistan to which Tehran was no party, and this created further complications very soon.

The Islamic summit resolution on Afghanistan was a considerable climb-down from the position the Islamic foreign ministers had held at their second conference at Islamabad in May 1980. Afghanistan was debated at Taif in a close-door session. The Afghan rebels were conspicuously absent. The resolution called for immediate and unconditional withdrawal of "foreign" troops from Afghanistan, without naming the Soviet Union. It called for a political settlement under UN auspices and within the framework of the UN resolution, giving up its earlier insistence that the search for a political settlement must be conducted within the confines of resolutions adopted at the Islamic meets of 1980.[36] Interestingly, Agha Shahi's stand at the Taif summit was considerably mellower than the strongly anti-Soviet rhetoric of Gen. Zia. One reason for the mellowness was the danger to Pakistan's stability emanating from a mass of disgruntled and angry Afghan refugees armed by Pakistan and its allies and friends. Pakistan could not afford to see these guns turned south. In fact, the restless Afghan refugees posed a double-edged predicament for Gen. Zia. He could not bend too much to the Soviet Union and be condemned for letting the refugees down. Nor could he delay a political settlement of the Afghan problem too long, thereby losing valuable time for sending the Afghans back home. If he escalated the conflict, he ran the risk of facing a Soviet armed attack.

From Taif, Shahi went to Tehran to talk to Iranian leaders, but failed to persuade them to join in the talks. The Iranian refusal and differences within the Pakistani military junta stiffened Shahi's position when he came to New Delhi on February 9 for the non-aligned foreign ministers' conference and at once became the star of a noisy, often raucous, show.

For six days the 90-odd foreign ministers sweated to produce a declaration that would reconcile the polarised positions of the pro-Soviet and pro-US groups over the tearing issues of foreign military intervention in Kampuchea and Afghanistan. The Declaration that finally emerged was a victory for the pro-US group—for the first time in the 20-year-old history of the nonaligned movement, a declaration was adopted which did not attack the United States by name, and blamed the two superpowers equally for the climate of confrontation and militarisation building up in the world, specifically in the Indian Ocean.[37] Of greater interest to participants and observers alike was the result of Kurt Waldheim's effort to bring Pakistan, Afghanistan and Iran together. The UN Secretary-General arrived in New Delhi on February 10 with a Peruvian official of the UN named as his representative to initiate the talks. He met with the foreign ministers of the three countries separately, but could not bring them together. Iran hotly refused to talk to Kabul until the last Soviet soldier left Afghanistan. Shahi would not meet Kabul's man except in the presence of Iran, and in no case would he meet Mohammad Dost of Afghanistan on Indian soil. Yet Shahi did not close the door on talks with Afghanistan. He had reason to be pleased with the phrasing of the Afghanistan part of the declaration, but he knew that it took Pakistan no closer to its goal, namely, an Afghanistan rid of Soviet troops. Perhaps Shahi had been asked by Gen. Zia to stall for some time until the American option had been once again exhausted. Or perhaps, as one report suggested, Zia was bargaining for a higher price from the Soviet Union—recognition by Moscow and Kabul of the Durand Line, which would help him get rid of the Pashtunistan problem.[38]

Pakistan or at least its foreign minister was now thinking in terms of "political consolidation" of South Asia, keeping all major powers out of involvement. In an exclusive interview to the writer in February 1981, Agha Shahi said that Pakistan wanted the South Asian region to stay out of superpowers' assertive competition and to emerge as a "viable independent political factor" in the arena of world politics. Pakistan wanted the countries of South Asia to build a regional edifice of "political cooperation," to "manage their own conflicts and devise mechanisms to settle their own differences through peaceful means," and to act together to defuse, if not prevent, a superpower confrontation leading to a conflict of unforseeable calamity for the human race. Pakistan wanted the states of South Asia to live peacefully with one another. As Pakistan's effable and astute foreign minister outlined Pakistan's regional perspective, it seemed for a moment that the congenital strategic divide between the two distant neighbours was about to be bridged. But no! For as Agha Shahi proceeded to outline his strategic regional thinking, the still sharp differences between Pakistan and India came into focus.

The region, Agha Shahi observed, had its deep-rooted differences as well as strong historical affinities. It was also profoundly influenced by what happened between the superpowers. In the 1980s, the superpowers had engaged in new mutually assertive competition and rivalry, triggered to a large extent by their parity of strategic power. He believed, however, that the superpowers were, or would be, moving towards "some kind of accommodation" for one another in the South Asian region.

This perception of the Pakistan foreign minister seemed to have sharpened his strategic thinking about problems and possibilities of regional cooperation. A great power confrontation in the region was pregnant with dangers for each country in the area—a point that India had been making since the beginning of the Afghan crisis. But when Agha Shahi spoke about the "ability of the region to settle its problems without leaving a sense of rankling injustices behind," he stressed that the creation of a "platform of political solidarity" in South Asia called for a symmetrical relationship between each of the regional countries and the superpowers.

Agha Shahi's basic concept of symmetry was non-alignment. "No one in the region must have a special relationship with either superpower." This, in his view, applied particularly to India because Pakistan perceived India's relationship with the Soviet Union as a "virtual alliance"—"you may not agree with this, but this is how we see it." The "special Indo-Soviet relationship," he indicated, created problems not only for other regional countries but also for the other superpower, and, of course, China.

Pakistan, he claimed, had no "special relationship" with the United States, nor was it seeking one even with Ronald Reagan in the White House. "We are in the process of reviewing our relations with the United States. Whatever happens as a result of the review, we will not ask for, nor accept a relationship that might infringe on Pakistan's independence and sovereignty or run against our nonalignment." Nor did Pakistan have a special relationship with China comparable to India's with the USSR, he asserted. "Our relations with China are good and have been free of clouds, although there is no 100 per cent agreement between us and the Chinese." However, Pakistan has signed no formal treaty with Peking, nor was China a superpower.

Pakistan, he claimed, had not become a part of the global or regional foreign policy design of the United States or China. The manner in which he stressed this point indicated that there had been some basic change in Pakistan's foreign policy strategic thinking since January-February 1980 when Gen. Zia offered Pakistan to Carter as a forward base of the latter's decision to contain and confront the USSR. In fact, Agha Shahi was more impressed with the fluctuations in the United States' policy towards Pakistan since the mid-sixties than with the blessings of the American connection. He even drew a contrast between the consistency of India's ties with the USSR and the instabilities of Pakistan's ties with the United States.

This, however, lent an edge to Agha Shahi's vision of India's Soviet connection. He did not exactly see India as a partner of Moscow's global foreign policy designs; India was too big for that, and had its own strategic goals. But he did see India's importance for Soviet global strategic designs, and was therefore particularly anxious that India maintained a "balanced" relationship with the superpowers, and not "tilt" towards Moscow.

The Pakistan foreign minister spelt out three concrete steps India could take in order to build a regional climate of "political consolidation." First, India's nonalignment should be "genuine". Second, within the framework of the Simla agreement there should be some progress for a settlement of the Kashmir issue. Third, India should have a greater appreciation of Pakistan's need to "modernise" some of its defence equipment.

On the last point, Agha Shahi was very emphatic, indicating that a more indulgent Indian view of Pakistan's shopping for modern arms would go a long way to build a climate of mutual trust. Agha Shahi did not mean that India had no appreciation at all of Pakistan's military needs. There was some appreciation in India, but not enough. With some regret he added that there was also inadequate appreciation in India of how much Pakistan's foreign policy had changed in the last four years. "Pakistan has walked out of SEATO and CENTO. Pakistan has embraced nonalignment as the basic concept of foreign policy. It has no security treaty with any major power." In contrast, India's foreign policy remained more or less unchanged, he said, adding in an undertone, "in a very altered and fast changing world."

Agha Shahi gave the impression that Pakistan's relations with the Soviet Union were improving slowly; no breakthrough was in sight.

He would not concede Moscow a conflict management role in the Persian Gulf and South Asia. "The management of conflict must be the prerogative of the regional powers themselves." He would even look ahead to a regional security system excluding all major powers. At the same time, Agha Shahi refused to recognise any power as a "regional influential" or "dominant regional power." That was hegemonism, he said, "All nations of course are not equal, but that's no reason why some nations should be recognised as more equal than others."

CHAPTER TEN

Asian Perceptions of Soviet Power

>Out of this nettle, danger, we pluck
>this flower: safety.
>*Henry IV*, Part I, II, iii, 11

The Soviet intervention in Afghanistan planted in the minds of Asian elites clear images of the USSR as the other global power. Asian nations *knew* that the Soviet Union was a superpower. They felt the impact of Soviet power since the 50s, when the USSR began to use military power as an instrument of foreign policy in the third world. But only when Moscow lifted 80,000 fully equipped troops to Afghanistan in less than two weeks, risking a major confrontation with the United States, did Asian elites *see* the might and power of the Soviet Union. The event quaked all regimes in the "arc of crisis". It scrambled the image-systems of some of the ruling Asian elites, jolted others' perceptions of the external world, the images of their immediate neighbourhoods, even their self-images. The intervention in Afghanistan was a culmination of the assertive diplomacy the USSR had been pursuing in the arc of crisis since 1975. Its impact on Asian minds was apocalyptic.

In this chapter, we try to assess and analyse elite perceptions of the Soviet Union *after* the Afghan intervention in three South Asian countries—Pakistan, India and Bangladesh. Perceptions strongly influence responses. South Asian perceptions of Soviet power influence each country's response to that power. To be sure, responses are influenced by other factors too, especially each country's perception of its own strength and weakness; its own role; of the other major actors who compete with the USSR. Furthermore, the Asian countries located in geographical proximity of the Soviet Union are handicapped, even crippled, by dependencies on outside powers. Nevertheless, these countries' responses to Soviet power are important not merely for their own foreign policies and domestic developments but also for the responses the US, the Western powers, Japan and China may build up to the phenomenon of Soviet power. In this context, South

Asian perceptions of Soviet power is of particular importance. This is so not only because of South Asia's close proximity to the USSR, but also because linkages have blurred geopolitical barriers between South Asia and the Persian Gulf, collapsing the two into a single geostrategic region of Southwestern Asia.

The three South Asian countries together constitute the subcontinent, home of nearly 800 million people, or one-fifth of mankind. The three partners of the subcontinent saw the intervention differently from one another. Pakistan, a neighbour of Afghanistan, and an ally of the United States and China, reacted with awe, verging on panic. Unlike Pakistan, India is one nation away from the USSR, and Moscow's most enduring friend in the third world. India was disturbed by the intervention, but more concerned about the arming of Pakistan by the United States than by the assertion of Soviet power. Bangladesh watched the event from a safe physical distance, but was nevertheless shaken as it immediately revived in its mind images of Indian intervention in the liberation struggle of 1971. The three countries, then, furnish a reliable barometer to measure the impact of the first display of Soviet military power in Asia on the image systems of three Asian elites each reacting in its own way to the same event.

THREE TYPOLOGIES OF RELATIONSHIP

The pattern of relations between each of the three South Asian nations and the Soviet Union has been far from symmetrical. In fact, the three countries provide three typologies of Soviet-Asian relationship. India and the USSR are close friends, if not allies. A congruence of interests, strategic, political and economic, bind them together. The relationship has survived the drift and scale of change in India, in the region, and in the wider international arena. Indians describe the relationship as "time-tested friendship," Russians as "traditional friendship." The relationship was gilded in 1971 with a 20-year friendship treaty which may have lost its emotional gloss, but retains its strategic glint.[1]

Pakistan's relations with the USSR has oscillated between prolonged unfriendliness and short spells of nonfriendliness. The relationship became mutually hostile after the Soviet move into Afghanistan. Pakistan's relations with the USSR have been determined by India's relations with the USSR; the enemy's patron and friend cannot be anything but an enemy. However, over the years a certain volume of nonpolitical and nonstrategic cooperation has grown between Pakistan and the Soviet Union. Pakistani leaders have often spoken about their intention to improve relations with the Soviets. President Ayub Khan conceded to Moscow in January 1966 a conflict manager's role in the subcontinent when he signed the Tashkent accords with India's Prime Minister, Lal Bahadur Shastri, in the wake of the India-Pakistan war four months before. Premier Zulfikar Ali Bhutto moved closer to Moscow by withdrawing Pakistan from SEATO and seeking admission to the nonaligned group. But the relationship never received the cement of shared interests and perceptions. It cooled off after Gen. Zia-ul-Huq came to power in a military coup in 1977. It reached its nadir after the Soviet intervention in Afghanistan.[2]

Bangladesh's relations with the Soviet Union has plunged from the peak of friendship to the bottom of unfriendliness. The Soviets played a significant role in the liberation of Bangladesh and in its emergence as a sovereign nation. Indeed, the Nixon Administration and many American analysts attributed the success of the Bangladesh liberation movement to the USSR rather than to India's decisive military victory over Pakistan in December 1971. The maiden blushes of Bangladesh as a nation glowed with warmth of friendship for the USSR and India. Relations with India was formalised in a 20-year treaty in 1972 largely resembling the Indo-Soviet treaty of the previous year. Though Soviet commitment to the security and development of Bangladesh was more symbolic than substantial, Bangladesh was seen by the outside world as belonging to the Indian (and therefore Soviet) sphere of influence.[3]

The friendship of Bangladesh and the USSR died in the blood of Sheikh Mujibur Rahman, creator of the new nation, when he was assassinated at his residence in Dacca in the night of 14 August 1975. The military-civilian regimes that have ruled Bangladesh since then, have lived in fear of India and therefore of India's far more powerful friend, the Soviet Union. The fear was muted for 18 months when the Janata Party ruled India, but returned in January 1980 as Indira Gandhi recaptured political power. If for the 18 months of Janata rule in India, Bangladeshi images of the USSR tended to soften, they hardened once again under the joint impact of two simultaneous unwelcome events—the Soviet intervention in Afghanistan and Indira Gandhi's return to power in India.

The three typologies of relationship, then, can be described as (1) uninterrupted friendship: India-USSR; (2) uninterrupted unfriendliness:

Pakistan-USSR; and (3) friendliness-turned-into-unfriendliness: Bangldesh-USSR. What is common in the three typologies is that Moscow's relations with India is the determining factor for Soviets' relations with Pakistan and Bangladesh. Pakistan is 600 miles away from the USSR; Bangladesh lies 2,000 miles to the South. Still India is the film through which both see the USSR. Whatever else the Soviet Union may be, to Pakistan and Bangladesh, it is, first and foremost, India's friend and patron.

COMMON FACTORS

At the time of the Soviet intervention in Afghanistan, the three South Asian neighbours, despite the difference in their political systems, and the disputes and schisms dividing them, had several political characteristics in common. The elite in each was fragmented, devoid of the cohesion of values and priorities of the past, far more intracompetitive than in the early years of independence. In December 1979 a lame-duck prime minister was presiding over a stop-gap government in India between the dissolution of one parliament and the election of another. The break in Congress rule in New Delhi, though only for two years, split the national elite into mutually opposed fragments; even among intellectuals, there were now "in" groups and "out" groups. Political stability was restored with Indira Gandhi's massive electoral victory; but the elite remained divided, and there was no national consensus on foreign policy, except, probably, on the need to prevent largescale arming of Pakistan by the United States. The fragmentation of the national elite into mutually opposed groups made different factions of Indians see the Soviet intervention in Afghanistan in different ways. No longer did the Indian national elite entertain a monolithic image of the Soviet Union. More significantly, the perception of the ruling elite—men and women in the government and their supporters outside—of the USSR was considerably at variance with the perception of the rest of the national elite.

The situation was far worse in Pakistan. In December 1979, the Pakistani president, Zia ul-Huq, was ostracised by the polite international society for hanging Zulfikar Ali Bhutto.[4] By twice going back on his promise to hold elections and by clamping down on Pakistan the harshest military rule in its chequered career, he isolated himself from the entire spectrum of the country's political life. Moreover, with a stagnant economy, crippling cost of petroleum, shortage of food, a $ 7.5 billion foreign debt burden and a defence budget that had quadrupled since the loss of Bangladesh, Zia ul-Huq was presiding over what most Pakistan-watchers agreed was the weakest and feeblest regime in Pakistan's history. The political climate in Pakistan was not one that could produce cohesive images of realities in the minds of the national elite. The ruling junta and its social and political allies, drawn mostly from Islamic fundamentalist elements and professional groups, were so alienated from the political mainstream that their images of realities projected through the tightly controlled mass media commanded little popular credibility and less response. Thus, the Pakistani government's image of the Soviet Union after the intervention in Afghanistan was entirely different from that of the country's largest political faction, the Pakistan People's Party founded by Bhutto, and led, after his death, by his wife, Begum Nusrat Bhutto. Even within the Pakistani military, there were differences over what the intervention implied and how the crisis created by it was to be tackled. An abortive coup attempted early March 1980 was perhaps fuelled by these differences. Gen. Zia-ul-Huq did not have much difficulty to quell it.[5] But he had to pay a price: a softer stance of the Soviet military presence across the border, and rejection of the "peanut" offer of US military and economic aid.

In Bangladesh, the civilian facade the military regime of Ziaur Rahman had been trying to put on since 1977 acquired a certain legitimacy by the time the Soviets moved into Afghanistan. But the intervention divided the political elite into two broad mutually fueding streams: those who backed Ziaur Rahman directly or indirectly and those who opposed him. The regime's political base was a coalition of conservative forces backed by the army. It received indirect but important support from the extreme left consisting of half-a-dozen Maoist or once-Maoist groups. Pitted against Ziaur Rahman's regime were the Awami League which had spearheaded the Bangladesh movement, its "front" organisations, and the pro-Moscow Bangladesh Communist Party (CPB). The stability of the regime can be judged by the fact that there have been eight attempted coups in Bangladesh since 7 November 1975, the latest one—dismissed by official spokesmen as a brief and inconsequential "unrest in the cantonment"—in June 1980. Bangladesh in 1980 was no longer known by the title of "international breadbasket" Kissinger conferred on it in 1972. It had received $ 7 billion in foreign aid, which increased its external dependencies so much so that 50 per cent of the 1980 budget and 70 per cent of planned public sector outlays in the Two-Year Plan covering 1978-80 were expected to come from external sources. Debt servicing consumed almost 16 per cent of export earnings. The balance of payment deficit had more than doubled between 1978 and 1980.[6]

The Soviet intervention in Afghanistan was seen in Bangladesh differently by different elite factions, the prism being set not so much by the USSR as by India. The Awami League, with its grassroot political base and its hold on the loyalties of large segments of the urban-rural population, entertained less malevolent visions of the Soviet Union and India. The hardest perceptions of both powers emanated from the Maoists and Islamic fundamentalists. Ziaur Rahman himself and his foreign minister, Shamsul Huq, skated the thin ice of opposing the Soviet lurch into Afghanistan, slowly improving relations with India, and tuning Bangladesh's foreign policy to the platform of Islamic nations without emulating the extreme fanaticism of Pakistan or Iran.

To sum up: in each of the three South Asian countries, the national elite was split into mutually opposing and competing factions. None of these countries had monolithic visions of the Soviet intervention in Afghanistan. The perceptions of each government clashed with the perceptions of major segments of the national elite. In Pakistan and Bangladesh, where the regimes are unstable, elite dissonance obliged governments to blunt the edges of their anti-Soviet attitudes. In India, on the other hand, the government of Indira Gandhi, with its massive parliamentary majority, had no problem in pursuing its own policy even if it met with bitter attacks from certain segments of the elite.

MIRROR IMAGES

On one crucial point the national elites of India, Pakistan and Bangladesh found themselves in total agreement. It was that the Soviet Union now was a truly global superpower, peer of the United States, if not with an edge over it. When, in January-February, Gen. Zia ul-Huq was bargaining with the United States over the quantity and price of military and economic aid, his main theme was that "one global power" had "invaded" Afghanistan, and it needed "another global power" to get the Soviets out. Chatting with a group of Indian reporters in February, Gen. Zia tried to show with the help of a wall map how Soviet influence was growing in the South and Southwestern region. "It is not a regional problem," he affirmed. "It is now a global problem. Russia is a superpower and to any action or reaction of a superpower there must be a global response."[7] This image of the Soviet Union was shared by critics of Gen. Zia's response to the Afghan intervention. *Muslim*, an English daily that occasionally reflects the political thinking of the Awami League, wrote in March, "Good or bad, kind or cruel, the Soviet Union is a superpower and it can neither be insulted nor blackmailed nor gunned out of Afghanistan. . . ."[8]

In Bangladesh, the government was so impressed with the Soviet Union's ability to intervene in the affairs of countries far from its borders that prime minister Shah Azizur Rahman, in justifying the arrest of a number of leaders of the relatively ineffectual communist party in April, accused the CPB of plotting "an Afghan-style revolution."[9] A little later, *Holiday,* a Maoist weekly, apprehended Soviet intervention in Bangladesh through a "proxy" power: India. "The threat lurks that Russian leaders might back and spurt India, at some opportune moment, to physically intervene in Bangladesh in just the same manner that the Kremlin had supported and planned Vietnam's Kampuchean exercise."[10] Echoing the same theme, *Dainik Sangram*, a daily close to the government, saw two Soviet gains from the $ 1.6 billion arms purchase deal concluded between Moscow and New Delhi: it made India "even more pro-Soviet" and it made Pakistan "even more frightened of India."[11]

The Indian perception of the Soviet Union as a global power was reflected in most Indian commentaries on the Afghan crisis. K. Subrahmanyam, director of the Institute of Defence Studies and Analyses, observed that in the mid-seventies, the world "entered the era of true strategic bipolarity" when the USSR, having already achieved nuclear parity with the US, also matched its adversary in interventionist power. In a "truly bipolar world" where two superpowers possessed "approximately equal" military capacity, "interventions could not remain the monopoly of one as had been the case earlier when the US dominated the international scene." Subrahmanyam went on to add that in the "first cold war," the Soviet Union yielded each time a superpower conflict threatened to escalate into a shooting war because it was the weaker power. "This is no longer likely because the two superpowers command nearly equal capabilities."[12] Participating in a discussion on the Afghan crisis in The *Times of India,* P.N. Haksar, one of the principal architects of India's successful 1971 strategy to deal with the Bangladesh liberation movement, confirmed Subrahmanyam's vision of the USSR. "The Soviet Union is a global power," mused Haksar. "It has global interests. Thus, the equation between them and the NATO system in particular looms very large. And if the rules of the game are thrown into doubt, obviously a state acts to protect what it regards as its security interests."[13] Adding another brick to the mosaic of Indian vision of Soviet power, Girilal Jain, editor of the *Times of India*, concluded, "The Soviet Union does not tinker with things. When it decides to act, it acts, with considerable force."[14]

South Asian perceptions of Soviet power fed on vivid pictures of Soviet military might on display in the rugged terrain of Afghanistan. It was all open to the glare of Indian journalists covering the Afghan crisis. "You do not have to look behind a door or under a charpoy to find Russian soldiers," reported Kuldip Nayar in the *Indian Express* in February. "They are there, right from the airport. You can see hordes of them, behind their guns and tanks."[15] J.D. Singh wrote in the *Times of India* that the Soviet troops in Afghanistan were "equipped with the most modern weapons capable of fighting a major war anywhere in Afghanistan and the neighbouring countries. The military hardware is impressive enough and includes 1,500 tanks, armoured personnel carriers, anti-tank rockets, artillery and anti-aircraft guns, bridging equipment, trucks mounted on tracks, and material for biological and chemical warfare. In addition to the army, there is a substantial Soviet air force presence in Afghanistan."[16] Pakistan had even closer visions of Soviet military power in Afghanistan. In the spring of 1980, Soviet troops almost knocked at the frontiers of Pakistan, though they never did actually touch the international boundary, nor cross it at any point in "hot pursuit" of Afghan rebels.

Not only the Soviet Union itself, but the United States and its allies also contributed to the formation and strengthening of South Asian images of Moscow's global power. Americans themselves proclaimed the decline of US power and the ascendance of Soviet might, and these proclamations were confirmed by the collapse of the Iranian monarchy and US setbacks in the arc of crisis. A good deal of American writing on the power equation, and its manifestations in the Persian Gulf got reproduced in Pakistani, Indian and Bangladeshi newspapers; perceptions of the relative power of the two superpowers generated by these writings were reinforced by the writings of British and French analysts, also reproduced in the South Asian press. It is interesting to note that Soviet writings contributed little to the formation of South Asian images of Soviet power for the simple reason that very little of these writings is printed in the subcontinent's press.[17]

VARIED IMAGES

Although South Asian elites had mirror images of the newly acquired global power of the Soviet Union, they had very different perceptions of why that power was applied to Afghanistan, what were the Kremlin's goals and objectives and what the impact of the intervention might be on regional and world politics. As noted, images in this context differed not only among the three national elites, but within each national elite also.

The darkest images formed in Pakistan—in the minds of Gen. Zia ul-Huq and his supporters; the Pakistani official perceptions of Soviet motives and goals almost mirrored those of the Carter Administration until the breakdown of the Pakistani-US military-economic aid negotiations. Thereafter, the images mellowed somewhat, but not enough to narrow the gap between Islamabad and Moscow or between Islamabad and Kabul.

Gen. Zia's perception of the grave implications of the Soviet action came out clearly in his address at the first conference of foreign ministers of Islamic nations held in Islamabad in the last days of January. We have noted this speech before, in chapter six; Gen. Zia's words bear repetition to give us as clearly as possible his visions of Soviet power. "It is the first instance since World War II when a superpower has made a sovereign and independent Muslim country the target of its attack," he declared. "We view this development with the utmost apprehension, because unless this trend to subjugate small countries through the use of force is arrested in time, world peace and the independent existence of small countries will be endangered. In plain words, if this precedent is allowed to perpetuate itself then what has happened in Afghanistan today could happen to another country tomorrow."[18]

Gen. Zia told Indian reporters that the Afghan issue was a global one. A superpower had overrun a neighbouring state, disturbing the equilibrium in the region. A "buffer" state had been vanquished in next to no time. Afghanistan had become a "big red wedge." The question was whether the wedge would move west to Iran or east to Pakistan. If it moved west, the entire Gulf area would be overrun. Either way, the prospects were grim. Zia said he was certain that the Soviets had larger geopolitical designs. Otherwise, the presence of 80,000 Russian troops in a rugged barren country "devoid of any mineral or natural resources" did not make any sense. The Soviet presence in Afghanistan was as much a threat to Pakistan as it was to India.[19]

Gen. Zia ul-Huq's perception of the geopolitical thrusts of the Soviet intervention in Afghanistan were shared by the Islamic-conservative elements in Pakistan. There was, however, one caveat. The Islamic world-view saw the United States pitted against the Islamic revolution in Iran and also as a major obstacle to the attainment of a national home for the Palestinians. Gen. Zia wanted to link Pakistan to the US initiatives to confront Soviet power in Southwest Asia. The contradictions between the Islamic-fundamentalist view and the geopolitical view came out in the open at an early stage of the Afghan crisis. *Pakistan Times*, the government-owned daily which reflected the junta's thinking, in one of its first comments on the Soviet intervention, saw it as a frontal drive against the "rising crescendo of Muslim rebellion," and the "spreading fire of Islam." It argued that the Soviet invasion had brought Muslims and Christians together to fight a "common enemy." Pakistan must therefore accept American help.[20] This sentiment was echoed by an Islamic daily, *Wafaaq*. Pakistan must not only accept help from the United States and China, it asserted, but also join with these countries to serve the Soviet Union with an "ultimatum" demanding immediate withdrawal from Afghanistan.[21]

Dissenting notes, however, were heard immediately among other segments of the Pakistani elite. *Muslim* cautioned the government against getting involved with "US activism" in the region, reminding it of what America had done, and was doing, to Iran.[22] *Sadaqat*, a Urdu daily, urged that Pakistan must not get entangled in a confrontation with the Soviet Union. "Pakistan's interest lies in trying, as far as possible, to ensure that its relations with the Soviet Union are not spoilt. . . . If the USA is indeed sincere about countering the Soviet aggression in Afghanistan, it should change its policy towards Iran."[23] *Viewpoint*, Pakistan's only notworthy leftist weekly, found the Soviet intervention "regrettable" even if it were made at Kabul's request, and "hoped that the Russian forces would leave soon." But it recommended a policy that had been firmly rejected by the military regime. What was happening in Afghanistan was that country's internal affair, it declared, and suggested that Gen. Zia resume negotiations with Kabul as soon as the "situation becomes clearer."[24] The *Pakistan Economist*, respected for its sobriety, asked Pakistanis to do some "hard thinking" on whether "it is a practicable proposition to build (the armed forces) for a role in which they have to remain counterpoised against two military threats—India on the east and Russia on the west." Siding with the United States, it added, "will mean a day-to-day and perilous living" for Pakistan.[25]

Pakistan Times projected a geopolitical view of the Soviet move into Afghanistan which betrayed the deep sense of insecurity that gnawed at the military-Islamic coalition that ruled Pakistan. According to this view, Afghanistan as a "buffer" between the divided subcontinent and the USSR was built into the partition of the empire into India and Pakistan, on the basis of which the British left in 1947. By "eliminating" the buffer, the Soviets actually denied the "viability of the successor countries in the subcontinent." The Soviet "occupation" of Afghanistan was the 1980 avatar of the ancient Anglo-Russian competition for the subcontinent, "a direct, albeit delayed, aftermath of the withering away of the British empire." If the two successor states stood together, the Soviets would not have so easily "trespassed the traditionally demarcated neutral zone." The present "precarious situation" was created in no little measure by India's "lack of realism." The newspaper gleaned from the pages of history a grim warning for India. "History tells—and it tells at the cost of India—that once the Khyber pass was cleared by a conqueror, the hordes pierced through to (the subcontinent's) southernmost point almost without resistance. The times might have changed but the geopolitical facts have not."[26]

The military-Islamic vision of the geopolitical sweep of the Soviet military presence in Afghanistan received jolts from three directions— from the political opponents of the martial regime, from the United States, and from India. It became clear even in the first weeks of the Afghan crisis that India stood as a solid barrier to the yoking of Pakistan to the engine of the Carter Doctrine.[27] The wide gap between the commitments Gen. Zia demanded of the United States and what Washington was prepared to offer could not be narrowed because India did not share the US-Pakistani view of the Soviet action. The collapse of the aid negotiations and Pakistan's rejection of the US package increased Pakistani doubts about the "credibility" of the

United States as an ally and made the Pakistani elite a little more aware of the weight of the Indo-Soviet friendship. *Maghribi Pakistan* saw in America's "new found love" for Islam an intention to "exploit the confrontation between Islam and communism for its overall global strategy against the Soviet Union." The main American interest lay in Persian Gulf oil, and "it is obvious that even if Russia moves towards Pakistan, the US reaction will be mild."[28] Another Urdu daily, *Jasarat*, warned that American aid "that subordinates our national and regional interest to US global policy," was "as dangerous" as Soviet aggression in Afghanistan.[29] *Viewpoint* believed that Pakistan must not "rush headlong into the blind alley of lining up, once again, with the United States."[30] A Pakistani analyst, Ashrad Ahmed Haqqani, observed towards the end of February that by pressing Moscow to withdraw its forces from Afghanistan, India had scored a major diplomatic success. "India has totally succeeded as far as the West is concerned." Haqqani listed four objectives of Indian diplomacy, two "fundamental," namely, (1) to prevent the arming of Pakistan; and (2) to be recognised by all the major powers as the dominant power in the region; and two "incidental and subsidiary" : to insulate the region from great power rivalries so that India's own predominance remained uneroded, and to keep the Soviet Union "as far away from its borders as possible." Huqqani came to the grim conclusion that India had realised its "fundamental" diplomatic objectives by threatening to move closer to the USSR if the United States transferred substantial quantities of arms and weapons to Pakistan.[30]

The proven potency of the Indian factor generated two contradictory pressures on the rulers of Pakistan—pressures to work with India to defuse the great power confrontation, and pressures to turn away from India and seek refuge in the "Islamic option." Gen. Zia flirted casually with the Indian option for a while in February and March, when he had two important visitors from India—foreign secretary Ram Sathe, and Mrs Gandhi's special envoy, Swaran Singh, a former foreign minister. He received some support even from elements not normally benign towards India. *Dawn*, for example, was enthused by Mrs Gandhi's efforts to get Soviet troops out of Afghanistan and stressed the "need for the two countries to seek to identify the issues of common interest and concern and explore broad areas of agreement.[32] *Viewpoint* urged Gen. Zia to emulate the model of Indo-Afghan relations to deal with Afghanistan.[33]

Gen. Zia, however, decided to hitch the Pakistani wagon to the star of the Islamic Foreign Ministers' Conference. Pro-regime analysts now identified India as the villain of the drama. Mushtaq Ahmed, writing in *Pakistan Times*, saw India's main objective to be "to weaken Pakistan to a point where Indian ascendency in the region is acknowledged by all the states on its periphery." He even suggested that India was "vitiating" Pakistan's relations with the Soviet Union. Moscow, he ventured, took a "less narrow" view of the issues involved. While India's "sole concern" was to keep Pakistan weak, this was not necessarily a Soviet objective for Afghanistan was part of a "broader international spectrum" for the Soviet Union.[34]

The biggest blow to the junta's hard-line perception of the Soviet military presence in Afghanistan came from Begum Nusrat Bhutto, widow of the former premier, and leader of the outlawed Pakistan People's Party, the single largest political force in the country. Begum Nusrat and her daughter, Benazir, were released from house arrest in April. Immediately after their release, both were interviewed by the *Guardian*, of London. Both saw the Afghan situation entirely differently. What was happening in Afghanistan, the Begum said, was an internal affair; Pakistan had no right to interfere. If the PPP were in power, it would not allow the Afghan refugees to wage a war of resistance from Pakistani territory. The Soviets had no intentions against Pakistan. Gen. Zia had "blown up" the "Afghan situation" to attract attention. "We would never forget that whenever we have had wars with India, the Afghans have never made use of that excuse to attack us from their side. We should not pay them back by allowing these people who call them mujaheddin, to use our territory to attack theirs. . . . If the Soviets came to Pakistan in hot pursuit, it will be fault of the government here."[35] Miss Bhutto shared her mother's perceptions of the Afghan situation and of the Soviet Union. Pakistan should have tried other means to resolve the crisis, and should not have rushed to the United States accusing the Soviet Union, whom she described as a "superpower and the fifth largest Muslim nation in the world." "We don't want to become pawns in anybody's hands. Our country must think for itself. The question is: how do you make these Soviet troops go back? You don't do it by closing all doors. You don't get results by cold war. You get results through detente.[36]

A few days before these interviews were given, Pakistani followers of Zulfikar Ali Bhutto and opponents to the martial regime living in London got together in a largely attended meeting and resolved to set up "a Pakistan government in exile" to conduct a mass struggle, even a military struggle if necessary, against the military regime.[37] Bhutto's son, a political aspirant, travelled to Kabul and lived there for several weeks in a symbolic demonstration of the PPP's rejection of the junta's response to the Afghan situation.

The perceptions of the Pakistani national elite of the display of Soviet power in Afghanistan, then, were split: the split images emanated from the deep polarisation between the military-Islamic coalition that had been ruling the country since August 1977 and the political elements which stood for restoration of representative government. Since the PPP is the major candidate for power if elections were held, it naturally saw almost everything differently from those who snatched away political power from its jaws in the coup in August 1977. Interestingly, however, the PPP perceptions of the Soviet Union and its interventionist might have elements of broad similarity with the perceptions of Indira Gandhi and her party. The PPP saw the intervention as a "local" event, an internal Afghan affair, and rejected the threat theory and the threat perceptions of the junta. It favoured a regional or nonaligned initiative to resolve the crisis; Miss Bhutto even welcomed the brief and barren initiative taken by Cuba in the spring of 1980 to bring Pakistan and Afghanistan together. It rejected confrontation with the USSR. It also rejected linkage with the USA to confront Moscow in Southwestern Asia. It did not invoke an Islamic response to the crisis. It wanted Pakistan-Afghanistan relations to be modelled on India's relations with Afghanistan. It remained an open question whether, restored to power, the Pakistan People's Party would entertain the same images of regional realities and of the Soviet Union as nursed by it in its winter of discontent. However, the fact that dominant political elements in both Pakistan and India should hold similar visions of the Afghan situation and of the USSR is a noteworthy fallout of the Soviet intervention in Afghanistan.

As Seen in Bangladesh

In Bangladesh, too, government perceptions of the Soviet intervention in Afghanistan were not shared by the mainstream of political opposition, but the polarisation was not as sharp as in Pakistan. President Ziaur Rahman kept a studiously cultivated poise of detachment, and the mass media were carefully orchestrated to mute criticism of the USSR. When government spokesmen attacked the Soviet Union for intervening in Afghanistan with military force, it was on foreign territory—at the Islamic meets in the Pakistan capital, at the Security Council, in the General Assembly of the United Nations. *But seldom on home territory.* Ziaur Rahman made a long statement in the National Assembly on 9 February 1980, in which foreign relations were said to have occupied a "considerable place." *But he did not even mention the Soviet intervention in Afghanistan.*[38] (If he did, his remarks were kept out of the mass media.) The National Assembly debated foreign policy for three days at the end of February. The foreign minister, Shamsul Huq, devoted exactly two sentences to the Afghan situation at the tail end of his 45-minute statement, making only two points: the Soviet intervention had taken all nations by surprise and it was an example of the strong attacking the weak.[39] Official statements issued in Dacca were almost always strikingly polite to the USSR. The Soviet action was deplored and condemned on grounds of high principle—it violated "all recognised principles of international relations," and posed a threat to the peace and stability of the South Asian region. The script was written by Ziaur Rahman. He followed it scrupulously on his official visits to foreign capitals—Peking or Manila or London or Washington.[40] His foreign minister read it at the two sessions of the Conference of Islamic Foreign Ministers in Islamabad, deliberately listing Afghanistan *after* Palestine as instances of injuries inflicted by the superpowers on the interests of Islamic nations. Like Pakistan, Bangladesh also relied on the Islamic conference mechanism to seek a political solution of the Afghan crisis. But its position was less rigid than Islamabad's. Bangladesh differed openly with India on the essentials of a peace settlement, insisting that the Soviets must first unconditionally withdraw their troops. At the same time, Ziaur Rahman proposed, at the height of the tension created by the Afghan crisis, a summit conference of six South Asian countries—Pakistan, India, Nepal, Bangladesh, Bhutan and Sri Lanka—with the elevating objective of creating something like a regional economic community.[41]

The regime's poise, however, proved to be evanescent as soon as even the remotest threat was seen to its stability. Its deep sense of insecurity was betrayed in its reaction to a political gabble of the relatively ineffectual Bangladesh Communist Party. The CPB issued a statement in February "welcoming" the help given by the Soviet Union to a distressed revolutionary regime, and called upon the people of Bangladesh to make an "Afghan-style" revolution.[42] The government panicked when thousands of its low-paid officials struck, and the strike was supported by the CPB. The CPB's call for an "Afghan-style revolution" brought forth the strongest attack to date on the Soviet intervention in Afghanistan—not from the government but its official daily, *Bangladesh Times*, "At the centre of the Kabul crisis," it declared, "are the fundamentals of international law which have been violated. The right of a nation to choose a government of its own is inviolable and this can never be suppressed under any pretext by any outside power. What has happened in Afghanistan is clear undermining of that right by the presence of foreign troops. The intervention has created apprehensions of destabilisation throughout the whole region, beyond Afghanistan's borders. And in a situation like this, the task is to be able to resist any threat to national sovereignty and independence."[43]

Outside the government, the national elite showed three different perceptions of the Soviet action in Afghanistan. The hardest images formed in the minds of conservative Islamic elements and Maoists; the softest came from the CPB and its allies and friends. In between stood the largest segment of the thrice-splintered Awami League (AL), still said to be the most popular political group. Abdul Malek Ukil, president of the main faction of AL, remarked that his party was opposed to any aggression anywhere in the world, but saw no point in "making such a row over the Soviet military presence" in Afghanistan. He believed that "some elements" were "taking advantage" of the event to shore up political gains.[44] The Jatiya Samajtantrik Dal, a coalition of assorted leftist groups, took an equally dour view of "Soviet expansionism" and "American imperialism."[45]

In March, the government arrested two dozen leaders of the Bangladesh Communist Party in the midst of accusations that the CPB was "conspiring" with other political forces to stage an Afghan-type revolution in Dacca. The target of Islamic and Maoist attacks from now on was India rather than the USSR. The Ganotantrik (Democratic) Front led by Mohammed Toha, a pro-Chinese leftist politician, called for unity of all patriotic forces to launch a mass movement against Soviet hegemonism and Indian expansionism.[46] The $ 1.6 billion Indian arms purchase deal with the Soviet Union resurrected the image of the Soviet-backed Indian intervention in Bangladesh in December 1971. *Dainik Sangram*, a daily close to the regime, pointed out that India imported 58 per cent of all arms flowing into the South Asian region from external sources between 1967 and 1976;

besides, it had its own armaments industry making tanks and supersonic jets: "This is what frightens the neighbouring countries,"[47] *Holiday*, the Maoist weekly, demanded abrogation of the Indo-Bangladesh friendship treaty.[48] One of the several Maoist factions asked for India's exclusion from the proposed South Asian summit, arguing that whatever India gained from it would also be the gain of the Soviet Union.[49]

INTENSE DEBATE IN INDIA

In India, no action taken by a major power produced a wider or more intense debate than the Soviet intervention in Afghanistan. The debate showed that different segments of the elite saw the Soviet action and its objectives differently from one another. Indian images of the Afghan situation fell broadly into four clusters. The *empathic* perceptions formed in the minds of the two major communist factions, the pro-Soviet Communist Party of India (CPI) and the independent Communist Party of India-Marxist (CPI-M); a powerful section of the intellectual-bureaucratic elite; and minority groups of the national bourgeoisie.[50] The *antipathic* images were projected by the Janata party, a section of intellectuals, a segment of the bureaucracy, and some small political groups. *Global-geopolitical* images emanated from several noted analysts of international affairs who saw the Soviet action as part of a larger Russian foreign policy geostrategic design. The Government itself, supported by a number of analysts, took a *regional* view of the Soviet action, refusing to be seduced by its global implications. The border line between the global-geopolitical and regional views were, however, not always clear. Some analysts perceived global implications of the Soviet lurch, but advocated a regional settlement.

All of these clusters of perceptions had several strands in common. All Indians saw the USSR as the *emergent* global power. Most Indians saw the United States as the *declining* global power. All Indians saw India as the leading regional power, with a stake of its own in the crisis. Most Indians saw a greater threat to India's regional predominance coming from the arming of Pakistan by the United States and China rather than from the Soviet Union with a military presence in Afghanistan. Few Indians were prepared to see Indo-Soviet friendship perceptibly weakened as a result of the Afghan crisis. Many Indians, however, wanted the friendship with the USSR to be "balanced" with improved ties with the United States and China.

The main debate raged between the global-geopolitical and regional clusters of perceptors. The global-geopolitical cluster, as noted, was less cohesive than the regional. Some geopolitical analysts had a threat image of the Soviet Union. They saw the Afghan intervention as a threat to the independence and sovereignty of small and weak nations, as an outflanking movement to grab, at the opportune moment, the oil wealth of the Persian Gulf, a bold attempt to extend Soviet influence in Asia. Other geopolitical analysts saw the USSR as The Other global power demanding of a reluctant United States its legitimate parity of influence in world affairs. Those who entertained the threat image of the USSR wanted India to join with other powers to contain the threat. Those who saw the USSR as The Other global power found no serious contradiction between Moscow's global interests in Southwestern Asia and India's regional interests as the leading South Asian power. There was, then, considerable congruence of The-Other-global-power image of the USSR and the regional image of the Afghan situation.

The regional image, as noted, was projected by Indira Gandhi herself and her government and party. This image was to a large extent determined by India's self-image as *the* independent regional power in South Asia. Roots of this Indian self-image run deep into Indian diplomacy since the 1950s. From the beginning of its career as a sovereign nation, India's principal foreign policy aim has been to be universally recognised as South Asia's dominant power. In the first decade-and-a-half of Indian diplomacy, this goal was pursued with efforts to have friendly cooperative relations with both superpowers. That gave India a favourable balance of power in the region and kept South Asia insulated from great power confrontation. India received substantial aid from both, and acted as a bridge between them during the peak of the cold war.

As detente began to sprout on a terrain once plagued by the cold war, the superpowers did not need bridges like India. From the mid-sixties therefore India's major foreign policy aim was to assert itself as the leading South Asian power. Soviet friendship made the assertion easier, but was not enough to stabilise India's primacy in the region beyond challenge and doubt. Indians see a challenge to their regional eminence every time Pakistan seeks to augment its military strength or strategic linkages. They suspect that the United States is not willing to make more than a casual rhetorical bow to India's regional preeminence. They see in each renewal of the US-Pakistani alliance and in each move towards the erection of a Sino-US axis a direct attempt to rob India of the substance of its status as South Asia's leading power. India's self-image of a major regional power, then, is not as secure as Indians wish it to be. It makes Indians extremely sensitive to any real or imagined attempt to limit India's role in South Asian affairs.

During the Afghan crisis, Indians felt that both superpowers were encroaching on India's regional pasture; both wanted to limit India's role as the region's number one power. However, the threat to India's regional eminence was seen to be coming *more* from the United States than from the Soviet Union. The threat coming from America was two-fold: the arming of Pakistan and the extension of a new cold war to South Asia. In order to arrest the threat, it became essential for India to localise the Soviet intervention, to see it as a defensive action of limited geopolitical import. Mrs Gandhi and her government saw the USSR as The Other global power, responding, by its Afghan intervention, to a series of US cold warish provocations—the SALT-II deadlock in the Senate, naval buildup in the Indian Ocean, the decision to deploy a new generation of nuclear missiles in Europe, creation of the Rapid Deployment Force and so on; they refused to see it as an unmistakable proclamation of the global reach of Soviet power. They saw the Soviet intervention as a defensive action aimed at securing an imperilled friendly regime in a land which had resided for 20 years or more in the Soviet sphere of influence, and at protecting the southern flank of the USSR. Mrs Gandhi did not approve of the Soviet intervention, much less support it. But she *understood* why the Soviets intervened, and wanted the rest of the world to understand it. For her, the danger lay in America's cold war response to the Soviet action. The action itself posed no particular threat to Pakistan unless Pakistan got involved in the American cold war design.[51] Mrs Gandhi's first priority was for the creation of conditions which could be used to pressure Moscow to withdraw its troops from Afghanistan and restore the status quo ante in South Asia. Indian diplomacy was therefore deployed with unprecedented vigour to seek a regional political settlement of the Afghan crisis, involving the regional powers and the USSR—directly, or indirectly through the Kabul regime. A regional political settlement would legitimise the Marxist regime in Afghanistan, but minimise—in the Indian government's perception—the impact of Soviet military power in a politically unstable area. It would leave India's regional eminence unimpaired, even slightly enhanced, for India would have played the role of regional peace-maker and conflict-manager. The friendship with the Soviet Union would remain unhurt, but India would emerge a bit stronger, a bit taller, in its own, and in the world's, estimate.

The-Other-global-power image of the Soviet Union did no offence to India's self-image as the region's dominant power. This was because of the decades-old congruence of Soviet and Indian strategic interests in South Asia; also because both had their quarrels and disputes with the United States and China. Thus, The-Other-global-power image of the Soviet Union came out clearly in a discussion between three noted strategic thinkers representing three distinctly different schools of strategic thinking—P.N. Haksar, K. Subrahmanyam and Girilal Jain. They broadly agreed that the present superpower tensions stemmed from American refusal to concede to the Soviet Union a parity of influence in the planet's affairs reflecting the approximate parity of strategic and global military power existing between them. The situation in Southwest Asia had become extremely serious because the "Americans are trying to keep (the oil) resources to themselves and their allies. Their effort, therefore, is to ensure that this area remains under their influence, to exclude the Soviet Union from it and to prevent, indigenously, political change which can deny them the oil.[52]

Those Indians who held threat perceptions of the Soviet military presence in Afghanistan also recognised the USSR as the emergent global power. They saw Soviet military power stationed in Afghanistan as constituting a direct and clear threat to India's regional primacy, even to its sovereignty and integrity. Images of the Soviet threat had different shades. Some were ideological; some moral. But most of the threat images were nationalist or geopolitical or both. The image of Soviet power as an ideological threat was entertained mostly by elements belonging to the right as well as the extreme left. The view that the Soviet intervention in Afghanistan was a cynical violation of international morality was widely shared and articulated; perhaps the most forceful articulation came from the prestigious newspaper *The Hindu*.[53] The nationalist-geopolitical threat view of the Soviet action, however, remained the main contender of the softer and more widely shared image we have outlined above.

The nationalist-geopolitical perception of the Soviet intervention led some Indians to see Moscow determined to bring the Persian Gulf region under its influence, an eventuality that they believed would be detrimental to India's regional primacy, even to its security. *The Hindu* reported in April that the Afghan crisis had helped to "hasten the process of Indian thinking on its defence strategy for the next two decades." This strategy, the report said, had to be based on the assumption that a major threat to India's security or regional interests could come from any one of the three powers—the United States, the Soviet Union or China—"either independently or in conjunction with others hostile to (India)." The new Soviet doctrine of "protective intervention," the report added, "has caused considerable concern even among friendly countries like India because of the uneasy feeling that what has happened in Afghanistan could happen to others with similar treaty relationships in certain circumstances."[54] Picking up the same theme from a very different angle, Bharat Wariavwalla, research associate at the Institute of Defence Studies and Analyses, warned that if the Soviets succeeded in snuffing out Afghan resistance and consolidating their power in Afghanistan, "the prospects for India are indeed grim." The grim prospect lay in a Soviet-Pakistan compact. "In the event of the Kremlin stabilising its hold on Afghanistan, Pakistan may well come to terms with the reality of Soviet power, particularly if the terms are attractive. . . . The implications for India of such a radically changed Soviet-Pakistan relationship could be grave. . . . The one unchanging goal of Indian foreign policy has been to shield as much as possible the subcontinent from external influences, and in the pursuit of this objective, it has sought limited and well measured Soviet support. But should the Soviet venture in Afghanistan succeed, this goal would be shattered. Indeed, India and the Soviet Union would become rivals for influence in the area."[55]

The Soviets indeed taught Indians to think the unthinkable and articulate the unutterable.

IMAGE OF ALLIANCE LEADER

When South Asian elites watched the Soviet Union straddling the Hindu Kush as a global colossus, they saw it not only as a military giant, but also as leader of an ideological fraternity of nations. The elites were surprised when the Soviets intervened with an impressive military force to protect a crumbling Marxist regime outside the East European bloc. Both in Pakistan and India, some analysts saw the intervention as an extension of the Brezhnev doctrine beyond the East European bloc.[56] While this vision sharpened in elite minds perceptions of their own respective countries' insecurity, it also enhanced the image of the USSR as a credible alliance leader. Even from those in Pakistan who took the darkest view of the Soviet power, the intervention coaxed out a certain amount of respect and considerable awe. [57] Analysts compared the two superpowers and pronounced the United States an undependable ally.[58] In India, even *The Hindu* which stands for friendly relations with US, was constrained to observe, "If past experience is any indication, the US has never fully stood by even its client States, let alone countries like India that are not prepared to subserve its global interests."[59] Girilal Jain expected the US to accept "the power realities in Afghanistan as it did in Europe." In the circumstances, it was only "proper", he concluded, that India had "refused to join any anti-Soviet chorus. . . .If the Indian attitude means in effect acquiescence in the reality of Soviet power in Afghanistan, it just cannot be helped."[60] A public opinion poll conducted for *India Today*, a Delhi-based mass circulation fortnightly, found a big majority of Indians living in 11 large cities see the USSR as the country they could trust most. The "can trust" image of the USSR was higher in the non-metropolitan cities than in the four metropolitan ones.[61]

Though the Soviet protective intervention to save a Marxist regime in Afghanistan did disturb fundamentalist and conservative elements among South Asian elites, the mainstream elite groups did not harbour hostile perceptions of a communist government ruling in the Hindu Kush.[62] In Pakistan, the anti-communist stance was predictably the hardest in the Islamic segment of the elite community. The anti-communism of the military junta wore democratic robes and was articulated in the demand that the Afghan people must have the right to choose their own government—a rather ironical and unconvincing posture struck by a regime which denied the same right to its own people. In circles opposed to the regime, there was a willingness to live with a communist Afghanistan on the basis of good neighbourliness.[63] In India too there was no dearth of people who were shaken by Sovietisation of Afghanistan. However, the mainstream Indian perception of a communist-ruled Afghanistan was tolerant. It was accurately articulated by K. Subrahmanyam in the *Times of India* : "If the Soviet presence in Afghanistan should end in due course, we are not interested whether Afghanistan still remains a communist country or not, though most probably it would."[64]

IMPLICATIONS OF PERCEPTION

The South Asian elite perceptions of the Soviet intervention in Afghanistan allow a number of generalisations with regard to the region's interactions with Soviet policies for Asia and the third world. The impact of Soviet power is firmly and unmistakably printed on the region's elite mental canvas. The USSR's credibility as a global power is high. Elite groups that are disturbed, alarmed or frightened by the sight of Soviet power are much larger in number and much more confused and scattered than the groups that are pleased with, or enthused by, it. In each of the South Asian countries, including Pakistan, there are now large constituencies prepared to live with Soviet global power in different norms of cooperative relationships. Even those who take a threat view of Soviet power, the compulsion to come to terms with it seems to be gathering momentum. The insecurities of the regimes, the tensions and conflicts inherent in the process of development and modernisation, the polarisations that are gradually shaping up in each South Asian society make the price of confrontation with the USSR too high for any government to pay. The ruling elites of South Asia, indeed of the entire third world, measure the might and power of the USSR generally with their measurement of the might and power of the United States. Their response to the emergence of the Soviet Union as a global power is conditioned to a large extent by the US response to the novel phenomenon. Should the United States recognise its adversary as a co-equal and concede to it a genuine partnership in the management of the international system, the rest of the world will find it relatively easy to adjust itself to the consequent change in world politics. If, on the other hand, the US refuses to recognise Soviet equality and determines to regain its own global superiority, the vast majority of the world's nations that are neither the Soviet Union's allies nor friends, will be faced with tearing dilemmas. They are not in a mood to fall in line with the US in its global confrontation with the USSR. Nor can they afford to fall out of step with the US beyond a certain limit. Indeed, the US would find confrontation with the Soviet Union without the support of its allies and friends as arduous and risky as its allies and friends will find detente with the USSR without the support of America. Policy choices on such slippery turf will then be determined mainly on the crucible of the national interest. Each nation will tailor its relationship with the USSR to fit its own interests. If this happens, the Soviets will have achieved one of their principal foreign policy objectives. For a full quarter century the Soviets lived and laboured in a world dominated by American power. In a decade they have shaken the US-dominated international system to its roots. The current decade will determine if the US can regain the leading position it has lost or if it has lost it for good.

CHAPTER ELEVEN

How to Live with Soviet Power

> Two stars keep not their motion
> in one sphere
> *Henry IV*, V, iv, 65

A remarkable change has visited world politics with the advent of the 80s: the United States and the Soviet Union confront one another in the third world with no third party screen falling between them. In its numerous engagements in third world conflicts since World War II, the United States always acted from behind the screen of an European ally whether it was Britain or France or Belgium or Portugal. When the Soviets too got involved in some of these conflicts, Washington and Moscow did not collide frontally. Even in Vietnam, the Americans were fighting the North Vietnamese and their allies and supporters in South Vietnam. Both President Johnson and President Nixon sought, and received, Soviet help to conduct peace negotiations with Hanoi even when Moscow was Hanoi's biggest aid-giver. In confronting the Soviets in the 80s, however, the United States can hardly produce an alibi.[1] Ironically, the former colonial powers of Europe, who once brought the US to the gray areas to defend their tottering empires or imperial interests, are now anxious to restrain America in its confrontation with the Soviet Union. In any case, they are reluctant to jump on to the American bandwagon and to contribute fairly to the crippling cost of confrontation.

Time magazine reported in mid-1980 that there was a widely shared belief, even among many of America's traditional friends, that US strength had declined so much that Washington "can no longer be relied upon as the leader of the Western alliance." Raymond Aron, one of the few delphic voices of our time, pronounced the stern verdict: "The United States is no longer Number One." Christoph Bertram, director of the London-based International Institute of Strategic Studies, observed, "In the past, the United States has been the undisputed leader, but the US that emerged from the 1970s was no longer always willing to provide this leadership, and even when she tried, she was no longer able to command the respect of her allies." Aldo Rizzo, noted Italian political commentator, remarked, "There is no sign of that concordance of views between Western Europe and the United States (over the Afghanistan and Iranian crises) that helped them through other grave crises."[2] Flora Lewis, Paris correspondent of the *New York Times*, summed up the present US-European relationship quite succinctly: "Europe and America have taken to speaking at, not to, each other."[3]

The Times, of London, which represents an European elite that is most respectful of American power, cautioned in a thoughtful editorial less than three weeks before the 1980 US presidential election that how strongly might Ronald Reagan and the American conservatives wish, the period when American power was undisputed and ideals untarnished "cannot be recaptured."

> It has been lost not, as is often alleged, by American weakness but because the world itself has changed. The Soviet Union has achieved military parity and is now able to deploy military force round the globe. Other centres of economic, political and military power have arisen with new states that are not willing to fall into line on one side or other of the East-West confrontation. At the same time, the United States itself has become militarily and economically vulnerable.
>
> No matter how much she may arm herself, the United States cannot control this world either directly or through regional proxies. Nor could she do so in collaboration with the Soviet Union because, even if these two powers could agree on the rules, the influence of the Soviet Union is also limited. There is, in fact, little hope of a new world order, economic, political or military. There is going to be turbulence, much of it involving states which do not see the world, or their own interests, in terms of East-West rivalry.[4]

If *The Times* line of reasoning is to be faulted, it is because of its inability or unwillingness to differentiate third world tubulances but lump them together into an awesome spectre defying the global powers and all international orders. The turbulence, however, is far more complex. It is domestic, regional as well as international; the three dimensions tend to mesh in this decade, trapping both local actors and external powers who may get involved in them. What make the

1980s a particularly dangerous decade is that in at least three strategically important third world regions—the Persian Gulf-Southwest Asia, the Middle East, and southern Africa—US and Soviet interests and roles directly collide with one another. In Latin America, Moscow's primary commitment is to the security and stability of Fidel Castro's Cuba.

The crucial question that divides the West today—divides even the United States—is whether military power alone can salvage Western interests in the third world and keep the Soviet Union at bay. West Europeans do not believe it can, nor do many members of the American foreign policy elite. *The Times* editorial cited above put the West European position forcefully. If the Western alliance were to defend its security, and especially its oil supplies against either local turbulance or Soviet expansion or a combination of the two, then, "its primary effort must be political." The Western alliance "must work to support areas of regional stability, economic prosperity, and political moderation which develop their own resistance to Soviet influence without being forced into East-West alignments."[5]

The Chinese are no less doubtful about US ability to summon the resources necessary to build up a credible wall of containment around the USSR. Deng Xiaoping in an interview with the editor of the *Christian Science Monitor* in December 1980 said, "The US alone is not in a position to deal with Soviet hegemonism. The Soviet challenge can only be coped with if the US strengthens unity with its allies and unites its own strength with all the forces that are resisting Soviet challenge, including the forces of the third world."[6]

SPLITS AND CLEAVAGES

A monolithic anti-Soviet global united front resides in Chinese fantasies rather than in the world realities of the 1980s. The actual situation is one of fragmentation of the foreign policy elites not only at the trans-Atlantic level but also in the United States itself. Indeed the foreign policy consensus lost in Vietnam is still to be regained in America. George Quester, of Cornell University, warned in 1980 that regaining the foreign policy consensus "may be fundamental to a new balance in American diplomacy."[7] The co-editors of *Foreign Policy* after taking a critical look at the past ten years of American foreign policy, came to the conclusion that "coalition building at home and abroad" might be the priority of US foreign policy in the 1980s.[8]

The foreign policy cleavage, observed Allen H. Barton, a Columbia University sociologist, cut across both the economically liberal and conservative groups even in the Republican party. In that party, he said, "there is a long-standing division between Eastern establishment moderates associated with the Council on Foreign Relations and the Trilateral Commission, and those who favour toughness at all risks: the Rockefellers, Scrantons and Percys vs. the Reagans, Connallys and Goldwaters." Foreign policy issues tore apart the Democratic party in 1972; the question of how to deal with the Soviet Union and Marxist and other revolutionary movements in the third world have not become less controversial since then. Political movements in the United States, Barton added, have therefore to come to terms with a world that does not fit American assumptions and ideologies. "Strategic doctrines and assessments of Soviet (and US) doctrines and intentions have polarised American elites into dove and hawk camps that mistrust and stereotype one another. The resulting debates bring forth the worst features of American political style: accusation of weariness and lack of virility against those trying to work for moderation, of creating a war mentality and trying to divert attention from domestic problems against those who favour increased military strength and involvement in the world balance of power." The net result of the polarisation is that in the United States today, there are no programmatic parties in the realm of foreign policy, only "loose aggregations of interests." Nor is a consensus in sight despite Reagan's pre-inauguration effort to put together a "bipartisan" foreign policy. As Barton puts it, "The ambiguous nature of remote realities and the emotional loading of the fears and hostilities involved are impediments to the creation of consensus or the maintenance of a coalition."[9]

Reagan's "bipartisanism" seems to have assembled a new foreign policy establishment drawn from the hawks of the two political parties as well as other aggregation of interests. Members of this new foreign policy establishment are laying down the lines of a tough US response to Soviet global power. For Paul Nitze, former director of the US Arms Control and Disarmament Agency, the "principal task" of America in the early 1980s to "check, blunt . . . (and) frustrate . . . Soviet strategies," which carry in their womb four foreign policy goals—"the political separation of NATO Europe from the United States . . . Soviet influence and control over the Persian Gulf . . . the encirclement and neutralisation of China . . . (and) trouble for the

United States... in the Caribbean."[10] Richard Pipes, of Harvard, visualises the "ultimate purpose" of Western "counter-strategy" to be "to compel the Soviet Union to turn inward—from conquest to reform."[11] Members of the hawk camp even question the legitimacy of the USSR as a partner of the international community.[12]

Four Missing Legs

Hawks and doves agree, however, that a confrontation policy must stand on four legs: elite unity and cohesion in America; cohesion and strength of the Western alliance; stable and reliable partners in the conflicted third world regions; and an economy that can bear the burden of rearmament without exploding at its social seams.

Each of these legs appears to be missing at the turn of the decade. The elite cleavage in America which we have mentioned already, puts powerful and authoritative voices on the other side of confrontation. George Kennan was one of the first to warn that Carter's response to the Soviet move into Afghanistan "revealed a disquieting lack of balance."[13] Alexander Dallin, of Stanford, affirmed that the "Soviet's Afghan invasion is not part of the implementation of a Master Plan of world conquest. It was a target of opportunity... low in cost."[14] Deborah Shapley, of the Carnegie Peace Foundation, argued that the consequences of shrugging off SALT-II could be bitter for the United States. "It seems an odd way to punish the Soviets for invading Afghanistan... (by) allowing them to build an unlimited number of nuclear warheads."[15] Alton Frye, director of the Washington-based Council on Foreign Relations, observed that the two superpowers "have much to gain from an effort to rescue SALT and to revive a sense of common purpose in such negotiations.... The two parties should consider a joint declaration inviting the participation of other states in monitoring the agreements."[16] The *New York Times* kept up sustained arguments against unrestrained militarism and for restoring the strategic arms limitation accords with the Soviet Union.

With regard to the European allies, the hawkish foreign policy establishment has high hopes but low expectations. Walter Laqueur, writing in *Commentary*, observed that "self-Finlandisation, the voluntary subordination of the European political order to the interests and wishes of the Soviet Union, has made considerable advance in recent years."[17] Concurring with this assessment, Fritz Stern, a Columbia University professor of history, wrote, "For the first time there is the possibility that if the present course is unchecked, the Europeans could drift without much consciousness into a situation approximating neutralism." The Soviet determination "to split the alliance," he said, was meeting with alarming success in Europe.[18] The US perception of the ambivalence of the allies was confirmed even by British responses to the Soviet intervention in Afghanistan. The foreign affairs committee of the British House of Commons found no evidence that the Soviet intervention was part of a grand strategy to extend Russian influence to the Gulf and threaten the West's oil supplies. The committee's policy recommendations agreed more with the continental mood than with the belligerence of Margaret Thatcher. It said that the West must check further Soviet "military aggression," whether this occurred in Europe or in the third world, and, at the same time, follow the principle of detente with the USSR.[19] The West Europeans were clearly reluctant to return to the tensions and uncertainties of the cold war years. What really motivated European prudence, said *Le Monde*, was "fear: not atomic fear—the Afghan affair doesn't change the balance of terror on which European security rests—but the permanent anguish of the time of the cold war, fear of being afraid, which is not a good adviser."[20]

In the 1980s, the Western alliance does not hinge on America alone, it also hinges on West Germany and France. The growing rapport between Bonn and Paris provides the contours of an emerging European coalition that may, during this decade, begin to function as a balancer between the US and the USSR, parallel to China. To be sure, West Germany and France do not agree on every aspect of East-West relations. France, with the legacy of de Gaulle, which has merged with its national psyche, takes a more independent military posture than Germany can afford in view of its heavy dependence on American nuclear power to defend itself from a Soviet attack. During the Afghan crisis Bonn was more reluctant than Paris to keep its distance from Washington. However, both were equally anxious to preserve and even increase their economic relations with the Soviet Union and neither therefore imposed trade sanctions in line with the United States. Soviet-West German trade had expanded sharply over the last decade from DM 2.8 billion in 1970 to DM 7.4 billion in 1979. Bonn and Moscow signed a massive DM 20 billion agreement in 1980 under which German steel pipelines and ancillary gear are to be sold to the Soviet Union in return for natural gas. One report said that it would not be far-fetched to believe that by the turn of the century West Germany could emerge as the most formidable trading partner of the COMECON countries.[21]

The economic aspects of European detente became all the more important in view of high inflation and alarmingly frequent cycles of recession afflicting the economies of the entire Western world. 1980 saw lengthening lines of the unemployed in France and Scandinavia; Margaret Thatcher's "monetarism" brought unemployment in England to a record high since World War II; even in West Germany shadows of an incoming recession became menacingly visible. The allies were not in a position to add substantially to their defence budgets in spite of their commitment to the United States that they would increase their defence spending by 3 per cent per year in real terms for five years. The *Economist* reported in November that while Britain had been able to keep the commitment in 1979-80 "after a bruising fight with the Treasury," and could come close to it in 1980, "there is hardly any chance of getting through even the third of the five years' commitment." Britain, the journal added, was "rapidly approaching another milestone in its long retreat from the front ranks of the world's powers." In 1970 Britain had decided to pull out from east of Suez and keep its military commitments confined to the defence of Europe. Now, in the early 80s, Britain would be obliged to drastically cut at least one of its three Services. Furthermore, the next Labour government in Britain would be under deep pressure from the party to initiate measures of unilateral disarmament.[22] The West German Bundeswehr of nearly half a million men is by far the biggest military force in Western Europe. The *Economist* said that it was, however, "an army still in search of an identity" and it had to cope with widespread hostility among the German youth to military service.[23] Even in Japan it was doubtful at the beginning of 1981 whether the government would be able to increase its military spending by 9.6 per cent over the previous year, as recommended by the defence ministry and pressed by the United States.[24]

The Western alliance, then, lacks the cohesion and unity of purpose essential for a credible and effective US policy of confrontation with, and containment of, the Soviet Union. The European allies see Soviet power, third world convulsions and their own security differently from the United States. In the language of the International Institute of Strategic Studies:

"For the United States, relatively secure in her geographic position and her military power, the security interest in co-operating with the Soviet Union was essentially limited to removing the danger of nuclear war, by regulating strategic arms competition and by reducing the danger of direct military conflict between the super-powers. A break-down in detente would not produce an immediate deterioration in American security. For most US allies, though, (and particularly those whose territory bordered the Soviet empire, like Norway, West Germany, Turkey and Japan) a deterioration in the East-West relationship would mean an increase in Soviet pressure and the loss of the advantages that detente had brought. This was especially clear in the case of West Germany—half of a divided country, with an isolated former capital, Berlin—for whom the improvement in East-West relations had brought the growth of contacts between the populations of the two German states and a reduction in the tensions over Berlin. . . .

"Third-world conflict and the Western response to it pointed to other areas of potential trans-Atlantic (and trans-Pacific) dissent. There was a clear difference in approach, not so much over the security challenge such conflict posed as over how to respond to it. The United States, with her global outlook and global means, was more ready to see threats to Western interests as Soviet-initiated challenges and more ready to contemplate military responses. Europe and Japan, on the other hand, instinctively interpreted these conflicts as indigenous and—with the occasional exception of France —were reluctant to consider military solutions. European instincts tended to follow short-run European interests. . . .

"As East-West security considerations superseded regional concerns over third-world crises, it would become increasingly difficult for the Western Alliance to accommodate these differences in outlook and method. The establishment of a US quick-reaction force to cope with threats to Western security in areas of primary strategic interest, like the Middle East, would also require greater American flexibility in the use of US military forces earmarked for threats in Europe and the Far East. Even more important, American support for the traditional security needs of the allies was bound to be weakened if Europe or Japan were unwilling to support American action in the Third World which was undertaken—at least in the US perspective—in defence of their interests as well.[25]

GULF AS CONFRONTATION TERRAIN

In the Persian Gulf, the crises in Iran and Afghanistan have reinforced one another to build a serious threat to US, West European and Japanese interests. US strategic thinkers, especially the hawks among them, see the Soviet threat to be the most immediate and gravest in the Persian Gulf. "The USSR is now poised along extensive stretches of territory bordering on two countries—Iran and Pakistan—one of which is rich in vital petroleum resources and both of which provide access to the sea lanes of crucial importance to international commerce and to the world's geopolitical balance,"[26] warns Helmut Sonnenfeldt, one-time aide to Henry Kissinger. The real objective of the Soviet Union is "control of the West's largest reservoir of oil in the Gulf," echoes Robert Moss, a contributing editor of *Saturday Review*.[27] "The Persian Gulf will pose the greatest challenge for US security in the 1980s of any region in the world," affirms an article in *Daedalus*, adding in the same breath that "the defence of Western interests will require . . . denial of the region to the Soviet Union . . . promotion of a moderately peaceful environment . . . and the cohesion of the Western alliance."[28] Samuel Huntington calls the Soviet intervention in Afghanistan "a hinge event,"[29] while Edward Luttwak is so impressed with the "quality of operational confidence" of Soviet troops in Afghanistan that he is constrained to warn that it will "lead to war unless we are very much luckier than we deserve to be."[30]

The US, however, feels more threatened than Western Europe because of its inability or unreadiness to tailor civilian petroleum consumption to what has come to be known as the Oil Crisis. American dependence on Gulf oil is of recent vintage. But it is increasing at an alarming pace—from 15 per cent of all oil imports in 1973 to 38 per cent in 1979; it will probably be as high as 45 per cent in 1985. The West Europeans are more dependent on Gulf oil, but less nervous and more ready to live with a regional situation not entirely favorable to Western interests. West Europeans are less than fully sympathetic to the American petroleum predicament in the Gulf because an average American consumes twice as much petrol as an average German and at half the price. The argument that America's unsatiable thirst for oil and its refusal to adopt a more prudent and restrained oil policy are at the root of US foreign policy activism in the Gulf region is freely articulated in European capitals. The West Europeans have developed a certain degree of dependence on Soviet oil and more on Soviet natural gas, while the East European countries are developing a stake in Persian Gulf oil. The Soviets too have registered their own "vital interest" in the Persian Gulf, not only because of an approaching oil crunch but also because the region's geographical proximity to the Soviet state. At the same time, Brezhnev has conceded that the US has a serious stake in Persian Gulf oil.

The instabilities in the Gulf region are not of Soviet making. But the unalterable fact that the region is next door to the USSR, Soviet interventionist capability, and the actual intervention in Afghanistan which has placed the USSR within tactical air strike distance from the Gulf area are factors that have added a visible Soviet dimension to the instabilities. The instabilities are extremely complex. An Iranian strategic thinker has aptly described them as "multiple (domestic, regional and external), murky (they are ambiguous in their origins and not clearly delineated as such), and interactive (they tend to be reinforcing rather than discrete autonomous or isolated events)."

> That developing states are rarely politically stable and seldom enjoy excellent relations with their neighbours is generally recognized, and is infrequently a cause for alarm in the Western world. What makes the Gulf region unusual, however, is the combination of circumstances that increase the prospects for sustained instability in a region where Western interests are uniquely reliant on order. First, the domestic stresses attendant on rapid modernization fueled by enormous oil revenues. Second, a political environment in which pressures from issues such as Palestine feed into persistent regional rivalries, and where multiple cleavages—ethnic, sectarian, linguistic—that overlap state boundaries often aggravate relations between neighbors. Third, the competition between the major external powers for influence and access intensifies these rivalries and instabilities, adding such divisive issues as alignment and orientation to the existing menu of instabilities. Western vulnerability, indigenous instability, and proximate Soviet military power combine to give the Persian Gulf an extraordinary importance to Western interests. The sensitivity to threats to these interests is acute, but it is also, by virtue of the multiple sources of threats, diffuse. It is the interactive nature of the threats that complicates the problem of the (analyst and) policy-maker in devising a response.[31]

This was the anatomy of Persian Gulf instabilities before the Iraqi invasion of Iran. The war between the two "oil powers" have continued for more than 120 days at the time of writing; an end is not in sight yet. The war and its aftermath will make restoration of any kind of order in the regional relationship extremely complicated and difficult.

It is in this volatile slippery terrain that the United States proposes to confront the USSR in the first place. An array of strong arguments greased with nationalist passions has been advanced to justify confrontation. It is argued that visible American military superiority, and readiness to use force where needed to protect vital US interests and commitments will restore international credibility in American leadership and breathe caution and restraint into Soviet foreign policy behaviour. The assembling of military power, building of military presence in crises-laden regions and readiness to use force do not necessarily mean that force will actually be used; indeed, it would be a more effective way to avoid war than detente or peaceful coexistence. It is further argued that deterrent American military force would restrain not only the USSR, but also local aggressors and reassure Washington's friends and partners in the various regions; once confidence in the United States is restored, third world governments will be willing to accept American help and will not hesitate to link their nations' security to US power. Thus order and discipline would be restored in regions now exceedingly destabilised by local conflicts, American weakness and an enhancement of Soviet military might.[32]

Behind this mosaic of arguments lies, barely concealed, a refusal to recognise the Soviet Union as a legitimate candidate for an equal status with the United States in the international system and its various regional subsystems. It dismisses the reasoning of those scholars and statesmen who do not perceive the Soviet Union as the principal cause of third world destabilities who stress the complexities of contemporary conflicts; regard excessive emphasis on military responses at the cost of effective and patient diplomacy to be counterproductive in the medium and long term even if it shores up some immediate success; who view a new superpower arms race as pregnant with the possibility of nuclear proliferation and as damaging both in economic costs and in its failure to restore regional and international stability. They do not share the militarists' optimism that the United States does command in the 1980 enough resource to meet at the same time the high cost of rearmament and the exacting demands of its own political economy. They doubt if European allies would back US military involvement in vital third world regions like the Persian Gulf, and whether the extreme plurality of conflicts and tensions, crisscrossing one another, would permit the United States to restore a viable order, domestically and regionally in that conflicted area.[33]

UNILATERAL US MIGHT

Unassured of allied backing and unsure of regional clout, the United States is obliged to rely on a programme of unilateral military buildup to wage confrontation and containment. The shape of things to come became clear in November 1980 when a few days after Jimmy Carter's defeat in the presidential poll, the US Senate passed, with 73 yeas and a single no, and with the minimum of debate, the largest ever military budget in history—$ 161 billion for fiscal 1981—$ 3.5 billion more than what the House of Representatives had allowed, and $ 6.2 billion more than what Carter had asked for. It was now estimated that in five years, 1980-1985, the US might be spending a trillion dollars on defence!

An integral part of the projected massive military buildup is the so-called "countervailing strategy" of "limited" nuclear war which Carter formally approved in the summer of 1980, six years after it had been mooted by James R. Schlesinger when he was Nixon's defence secretary. Anchored on new mobile MX missiles and the new Cruise missiles, the "countervailing strategy" is designed to ensure a most accurate second strike capability against "the things that the Soviets value most"—their war-supporting industry, command bunkers, nuclear storage sites, lines of communication, airfields, missile silos and other vital resources and facilities."[34] Cabinet officers as well as members of the foreign policy establishment began to talk freely about theatre and tactical nuclear war should the US have to meet its adversary in the unfavourable terrain of the Persian Gulf.

> The worst aspect of the "new strategy" is that it would tend to make nuclear war more nearly acceptable—hence more likely. If leaders come to believe, and the public accepts, that a nuclear war can be "limited" to military targets only, and can even be won, nuclear war becomes no longer "unthinkable" and the object of a national policy no longer will be to avoid it but to win it when it comes.

That being the case, any president or Soviet leader in some future crisis is more likely to order a nuclear strike—for "limited" purposes—than has been the case while the obliteration of the human race—whole nations, at least—was thought to be the certain consequence of a nuclear exchange.[35]

The US military buildup programme is triggered by two factors, one American, the other Soviet. The American factor is the lead hawks in America believe the US has established in the production of a new generation of sophisticated strategic weapon systems; once these weapons systems are operative, they argue, the US could restore its strategic superiority over the USSR. The other factor is the emergence of the USSR as a co-equal global power which many Americans find it difficult to live with as a permanent fact of international relations. Others, however, doubt if the US can achieve a strategic edge. A *New York Times* report says that few in the US seriously doubt that the Soviets in this decade could easily acquire an ability to make the MX (estimated to cost $ 34 billion, but likely to be even two or three times more costly by the time it is actually produced) vulnerable to a surprise strike. It said the Soviets could match every strategic weapon the US could deploy or any nuclear war strategy the US might design.[36] A Soviet arms control specialist who took part in negotiations with the US for conventional arms control accords told the writer in February 1981 that the Soviet Union "will not permit the United States to achieve strategic superiority." The Soviet ability to match the new generation of US strategic weapons systems was confirmed by Andre Fontaine, strategic analyst of *Le Monde*:

> Considering the disparity of conventional weapons, the United States would not be able to wage war on the Soviet Union except by committing its nuclear capability. But the whole idea of deterrence has been conceived with the object of preventing one or the other of the superpowers from resorting to nuclear arms. Let's make no mistake: the USSR today has every effective means for "dissuading" the US from taking this course.[37]

Some experts believe that the American inferiority in conventional arms is insurmountable particularly in regions close to the Soviet heartland such as the Persian Gulf. Others point out that the military balance between the US and the USSR cannot probably be redressed before the end of the decade, if then.[38]

The projected American military buildup has to be attempted amidst three major changes in the American global strategic position. First, the era of US economic self-sufficiency has passed. Apart from oil, the US must import 15 minerals and other raw materials to keep its industry going in war and peace. To maintain the flow of these raw materials in times of war requires increasing allocations for more sea-control ships and surveillance aircraft and for more expanded research and development in anti-submarine warfare. Secondly, the regions which provide these raw materials are exceedingly unstable. West Asian oil and African copper and crome are militarily vital American imports. To be able to flaunt a credible rapid deployment force, the US would need an armada of new long-range transport aircraft. Thirdly, the Soviet Union and its Warsaw Pact allies have attained superiority, first in quantity and lately in quality, in conventional and theatre nuclear forces. The NATO decision to proceed with the deployment in Europe of 572 mobile Pershing-2 ballistic missiles and ground-launched Cruise missiles, also mobile, could give the West parity in theatre nuclear weapons by 1985 at the earliest. "That projection assumes that the Russians will not develop and deploy an improved version of their SS-20 mobile missile and a heavy bomber of greater range and payload than the Backfire." According to US officials who negotiated the SALT-II treaty with Moscow, the Soviets have actually begun developing a new type of long-range bomber. The favoured prototype is the TU-160 which the officials said was a Soviet version of the B-1 bomber which Carter killed in 1979.[39]

One of the most crucial questions relating to arms buildup is whether the economic afflictions of the United States will permit the transfer of largescale resource for a sustained rearmament programme. *Fortune* magazine warned towards the end of 1979: "Uncertainties about the US economy in 80s have to do not only with energy, inflation and productivity, but also ... with questions about the nation's ability to devise ... and carry out effective long term policies."[40] More than a year later the *Economist* reported: "When Mr Reagan moves into the White House ... he would be faced with rising inflation, spiralling federal spending, sky-high interest rates and an economy which could be heading for its second downswing within 12 months. None of these is likely to be improved by Mr Reagan's election promise of income tax cuts—indeed, by concentrating the cuts on personal taxes, rather than making changes that will stimulate business investment, the Reagan administration could make matters worse."⁴¹ Several American scholars visualise a continuing conflict and clash between economic stringencies and military needs. In the words of Robert W. Hartman, of the Bookings Institute, "there is an increasing realisation that the government pie cannot keep going at past rates and if you give more to defence you must give less to everything else."⁴²

ARMS AND BASES

How much more should be given to a new defence buildup and what might be the action's social and political costs were questions that seized the Carter administration as soon as it was inaugurated in January 1977. The debate within the government was initiated on the basis of the Presidential Review Memorandum No. 10, or RPM-10, drawn up by the national security council. The debate exposed deep divisions in the entire US foreign policy elite, pitting "doves" against "hawks". People disagreed about everything—on the nature of the threat the United States faced, on American response to the threat, on the force level required for a credible response, on how much the US could count for what kind of support from its allies and clients, and on the economic and social spin-off of a substantial military buildup.⁴³ As the tearing debate went on, it seemed that Carter would lean towards both sides which made many people eventually to question the timber of his leadership. It also became clear that whatever volume of defence buildup might be allowed would be justified on the visible global might of the USSR. Thus, in July 1977, defence secretary Harold Brown declared in a major speech, "Whether we like it or not, the Soviet leadership seems intent on challenging us to a major military competition. ... The most evident—and dangerous—features of the challenge arise from the steady annual increases (in real terms) in the Soviet defence budget, the buildup and improvement of Soviet strategic nuclear force, the modernisation of Soviet ground and tactical air force in Eastern Europe, and the growing sophistication of Soviet naval forces, which include a gradually expanding capacity to project military power at considerable distances from Russia itself."⁴⁴

With Mr Ronald Reagan in the White House, the United States has to live with Soviet global power with vastly enhanced American global power. This new military competition between the two *global* powers will dominate international relations all through the 1980s. It is a confrontation very different from the cold war of the 1950s and early 1960s, for, as already noted, the US has to take on Soviet global power, without the advantages it enjoyed in the earlier decades in terms of its leadership of the Western world, its economic health, its stable treaty-bound relationships with a host of third world nations.

The new confrontation will spawn third world geopolitical regions with increasing intensity; at the beginning of the decade, its focus is on the Persian Gulf-South Asian area. Simmering conflicts may erupt into military collisions any time in the other critical regions— the Middle East, southern Africa, Southeast Asia, the Indian Ocean and the subcontinent. In all these regions the new global power confrontation has already generated fresh arms races; the two superpowers have thrown away whatever restraints they had seemingly agreed to observe—though informally—as a result of their tentative dialogues in the late 1970s on control of arms transfers to the third world. The United States and the USSR have been for over a decade the two major suppliers of weapons and services to client states in the third world. Though experts differ on the relative volume of arms transfers by the two superpowers—one estimate placing them almost neck to neck, another placing the US way ahead of the USSR[45]—there is solid evidence that arms transfers on a significant scale generate regime instabilities, sometime lead to, or are created by, regime change, at other times generate or intensify internal or inter-state conflicts. Between 1968 and 1977, as many as 12 third world countries—two each in Southeast Asia and the Gulf region, three in the Middle East-North Africa, four in sub-Saharan Africa, and one in Latin America —switched off from one power bloc to another as the principal source of arms and weapons as a result of regime change (3), or change in supplier's or client's policies (9).[46] During the writing of this volume, the US-Soviet confrontation generated an arms race between Pakistan and India after a fairly long period of arms stability; Iran and Iraq were fighting a four-months-old war with American and Soviet arms and weapons; Afghan rebels were engaging the Kabul regime with weapons supplied by China, Pakistan, Egypt and Saudi Arabia; Japan entered the world arms bazar as an exporter of weapons; and the US was hunting for base facilities along the entire Indian Ocean littoral.

Indeed bases and staging points for extended logistics have become an integral aspect of the new global power confrontation. Since the

1970s the two superpowers have been conducting "base" diplomacy in an increasingly volatile international milieu and with mixed fortunes. The countries involved in "base" diplomacy included Egypt, Somalia, Angola, Mozambique, the Azore islands, Turkey, Greece, Malta, Bahrain, Iraq, Syria, Libya, Kenya, Thailand, Philippines and Vietnam; in 1980 to this list were added Ethiopia, Iraq, Oman and Pakistan.

In the Persian Gulf, the United States signed a military-economic agreement with Oman which, with Iran in the north, covers the entrance to the Gulf. The agreement permits the US to use Oman's military facilities in an emergency, and commits the US to Oman's security. In 1980-81 the United States was planning a chain of military facilities along the northwestern coast of the Indian Ocean. Reports said that naval facilities or bases had been, or were being, acquired in Egypt, Kenya and Somalia. By the spring of 1980, the US assembled 52 warships in the Indian Ocean and 20 in the Arabian Sea. The armada was led by two aircraft carriers, the *Nimitz* and the *Coral Sea*; between them they could launch more than 150 warplanes, if needed. The buildup included B-52 bombers, and received cooperation from Israel, Egypt and Somalia.[47] The US naval buildup caused, and was caused by, an increased Soviet naval presence in the Indian Ocean and the Arabian Sea.[48] Militarization of the Indian Ocean perturbed the littoral states, especially after the US made known its decision not to attend the proposed UN conference on the Indian Ocean in 1981. India felt particularly threatened.[49]

There is, then, a growing linkage between confrontation, arms transfers and strategic access in the major third world geopolitical regions. As a recent US study puts it, "Resource shortages, both existing and expected—most notably in oil but involving numerous other commodities—have served to focus renewed attention on real or hypothetical requirements for protecting sea lanes and for controlling maritime chokepoints and on the importance of staging areas for military intervention contingencies. The apparently declining salience of cold-war ideological conflict, following upon the final collapse of former colonial empires, has rendered base acquisition and retention a more competitive business. Various forms of strategic access have become important, tangible items of exchange, providing considerable leverage for smaller powers in bargaining over military and economic aid. Meanwhile, the Soviets' development of a blue-water navy and a long-range air transport logistics capability has expanded the superpowers' competition to global dimensions, involving all three oceans and their littorals. Finally, there is the greatly increased sensitivity on the part of smaller nations to the symbolic import of compromised sovereignty inherent in granting strategic access to others, which often provides a visible target for internal opposition groups."[50]

Implications of total confrontation with the USSR has generated a debate in the US foreign policy establishment on how much and what kind of confrontation should be practicable in the 1980s. Three positions seem to have emerged. The hardest position, represented by one of its protagonists, Norman Podhoretz, is that the current confrontation is, or must be, one between two irreconcilable ways of human existence, two ideological universes that just cannot live together as equals. "In resisting the advance of Soviet Power . . . we *are* fighting for freedom and against Communism, for democracy and against totalitarianism," Podhoretz affirmed in 1980. Podhoretz was disturbed by the lack of a moral purpose in the currently roused American nationalism; this lack, in his thinking, betrayed the absence of an American sense of direction: "Without such clarity, the new nationalism is unlikely to do more than lead to sporadic outbursts of indignant energy."[51] Striking a medium posture, Robert W. Tucker, who has been persistently pressing since the midseventies for a formidable American military presence in the Persian Gulf, which would virtually amount to American military control of the region's petroleum, called in 1981 for "a limited policy of containment" rather than a strategy of total confrontation. "In the present circumstances . . . a return to the expansive version of containment, if seriously intended, is likely to place us on the most dangerous of courses with the Soviet Union. For that policy must in effect convey the message to Moscow that the clock is to be set back at least 15 years, that the status of equality accorded to the USSR by the late 1960s is henceforth to have largely a honorific significance, and that the United States no longer intends to accept the Soviet Union as a global power." Tucker conceded that an American attempt to deny the Soviets the status they had won at considerable cost would, "at best," further exacerbate America's relations with its allies, "at worst," lead to an open rupture and "to the greatest diplomatic defeat for this country in the postwar period." Tucker therefore concluded that "the containment of today and tomorrow will have to make concessions and compromises in areas of contention where concession and compromise were once spurned. And if it is at all prudent, a refurbished containment will, wherever possible, avoid measures which at once sharply exacerbate the relationship with the Soviet Union and make the prospect of its future amelioration virtually impossible." Tucker specifically warned against even a de-facto military alliance between the US and China, which would "seal the Soviet-American relationship in a fixed and truly dangerous mould by making it hostage to our relations with China."[52]

The softest confrontation line was put forward by a third US specialist on Soviet affairs, Robert Legvold. Writing in *Foreign Policy* in the fall of 1980, Legvold offered a slightly modified version of the pattern of Soviet-US relationship that Kissinger and Brzezinski tried to follow in two markedly different concepts and styles. Legvold called his own version "containment without confrontation." This policy "must proceed on two tracks: one of firmness, military strength (but not by seeking military superiority); the other of cooperation, the extended hand, and a renewed interest in dealing with problems jointly rather than in turning problems against each other." The first track would provide for increased American military power in the belief that this would draw the line that the Soviets could cross only at the risk of war. The second track would provide incentives for cooperation in such areas as arms control and international security, with "a serious attempt to open the one area of detente that never got started, namely, crisis management" (in the third world).[53]

It is clear, then, that at the beginning of the 1980s, the American foreign policy elite is sharply split on almost every aspect of the phenomenon of Soviet global power. There is no agreement on the actual substance of Soviet power, the primary objectives of Soviet power, nor on what should be the best and most effective American response to it. If there is a consensus in America at all, it is on the need to refurbish its military power and reestablish its military presence in critical regions. How much additional military power the United States must acquire, how precisely this power should be used, what its impact would be on the USSR and on America's allies and clients are, once again, questions that split the foreign policy elite rather than unite them. This elite division in the US is a striking paradox generated by international change. Twentyfive years ago, much less Soviet power united the US elite on the platform of the cold war. Now, the vastly augmented Soviet power splits the elite in the US, the US and its allies, the US and its third world friends and clients.

This paradox was confirmed in the intermeshing crises in Iran and Afghanistan. The Soviets had little to do with the American debacle in Iran, but the debacle itself was seen by all international actors as a major gain of the USSR. The intervention in Afghanistan was an obstreperous assertion of Soviet power as a factor that must be taken into account in the management of crises in the Persian Gulf region, whatever else might also have been its motivating force. Few countries outside the Soviet system endorsed the Afghan intervention; as many as 104 members of the United Nations voted twice in the General Assembly urging complete withdrawal of Soviet forces. But no one was ready to take on the Soviet Union. There was widespread support for American muscle-flexing. But the allies were reluctant to keep in step with the United States, friends and clients were afraid of being openly seen in American company. Pakistan asked for a formal treaty-bound US commitment to the preservation of its internal integrity and external security, but the Pakistani military saw India, and not the USSR, as the main source of threat. Even Saudi Arabia refused to place its naval bases at US disposal and regarded the Israeli occupation of Jerusalem to be no less a threat to Islam than the Soviet intervention in Afghanistan.[54] The allies did not participate except cosmetically in economic sanctions against the USSR; some of them took part in the Moscow Olympics. Argentina and Brazil did not halt wheat exports to the Soviet Union, nor did Canada and Australia after an initial period.[55] China was more than willing to fight its number one enemy to the last American.

It does not, of course, mean that nations will behave with similar absence of anger if the Soviets continue to make reckless use of military power to garner foreign policy gains. What it means is that the intervention in Afghanistan was not *really* seen by most nations as the watershed in international relations Americans perceived it to be. It was bad. It was deplorable. But the Soviets were not without a credible case. In southern Africa and Ethiopia, Soviet "proxy" intervention enjoyed African support. No one blamed Moscow for its massive help to North Vietnam. In the event of another Arab-Israeli conflict, the Soviets will be lauded if they intervene on behalf of the Arabs. The Soviets will be acceptable to the nations as a global power if their might is not used to violate the sovereignty of independent countries, nor to block the process of evolutionary change within the Soviet system. The Soviets will risk the formation of a global coalition against them if they use military power to topple non-radical regimes

How to Live with Soviet Power 243

or prop up pro-Soviet revolutionary governments. From available evidence of the conduct of Soviet foreign policy, it seems to be unlikely that the Soviets would do another Afghanistan in the near future.

It is argued elsewhere in this volume that the Soviet leadership will wage "peace" instead of war in response to Mr Reagan's confrontation strategy—peace aimed at consolidating what Moscow has gained in the third world, to recover from the losses it has suffered, to distance the US from its allies and clients, to fan elite cleavages in America, to watch how military buildup aggravates America's economic and social problems: in short, as a strategic weapon of foreign policy no less ambitious in the sweep of its objectives than the instrument of force. Of course, Moscow's "peace strategy" in the 1980s will also include the application of military power in two areas, namely, the defence of the USSR and the socialist system, and, in situations of unmistakable opportunities running a low risk of defeat. To be more specific, the Soviets will not hesitate to use force, as diplomacy of last resort, to defend the socialist system in Poland, nor, in all probability, to intervene in northern Iran in the event of a clearly visible US invasion of Iran from the south.

LIVING WITH SOVIET GLOBAL POWER

In two different global scenarios, most nations of the world will find it easier to try to live in peaceful coexistence with the Soviet Union as a global military power. The first is a scenario of a substantial and durable retreat of US power, a major folding up of America's role as the policeman of the non-communist world. The second scenario is that of American acceptance of the USSR as a co-equal global power, a mosaic of mutual accommodation defining their living together in a planet that is not too small to bear the weight of both of them.

The first scenario silhouted in 1975 after the American debacle in Vietnam; in an ambience perceived to be marked with a retreat of US power from part of the global arena, nations hitherto dependent on the US for security began to extricate themselves from formal security ties or maintain a certain cultivated distance from America's worldwide strategic presence; even such staunch pro-US nations as Japan and Iran started thinking in terms of, and articulating, somewhat antonomous foreign policy preferences.[56] Soviet diplomacy assumed a global sweep it did not previously possess. Indeed the

Soviets launched a diplomatic offensive to replace the US inter-linked military pacts global security model with their own model of collective security based on principles of peaceful coexistence, which, in effect, aimed at formalising the detachment of third world countries from the US security system rather than their attachment to a new Soviet global or regional security design.[57]

The low response to the Soviets' collective security diplomacy in Asia proved that, in the first place, Moscow still was not seen by most third world nations as having replaced the US as the planet's leading power; secondly, that Moscow's military power was by no means matched by economic power without which no nation can aspire to actual global leadership; and thirdly, that the USSR and most third world nations, including those who had concluded friendship treaties with Moscow, were still separated from one another by different ideologies, conflicting national interests, and deep-rooted mistrust of third world ruling elites in Soviet blandishments.

The second scenario—US recognition of the USSR as a co-equal—was sketched by detente, and, overall, it produced a handsome harvest of foreign policy gains not only for the Soviet Union but also for a large number of countries belonging to each of the three worlds in which it is now a habit of mankind to divide the planet. Detente induced several third world countries that had kept themselves studiously away from the Soviet Union, to turn cautiously to Moscow for economic and even arms support. Detente, however, was seen very differently by the Soviet Union and the United States. To Moscow, detente was an "objective reality" delivered by a decisive qualitative change in the balance of world forces—decline of the "imperialist" global hegemony and a sharp increase in the military and economic power of the socialist bloc. It also increased prospects of revolutionary change in developing countries. To the United States, detente was a strategy to tame the USSR to work for betterment of the existing international system rather than for its revolutionary transformation, and to preserve the status quo in the third world, which meant allowing gradual, but resisting revolutionary, change. Most third world elites saw detente as it was seen in the United States, not in the Soviet Union. In other words, on a general level, third world ruling elites agreed with the United States that detente offered the two power blocs a historic opportunity to work together for a better, more orderly and less stratified world order, and that it would broadly help third world regimes to better manage the increasingly attritious tasks of development and social change.

Third world ruling elites, then, do not wish to see a spatial expansion of the Soviet Union's global power and influence. Most of these elites would feel comfortable in a world order based on formalised equality of the two global powers in case the new balance of global forces does not destabilise the regimes over which they themselves preside in the vast majority of developing nations. Third world regimes, in other words, welcomed detente to the extent it gave them greater autonomy in international relations and increased their options in the realm of aid and trade. It is noteworthy that the major third world platforms to press for desired change in the world economic order—OPEC and the North-South front of international relations—emerged in the ambience of detente.

Detente stimulated human quests for a better world. It encouraged intellectuals to develop global approaches to global issues and problems. The decade of the 1970s demonstrated that it was no longer possible for a single nation or combination of nations unilaterally to set the terms of international cooperation or manage the international system. Scholars all over the world including the Soviet Union and Eastern Europe but mostly in the United States began to see issues like energy, pollution, interdependence, management of structural and rapid social change, the impact of communications technology on societal and inter-societal relations in global perspectives, and to seek global remedies. In short, detente introduced a process of global learning aimed at mankind's preparation to face perhaps a far more tumultuous twentyfirst century whose footsteps were audible to discerning ears.

The learning process remained constrained because neither the USSR nor the US accepted detente as more than a tactical foreign policy concept, its future mortgaged to short-term, visible gains. The Soviets kept their distance from the North-South platform, claiming that the issues and problems were the legacy of imperialism and must therefore be resolved between the newly liberated nations and their erstwhile masters. At the same time, the Soviets deployed their propaganda resource to radicalise the South's stand at bargaining forums, that is, to aggravate the crisis of confidence between the developed and developing nations. And the Soviets actively intervened in southern Africa to help revolutionary forces capture power in Ethiopia, Angola and Mozambique.

The United States, apart from *not* making any noteworthy concessions to the South on major economic issues, made the mistake of blending revolutionary ferment in third world countries and Soviet might into a threat theory of unprecedented proportions. The traditional American inability to comprehend revolutionary upsurge in the third world and America's strong economic and political-strategic linkage with reactionary regimes and ruling elites reinforced US proclivity to perceive the Soviet Union as the villain of revolutionary upheavals in the developing world. That this only confirmed the "natural allies" theory of Leninism did not cause any concern among American policy-makers.

But the United States lost a great opportunity to mobilise the developing nations' support to persuade the Soviet Union to "behave" in the third world. Soviet-Cuban active intervention in Angola and Ethiopia raised no protests in the third world, not even in Africa, because Moscow and Havana backed forces that enjoyed considerable African nationalist approval. The British-US endorsement of Marxist Robert Mugabe as prime minister of the first black-majority regime in Zimbabwe, on the other hand, led to a significant setback for Soviet diplomacy. An ability to distinguish between a genuine revolutionary situation in a third world nation and the Soviet Union was a remarkable improvisation in American foreign policy. If it did not receive the appreciation it deserved, it was partly because soon after the Zimbabwe settlement, President Carter was overtaken by the Iranian revolution, and perceived the oil wealth of the Persian Gulf falling under the shadow of Moscow's extended military power. If the maiden stirrings of President Reagan's foreign policy are indications of thrusts to come, the United States will once again "adopt" reactionary, repressive regimes in the third world, and link militant nationalist-revolutionary movements and forces with Soviet military power.

American ability to stem the tide of radical or revolutionary change in the third world is as limited as Soviet ability to engineer third world revolutions. The history of the post-war decades shows that the Soviets have done well only where they have been able to help indigenous radical or revolutionary movements locked in protracted struggles against imperialism. The third world is still largely the economic backyard of the first world of industrialised developed free-market countries. A process of detachment has begun. It is not a simple process moving in a single direction. It is a multiple, complex and volatile process that tests the timber of both international capitalism and international communism. One sure way to tame the Soviet Union and yoke it to a heterogenous international system is to let the number of third world nations dependent on Soviet resources for development *increase*. One Afghanistan has cost the Soviet Union credibility of many third world ruling allies as a realiable friend that would protect their regimes and—more important—themselves. A few more interventions a la Afghanistan, and the USSR has united the largest part of the third world against it![58]

This decade is probably destined to witness the growing isolation of both the United States and the Soviet Union in the lonely grandeur of their respective global military power. The two goliaths are moving towards mutually recognised equality along a tortuous zigzag road laden with mines of confrontation, containment, competition and deterrence. Their quest for relative military superiority must proceed along lonely tracks, with little actual help from allies and friends. Their adversary relationship is steadily spending itself even as they reach for each other's throat. The Soviet system, far from being able to "bury" industrial capitalism, seeks a long-term honeymoon with it, without agreeing to "behave" in the third world. It is beyond Soviet capability to dwarf the world status of the United States. That business is best left to the rulers of America! Similarly, it is beyond the ability of the United States to "punish" the Soviet Union or bring about internal explosions in the Soviet system. The Soviet system shows a hundred chinks, but it will not burst at the seams American academic experts keep pathologically zeroing on for the meanest line of crack. The only strain that will probably break the Soviet system is one of serious reverses in a third world war with the Western powers led by the United States. But the Soviet Union can make that war as unacceptable to its adversaries as it is to itself.

An American confrontation—even containment—may indeed be what the Soviet and East European leaders would welcome in the early 1980s to bring their societies to stricter order, to get rid of some of the deviant tendencies these societies have shown since winds of evolutionary change began to blow in after the death of Stalin.[59] The Soviet system has grown up and acquired its present stature in a hostile world, amidst civil war, foreign intervention, a world war, and a cold war. It may find it easier to operate in a world in which the dividing lines are clear, firm and stable. Confrontation by the United

States may help the Soviet leaders work more successfully on the differences that have come to exist between Western Europe and America. Confrontation will not bend the Soviet Union in the 1980s, though it did in 1962. The USSR is still very largely a self-sufficient economy, far less dependent on the outside world for minerals and essential raw materials than the United States. The United States alone cannot hurt the Soviet Union by denying it trade and technologies; even if the Western powers impose collective economic sanctions —an event not easily believable—the Soviet system will survive by tightening the belt. A cut off of all grain shipments from the West will not deprive the Russian of his daily bread. He will have to make do with little meat; he will probably stoically return to his old, unforgotten diet of patriotism, pride, anger and hatred on which he survived long difficult years. In ony case by the end of the decade the Soviets may well become self-supporting in grains, considering the investments that are going into agriculture regardless of cost. Confrontation could only add intransigence to Soviet global might, make it more truculent. The danger is all the more clear because the men who will soon succeed the present aging Soviet leaders in the highest echelons of power are believed to be made of tougher stuff, more accustomed to Soviet 'power', less exposed to the indigent days of the Bolshevik regime.

The new confrontation, then, is far more dynamic than the cold war of the 1950s and 1960s when the world balance was clearly favourable for the United States. It is dynamic because it will be waged in the extremely "soft" terrain of crises regions in the third world, and because it threatens to mesh superpower conflicts with volatile third world convulsions. The new confrontation may lead to military interventions by *both* superpowers in third world countries or regions, each acting under the assumption that it could get away with political or military plums. Certain elements in the Reagan administration are said to believe that the easiest way to restore third world confidence in American Power is to inflict punishment on one or two countries in Asia and Africa that are closely linked to the USSR. This kind of policy, put into operation, could lead to a US-Soviet collision.

The current confrontation is more dangerous than the cold war in another respect also. It is taking place amidst a new strategic arms race which, if allowed to run, will make strategic arms control more difficult of achievement because of fresh complexities in verifying and monitoring implementation. At the same time, there are strong reasons, outlined above, that should breathe caution into confrontation in the 1980s. There are objective realities which, activised, could prevent confrontation from engulfing the entire spectrum of world politics. If the middle powers refuse to be sucked in, they will be able not only to keep their own distance from confrontation, and defuse an oncoming conflict, but also induce the superpowers to wage confrontation within tolerable limits of risks. The middle powers could then reduce confrontation to a transient face-off peculiar to US-Soviet relations, a deplorable but inevitable worsening of relations before they could get durably better. If a mere five years of detente frightened Americans that their corporate universe was collapsing into the extended arms of the bear, it only shows that detente or coexistence is still alien to the grain of American power. Reagan believes that he has his tryst with that power to put it back again at the centre of the planet. Only when Americans realise that this cannot be done, that the world in which this happened is now history, will they take a fresh hard look at the grammar of living together with a second global power.

As the Goliaths duel, others must see to it that they do not inflict irreparable damage on an afflicted planet. The world today has a cluster of middle powers spawning the continents, who can join together to protect the present and future worlds while the global powers gnash their teeth and flaunt their claws in the process of settling their own terms of coexistence. Thereby the middle powers can ensure that the globe's future is not hostage to superpower confrontation. It is not a question of being non-aligned in a new cold war. Nonalignment is as dated a doctrine of international relations in the 1980s as the cold war is. The newly emergent and emerging powers—Germany, France, Japan, Canada, Australia, Brazil, Mexico, Nigeria, Indonesia and India—form a new category of nations with individual and collective interests that surpass their respective linkages with one or the other global power. They stand to gain little and lose a great deal, individually and collectively, if confrontation and containment becomes global and threatens much of what mankind has learnt in recent years of the art of living together in a crowded, resource-strained, disparities-laden, unequal but only world. The learning has not been much, it has only begun; but there has been a lot of effort, and many contending thoughts have bloomed.

This decade, then, does not have to be the decade of confrontation of the two global powers. It can be made the decade of the middle powers bound together by a single shared goal: to protect much of mankind from destruction. For that will be the deadly gift of confrontation if it leads to nuclear war which it very well may.

Notes

CHAPTER ONE

[1] Between 1971 and 1979 Bangladesh received more than $7 billion in aid. More than 50 per cent of the national budget of 1979-80 and more than 70 per cent of the planned public sector outlays in the Two-Year Plan of 1978-80 were expected to come from foreign donors.

New York Times, 6 June 1978; *The Statesman* (Calcutta), 6 June 1978; Marcus Franda, *Ziaur Rahman's Bangladesh Part II: Poverty and Discontent*, American Universities Field Staff Reports 1979.

[2] In fact, Soviet political influence in the entire Persian Gulf area in 1978-79 was far from strong. Moscow had extensive economic and trade relations with the Shah's regime, but very little political clout. In January 1979 Shahpur Bakhtiar accused the Soviet Union and its followers in Iran of fomenting trouble in Iran. Moscow reacted angrily, a *Tass* statement warning that such accusations "can darken substantially the development of relations between Iran and the USSR." *Pravda* saw the "threat of military dictatorship" in Tehran and called Bakhtiar a US agent. A CIA report claimed in February 1979 that clandestine radio stations operating from Soviet territory preached revolution and instructed Iranians on how to organise riots. However, Alfred Wholstetter writing in the *New York Times* in January 1979 on the situation in Iran saw no evidence of Soviet influence on the Iranian political forces.

See *New York Times*, 28 January 1979; *International Herald Tribune*, 6 December 1979; *Tehran Journal*, 18 January 1979; *New York Times*, 22 February 1979; *Pravda*, 19 January 1979; and *Tass*, 15 January 1979.

[3] *New York Times*, 6 January 1980.
[4] *New York Times*, 18 November 1979.
[5] *New York Times*, 16 December 1979.
[6] *Ibid.*
[7] The text of the message can be found in the *New York Times*, 22 January 1980.

"It was the hard, anti-Soviet address that largely reflected Brzezinski's views rather than those of Vance. Said a senior State Department official, 'Brzezinski has finally got his cold war.' Indeed it struck some foreign policy experts as ironic that Brzezinski's longstanding advocacy of a tough line had apparently been vindicated by a crisis that his arguments, his Moscow-baiting and his tilt towards Peking may have helped to cause." *Time* magazine, 4 February 1980.

[8] *New York Times*, 5 January 1980.
[9] *The Nixon Doctrine*, Washington, American Enterprise Institute for Public Policy Research, 1972, p. 58.
[10] *Ibid.*, p. 6.

252 Afghan Syndrome

11. *New York Times*, 28 January 1980.
12. *Hindustan Times*, New Delhi, 6 March 1980.
13. *The Hindu*, Madras, 27 January 1980.
14. *New York Times*, 6 January 1980. For a more detailed exposition of Luttwak's views, see his "After Afghanistan, What?" *Commentary*, New York, April 1980.
15. *New York Times*, 27 January 1980.
16. *Indian Express*, New Delhi, 4 February 1980.
17. *Hindustan Times*, 6 March 1980.
18. *Washington Post*, 8 February 1980.
19. Jimmy Carter's diplomatic efforts to mobilise allies and friends in support of his confrontation policy met with an early setback. The allies, with the sole exception of Britain, refused to cut down on trade with the Soviet Union. There was practically no support for confrontation. At a meeting in Brussels in January 1980, EEC foreign ministers failed to agree on a common line to be taken with regard to the Soviet Union. The only consensus to emerge was a statement condemning the Soviet intervention in Afghanistan and calling for immediate withdrawal of Soviet troops. Mr Carter warned the allies in Rome in June that Europe could not be an island of detente. The *New York Times* asked in an editorial in June "What kind of alliance is this anyway?" The United States, it said, "had always been ambivalent about detente while detente had become a way of life in Western Europe especially in West Germany which had been pursuing it for 11 years." (See also Notes to Chapter Four)
20. *The Hindu*, 2 February 1980. *New York Times*, 6 January 1980.
21. *Guardian*, London, 20 February 1980.
22. *New York Times*, 13 June 1980.
23. *Times of India*, New Delhi, 30 December 1979.
24. *The Hindu*, 1 January 1980.
25. *Tribune*, Chandigarh, January 2 1979.
26. *Times of India*, 1 January 1980.
27. *Indian Express*, 1 January 1980.
28. *Hindustan Times*, 1 January 1980.
29. Bhabani Sen Gupta, "The Necessity of Choice," *Seminar*, New Delhi, No. 246, February 1980.
30. Numerous reports of smallscale help to the Afghan rebels from Pakistan, China, the United States and Iran appeared in the Indian press all through 1979. For a somewhat comprehensive report see *Indian Express*, 10 December 1979. Also, Michael Kaufman's report in *New York Times*, 6 September 1979. (See also Notes to Chapter Two)
31. *Times of India*, 3 January 1980.
32. It was not a formal treaty approved by Congress but an executive agreement. The agreement failed to get Pakistan American military support in the two wars with India in 1965 and 1971. See Stephen P. Cohen, "South Asia and US Military Policy" in Lloyd I. Rudolph and Susanne H. Rudolph (eds.) *The Regional Imperative*, New Delhi, Concept Publishing Company, 1980, pp. 101-124.
33. *New York Times*, 6 January 1980.
34. *New York Times*, 25 February 1980.

35 *APN*, Moscow, 22 and 25 January 1980.
36 *Peoples Daily*, Peking, 1 January 1980.
37 *Ibid.*
38 *Ta Kung Pao*, Hong Kong, 3 January 1980.

CHAPTER TWO

1 Asghar H. Bilgrami, *Afghanistan and British India 1793-1907, A Study in Foreign Relations*, New Delhi, Sterling Publishers, 1972, pp. 201-213. The delicate negotiations, often made extraordinarily difficult by the bellicosity of the press and "public opinion" in Britain and Russia, involved three of the best known British prime ministers—Disraeli, Gladstone and Salisbury.

2 *Ibid.*, pp. 276-278. Also, Bisheshwar Prasad, *The Foundation of India's Foreign Policy, Imperial Era* 1882-1914, Calcutta, Naya Prokash, 1979, pp. 304-306. The buffer concept was rejected by the British-Indian Government and by Afghanistan too.

3 Louis Dupree, *Afghanistan*, Princeton, N.J. Princeton University Press, 1973, also, F. Halliday, "Revolution in Afghanistan," *New Left Review*, (London), November-December 1976.

4 Louis Dupree, "Afghanistan Under the Khalq," *Problems of Communism*, July-August 1979.

5 *Ibid.* The narrative of the Afghan revolution owes a great deal to Dupree's article.

6 On April 28, the Revolutionary Council appointed a 21-member cabinet. None of the 21 denied their Leftist leanings and none had ever expressed loyalty to any country other than Afghanistan. None had ever attended or been invited to attend international Communist meetings. *Ibid.*

7 *Ibid.*

8 *Ibid.*

9 *Strategic Survey 1979*, London, International Institute for Strategic Studies, pp. 32-33.

10 *Ibid.*

11 This summary of events is based on newspaper reports in India, Britain and the United States. The Soviet troops apparently were ordered to keep a low profile. A *Guardian* report by Liz Thurgood printed in *The Hindu* of 30 January 1980, said, "The Red Army has orders to return fire but not to initiate shooting ... The officers believe with what seemed to be a very real sincerity that they are not an occupation army and certainly do not reckon with being the biggest threat since World War II. 'We are here to help a friendly country,' said one. 'This was not an invasion, we cannot understand why the BBC and the Voice of America are saying these things.' They see their roles as saving Afghanistan from Chinese and Pakistani interference."

12 Demchenko's profile of the new Afghan government and the Revolutionary Council makes it clear that the Afghan revolution was what in Marxist-Leninist political theories is called "democratic" though the leadership was firmly in the grasp of communists; both included non-communist nationalists and republicans. Demchenko shed no light on whether Babrak Karmal was in Kabul when the

Soviet troops arrived or whether he was transported by the Soviets. He took some pains, however, to affirm Karmal's revolutionary and patriotic credentials.

13 *Indian Express*, 9 February 1980.

14 *Times of India*, 30 January 1980, 2 February 1980. In a subsequent report in *Times of India* (8 February 1980), Singh wrote: "The feeling that the Afghans have been reduced to the status of second class citizens in their own country hurts deeply. An Afghan military officer told me, 'My weapon has been taken away and I am searched by a 'Shourvi' (Soviet) when I go to my office every day. Most of the day I just drink cups of tea and am assigned no work. The Soviet advisers have taken over, and they take all decisions."

"Communist influence in Afghanistan is confined to a small group of educated persons, particularly university students, while the bulk of the population remain deeply religious. Conscious of the fears of the Muslims about the revolution, the government has launched a campaign to win them over to its side. The government has issued a lengthy message condemning the atrocities committed by the overthrown Amin regime against the notable learned clergy, seeking the cooperation of the Muslim leaders in building a society based on real social justice. It stressed the profoundly national and democratic character of the revolution and described it as a powerful manifestation of the will of 'our Muslim masses to achieve their long-cherished aspirations'. It reminded the people that the Soviet Union had supported the Muslims of the world including the Arabs in their struggle against imperialism and zionism." *Times of India*, 26 January 1980.

"Karmal, though a Marxist, is also a devout Muslim. He has given repeated assurances about his profound respect for the sacred religion of Islam and 'our national customs and traditions'. , ." Tarakki had in the initial days of the revolution shown deep respect for the sentiments of the Muslim masses. He avoided using terms like Marxism and Communism so as to inflame orthodox religious sentiments. However, the programme of socio-economic reforms announced by mid-1978, coupled with the change of colour of the national flag from green to red and the use of the prefix 'comrade' before the names of Afghan leaders, led to the alienation of the majority of Muslims. The Mullahs were upset by many of the reforms such as the ban on usury and on the sale of women for marriage (Hoqmohr) and distribution of land to the tiller. They feared that these reforms would reduce their hold on the masses. Big landlords and moneylenders used the Mullahs to incite their followers against their government. The Mullahs were also helped in their propaganda from across the Afghan borders—from Pakistan, Iran and Saudi Arabia. The government's overreaction in adopting strong arm methods to deal with its opponents further exacerbated Muslim sentiments. Amin purged the government, the party, the army and the administration in general of his rivals and sought to cow down the people into submission through a reign of terror. There is not a single household in Afghanistan, it is said, that escaped the brutal repression by the regime. The task facing Karmal is not an easy one. He must not offend orthodox Muslim sentiments and yet he cannot sacrifice the demands of the revolution for socio-economic reforms. It requires a good deal of tightrope walking. But it needs to be mentioned that of all the three top leaders thrown up by the revolution, Mr Karmal is the best suited for it. . . . He has the reputation of a pragmatist. At 50, he is the youngest of the heads of state since the 1978 revolution. He has charisma. Son of the commander-in-chief of the armed forces of southern Afghanistan and governor of Paktia during the royal regime, Karmal has always managed to temper revolutionary idealism with the needs of a given situation. He was close to King Zahir Shah during his reign. . . . The Parcham faction was therefore nicknamed as the Royal Communist Party of Afghanistan. After Daoud Khan toppled the king and set up a republican regime (1973-78) Karmal, at Moscow's behest, cooperated with his government unlike the Khalq which refused to do so." *Times of India*, 18 February 1980.

[15] According to B.K. Joshi, London correspondent of *Times of India*, British defence experts estimated a month after the Soviet intervention that the level of deployment of forces had achieved Russia's main objective of ensuring that there was no further deterioration in the political situation in Afghanistan. "But the assessments say that the Soviet Union would require double the force if it attempts to subjugate the insurgents operating from Pakistan. They assert that the Soviet presence in the countryside is still tenuous, although their troops are in control of the main towns and lines of communication." *Times of India*, 31 January 1980.

[16] Paval Mezentsed, "Manufactured Issue and the Reality." *New Times*, No. 47, November 1980. This is one of a few accounts from the Soviet side of how Russian and Afghan troops dealt with the Afghan insurgency.

[17] *New York Times* confirmed in February that the CIA had started a covert operation to supply weapons to Afghan rebels. The operations were approved by a special coordination committee chaired by Brzezinski and then by Carter himself. As required by law, seven Congressional committees were informed. It was the largest CIA operation since what it did in Angola in 1975. The rebels were being supplied Soviet designed light infantry weapons obtained from Egypt, China and the underground arms market in Eastern Europe. The weapons were being supplied through Pakistan. Iran too was said to have offered limited quantities of arms to the rebels. Egypt announced that it was training the Afghan rebels and sending them back with weapons. *The Hindu*, 17 February 1980.

[18] Demchenko in *International Affairs*, Note No. 12.

[19] *Times of India*, 5 February 1980.

[20] *New Times*, No. 5, February 1980.

[21] There was a spate of reports in the world press about the exploits and fortunes of the Afghan rebels, most of them proven fanciful in various degrees. There was no doubt stubborn and protracted resistance in several provinces, especially in the region close to the Iranian border. But from the beginning of the intervention it was clear that sooner rather than later the Soviet troops would bring the insurgency under control. The rebels had no unifying political programme, nor political leadership. Afghanistan could not be a Vietnam for the Soviet Union. For more sober appraisal of the rebel situation, see the *Christian Science Monitor*, 12 July 1980; Peter Niesewand's report in the *Guardian Weekly*, 4 January 1981; Ian Hamel's report in *Le Monde*, 12 November 1980. While Hamel found the insurgency on the verge of collaspe, Niesewand focussed more on the Soviet's military problems in Afghanistan, giving the impression that the insurgency, though no threat to the Soviet control of Afghanistan, would still be a nagging problem of attrition. The Soviets, on the other hand, appeared by October 1980 to be sanguine that the insurgency was no longer the main problem in Afghanistan;

the main problem was Pakistan's and Iran's refusal to normalise relations with the pro Soviet communist regime in Kabul. See Mikhail Ilynsky, "The Revolution Forges Ahead," *New Times*, No. 52, December 1980. See also Zalmay Khalilzad, "Soviet occupied Afghanistan," *Problems of Communism*, November-December 1980.

22*New York Times*, 13 January 1980.

23When the next Islamic summit was held in Saudi Arabia in January 1981, the Afghan rebels practically ceased to be a political factor in a negotiated political settlement of the Afghan crisis.

24Rakshat Puri in *Hindustan Times*, 6 January 1980. This point was made by the writer of this volume at a seminar on the Soviet intervention in Afghanistan he took at the Institute of Defence Studies and Analyses, New Delhi, on January 3, 1980.

25*Guardian*, 24 February 1980.

26For the most revealing account of the Baluchi rebellion against Pakistani rule, see Selig S Harrison, "Nightmare in Baluchistan," *Foreign Policy*, Fall, 1978; for a detailed account of the Baluchi nationalist movement, see Inayatullah Baloch "Afghanistan-Pashtunistan-Baluchistan," *German Foreign Affairs Review*, Hamburg, Vol. 31, 3rd Quarter, 1980.

27*The Statesman*, New Delhi, 7 February, 1980.

28As reported in *Times of India*, 12 February 1980 and *Indian Express*, 12 February 1980. In April, the Associated Press reported that Pakistan was forming a new army corps in Baluchistan and described this decision as "the biggest defensive military step" taken in Pakistan since the Soviet intervention in Afghanistan, *Amrita Bazar Patrika*, Calcutta, 25 April 1980.

CHAPTER THREE

1Henry Kissinger, *The White House Years*, New Delhi, Vikas Publishing House, 1979, p. 114.

2*The Department of State Bulletin*, Washington DC, July 3, 1967. Brzezinski who was then a member of the Policy Planning Division of the Department of State saw evidence of the USSR's lack of global power in its inability to defend its interests "even in an area of its regional predominance—in Berlin. ... It had no military capacity to fight in Cuba, or in Vietnam, or to protect its interests in the Congo." Brzezinski foresaw that the "paramountcy" of American military power would end in the 1970s.

3Richard P. Stebbins and Elaine P. Adam (eds), *American Foreign Relations 1975: A Documentary Record*, New York, New York University Press, 1977, pp. 561-62. Kissinger was briefing U S. ambassadors at a meeting in London in December 1975.

4*Ibid*. Helmut Sonnenfeldt, Counsellor of the State Department, and a long-time Kissinger aide, evoked a noisy controversy with his remark at the same meeting that the United States must "strive for an evolution that makes the relationship between the East Europeans and the Soviet Union an organic one," avoiding "any excess of zeal" but "responding to the clearly visible aspirations in Eastern Europe for a more autonomous existence within the context of strong

Soviet geopolitical interest." This was the reverse of containment. The observations were taken by Kissinger's critics to reflect his thinking on the emerging pattern of Soviet-US relationship. *Ibid.*, pp. 565-569.

5. *The White House Years*, pp. 129-30, Kissinger realised that it would not be easy to "sell" linkage to Moscow, nor even to the US. "Linkage, however, is not a natural concept for Americans, who have traditionally perceived foreign policy as an episodic enterprise. Our bureaucratic organizations, divided into regional and function bureaus, and indeed our academic tradition of specialization compound the tendency to compartmentalize. American pragmatism produces a penchant for examining issues separately: to solve problems on their merits, without a sense of time or context or of the seamless web of reality. And the American legal tradition encourages rigid attention to the 'facts of the case,' a distrust of abstractions."

6. *Time*, 14 January 1980.

7. The Soviets take a dialectical view of detente, that is, normal relations between nations with different social and political systems, and "the battle of ideas" and "social forces"; the two must go together. For a recent exposition of the Soviet perspective of detente, see N. Kapchenko, "Socialist Foreign Policy and the Struggle of Ideas," *International Affairs*, No. 9, 1980.

8. *Time*, 14 January 1980,

9. *New York Times*, 20 and 26 January and 3 February 1980.

10. Stanley Hoffman, "A View at Home: The Perils of Incoherence," *Foreign Affairs*, Special Number: America and the World, 1978.

11. *New York Times*, editorial, 1 June 1980: US exports to the third world has tripled since 1975. Agricultural products constitute over 20 per cent of all US exports and the great bulk of US grain exports go to the communist countries and non-communist developing nations, *Time*, 21 January 1980.

12. "The Perils of Incoherence," Note No. 10.

13. *New York Times*, 3 February 1980, Winston Lord, president, Council on Foreign Relations, and a former head of the State Department's Policy Planning Division, observed, "In the near-term, the emphasis has to be on building up our strength. But we've got to find a way to keep the world from blowing up and that means you can't throw all the co-operative elements of Soviet American relationship out of the window." *Ibid.* "1½ wars" means a major nuclear war and a local war in the third world at the same time.

14. *New York Times*, 2 February 1980.

15. *Newsweek*, 12 June 1978.

16. *New York Times*, 2 February and 1 June 1980. It should be noted that of the $ 44 billion of total aid given by the US to developing nations since 1945, $ 22 billion in principal and interest had been repaid by 1978. The great bulk of the aid money had been spent by the recipient nations buying goods and services in the United States. See *New York Times* editorial, 1 June 1980.

17. *Newsweek*, 12 June 1978.

18. *Ibid.*

19. *Ibid.* Brzezinski was quoted by *Newsweek* to have made this observation on US-Soviet relationship: "The public interprets detente as total accommodation. (But it) must understand that this is a long-haul relationship, and not swing back

and forth between euphoria and belligerency. If you bear in mind the nature of the relationship, one is not so optimistic about grand solutions and not so pessimistic about grand failures."

20 *Time*, 14 January 1980.

21 *Newsweek*, 11 December 1978. Kissinger told *Time* magazine in May 1980, "The absolute imperative to get across to the Soviet Union is that their definition of detente is simply not acceptable. Their definition of detente is to be permitted to defeat us peacefully. They either have to accept that they cannot undertake a geopolitical offensive, or they have to give up detente. They have to make a choice. ... I would tell the Soviets that there will be no talks in economic and arms control areas until there is progress towards agreed restraint in international conduct." *Time*, 12 May 1980.

22 How quickly, almost instantly, the self-image of the US changed in 1979 is vividly illustrated on the columns of *Newsweek*. It reported in its issue of February 9, "For all his problems, Carter enjoyed some geopolitical advantages. The superpower rivalry—seen in the Nixton-Kissinger era as a 'triangular' relationship—more closely resembles a 'V'. The growing hostility between Moscow and Peking has removed the third side of the triangle, while Washington—the only superpower having normal relations with the other two—controls the point of the 'V'. Thus, the US is in a favourable position to play off Moscow and Peking against each other—or to get along with both." On February 26, *Newsweek* had this to say about the US position in world politics: "Only a few months ago, (Carter's) fortunes had ticked upward after the Camp David triumph, the breakthrough to China and the prospect of a second-stage strategic arms limitation agreement (SALT-II) with the Soviet Union. Now the Mideast peace process had stalled, and a valued ally, the Shah of Iran, had fallen. A SALT pact was still within reach—but ratification by the Senate seemed chancy. And the new relationship with China backfired when Peking launched a massive incursion into Vietnam late last week. Even a fight between Communists could turn out badly for Carter if the Russians intervened to support their Vietnamese allies. And with its new Chinese friends on the warpath, the US could hardly demand good behaviour from Moscow in any world trouble spot."

23 *Newsweek*, 5 March 1979.
24 *Newsweek*, 11 December 1978.
25 *New York Times*, 16 and 23 December 1979.
26 *New York Times*, 28 September 1979.
27 *New York Times News Service, The Hindu*, 17 February 1980.
28 *Ibid*.
29 *Ibid*.
30 *Ibid*.
31 *Ibid*.
32 Interview with *New York Times*, 6 March 1980.

CHAPTER FOUR

1. V. Gaurilov, "The Soviet Union and the System of International Relations," *Mirovaya Ekonomika i Mezhdunarodnye Otnosheniia*, No. 12, 1972; V. Gantman, "A Policy that is Transforming the World," *Kommunist*, No. 7, signed to press, 8 May 1973; Bhabani Sen Gupta, *Soviet-Asian Relations in the 1970s and Beyond*, New York, Praeger Special Studies, 1976, Chapter 1. The Soviet world-view in the current period perceives "a kind of bipolarity" between the USSR and the US because of the exclusive strategic relationship. The US no longer occupies the pivotal place in Soviet foreign policy in view of the changed correlation of forces within the capitalist system. See also E. Shershnev, *On the Principle of Mutual Advantage: Soviet American Economic Relations*, Moscow, Progress Publishers, 1978.

2. This is all the more so because the great majority of Sovietologists in the US are men and women of Slavic origin when they are not refugees from the USSR and Eastern Europe.

3. The USSR extends from the Baltic Sea to the Pacific Ocean, 3000 miles from north to south. It is the world's largest country. Its GNP grew in the 1970-75 period by 3.8 per cent annually, but has since slowed down. It has a labour force larger than the entire Western community put together with largescale utilisation of women in industry, some 50 million women, 51 per cent of the total, being in paid employment in 1974. Per capita consumption rate has been growing at 3.5 per cent a year. Thirty per cent of the GNP goes to investment, much larger than in the US. In productivity, the USSR "has nowhere to go but up . . ." Abram Bergson, "Soviet Economic Slowdown," *Challenge*, vol. 20, No. 6, January-February 1978; David Lane, *The Socialist Industrial State*, London, George Allen & Unwin, 1976, p. 195; J. Wilezynski, *The Economics of Socialism*, London, Allen & Unwin, 1977, Chapter 8.

In January 1981 the Central Statistical Board of the Soviet Union reported on the economic performance of the 10th Five Year Plan 1975-80. The national income extended by 16 billion roubles in 1980 over 1979 to exceed the sum of 45 billion roubles (in real terms). Three quarters of the income went for consumption. Four-fifths of the national income were invested in housing, social and cultural development. Industrial output rose in value to 627 billion roubles and agricultural output to 121 billion roubles. The volume of foreign trade, the bulk of which is with the socialist countries, reached almost 92 billion roubles. The 1980 industrial plan was fulfilled by all the constituent republics. Compared to 1979, production in 1980 rose by 3.6 per cent. As many as 240 large industrial enterprises went into operation in 1980.

The total grain crop amounted to 189.2 million tons or 10 million tons more than in 1979. A record harvest of raw cotton, 9.96 million tons was obtained. Real per capita income increased by 3.5 per cent. *New Times*, No. 5, January 1981.

4. Contrary to popular impression, Soviet agriculture has made impressive gains in the post-war period. Farm output has increased $2\frac{1}{2}$ times between 1950 and 1977— an annual growth of 3.5 per cent, almost double the rate of growth in the US. Massive investments have been made in agriculture, $ 78 billion in inputs and resources, compared to $ 10.5 billion in the US. Total productivity in agri-

culture in the 1951-77 period grew at the rate of 1.2 per cent per annum as against 1.6 per cent in the US. The Soviets import large quantities of grain because they use wheat for animal feed. During the period 1971-72 to 1975-76, wheat feed constituted 34 million tons per year or 37 per cent of total wheat consumption in the USSR. These achievements have to be seen in the context of the heavy geo-climatic constraints under which agricultural operations have to be performed. Weather fluctuations can make more than 50 per cent difference in output. Only 10 per cent of the total area of the USSR has sufficient moisture and adequate heat supply for all crops. According to an American expert, "the 1981-85 average grain output target of 238-243 million tons appears attainable if weather is not exceptionally unfavourable and if planned resources are made available." Another less optimistic US expert says Soviet grain output may not exceed 235 million tons for 1985. *Soviet Economy in a Time of Change*: A Compendium of Papers submitted to the Joint Economic Committee, US Congress, Washington DC, US Government Printing Office, 1979, vols. 1 and 11. The compendium contains six papers on Soviet agriculture.

[5] A Harvard study of Soviet citizen behaviour says that Russians expect their leaders "to be the main source of initiative in the inauguration of general plans and programmes and with provision of guidance and organisation for their attainment. The Russians do not seem to expect initiative, directness and organizedness from an average individual." Russians are "passively accommodative to the apparent hard facts of situations," and are less problem-solving oriented than Americans. Alex Inkeles, Eugenia Hanfmann and Helen Beier, "Model Personality and Adjustment to the Soviet Sociopolitical System" in Alex Inkeles (Ed.), *Social Change in Soviet Russia*, Cambridge, Mass. Harvard University Press, 1968, pp. 115-122. Also Z. Gitelman, "Soviet Political Culture: Insights for Jewish Emigres," *Soviet Studies*, vol. 29, No. 4, 1977.

[6] Several US Sovietologists discount the possibility of an Islamic revolt in the Soviet Union. Richard Pipes, of Harvard, a hawk, observed at the height of the Afghan crisis, "I don't see fear of violence on the part of Moslems of Soviet Central Asia. It is a subject on which I have worked for a long time. There is no evidence that they are restless; they are under thorough control. *New York Times*, 10 February 1980.

[7] *Time*, 23 June 1980.

[8] Roy A. Medvedev and Zhores A. Medvedev have discounted the theory that an intense power struggle led to the resignation of Khruschev in 1964. From their *Khruschev: The Years in Power*, New York, Columbia University Press, 1976, it seems that Khruschev had to quit because his policies had gone wrong. The resignation of Kosygin in 1980 drew from Brezhnev a public tribute to his services to the USSR, a departure from norm. It seems that US and West European experts are too eager to discover "power struggle" in any personnel shift at the top levels of the Soviet hierarchy. The fact that Brezhnev paid tributes to Kosygin a day or two *after* his resignation was accepted by the politbureau was interpreted in the West as his initial "reluctance" to do so. When *Pravda* announced on November 18, 1978 the resignation of Kiril Mazurov, a politbureau member for ten years "because of health and at his own request," Western media and specialists at once smelt a power struggle for the reason that Mazurov was not *known* to be in failing health. It is, however, the norm in the Soviet Union not to publicise

personal affairs of public men.

[9]Jerry F. Hough, "The Generation Gap and the Brezhnev Succession," *Problems of Communism*, July-August 1979; Jane P. Shapiro, "The Soviet Leadership Enters the 1980s," *Current History*, October 1980. According to Miss Shapiro, the next generation of Soviet leaders were born in the decade after the revolution; experienced the Great Purge as children of victimised fathers; are far better educated ("virtually all have graduated from a post-secondary institute or a university"); have had years of training and experience in industry or agriculture; have had several years of ideological schooling but are, at least on the surface, less ideologically oriented; have had greater contact with Westerners; and came to political maturity in the 1950s as the Soviet Union rebuilt itself as a leading world power and subsequently as one of the world's superpowers. See also Jerry F. Hough. *The Soviet Prefects*, Cambridge, Mass. Harvard University Press, 1969; "The Brezhnev Era: The Man and the System," *Problems of Communism*, May-June 1970; T.H. Rigby, "The Soviet Leadership: Towards a Self-stabilising Oligarchy," *Soviet Studies*, October 1970.

[10]A surfeit of studies exist on the state of the armed strength of the USSR. The most reliable annual surveys are issued by the International Institute of Strategic Studies, London. *Military Balance* offers inventories of armed forces of all nations, giving the pride of place to the US and the USSR; *Strategic Survey* analyses the developments, trends and processes in international strategic relations. For short but reliable accounts of Soviet strategic and conventional military power, see the following recent Adelphi Papers published by the IISI: *The Future of Strategic Deterrence*, Part I and II, (1980); *New Conventional Weapons and East-West Security*, Part I and II, (1978); *The Future of Land-based Missile Forces* (1977) *and Sea Power and Western Security: The Next Decade* (1977).

Soviet defence expenditure is a controversial issue. According to the German specialist, W.T. Lee, the Soviet defence budget for 1979 came to $ 116-162 billion, leaving a wide margin of speculation. The CIA put the dollar equivalent of the 1979 Soviet military budget at $ 165 billion. A Chinese estimate placed it at 102 billion roubles, while the Soviets themselves said that their defence budget amounted to 17.2 billion roubles (83 (US) Cents=1 rouble). Lee says Soviet defence expenditure has been growing since 1970 (price base) at an annual rate of 8-10 per cent; the CIA estimate is 4.5 per cent; the Chinese estimate is 8.26 per cent. Lee calculates that defence claims 14-15 per cent of the Soviet GNP; CIA says it is 11-13 per cent; the Chinese claim that it is above 15 per cent. *The Military Balance* 1980-81, IISS, London, page 13. An American economist, Victor Perlo, describes the CIA estimate of the Soviets' 1981 defence budget as "misleading and heavily biased" against the USSR. The Soviet defence allocation for 1981, according to Moscow, is $ 25.4 billion, and the U.S. allocation is $ 174.4 billion. *Times of India*, 15 February 1981.

The Soviets put their 1968-80 defence expenditure at 227.2 billion roubles or about $ 378 billion as against $ 1174.9 billion for the United States. The Soviets also claim that their defence spending in 1980 amounted to 17.1 billion roubles and is planned at 17.05 billion roubles in 1981, that is about one-sixth of the US military budgets for these two years. *New Times*, No. 5, January 1981.

[11]Cost comparisons between US and Soviet weapons indicate that the Soviets can produce tanks at about 50 per cent less cost than the Americans and jet

engines at more than 60 per cent less. Lower costs generated by Soviet design process are likely to prevail across a large variety of equipment, especially when based on mature technologies. Arthur J. Alexander, *Decision-Making in Soviet Weapons Procurement*, Adelphi Paper No. 148, IISS, 1978-79, p. 63.

12 Clarence A. Robinson, Jr. "Soviets Push for Beam Weapons", *Aviation Week and Space Technology*, 2 May 1977; David Holloway "Technology and Political Decision in Soviet Armaments Policy," *Journal of Peace Research*, No. 4, 1976; Nicholas Daniloff, *The Kremlin and the Cosmos*, New York, Alfred A. Kropf, 1972. There are several Rand Corporation Studies dealing with technological developments relevant to charged-particle beam research in the USSR. Alexander (No. 11) notes that a "key role in the Soviet military R & D has been given to design bureaux and their chief designers . . . .With their responsibilities designers possess a degree of autonomy in running their organisations uncommon in the Soviet Union" (pp. 23-24). A US government review identified "hundreds of laboratories and thousands of top scientists" working on the technology necessary to produce high-energy beams. Robinson, p. 21.

In naval armaments, "The outlook is one of a diminishing American technological lead but prevailing American advantage over the next decade, in the absence of deliberate cooperation in the West with Soviet technological aims." Worth H. Bagley, *Sea Power and Western Security: The Next Decade*, Adelphi Paper No. 139, IISS, 1977, p. 34. See also *Military Balance 1980-81*, IISS, pp. 3-4.

13 The Soviets affirm that they have no military doctrine of nuclear war and that Soviet military doctrine is not geared to a strategy of fighting and winning a limited nuclear war. At the same time, Soviet spokesmen leave no doubt in anyone's mind that the USSR will not allow the US to upset the present balance of strategic forces in America's favour. See Lt. Gen. Mikhail Milshtein's interview to *International Herald Tribune*, August 28, 1980. General Milshtein said, "the Soviet Union will never permit parity to be upset," and added, "If anyone thinks the United States can inflict irreparable losses on the Soviet Union and avoid such irreparable losses itself, he is under the deepest illusion."

14 Between 1946 and 1975, the United States employed its armed forces in 215 incidents *for political purposes*; which works out at 7.2 incidents per year; only three of these actions took place in South Asia, all related to wars between India and its neighbours. Seventythree of these 215 incidents involved the Soviet Union, 30 China, and 25 Cuba. While 92 actions involved Europe between 1946 and 1955, the gravity of the use of force without war shifted to the third world since the mid-fifties. "As the Soviets gained in nuclear strength relative to the United States, especially after the mid-1960s, the United States employed its armed forces less frequently for political objectives." Barry M. Blechman and Stephen S. Kaplan, *Force Without War; US Armed Forces as a Political Instrument*, DC, The Brookings Institute, 1978, Chapter 2.

Blechman and Kaplan wrote in 1977: "One conclusion that runs counter to presently prevailing views concerns the effect of the US-Soviet strategic nuclear balance on the relative fortunes of the super-powers. We did not find, as is often maintained, that the United States became less successful in the use of armed forces for political objectives as the Soviet Union closed the US lead in strategic nuclear weapons. Soviet political and/or military involvement in an incident, on the other hand, was of great significance. Outcomes tended to be less favourable from the US perspective when the Soviet Union was involved in an incident. Outcomes were particularly less favourable when the Soviet Union threatened to, or actually employed, her own armed forces in the incident. Interestingly, this finding pertained more to the short term (six-month) success rate than to the longer term outcomes." "Armed Forces as Political Instruments." *Survival*, July-August 1977.

15Burma, Guyana and Mozambique are reported to have begun to distance themselves from the USSR. *Time*, 23 February 1981.

16For Soviet view of states like Angola, Ethiopia and Yemen, see V.Y. Chirkin and Y.A. Yudin, *A Socialist-Oriented State: Instrument of Revolutionary Change*, Moscow, Progress Publishers, 1978.

17*Hindustan Times*, 9 December 1980. This was the first time since the emergence of the triangular relationship that a Chinese leader publicly threatened to use China's Soviet card.

In an interview given to Earl W. Foek (ed.), *Christian Science Monitor* in December 1980, Deng spelt out the basic requirements of Sino-Soviet rapprochment. "The Soviet Union must do something real in order to show that it has changed its strategy, that it has given up hegemonism. For instance, it must reduce its troop levels along the Sino-Soviet border from one million men at least to the level of Khruschev's time. It must withdraw its troops from Mongolia, Afghanistan, from Southeast Asia. If the Soviet Union is able to do all the things I've mentioned, then from tomorrow . . . there will be an improvement in our relations." *The Hindu*, 26 December 1980.

18The 34th CMEA session, held in Prague in June 1980, was attended, from outside the Soviet bloc countries, by Yugoslavia, Laos, Angola, Afghanistan, Yemen, Mozambique, Ethiopia, Vietnam and Kampuchea. Afghanistan was given an observer status. The session "gave a positive assessment of the implementation of agreements on cooperation between the CMEA on the one hand and Yugoslavia, Finland and Mexico on the other." Over the 1971-1980 period the national income of the CMEA countries "will grow, according to preliminary estimates, by almost 70 per cent, while industrial production is to rise by 90 per cent and the volume of trade will increase fourfold and top, for the first time ever, the 200,000 million rouble mark (one rouble=83 (US) cents)." Y. Shiryaev, "The Coordinated Strategy of Cooperation for the 1980s," *International Affairs*, No. 9, 1980.

The prolonged workers' and peasants' agitation in Poland in 1980-81 dramatised the problems the country faced as a result of rapid industrialisation without streamlining the political system. However, both in Western Europe and the Soviet Union, as well as in the United States, there was no visible wish to let the Polish situation boil up to a level at which Soviet military intervention would be inevitable. By March 1981 the situation in Poland seemed to have been brought under control. Successive changes in the top personnel of the government indicated an attempt to narrow, if not bridge, the gulf between the regime and the people. The Polish turmoil, kept within limits, should lead to significant change in Polish and perhaps East European communism.

19*Times of India*, 9 December 1981.

20Bhabani Sen Gupta, *Soviet Asian Relations in the 1970s and Beyond*, Note No. 1, pp. 15-18. Also, V. Li, "The Newly-Free Countries' Problems of Social and Political Development," *International Affairs*, No. 11, November 1980.

[21]M.K. Bunkina, *USA versus Western Europe: New Trends*, Moscow, Progress Publishers, 1979, pp. 176-186.

Detente in Europe has now an infrastructure of political accords and mutual economic advantages. It is therefore a stable trend. It is not yet a stable process because the division of Europe between the NATO and Warsaw Pacts towers over the infrastructure of detente, while political turmoil in Eastern Europe, such as the 1980-81 turbulances in Poland, strains European detente, sometime threatening to dislocate, if not dismantle, the infrastructure. On the other hand, the detente infrastructure will be stronger if the natural gas agreements now in the pipeline are fully implemented. The delicate task before Soviet foreign policy decision-makers is to preserve and strengthen European detente, defend the socialist system in Eastern Europe from internal turmoil and external pressure, and blunt American confrontation. For the West European governments, the no less complex foreign policy task is to protect and steadily build on detente, limit the superpower confrontation, and, at the same time, stem any sharp increase in the Soviet Union's global power and influence.

Trade between Western Europe and the Soviet bloc came to a hefty $ 15.8 billion in 1978. (*Time*, 30 June 1980). The Soviet Union's own trade with the major West European countries in 1979 were: Germany—exports $ 2.8 billion, imports $ 3 billion; Italy, exports $ 8.9 billion, imports $ 1.7 billion; France, exports $ 1.8 billion, imports $ 1.6 billion; Britain, exports $ 1.4 billion, imports $ .75 billion. Percentagewise, however, the trade was not very significant for the European countries—2.2 per cent for Germany, 1.9 per cent for France, 2 per cent for Italy and 1.1 per cent for Britain. Americans argue that Western Europe can live without trade with the Soviet bloc. Secretary of State Cyrus Vance warned the allies in March 1980 that it would be shortsighted and dangerous for them to seek to enjoy the benefits of detente while leaving the task of deterring the Soviet Union to the United States. West Europeans, however, do not object to deterrence, but to confrontation and cold war. "In crisis situations one must both talk to the other side and listen to what they have to say so that crisis are blunted rather than sharpened," observed Chancellor Schimdt in February 1980. The Europeans did not join in Carter's economic sanctions against the USSR. Three months after the imposition, *Time* magazine reported that the sanctions did not really hurt the Soviet Union. Official American sources conceded that Moscow could buy at least six million tons from non-American grain exporters; unofficial experts put the figure at 11 million tons. The largest single new grain supplier to the Soviet Union was Argentina which signed a long-term agreement with Moscow in July 1980 to export 22.5 million tons of corn, sorghum and soyabean in the next five years. The *New York Times* reported in June 1980 "No division within the alliance is more critical or deeprooted than that over how to deal with the Soviet Union." The *Observer* said in July, "The strengthening of trade links with the communist bloc during a decade of Ostopolitik, the importance for Germans of the flow of millions of West German visitors to East Germany each year are developments that often get overlooked by Washington. The difference between Bonn and Washington may be only a matter of approach, but it is beginning to get structural." *The Observer*, 24 July 1980; *New York Times*, 22 June 1980; *Ibid*,

July 18, 1980; *Observer* Service, *Amrita Bazar Patrika*, 25 February 1980; *New York Times*, 27 January 1980; *The Hindu*, 5 March and 8 June 1980; *International Herald Tribune* News and Feature Service, *Times of India*, 21 July 1980.

22V. Abarenkov, "US Policy: Escalating the Arms Race and Aggravating the World Situation," *International Affairs*, No. 11, November 1980; A. Matveyev, "Who is Generating Tension in Southeast Asia?" *International Affairs*, No. 10, October 1980; N. Vasin, "Iran and US Imperialism," *International Affairs*, No. 5, May 1980; L. Medvedko, "The Persian Gulf: A Revival of Gunboat Diplomacy," *International Affairs*, No. 12, December 1980.

23*Indian Express*, 9 December 1980.

24*Time*, 23 June 1980.

25*Ibid*. "For the Soviet Union (her specific concern to curb American military potential apart), the purpose of bilateral detente with the United States is political; she wishes to be recognised by the leading world power as the equal co-manager of international affairs." Bertram Christoph in his Introduction to *The Future of Arms Control: Part I*, Adelphi Paper No. 141, 1978, p. 3.

CHAPTER FIVE

1Louis Dupree, "Afghanistan Under the Khalq," *Problems of Communism*, July-August, 1979. Dupree, one of the most knowledgeable scholars on Afghanistan, believed, while writing this article in the summer of 1979, that the Soviets would not intervene in Afghanistan with military force. Also, *New York Times*, 23 March 1979.

2*Ibid*. Also, Louis Dupree, "USAID and Social Scientists Discuss Afghanistan's Development Prospects," American Universities Field Staff *Reports*, Vol. XXI, No. 2, April 1977.

Business Week, New York, in its issue of 29 September 1980, however, suggested that "hunger for Afghanistan's important and strategic minerals was an incentive for the Soviet invasion and attempt to annex Kabul to the Soviet bloc." This analysis argued that the April 1978 "coup" was designed to halt Daoud's move to weaken Afghanistan's economic linkages with the USSR. In 1977 Soviet experts made a geological study of Afghanistan showing substantial deposits of copper, oil, gas, barite, bauxite, beryl, iron ore, fluorspat, coal and chrome ore. According to *Business Week*, this study has been translated by the UN Development Programme.

3Dupree, Note No. 1.

4*Times of India*, 8 January 1980.

5*Indian Express*, 28 December 1979.

6*The Statesman* (New Delhi), 26 January 1980.

7The theme that the US reneged on accords solemnly arrived at occurred repeatedly in Soviet formulations, especially after Carter formally asked for indefinite postponement of the Senate consideration of the SALT-II treaty. In this connection, the observation of Cyrus Vance, Carter's Secretary of State till 1980, on the Soviet record on compliance with agreements formally reached merits to be cited. Interviewed by *Time* magazine in April 1978, Vance said, "The Soviets are tough negotiators. They strike a very hard bargain. They have very clearly in their minds what their self-interests are, and they will doggedly pursue those interests. Negotiating with the Soviet Union is a sometimes frustrating experience, but at the end of the road, when you reach an agreement, they stick to their bargains. In the past, we've reached an agreement with them in which other parties are involved and one of their friends moved away from the bargains we had reached. I brought this to the attention of the Soviets and within hours, in the middle of the night, they corrected the situation, saying, our reputation is behind that agreement, this is unacceptable, and the situation was straightened out by the next morning." *Time*, 24 April 1978.

[8] In accusing Jimmy Carter of using the Afghan crisis to strike a tough anti-Soviet posture in order to influence the US electorate, the Soviets were in the company of Carter's opponents like Senator Edward Kennedy and Senator Anderson. Readers should note the use of the phrase "most reactionary circles" in the *Pravda* commentary. Contemporary Soviet analyses of US affairs make a distinction between "reasonable" and "reactionary" elements in the US foreign policy elite. Among the "reasonable" Soviet analysts place many conservatives too. By "reactionary", Soviet analysts generally identify the hard core of the military-industrial-academic complex.

[9] *Guardian*, 29 January 1980. Several politbureau members took up the cudgels to defend the Soviet action in Afghanistan. One of them, Kirilenko, declared on February 20 that the US Government was adopting a "militarist and hegemonist policy of force and diktat." The Soviet Union would upgrade its defence capability to counter "any aggressor wherever it might brandish its sword against us." *Times of India*, 21 February 1980.

The Soviet ambassador to Japan, Polyanski, disclosed that "three successive Afghan governments had sought Soviet military aid to quell rebellion on 14 occasions. But we decided to step in only when the Afghan revolution was in danger of being disrupted by outside forces." *Indian Express*, 6 March 1980.

The Soviets quietly ignored Carter's February 28 deadline for withdrawal of Russian troops from Afghanistan. On that date there were 1,00,000 Soviet troops in Afghanistan. *Indian Express*, 21 February 1980.

[10] *Pravda*, 23 February 1980; *New York Times*, 23 February 1980; *Times of India*, 23 February 1980. The entire text of Brezhnev's interview was printed in the *Indian Express* by the Soviet embassy in New Delhi as a "sponsored feature."

[11] *Hindustan Times*, 23 February 1980.

[12] *Ibid*. The Soviet leaders were making their own election speeches as election to the Supreme Soviet took place in February.

[13] *Pravda*, 9 March 1980.

[14] *Times of India*, 8 March 1980.

[15] *The Hindu*, 13 February 1980.

[16] *Times of India*, 9 February 1980.

[17] *Times of India*, 22 January 1980.

[18] *Indian Express*, 10 February 1980.

[19] *Indian Express*, 23 January 1980.

[20] *Ibid*.

[21] *New York Times*, 9 December 1979.

[22] *Ibid*.

23 *Ibid.* US intelligence reports said that the USSR were mobilising 1,00,000 troops for exercises northwest of Iran. A State Department spokesman, however, added that there was no indication "at present" that these forces were being put together for an intervention in Iran. *Indian Express*, 10 February 1980.

24 *International Herald Tribune*, 6 March 1980.

25 *New Times*, No. 32, August 1980. For a deeper understanding of the Western view of Soviet policy towards Iran, see Shahram Chubin, *Soviet Policy Towards Iran and the Gulf*, Adelphi Papers No. 157, London, International Institute of Strategic Studies. Spring 1980.

26 *Times of India*, 12 January 1980.

27 *Indian Express*, 2 February 1980.

28 *The Times*, 16 February 1980.

29 *Times of India*, 6 March 1980.

30 *Indian Express*, 9 March 1980.

31 *Times of India*, 8 March 1980.

32 *The Hindu*, 11 April 1980. Earlier, in February, Karmal told Kuldip Nayar that it was neither possible nor necessary to set any time limit for the withdrawal of Soviet forces from his country. "They are here to consolidate the gains of our revolution, protect our land and secure peace in the region," he said. "As long as there are dangers from outside, the Russians will stay." Karmal alleged that there was a joint plot by the Americans, the Chinese and the Pakistanis to attack Afghanistan on January 6. "But the Russian forces which arrived on December 27 foiled the plot." *Indian Express*, 9 February 1980.

33 *Indian Express*, 16 April 1980; *New Times*, No. 18, May 1980.

34 *Indian Express*, 25 February 1980; *Hindustan Times*, 29 February and 24 March 1980.

35 *Indian Express*, 26 February 1980.

An Associated Press report said that the Karmal government "has virtually broken down." Nearly all stores except those selling perishable goods remained closed for five days. About 300 civilians and an unknown number of Soviet and Afghan troops were killed in street battles, according to Pakistani sources. *Tass*, quoting Kabul reports, blamed the disturbances on the US, China, Pakistan and Egypt. Kabul and Moscow reports said that hundreds of civilians helped Russian and Afghan troops restore order. *Indian Express*, 26 February 1980. The Soviet stand on Afghanistan seemed to have hardened as a result of the Kabul disturbances, *The Hindu*, 26 February 1980.

36 *The Hindu*, 26 February 1980.

37 *Times of India*, 27 February 1980.

38 *Ibid.*

39 *Ibid.*

40 *Times of India*, editorial, 16 June 1980.

41 *Times of India*, 12 July 1980.

42 *Times of India*, 2 July 1980.

43 *Times of India*, 20 July 1980.

44 *Times of India*, 5 July 1980.

45 *Time*, 25 August 1980.

46 The Soviets stoutly proclaimed the "proletarian internationalism" aspect of

their Afghan intervention; it was clearly and explicitly aimed at securing a Marxist-led revolution from capitalist-imperialist subversion. The Afghans used to be "friends", now they were "brothers." This line of defence was particularly projected to rebut criticism from several West European communist parties, notably the Communist Party of Italy. See A. Ulansky, "Old Friends, Brothers Today," *New Times*, No. 43, October 1980.

CHAPTER SIX

[1] *Indian Express*, 13 January 1980.

[2] See the author's "The Necessity of Choice," in *Seminar* (New Delhi, No. 246, February 1980).

[3] See the author's "South Asia and the Great Powers," in William E. Griffith (ed.), *The World and the Great Power Triangles*, Cambridge, Mass., MIT Press, 1975, pp. 225-231.

[4] "The Necessity of Choice," Note No. 2.

[5] *The Hindu*, 20 January 1980.

[6] *Ibid.*

[7] *Indian Express*, 30 January 1980.

[8] *The Hindu*, 31 January 1980.

[9] *Indian Express*, 1 February 1980; *Hindustan Times*, 1 February 1980. "The dialogue—which was more in the nature of a monologue, with Mrs Gandhi talking at a stretch for more than half an hour after Mr Clifford had repeated his set speech—was not intended to bridge the gap and bring the two countries together to embark on any joint action." *The Hindu*, 1 February 1980.

[10] According to the *Los Angeles Times*, Clifford outlined the American position in some of the strongest language yet. "They (the Russians) must know that if they head for the Persian Gulf, that means war. If there is any temptation to go to Pakistan, then that will also bring grave difficulties." With regard to India's fears about the use of arms supplied to Pakistan, Clifford said, "We intend to be present, we will be there to ascertain that the arms are used in the way they are intended. I assume there would be military advisers." *Indian Express*, 2 February 1980

[11] *Times of India*, 23 January 1980.

[12] *Times of India*, 2 February 1980.

[13] It is of some interest that this report did not appear in any other Indian newspaper, nor did it stimulate any public discussion. Towards the end of 1980 a ranking military intelligence officer even feigned total ignorance of *The Hindu* report.

[14] *New York Times*, 1 February 1980.

[15] *Indian Express*, 23 January 1980.

[16] *Indian Express*, 31 January 1980.

[17] *Hindustan Times*, 31 January 1980.

[18] *Hindustan Times*, 23 January 1980.

[19] *Hindustan Times*, 2 February 1980; *Indian Express*, 21 January 1980.

[20] *Times of India*, 31 January 1980.

[21] *The Hindu*, 21 January 1980.

22 *The Hindu*, 25 January 1980.
23 *Indian Express*, 24 January 1980.
24 *Times of India*, 6 February 1980; *Indian Express*, 6 February 1980; *The Hindu*, 6 February, 1980.
25 *The Statesman*, 7 February 1980; *Indian Express*, 7 February 1980.
26 *Times of India*, 7 February 1980.
27 *New York Times*, 1 June 1980. India manufactures 60% of its own arms requirements including Soviet-designed MiG-23's. Under the new deal, India is to get later model MiG's, battle tanks, artillery and naval material. In 1979 India struck a deal to buy deep-penetration Jaguar planes from Britain at a cost of $ 1.2 billion.
28 See also *Times of India* and *Indian Express* of 20 February 1980; *Hindustan Times* of 11 February 1980 and *The Stateman* of 9 February 1980 for reports of Indian officials' talks with officials of these countries.
29 *The Statesman*, 10 February 1980.
30 *Times of India*, 12 February 1980.
31 *Ibid*.
32 *Indian Express*, 12 February 1980.
33 *Times of India*, 12 February 1980.
34 *Ibid*.
35 *The Hindu*, 12 February 1980.
36 *The Hindu*, 13 February 1980.
37 *The Hindu*, 14 February 1980.
38 *Indian Express*, 14 February 1980.
39 *Hindustan Times*, 14 February 1980.
40 *Times of India*, 14 February 1980.
41 *The Hindu*, 15 February 1980. Both countries resolved to further develop and strengthen the mutually beneficial bilateral relations. Thus, from the beginning India and the USSR agreed to separate their differences over Afghanistan from the arena of bilateral friendly relations. This implied that the Soviet military presence in Afghanistan was not seen by Mrs Gandhi as a strain on the bilateral relationship. *Pravda* in a commentary on February 18, did not refer to Afghanistan at all, but said that the Soviet Union and India had decided to strengthen their ties in the context of the friendship treaty.
42 *Times of India*, 13 February 1980.
43 *Indian Express*, 14 February 1980.
44 Some extracts from Indian newspapers' editorial assessment of the Gromyko visit:

Indian Express (February 15):
'Let alone a time-span for the pullout, the Soviet Union has not given a specific assurance of its intention to withdraw.''

Times of India (February 15):
"The Soviet Union's and India's positions on Afghanistan remain as far apart at the end of Mr Gromyko's three-days visit to New Delhi as they were before ... the Soviet foreign minister has taken an extremely tough stand in his discussions with the Indian Prime Minister and minister for external affairs.''

Hindustan Times (February 15):

"The withdrawal of Soviet troops from Afghanistan is the only step which can halt the current drift to disaster. The Soviet Union would do well to realise this, and also Pakistan's predicament to which it has been singularly insensitive. Indeed, Pakistan's dilemma is all the greater because all the Islamic States, including Iraq, whose ties with the Soviet Union are close and warm, have taken a serious view of the invasion of Afghanistan and would frown upon any indication of Islamabad's hostility to the refugees from the other side of the border. Here lies the crux of the problem. It is the shelter granted to the refugees which Moscow views as deliberate stoking of guerrilla activities in Afghanistan. But even if it is conditioned to regard Pakistan as a hostile country friendly to the US and China, it should understand that there must be something very wrong and ominous about the Afghan adventure for even genuine friends of long standing like India and Iraq to feel disturbed."

[45] *Times of India*, 21 February 1980.
[46] *The Hindu*, 29 February 1980. For denial of the arms deal report, see *Hindustan Times*, 15 February 1980.
[47] *Ibid*.
[48] *The Hindu*, 25 March 1980.
[49] *Ibid*.
[50] *The Hindu*, 16 February 1980.
[51] *Indian Express*, 16 February 1980.
[52] *The Hindu*, 21 February 1980.
[53] *The Hindu*, 2 March 1980.
[54] *The Hindu*, 24 February 1980.
[55] *Indian Express*, 25 March 1980.
[56] *The Hindu*, 28 March 1980.
[57] *Indian Express*, 10 April 1980; *Vhe Hindu*, 6 April, 1980; *Hindustan Vimes*, 8 April 1980; *Vimes of India*, 8 April 1980.
[58] *Hindustan Times*, 8 and 10 April 1980.
[59] *The Hindu*, 8, 9 and 11 April 1980.
[60] *Times of India*, 9 April 1980.
[61] *Indian Express*, 10 April 1980.
[62] *Indian Express*, 11, 12, 13 and 16 April 1980; *Hindustan Times*, 15 April; *The Hindu*, 16 April 1980.
[63] *The Hindu*, 10 May 1980.
[64] *Indian Express*, 9 May 1980; *Hindustan Times*, 9 May 1980; *The Hindu*, 10 May 1980; *The Hindu* correspondent wrote that the "real problem" was how to make the Karmal regime acceptable to the Afghan people once the Soviet troops had been withdrawn.
[65] See, for instance, *Indian Express* and *Times of India* editorials of 10 May 1980.
[66] *Times of India*, 15 May 1980.
[67] *The Hindu*, 17 May 1980. The Afghan proposal was preceded by a Pakistani suggestion that a "government of national reconciliation" be formed in Kabul including representatives of rebel groups. *Hindustan Times*, 21 May 1980.
[68] *Times of India*, 17 and 18 May 1980; *The Hindu*, 17 May 1980; *Indian Express*, 17 May 1980; *Hindustan Times*, 20 May 1980.

69 *Indian Express*, 20 May 1980. *The Hindu*, 23 May 1980.
70 *Hindustan Times*, 29 May 1980. The newspaper's diplomatic correspondent said that Brezhnev's offer "brings the Soviet Union within negotiating distance of Pakistan..."
71 *Hindustan Times*, 4, 7 and 11 June 1980; *Indian Express*, 7 and 8 June 1980.
72 *Times of India*, 18 June 1980.
73 For the Soviet announcement, see *Times of India*, 23 June 1980. For Indian press reaction, see *Times of India*, editorial of 25 June 1980; *Indian Express* editorial of 26 June 1980; *Hindustan Times* editorial of 25 June 1980. An official spokesman in New Delhi described the news as "pleasant" and related the Soviet decision to Mrs Gandhi's suggestion to Gromyko in February that there should be a partial withdrawal of Soviet troops. *Times of India*, 23 June 1980. In Washington and West European capitals response was skeptical while the Chinese saw the Soviet move as "deceptive." *The Hindu*, 23 June 1980; *Times of India*, 23 June 1950. Some units were, in fact, withdrawn from Afghanistan.
74 *Indian Express*, 27 July 1980; *Hindustan Times*, 28 July 1980; *The Hindu*, 27 July 1980.
75 *The Times*, London, 17 and 20 October 1980; *Guardian*, 7 October 1980. *The Times* correspondent reported, "In tones of ringing defiance, President Brezhnev... declared that the revolution in Afghanistan was irreversible and the world had better understand the fruitlessness of trying to interfere in the country's internal affairs." During the visit the Soviets gave Karmal "a written undertaking that it will keep its troops in Afghanistan until opposition to his Marxist government has been crushed."

For Mrs Gandhi's endorsement of the "Brezhnev doctrine" for the Persian Gulf, see *Indian Express*, 20 December 1980; for West European interest, *Times of India*, 18 December 1980; *Hindustan Times*, 20 December 1980.

CHAPTER SEVEN

1 *New York Times*, 6 September 1979.
2 *Pakistan Times*, 23 January 1980; *Indian Express*, 23 January 1980. Agha Shahi sought to play down the Chinese note in boosting the armed strength of Pakistan. No new aid plan had been agreed on, the amount of possible future assistance was not even discussed, he maintained.
3 *Pakistan Times*, 28 January 1980.
4 *Indian Express*, 28 January 1980. Gen. Zia offended Indian sensibilities by bracketing the "people of Kashmir" with the people of Palestine; both, he said, were "yearning for the restoration of their rights." This drew an instant protest from the Indian ambassador who walked out.
5 *Indian Express*, 31 January 1980. The Pakistan embassy in New Delhi protested Nayar's report that Gen. Zia's attitude to India had hardened. A statement issued by the ambassador, Abdul Sattar, said that Pakistan was keen on continuing "an earnest and sincere dialogue" with India on the situation in the region. *Times of India*, 1 February 1980.

Visiting an Afghan refugee camp near the Khyber Pass, Kuldip Nayar wrote, "Except slogans like 'communism meets its own death at the hand of Islam', on a few walls in Peshawar, I have not found any fervour in the town, or for that matter, anywhere else in Pakistan in the last seven days for the Afghan cause." *Indian Express*, 2 February 1980.

[6]*New York Times*, 3 and 4 February 1980; *Pakistan Times*, 1-7 February 1980; *Dawn*, 5 February 1980.

[7]*The Hindu*, 2 February 1980.

[8]*Indian Express*, 3-5 February 1980; also, *Times of India* and *Hindustan Times* of the same date.

The basic weakness of the US-Pakistan relationship was stressed by William Borders in the *New York Times* of January 20, 1980, "The United States Embassy here, a modern red brick building at the edge of the grey-green Himalayan foothills, has been a burned-out, empty shell since it was attacked two months ago by a howling mob of Islamic zealots. Two Americans died in that fire, and many of the survivors are privately incensed at the Pakistani Army's sluggish response to the attack. Now the American diplomats work in temporary quarters, living alone because the State Department, fearing further violence, ordered the evacuation of their wives and children.

"This is an odd sort of ally upon which to build a regional United States policy—an uncertain choice for the linchpin in an area reaching from Turkey to Indochina. But it is also, as an American in Washington put it, 'the only choice we've got.' The Soviet invasion of Afghanistan, just across a long and troubled border, has forced Pakistan and the United States into the same corner, obliging American re-evaluations of a once cordial relationship that has lately become tortured. The other onetime United States ally in this region—Iran—is no longer in the running, and the future foreign policy of India under a resurgent Indira Gandhi is a source of concern to Washington."

The plan to massively rearm Pakistan drew strong criticism from several American sources. The *New York Times* asked Carter on February 7 to disclose what precise commitments had been made to Pakistan. "Americans should not have to hear from President Zia of Pakistan about how and when American forces might join Asian battles.... He (Brzezinski) is banking on the Pakistanis to act more like the fighting Poles than the docile Czechs of 40 years ago. But in measuring allies in Asia, Americans are more likely to recall Washington's more recent boasts about the bastions of Saigon and Tehran." The *Washington Post* ridiculed the Brzezinski mission in a front page cartoon on February 8. James Wechsler, a syndicated columnist, wrote "Perhaps the most dismal performance was staged by Brzezinski on his expedition to Pakistan. More important than these exuberant excesses, of course, was his apparent commitment to an American readiness to go to war if Pakistan—ruled by a wretched vulnerable despot named General Zia ul-Huq—is attacked. Certainly a Russian rape of Pakistan would be a grim dangerous event. But was it the business of Brzezinski to announce that this would trigger war—as if he were unaware that Congressional sanction is required for such a decision? Is Gen. Zia worthy of such commitment under any circumstance?"

[9]*Times of India*, 4 February 1980.

[10]*The Hindu*, 7 February 1980.

[11]*Ibid.*

[12] *The Hindu*, 8 February 1980.
[13] *Ibid*.
[14] *Indian Express*, 18 February 1980.

Aga Shahi said that Gromyko had attempted to sidetrack the real issue which was Soviet armed intervention in Afghanistan and the universal appeal for withdrawal of Soviet troops. He "deeply regretted" Gromyko's statement that the US was scheming to convert Pakistan into a hot bed of tension and a springboard for aggression against Pakistan. Shahi said he was disappointed that the talks between Gromyko and Mrs Gandhi did not bring out a Soviet commitment to withdraw troops from Afghanistan. He said Pakistan wanted good relations with the Soviet Union and Soviet withdrawal from Afghanistan would help this process.

Shahi also suggested an internationally recognised neutral status for Afghanistan on the model of Austria which he said would satisfy the best interests of peace and stability in the region.

[15] *Dawn*, 19 February 1980.

Gen. Zia apparently realised that there was no meeting ground between his and India's regional strategic thinking. "The Indian view is that any attempt to confront Soviet presence in Afghanistan with a matching military buildup in Pakistan will only intensify the prevailing tensions in the region. The best way of inducing the Soviet Union to pull out would be for the regional states to get together and exert their collective influence to impress upon Moscow that the continued presence of its forces would be politically counterproductive, whatever the initial excuse for intervention. If Pakistan is prepared to go along with India in trying persuasion first, before lining up with US and China, in meeting the Soviet threat with military means, Mrs Gandhi would be in a better position to tell Mr Gromyko that the sooner the Soviet troops were withdrawn the better it would be for all concerned including the Soviet Union in the highly dangerous situation that was now developing in the region." *The Hindu*, 5 February 1980.

[16] *Hindustan Times*, 20 February 1980.
[17] *Hindustan Times*, 2 March 1980.
[18] Aid commitments from European nations to Pakistan were either modest or none at all. Pakistani officials were disappointed by a seeming decline of interest on the part of donor nations. Saudi Arabia was negotiating with Pakistan to provide up to $ 750 million to help in a military buildup. The spurning of the high profile aid offer was viewed by the Carter Administration as another blow to US diplomacy now under fire from several directions for "mistakes and inadequacies." *Washington Post*, 8 March 1980.

The *Post* said in a later report that Pakistan was asking for about $ 1.5 billion a year in economic aid from a variety of sources including the US. "An existing economic consortium contributes about $ 700 million yearly. Aid from the Persian Gulf Sheikdoms brings the expectable total to about $ 1 billion a year. The US is seeking to persuade its European allies for new contributions for Pakistan but so far with limited success." Cited in *The Hindu*, 30 February 1980.

[19] Cited in *Times of India*, 9 March 1980.
[20] *Ibid*.
[21] *Pakistan Times*, 7 March 1980; *Times of India*, 7 March 1980. In the United States, even the idea of transferring large quantities of arms to Pakistan under

274 *Afghan Syndrome*

the 1959 treaty had been opposed in January by *New York Times* which wrote in an editorial on January 6, "It does not automatically follow from the 1959 treaty that America must enter into open ended arms sales to a divided country ruled by an erratic Islamic fundamentalist. As Iran attests, selling costly hardware to a country cannot of itself assure the stability of a vulnerable regime. Pakistan's General Zia is so unsure of his hold that he has postponed elections four times. He has been unable to quell Baluchi and Pathan insurgents and has filled prisons with dissidents. Where and at whom would he aim American weapons?"

[22] *Indian Express*, 9 March 1980. The report quoted a US Government analyst for its source.

[23] *Times of India*, 8 March 1980.

[24] *Times of India*, 26 March 1980.

[25] *Times of India*, 29 July 1980. Bhutto's son, Murtaza Ali Bhutto, who lives in England, paid several visits to Kabul and sought to organise a Pakistan-Afghanistan "leftist front." *Times of India*, 29 April 1980; *Hindustan Times*, 29 April 1980.

[26] Bhabani Sen Gupta, "India Vies with Russia For Pakistan," *Amrita Bazar Patrika*, Calcutta, 13 May 1980.

[27] *Pakistan Times*, 12 May 1980.

[28] *Dawn*, 17 and 18 May 1980; *Pakistan Times*, 23 May 1980. *The Hindu*, 17-19 May 1980; *Indian Express*, 17-18 May 1980.

[29] *Guardian*, 18 May 1980; *Pakistan Times*, 17 May 1980.

[30] *The Hindu*, 2 June 1980; *The Statesman*, 19 June 1980.

[31] *The Hindu*, 13, 16 and 28 June 1980; *Times of India*, 27 June 1980.

[32] *Times of India, Indian Express, Hindustan Times*, 15-17 July 1980.

[33] *Amrita Bazar Patrika*, Calcutta, 15 July 1980.

[34] *The Hindu*, 31 August 1980.

[35] *Daily Telegraph*, 1 April 1980. The report added "The real threat to Gen. Zia comes from two sources, one from the brother generals who feel he must go before he does any more damage to the prestige of the army and the other from younger officers who are more open in their disenchantment."

CHAPTER EIGHT

[1] *White House Years, op. cit.*, pp. 1058-74.

[2] *Ibid.*

[3] Li Xiannian, a deputy prime minister of China, said while on a visit to the United States, that the Karakoram highway would "allow us to give military aid to Pakistan." This highway which links China with Pakistan through some of the world's tallest mountains, gives China land access to the Arabian Sea in the event of a Soviet blockde of its constlines. In 1979 Seymour Topping, of *New York Times*, and his wife were the first foreigners to be permitted to travel part of the Pakistani length of the highway. *Hindustan Times*, 4 December 1979; *New York Times*, 3 December 1979. For an earlier report, see *New York Times*, 28 January 1979.

[4] The talks were resumed in August 1979 at the level of deputy foreign ministers nad broken off early January 1980.

⁵Deng hobnobbed with topmen of corporate Japan. Many of these men had high hopes about capturing China's huge potential market. "The Japanese feel that the combination of China's resources, Japan's technological abilities, their geopolitical closeness and ageold cultural ties give them a collective wedge over competition from the United States and European rivals." Deng, however, was quite candid about China's backwardness. In a chat with reporters, he said, "When your face is ugly, you shouldn't pretend to be beautiful." Deng's visit led to an eight-year $ 20 billion deal exchanging Chinese oil and coal for Japanese plants and technology. The eight-year trade pact signed in 1977 was extended by five years, envisaging a total turnover of $ 100 billion. China placed firm orders for $ 5 billion worth of plants and seemed close to buying $ 5 billion worth more. China agreed to sell Japan 15 million tons of oil in 1982, up from 7 million tons in 1978. Japan reportedly agreed to buy Chinese crude not for its merits but for "higher reasons of state." *Far Eastern Economic Review*, 3 March, 1978.

⁶*News Week*, 12 February 1979.

⁷*Ibid. New York Times*, 3-5 February 1980.

⁸In 1979 the State Department and the Pentagon were pressing Carter for two different lines of China policy. The Pentagon prepared a study in April for Defence Secretary Harold Brown which ascribed to China a "pivotal role" in the global balance of power. It would therefore be to American benefit "to encourage Chinese actions that would heighten Soviet security concerns." The study reached the conclusion that the US should bolster China's military potential so that Peking could assist the West in a war with the Soviet Union.

The State Department, however, was resisting pressure from the Pentagon and the national security setup in the White House to abandon the policy of "even-handedness" and forge military linkage with China. "State Department officials expressed concern about a number of articles in recent days that, by design or coincidence, left the impression that the United States was seeking to retaliate against Moscow by favouring Peking. . . . Some officials have gone so far as to charge that Zbigniew Brzezinski . . and Defence Secretary Harold Brown are trying to foster an impression that the United States is retaliating the troop issue (in Cuba) by strengthening its ties with China despite the President's decision not to do so." *New York Times*, 4 and 5 October 1979.

⁹*New York Times*, 23-27 May 1980; *Time*, 9 June 1980; *The Hindu*, 1 June 1980.

On the eve of Brown's visit to Peking, the Pentagon drafted a report analysing the possibility of granting China $ 63 billion in aid for modernisation of its armed forces.

In 1979 alone 308 Chinese delegations visited the United States. Among the Carter cabinet members to visit Peking during 1978-80 were Brzezinski (1978), Mondale, Kreps and Califano (1979) and Brown (1980).

The Western summit at Guadeloupe in France in January 1979 made China "something like the 16th member of NATO," *Newsweek*, 12 February 1979.

¹⁰*The Hindu*, 2 June 1980; *New York Times*, 1-4 June 1980. For Indian reaction to the US decision to sell arms to China, see *Times of India* and *Indian Express* editorials of 2 June 1980. The US also lifted the embargo on West European sale of "high technology" to China.

¹¹*New York Times*, 11 August 1979.

[12] *New York Times*, 11 July 1980.

[13] This train of thinking was noticed in numerous articles in the Soviet journals like *International Affairs* and *Far Eastern Affars* in 1980. See, for instance, "Leninism and the Problems of China" in *Far Eastern Affairs*, No. 3, 1980; and a series of 9 articles on China in the same issue; V. Andreyev, "The Partnership Between Peking and Imperialism—A Threat to Peace and Independence," *International Affairs*, No. 11, 1980.

It was clear from the contents of articles on China printed in these two Soviet journals in 1980 that in the USSR itself China scholars differed in their analyses of trends and processes in the People's Republic. One school believed that the de-Maofication process, tortuous and uneven though it was, was pregnant with possibilities of China's return to normal relations with the USSR. The other school was convinced that the Chinese leaders who were trying to bury Maoism were no less anti-Soviet than the Maoists. *Far Eastern Affairs*, No. 4, 1980 published extracts from Deng's report at the meeting of cadres of Peking's People's Assembly House on 16 January 1980.

Numerous reports appeared in the world press in 1980 of continuing struggles within the top Chinese leadership. The "power struggle" became very intense in July-August, leading in the autumn fall of Hua Guofeng from prime ministership. See Fox Butterfield's report in *New York Times*, 13 July 1980; Ross Terril, "China Faces the Perils of Cutting a Myth Down to Size," *New York Times*, 3 August 1980.

[14] *Times of India*, 2 June 1980.

[15] An Indian foreign office official who did not wish to be identified. *The Hindu*, 29 August 1980 reported that the Chinese had actually stopped "gifting" arms to Pakistan.

[16] *Tass* report was cited in *Hindustan Times*, 4 May 1980.

[17] For reports of Gen. Zia's visit to Peking, *Times of India*, 3-6 May 1980; *New York Times*, 5 May 1980. For Indian reaction to the Chinese non-response to Gen. Zia's reference to the Kashmir issue, see *Times of India* editorial of 9 May 1980.

Zia had said in a television interview on March 1 that China had given Pakistan "a good deal of military hardware" and would continue to do so. China was assisting Pakistan with the supply of MiG-19s, tanks and gunboats. The Chinese were also setting up two large complexes, one for reconditioning tanks and the other to recondition MiGs. Zia said that the Karakoram highway which linked Pakistan and China and had been built with the blood of Chinese and Pakistani engineers had great potentiality and capability. "It is a question of when it is to be used." *Times of India*, 2 March 1980.

[18] *The Hindu*, 15 March 1980.

[19] India had refused to discuss a quid pro quo in 1960 and after the 1962 border war. See Bhabani Sen Gupta, *The Fulcrum of Asia*, New York, Pegasus, 1968, Chapter 4.

[20] *The Hindu*, 19 April 1980; *Times of India*, 19 April 1980; *Indian Express*, 19 April 1980.

[21] *The Hindu*, 4 May 1980.

[22] *Indian Express*, 10 May 1980.

[23] *Times of India*, 15 May 1980.

24 *The Hindu,* 17 May 1980.
25 *Ibid.*
26 Inder Malhotra. "India, China and Pakistan: Shift in Triangular Relations," *Times of India,* 15 May 1980.
27 Deng did this in an interview with a visiting Indian editor, *Times of India,* 22 June 1980.
28 *The Hindu,* 3 July 1980.

Xinhua, in a long commentary, backed the offer of Deng Xiaoping. It also provided the rationale behind the Chinese offer: "Development of Sino-Indian relations in such a serious situation (in the region) will undoubtedly exercise a positive influence on world affairs, Asian affairs in particular. Such positive influences should by no means be neglected." *The Hindu,* 26 June 1980. Deng's concept of a package deal received widespread support in the Indian press.

29 *People's Daily* article was cited in *Times of India,* 26 June 1980. Wire services from Peking pointed out that China was "giving up" its "claim on 93,000 square kilometres of Indian territory in the central and eastern sectors of the border' and expected to "give up" its own claim on "35,000 square kilometres of Chinese' territory in the Karakoram chain in the west."

The Colombo newspaper *Sun* quoted a Chinese vice-foreign minister, Han Nienlong, as saynig that China was adopting an "active" attitude towards improving relations with India. "It will not do anything harmful to Sino-Indian relations. . . . But I should also tell some leaders of the Indian government not to speak unfriendly words which are not conducive to improving Sino-Indian relations. This is not right to do. We raised this with the Indian government. We think one's words should be in conformity with one's deeds." *Times of India,* 26 June 1980.

The Hindu's Tokyo correspondent reported that "all *Xinhua* reports from Beijing on the Zia visit strongly suggest China's desire that while Pakistan should be helped to meet any eventuality, emphasis should also be on efforts to find a peaceful solution which would lead to the withdrawal of Soviet troops from Afghanistan and the restoration of that country's genuine independence and not on the basis of military confrontation which would only heighten tensions.

"Gen. Zia spoke of Pakistan's policy of developing good neighbourly relations with India and pursuing the path of normalising relations with New Delhi in accordance with the Simla agreement. For its part, China also seems to be quietly pressuring Pakistan towards improving ties with India.

"The reasons for this are obvious. Continued tension between India and Pakistan would not only contribute to greater instability in South and South-East Asia but have the unfavourable effect of deviating China from its present great preoccupation of speedily building up and modernising its economy. It would also retard the process of full normalisation of Sino-Indian relations." *The Hindu,* 11 May, 1980.

30 Andre Fontaine, French strategic expert, saw certain developments in China, like the posthumous rehabilitation of Liu Shaoqi, who was dubbed as "China's Khruschev" by Mao, and the dropping of the charge that the USSR had ceased to be a socialist country, indicating that there were possibilities of a thaw in Sino-Soviet relations. He wrote: "The Cninese have now had to accept the fact that the

West does not dare sell them arms, that the United States shied away from a Chinese proposal they should work together to help the Afghan resistance (who are still having to make do with their ancient and broken-down rifles), that the aid the Americans were able to come up with for Pakistan was purely symbolic, that in the Iranian affair they have successively displayed naivete and irresolution, and lastly that the peoples of the West are becoming increasingly hostile towards China.

"If ever the Chinese went through the motions of patching up their quarrel with the Russians, we may be quite certain that it would not be because they suddenly saw in them the socialist and revolutionary virtues whose absence they had denounced since the Khruschev era. It would be because they had finally come to the conclusion, as Stalin did in 1939 in his dealings with the French and the British, that the Western countries were decidedly too weak, too divided among themselves, and, in fact, too stupid for any further reliance to be placed on them." *Le Monde* News Service, *Times of India*, 7 May 1980.

Marian K. Leighton, an analyst at the national foreign assessment centre of the CIA, wrote in an article printed in the *Wall Street Journal* of 12 February 1981: "There is a further danger that the growing strength and influence of the Soviet Union in Asia will erode Peking's confidence in close Sino-American ties and bolster the position of those in the Chinese leadership who reportedly favour a rapprochement with the USSR." *Indian Express*, 14 February 1981.

31*The Hindu*, 7 August 1980. It was even reported in the Indian press that the power struggle in China made Huang Hua's position uncertain and that he might soon be replaced as foreign minister by someone more unequivocally linked to Deng Xiaoping.

32A section of the foreign policy elite in India argued that since China no longer posed a credible threat to India, New Delhi should not hasten to sew up a border deal with Peking. China had no consistent foreign policy, wrote Girilal Jain, editor, *Times of India*; it was difficult to deal with it. Besides, India could wait: "India does not have much to gain from China's friendship, the northern border has been tranquil for over a decade. Beijing can threaten peace there only at its own peril. Pakistan is in no position to serve as a proxy for China to embarrass or harass this country. New Delhi's capacity to influence Soviet policy in Afghanistan cannot improve as a result of better ties with Beijing. Since India's and China's economies are not complementary, the scope for trade between the two is rather limited. New Delhi would have had a strong incentive to go out of its way to seek friendly relations with Beijing if it regarded the Soviet intervention in Afghanistan as a long-term threat to the region's and India's own security."

33China took a dark view of the Taiwan Relations Act passed by the US Congress in March 1980 and approved by Carter in April. With Ronald Reagan in the White House, China was perturbed in the early months of 1981 that this piece of legislation might be implemented. The Chinese made it clear that revival of the Two China theory by the United States would spell the end of the Sino-American friendship. See "US 'Taiwan Relations Act' " in *Peking Review*, No. 2, 12 January 1981. The possibility of a sharp deterioration in Sino-US relations created a certain ambivalence in China's stance on the USSR early 1981. Writing in *Peking Review*, No. 3, 9 January 1981, an analyst observed, "Whether there will be any change in Sino-Soviet relations *mainly* depends on whether the Soviet

Union will change its social-imperialist policy and abandon its hegemonist ambitions," (italics supplied). Evidently, there could be other factors too leading to an improvement in Sino-Soviet relations. For China's gloomy view of the growing independence of Western Europe in world affairs, see "West Europe's Independent Role," *Peking Review*, No. 2, 12 January 1981.

34*Peking Review*, No. 4, 26 January 1981.

CHAPTER NINE

1*Pravda*, 10 May 1980.

2Cyrus Vance resigned protesting the failed U.S. commando raid on Tehran on 25 April 1980. He saved what James Reston described as "the best speech of his long and distinguished career," for the Harvard commencement in May. Vance said, "Neither we nor the world can afford an American foreign policy which is hostage to the emotions of the moment. We must have in our minds a conception of the world we want a decade hence. The 1990 we seek must shape on action in 1980 or the decisions of 1980 will give us a 1990 we will regret." *New York Times*, 8 June 1980.

Columnist Jack Anderson reported in August that the Carter administration had prepared plans and fixed a "tentative date" for mid-October for "an invasion of Iran" to rescue the 52 hostages held in Tehran since 4 November 1979. This report was denied by the White House but Anderson stood by it. *Indian Express*, 17-18 August 1980.

3When Eric Gonsalves, secretary in the Indian External Affairs Ministry, went to Washington in February 1980, he noted a "positive shift" in the American stand towards a diplomatic rather than a military response to the Afghan crisis. *The Hindu*, 28 February 1980.

4The process was interrupted after Jimmy Carter's defeat on 4 November 1980. No negotiating process between Moscow and Reagan administration began till February 1981 but the new Secretary of State, Alexander Haig, had some preliminary conversations with the Soviet ambassador, Antoly Dobrinyn.

5*The Times*, 8 September 1980.

6*International Herald Tribune*, 21 September 1980.

7See the writer's interview with Agha Shahi in *India Today*, 15-28 February 1981.

8See Kuldip Nayar's report in *Indian Express*, 10 October 1980.

9*Indian Express*, 18 September 1980. No second instalment of Soviet troop withdrawal occurred till the end of February 1981.

10These proposals were put up in various garbs to the French President, the West German Chancellor and the U.S. Secretary of State.

11These proposals were clearly aimed at the second Islamic foreign ministers' conference in Islamabad. The proposals were received in the world with a mixture of interest and skepticism. Kabul Radio quoted Indira Gandhi as saying that the Afghan proposal were "balanced" and would "help ease off tensions." *Times of India*, 18 May 1980. The proposals had an impact on the Islamic conference, as noted in chapter seven.

12*Times of India*, 21 February 1980.

13*Indian Express*, 26 February 1980.

14. *Indian Express*, 28 February 1980.
15. *Times of India*, 26 February 1980.
16. *Indian Express*, 28 February 1980.
17. *Hindustan Times*, 28 February 1980.
18. *Times of India*, 7 March 1980.
19. *Hindustan Times*, 16 March 1980.
20. *Ibid.*

21. Selig S. Harrison, senior associate of the Carnegie Endowment for International Peace, suggested a settlement with the Soviet Union of Afghanistan by providing for "Finlandisation" of Afghanistan and neutralisation of Pakistan and Iran. Writing in the *Foreign Policy* magazine of Winter 1980-81, Harrison said "Finlandisation" had given Finland three decades of stability and prosperity and might offer the only slender hope left for getting the Russians out of Afghanistan. "Even if a withdrawal occurred in stages over several years, a formal commitment to the principle of total withdrawal by an agreed target date would greatly help forestall the current growth of tensions between Washington and Moscow."

Moscow would have to be satisfied that substantial resistance elements were ready for a return to the previous Soviet-tilted brand of neutralism, and would agree to Finland-style security arrangements providing for the right of Soviet re-entry if Afghanistan, or the Soviet Union through Afghanistan, should become the target of military aggressions. "The key to a political settlement lies in whether the (ideologically neutral) tribally based elements succeed in their effort to isolate the (Islamic) fundamentalist leadership..." Finlandisation would have to be accompanied by a regional security agreement containing explicit mutual inspection procedures.

In return for agreeing not to give help or sanctuary to resistance groups (now based in Peshawar) Pakistan and Iran should seek Soviet pledges barring support to Baluch and Pashtu separatist movements.

An enduring settlement would also require understandings between America, the Soviet Union and China designed to insulate Pakistan and Iran from great power rivalry. This would rule out military alliances, one-sided military aid dependencies and the use of Pakistani and Iranian territory for intelligence surveillance of the Soviet Union.

"Just as Sweden stayed out of the North Atlantic Treaty Organisation to make Finlandisation possible, so Pakistan and Iran would have to be neutral."

The relationship between Finland and the USSR, formalised in the treaty of friendship of 1948, is based on certain geopolitical realities. These were outlined by President Kekkonen of Finland in a Washington speech in 1961. A deterioration in Finnish-Soviet relations would serve the interest of no one, he said. "It would, of course, do no practical harm to the Soviet Union, it would be of no benefit to any foreign power and it would not help Finland in the least. Quite the contrary." The Western powers, he said, would be neither able nor willing to give finland effective support against the Soviet Union. "Nor would Finland be willing to accept support that would place her in the very dangerous position of an "outpost" against the Soviet Union. Therefore, when for some reasons or other signs of a political crisis between Finland and its Eastern neighbours have appeared, as in 1958 and 1961, Finland has always sought to solve the problems without outside support. By always treating issues that arise in her relations with the Soviet Union bilaterally, Finland has tried to show the Soviet Union that her policy does not serve any foreign interests,"—Urho Kekkonen, *Neutrality: The Finnish position*, 1973, Heinemann, London, pp. 9-10.

Afghanistan stood virtually "Finlandised" prior to the April 1978 revolution. The efforts of the late Shah of Iran to reduce Afghanistan's dependence on the USSR probably persuaded Moscow that the relationship was less than stable.

22 This was reiterated almost in any major Soviet pronouncement in Afghanistan.

23 *Times of India*, 17 May 1980.

24 *New York Times*, 1 June 1980.

25 *Indian Express*, 27 June 1980.

26 *New York Times*, 21 June 1980.

27 *New York Times*, 23 June 1980.

28 *Indian Express*, 27 June 1980; *The Hindu*, 21 June 1980.

29 US officials also talked about "transitional arrangements" which were rejected by the Soviets and objected to by the French President. *The Hindu*, 27 June 1980; *Hindustan Times*, 29 June 1980.

30 *The Hindu*, 27 June 1980.

31 *Times of India*, 28-29 July 1980. Gelb is a former director of the State Department's Bureau of Political-Military Affairs.

It is interesting to note how the vicerogenic compulsions of world politics are building frameworks of cooperation between the USSR and the advanced capitalist countries even as, psychogenic elements assault the same frameworks. Giovanni Agnelli, leading Italian industrialist, held in 1980 that the most serious mistake made by the United States was the decision to block the development of large potential oil and gas fields of Eastern Siberia. This view was shared by Samnel Pisar, former economic counsellor to President Carter. Pisar agreed with Agnelli that the failure of the US-Soviet oil and gas deal was a great opportunity lost for world peace. According to Pisar, Soviet trade with the US and East-West economic and technological collaboration are the only feasible alternatives to the increasing danger of military confrontation. *Indian Express*, 15 July 1980.

With a grim touch of irony for the US confrontation Policy, West Europeans stepped in boldly in 1980-81 where Americans feared to trod. A gigantic Soviet-West European deal to develop the world's largest untapped proven reserves of natural gas in Western Siberia (estimated at 26 trillion cubic metres) was reported in February 1981. The participating Western countries included France, Belgium, the Netherlands and Western Germany. The Soviet project is to build a natural gas pipeline for the remote Siberian peninsula, 3,000 miles across the heart of Central Russia to Western Europe. The West European partners are to lend the Soviets $ 10 billion to $ 15 billion to cover the entire construction cost of the project and provide their best technology and equipment in return for a supply of 40 billion cubic metre of natural gas annually, starting in 1986 at the earliest. Already a consortium of 20 West German banks has agreed to provide $ 5.2 billion and a group of French banks was expected to contribute $ 4 billion. The steel mills of Western Europe, starved of orders, saw big profits from the sale of extensive gas pipes. Two US firms were also looking for a share of the construction contract.

When the project is fully operative, West Europe will get 25 per cent of its natural gas from the USSR as against 9 per cent in 1980. France and Germany will get more than 30 per cent each. For the USSR, the project will not only ease the petroleum situation considerably, but also mean a covetable economic bonanza. Once the Soviets have paid off the foreign loans in eight to ten years, the gas supplies to Western Europe will earn considerable foreign exchange with which the Soviets should be able to further develop Siberia's natural gas and oil fields, and import technologies for agricultural and industrial development in general.

The Soviet-West European natural gas deal went against the grain of US confrontationist policy and raised growls and snarls in Washington. A report by the Senate Energy Committee warned in December 1980 that the pipline could split the NATO alliance because it would reduce Western resistance to Soviet pressure. "The USSR can strengthen its economic influence over the West and reduce cohesion among the US and its allies on political, economic and military matters to the extent that it can increase its gas exports to Western Europe," the report concluded. *Time*, 16 February 1981.

The Soviet-West European project erodes the US claim that in view of an approaching oil crunch, the USSR is casting covetous eyes on Persian Gulf oil. The Soviets appear to be keen on developing Siberian oil and natural gas reserves to such an extent that they can offer to the West Europeans a stable, assured and adequate source of energy for a considerable period of time. The prospects are bound to appear tantalising to Japan also.

[32]*Indian Express*, 4 and 23 January 1981; *The Hindu*, 7 and 26 January 1981; *Times of India*, 14 January 1981.

[33]The Afghan education minister, Dr Anahita Ratebzad, was in New Delhi in the first week of January, while Ram Sathe visited Kabul early February. On both occasions the Afghan peace proposals were discussed.

[34]For excellent but different analyses of the Pakistani response to the Soviet-Afghan peace move, see Pran Chopra, "Unreal Hopes in Pakistan," *Hindustan Times*, 29 January 1981 and Inder Malhotra, "From Taif to New Delhi: A Diplomatic Maze," *Times of India*, 29 January 1981.

[35]*Times of India*, 19 January 1981.

[36]"From Taif to New Delhi . . ." Note No. 34, *Times of India*, 29 January 1981.

[37]*Times of India* and *Indian Express*, 10-14 February 1981; *New York Times*, 14 February 1981.

[38]"From Taif to New Delhi. . . ."

CHAPTER TEN

[1]The Janata government which was in power in India from March 1977 to August 1979 went back on its election pledge to abrogoate the Indo-Soviet treaty. Its policy of "genuine non-alignment" left the strategic content of the treaty unaffected. See S.C. Gangal, *India's Foreign Policy*, New Delhi, Young Asia Publications, 1980, for relevant documents. For genesis of the treaty, see the author's chapter in William Griffiths (ed.), *The World and the Great Power Triangles*, Cambridge, Mass. MIT Press, 1975. For the treaty's significance for

Indo-Soviet and Soviet-Asian relations, see the author's *Soviet-Asian Relations in the Seventies and Beyond: An Interperceptional Study*, New York, Praeger, 1976, ch. 5.

[2]William J. Barnds, "The Communist Powers and South Asia," *Problems of Communism*, November-December, 1977; Satish Kumar; *The New Pakistan*, New Delhi, Vikas, 1978, pp. 132-33; G.W. Choudhury, *India, Pakistan, Bangladesh and the Major Powers*, New York, Free Press, for the Foreign Policy Research Institute, 1975.

[3]President Nixon even paid a left-handed tribute to the USSR for its restraining role in the India-Pakistan war. See *US Foreign Policy for the 1970's: The Emerging Structure of Peace*, Washington DC, US Government Printing Press, 1972. Also, James Reston, "Who Won in India?" *New York Times*, 17 December 1971.

[4]Gen. Zia ignored requests even from friendly countries like the United States and Saudi Arabia to spare Bhutto's life. The Janata regime in India was one of the few governments that did not plead with Gen. Zia, but Indira Gandhi strongly condemned the hanging, which improved her image in the Pakistan People's Party.

[5]Delia Denman, "Zia Regime Under Pressure," *Far Eastern Economic Review*, carried in *Times of India*, 14 April 1980; Girilal Jain, "Abortive Coup in Pakistan," *Times of India*, 19 March 1980. The Pakistani military police arrested a former Major-General, Tajmal Hussein, for an alleged attempt on Zia's life. *The Hindu*, 25 March 1980; see also *The Hindu* editorial of March 21, questioning the stability of the Zia regime. For reports of Zia's compromise with the Generals, see B.K. Joshi's report in *Times of India*, 25 March 1980.

[6]*Holiday*, (Dacca weekly), 22 June 1980.

[7]*Indian Express*, Delhi, 18 February 1980.

[8]*Muslim* (Urdu), 7 March 1980; translated into English.

[9]*Holiday*, 6 April 1980.

[10]*Holiday*, 18 May 1980.

[11]*Dainik Sangram* (Bengali), 31 May 1980; translated into English.

[12]K, Subrahmanyam, "The Second Cold War," *Times of India*, Delhi, 23 July 1980.

[13]"Cold War at our Doorstep," *Times of India*, Sunday Review, 22 June 1980.

[14]*Ibid*.

[15]Kuldid Nayar, "Will Soviet Troops Withdraw?" *Indian Express*, 13 February 1980.

[16]J.D. Singh, "Moscow's Aims in Afghanistan Unclear," *Times of India*, 31 January 1980.

[17]While the major Indian newspapers printed over 500 articles on the Afghan crisis written by American, British and French analysts, they printed none by a Soviet analyst. Soviet viewpoints were carried in wire service reports. The Soviet embassy in New Delhi had to buy space to get full texts of Brezhnev's interviews with *Pravda* reproduced in a major Indian newspaper.

[18]*Pakistan Times*, 28 January 1980.

[19]*Indian Express*, 31 January 1980.

[20]*Pakistan Times*, 1 January 1980.

[21] *Wafaaq* (Urdu daily), 30 December 1979; translated into English.
[22] *Muslim* (Urdu daily), 30 December 1979; translated into English.
[23] *Sadaqat*, (Urdu), 1 January 1980; translated into English.
[24] *Viewpoint*, 6 January 1980.
[25] *Pakistan Economist*, 5 January 1980.
[26] *Pakistan Times*, 2 and 26 January 1980.
[27] This was conceded by the Pakistan foreign minister, Aga Shahi in his statement announcing the rejection of the American aid package, *Pakistan Times*, 7 March 1980.
[28] *Maghribi Pakistan* (Urdu), 3 February 1980; translated into English.
[29] *Jasarat*, (Urdu), 2 February 1980; translated into English.
[30] *Viewpoint*, 24 February 1980.
[31] *Nawai Waqt*, (Urdu), 26 February 1980; translated into English.
[32] *Dawn*, 22 January 1980.
[33] *Viewpoint*, 27 January 1980.
[34] *Pakistan Times*, 16 April 1980.
[35] *Indian Express*, 14 April 1980.
[36] *Indian Express*, 18 April 1980.
[37] *Indian Express*, 25 March 1980.
[38] See report of speech in *Bangladesh Times*, the government's own paper, 10 February 1980.
[39] *Bangladesh Times*, 27, 28 and 29 February 1980.
[40] For Ziaur Rahman's formal speeches while on a state visit to Manila, see *Bangladesh, Observer*, 27 May 1980; his speeches in London were strikingly similar.
[41] *Times of India*, 21 May 1980.
[42] *Bangladesh Times*, 15 January 1980.
[43] *Ibid*.
[44] *Bangladesh Observer*, 11 January 1980.
[45] *Bangladesh Times*, 7 February 1980. Another pro-Awami League daily, *Sangbad* (News) disparaged the Islamic face of the protest against the Soviet intervention. "The very forces which opposed the liberation struggle in the name of Islam are in the field today in distant Afghanistan, once again with the cry to save Islam." 12 January 1980; translated from Bengali.
[46] *Bangladesh Times*, 22 June 1980.
[47] *Dainik Sangram*, 31 May 1980.
[48] *Holiday*, 18 May 1980.
[49] *Bangladesh Times*, 30 May 1980.
[50] The CPI-M appeared to be less enthusiastic about the Soviet intervention than the CPI. The Marxist party supported the Soviet action in January at a meeting of its national executive attended by less than half of the members; the announcement immediately drew criticism from the party's leaders in West Bengal. Since then the CPI-M has not commented on the Soviet intervention at all. The party's "foreign policy" expert, Surjeet, described the intervention as "regrettable" while speaking at a meeting of Delhi University students. However, the CPI-M has been highly critical of US, Chinese and Pakistani responses to the Afghan situation.

51This was the burden of 21 interviews Indira Gandhi gave to foreign newspapers or television networks between January and April 1980; also of her major speeches in India.

52As in n. 13. The quotation is from Subrahmanyam, with which the two others agreed.

53See the editorial of 1 January 1980; *The Hindu* was the only national paper to demand abrogation of the Indo-Soviet Treaty.

54*The Hindu*, 6 April 1980.

55Bharat Wariavwalla, "Soviet Presence in Afghanistan," *Times of India*, 5 July 1980.

56See, instance, A.S. Abraham, "Moves on Afghanistan," *Times of India*, 4 July 1980; *The Hindu* editorial of 1 January 1980: *Pakistan Times* editorial of February 2, and *Dawn* editorial of January 5.

57*Pakistan Economist*, 5 February 1980.

58*Maghribi Pakistan*, 3 February 1980.

59G K. Reddy, "Towards a New Balance," *The Hindu*, 24 February 1980.

60*Times of India*, 16 April 1980.

61*India Today*, 1-15 October 1980.

62The April revolution was, however, criticised for its political style and evident weaknesses.

63See Begum Bhutto's interview in *Guardian*, n. 35; also, *Viewpiont*, 27 January 1980.

64As in n. 13.

CHAPTER ELEVEN

1Zbigniew Brzezinski wrote in *Encounter* in 1968 that once the Soviet Union achieved nuclear parity with the United States, there would be, for the first time in history, "two overlapping global military powers." Once the Soviet Union matched American long range air-and sea-lift capabilities for projecting force into distant regions, there would be growing "probabilities of a new type of confrontation—a direct one between US and Soviet intervention forces."

Cited in Hedrick Smith, "Russia's Power Strategy," *New York Times Magazine*, 27 January 1980.

2*Time*, 30 June 1980.

3*New York Times*, 23 March 1980.

4*Times*, London, Editorial, 17 October 1980.

5*Ibid*.

6Interview with Earl W. Freth, *The Hindu*, 26 December 1980.

7George Quester, "Consensus Lost," *Foreign Policy*, Fall 1980. The same point is made in a different way by Carl Gersham, "The Rise and Fall of the new Foreign Policy Establishment," *Commentary*, July 1980.

8Charles William Maynes and Richard H. Cullman, "Ten Years of Foreign Policy," *Foreign Policy*, Fall 1980.

9Allen H. Barton, "Fault Lines in American Elite Consensus," *Daedalus*, Summer 1980.

10Paul Nitze, "Strategy in the Decade of the 1980s," *Foreign Affairs*, Fall 1980.

[11] Richard Pipes, "Soviet Global Strategy," *Commentary*, April 1980.
[12] See, for example, Jeremiah Novak's article in *Worldview*, August 1980.
[13] *New York Times*, 1 February 1980.
[14] Alexander Dullin, "Russia's Afghanistan Move," *The Center Magazine*, May-June 1980.
[15] Deborah Shapley, "Shrugging off SALT: The Consequences May Be Bitter," *The New Republic* 7 June 1980. See also Lawrence Caldwell, "SALT-II and the Strategic Relationship," *Current History*, October 1979.
[16] Alton Frye, "How to Fix SALT," *Foreign Policy*, Summer 1980.
[17] Walter Laqueur, "Euro-Neutralism," *Commentary*, June 1980.
[18] Fritz Stern, "Europe's Release from Greatness," *The Center Magazine*, July-August 1980.
[19] *Times of India*, 5 August 1980.
[20] Cited by Flora Lewis in *New York Times*, 13 January 1980.
[21] *The Observer*, London, 24 June 1980; *New York Times*, 13 January 1980.
[22] *The Economist*, London, 24 November 1980.
[23] *Ibid*.
[24] *Idid*
[25] *Strategic Survey 1979*, London, The International Institute For Strategic Studies, pp. 7-8.
[26] Helmut Sonnenfeldt, "Implications of the Soviet Invasion of Afghanistan on East-West Relations," *The Atlantic Community Quarterly*, Summer 1980.
[27] Robert Moss, "Reaching for Oil: The Soviets' Bold Middle East Policy," *Saturday Review*, 12 April 1980.
[28] Sharham Chubin, "Security Interests in the Persian Gulf," *Daedalus*, Fall 1980.
[29] Samuel Huntington, "Iran and Afghanistan: Turning Points for America?", *Public Opinion*, February-March 1980.
[30] Edward Luttwak, "After Afghanistan, What?" *Commentary*, April 1980.
[31] Sharham Chubin, "Security Interests in the Persian Gulf," *Daedalus*, Fall 1980.
[32] This was the line of argument in numerous articles published in American journals in 1979-80. See Francise Fukuyama, "A New Soviet Strategy," *Commentary*, October 1979; Edward Luttwak, "After Afghanistan, What?" *Commentary*, April 1980; Donald Rumsfeld, "The State of American Defence," *Orbis* Winter 1980; Adam B. Ulam, "How To Restrain the Soviets?" *Commentary*, December 1980; Robert W. Tucker, "The Purposes of American Power," *Foreign Affairs*, Winter 1980-81. See also a series of articles in *Daedalus*, Fall 1980, under the topic, "US Defence Policy in the 1980s." Among the contributors are Sydney D. Drell, Colin S. Gray, David Hollway, Richard Pipes, Henry Rowen and Allen S. Whiting.
[33] This line of reasoning was noticed most on the pages of the journal, *Foreign Policy*, and the newspaper, *New York Times*.
[34] *New York Times*, 17 August 1980.
[35] *Ibid*.
See also Colin S. Gray and Keith Payne. "Victory Is Possible," *Foreign Policy*, Summer 1980; the US Defence Secretary, Harold Brown's statement in *Times of India*, 10 February 1980; Brzezinski's statement in the *Times of India*, 23

February 1980; N. Ravi's despatch in *The Hindu*, 4 February 1980; and T.V. Parasuram's report in *Indian Express*, 3 February 1980.

[36]*New York Times*, 17 August 1980; *New York Times*, 23 March 1980.

[37]Andre Fontaine, "Deterrence for How Long," reprinted in *The Hindu*, 7 August 1980.

[38]Fred Charles Ikle, in *New York Times*, 5 February 1980; also *New York Times* News Service, *The Hindu*, 26 January 1980.

[39]*Ibid*.

[40]*Fortune*, 8 November 1979, 14 July 1980 and 1 December 1980. See also "The 1980s: Perdition or Paradise?" *USA Today*, July 1980 for a gloomy forecast by Harold Ehrlich who says that the 1980 recession "could last a lot longer than the one of 1974-75."

[41]*The Economist*, November 1980; *The New Leader*, 17 November 1980; *The New Republic*, 22 November 1980.

[42]*New York Times*, 8 June 1980. Professor Hartman added "It raises questions about whether the United States has economic resources adequate for supporting large military establishment needed to preserve the global role the nation has carved out for itself. In the 1960s Great Britain was confronted even more starkly by the same question and with its economy deteriorating pulled its military ambitions back east of Suez."

"This nation is on the precipice of an economic, political, military and social crisis that may shadow the crisis of the 1930s. The present situation contains once again the potential for mass unemployment. But it also contains the potential for hyperinflation, an economic catastrophe unfamiliar to most Americans." Leonard A. Rapping, *New York Times*, 23 March 1980.

[43]Bruce Palmar, Jr. (ed.), *Grand Strategy for the 1980s*, Washington D.C., American Enterprise Institute for Public Policy Research, 1978, p. 21. This volume, written by four retired Generals of the US Army and a retired Admiral of the US Navy, foresaw a fairly long period of intense and direct competition between the US and the USSR in almost all the major geopolitical regions of the world with the probable exception of Latin America.

[44]Department of Defence (Public Affairs), News Release Nos 353-77, p. 2.

[45]The Stockholm International Peace Research Institute (SIPRIP, valuing arms transfer only by the cost of major exported weapons, came to the conclusion that in the 1967-76 period, the US delivered $ 14.8 billion and the USSR $ 14.6 billion worth of arms in constant 1975 prices. The US Arms Control and Disarmament Agency (ACDA), on the other hand, in its *World Military* Expenditure and Arms Trade 1967-78 (WMEAT) concluded that the US exported $ 30 billion and the USSR $ 15.5 billion worth of arms and services, in current prices, during the same period. The CIA claimed that the dollar value of Soviet arms transfers closely approximated the value of US exports. SIPRI: Arms Trade Registers: The Arms Trade with the Thrid World, MIT Press, Cambridge, Mass., 1975: *SIPRI: World Armaments and Disarmament, SIPRI Yearbook, 1975, 1976, 1977, WMEAT 1967-76*, Washington DC, ACDA, 1978. See also Amelia Leiss, "Changing Patterns of Arms Transfers," Report C/70-2, Center for International Studies, MIT, February, 1970.

[46]Michael Mihalka, "Supplier-Client Patterns in Arms Transfers: The Deve-

loping Countries 1967-76" in Stephanie G. Neuman and Robert E. Harkavy (eds.), *Arms Transfers in the Modern World*, New York, Praeger Special Studies, 1973, p. 73.

47*Indian Express*, 14 February 1980.

48The Soviets had 26 Navy ships in the Indian Ocean and the Arabian Sea, of which 10 were combatants. *Ibid.*

Derek Davies reported in the *Far Eastern Economic Review*, 9 January 1981 that Soviet forces were building naval facilities on the Dahlak Archipelago, sparsely inhabited islands fifty miles off Ethiopia's major port of Massawa and 250 miles north off the Bab al Mandab Straits, which links the Red Sea and the Gulf of Aden and divides Africa from Arabia.

49At the time of writing in February 1981, the Soviet Union was making strong diplomatic efforts to persuade the major littoral governments to hold the conference in 1981.

50Robert E. Harkavy, "The New Geopolitics: Arms Transfers and the Major Powers' Competition for Overseas Bases," *Arms Transfers in the Modern World*, Note No. 45.

51Normal Podhoretz, *The Present Danger*, New York, Simon and Schuster, 1980, pp. 100-01.

52Robert W. Tucker, "The purposes of American Power," *Foreign Affairs*, Winter 1980-81.

53Robert Legvold, "Commitment Without Confrontation," *Foreign Policy*, Fall 1980.

54Several reports in the American press in 1980 suggested that relations between the US and Saudi Arabia were less than warm. *New York Times* correspondent in Riyadh reported in March that there were indications that the special relationship of 50 years between the US and Saudi Arabia was "gradually cooling." The key question is "Where does Saudi Arabia's long-term securities lie—traditional alliance with the United States or with the surrounding Arab world and, beyond, with the third world and the wider world of Islam? The answer seems to be that Saudi interests are increasingly at odds with the United States' objectives ... the Saudis still see themselves as part of the Western alliance. But they are beginning to see another layer of international and regional considerations." *New York Times*, 9 March 1980. See also Peter Lubin, "Our Saudi 'Friends'," *New York Times*, 30 December 1979; and David Hirst "Saudi-US Relations on Collision Path?" *The Guardian*, reprinted in *Indian Express*, 29 August 1980.

55In July 1980 Argentina signed a long-term agreement to supply to the Soviet Union 22.5 million tonnes of corn Sorghum and Soyabean over the next five years. The agreement was concluded despite American efforts to line up Argentina behind President Carter's trade sanctions against the Soviet Union. *New York Times*, 28 July 1980.

Argentina had $ 355 million worth business deals with the Soviet bloc in 1979-80 including grain exports worth $ 150 million. *Times of India*, 22 January 1980.

56Bhabani Sen Gupta, *Soviet-Asian Relations in the Seventies and Beyond: An Interperceptional Study*, New York, *Praeger* Special Studies 1976, Chapters 6 and 7.

[57] For details of the Soviet Union's Asian security diplomacy see *Ibid.*, Chapter 3.

[58] "The Russians have suffered repeated rebuffs in Iran and have alienated most of the Muslim world by their intervention in Afghanistan. And in Afghanistan itself they are stuck in an unwinnable guerrilla war, squandering men, material and world prestige. Overseas adventures have not been going well: Angola has not proved to be such a valuable gain, Cuba is still costing about $ 8m a day to support, Ethiopia is a drain on Soviet arms and supplies and has been noticeably slow to transform itself into an orthodox communist state, and the Vietnamese are as stubborn and costly as allies as they were enemies to the Americans. The Vietnamese attempt to dominate Laos and Kampuchea has rallied most of South-East Asia against their Soviet patrons." Michael Binyon, "Is the old nightmare coming true?" *The Times*, London, 22 October 1980.

[59] This point is made obliquely by Adam B. Ulam, "How to Restrain the Soviets?" *Commentary*, December 1980.

Index

ASEAN, 76, 162, 168
Afghan Revolutionary Council, 35-37, 39-40
Africa, 51-52, 54, 61, 75, 90, 133, 192, 242, 245, 248
  North, 60, 75, 238
  South, 51, 59, 63, 74n, 76, 80, 225, 238
Ahmed, Mushtaq, 211
Ai-ping, Chang, 163
Algeria, 75, 91, 114, 134, 153, 183, 185
Amanullah, 31-33
Amin, Hafizullah, 13, 15, 18, 22-23, 25, 35-41, 47, 85, 97-98, 114, 143
Amnesty International, 98
Andropov, 12
Angola, 27, 50, 74-76, 78-80, 239, 245
Arab, 81, 141, 154, 242
Arab-Israeli Conflict, 192
Argentina, 162, 242
Arkhipov, I.V., 125
Aron, Raymond, 83, 223
Asia, 2, 6, 30, 47, 51, 130, 133, 138, 192, 198, 216, 248
  Central, 30
  East, 113
  Perceptions of Soviet Power, 199
  South, 2, 12, 16-17, 19-22, 75, 89, 104, 107-108, 111, 113-14, 122, 125, 130, 132, 139, 145, 157, 160-61, 169, 172-73, 175-178, 182-83, 187, 195-96, 199-200, 202, 204, 206-7, 213-14, 216-17, 219-21, 238
  Southeast, 75-76, 161, 164, 238
  Southwestern, 18, 21, 33, 46, 60, 89, 143, 151, 168, 182, 200, 212, 216, 218, 225
  West, 54
Australia, 68, 242, 249

Austria, 94, 114, 155, 184, 186
Awami League, 203-5, 214
Azore islands, 239
Azzam, Salem, 44

Bahrain, 239
Bajpai, K.S., 19
Bangladesh, 2, 13, 16, 59, 107, 116 183, 199, 201-3, 205-6, 212-14
Bangladesh Times, 214
Bangladesh War, 74, 160, 166
Barnett, Doak, 168
Barton, Allen H., 226
Bazarghan, 93
Belgium, 80, 223
Benazir, 211
Bertram, Christoph, 223
Bhutan, 183, 213
Bhutto, Begum Nusrat, 203, 211
Bhutto, Zulfikar Ali, 2, 46, 141, 143, 152, 158, 201-3, 211
Bialer, Sewryn, 71
Biao, Geng, 165
Bolshevik revolution, 33, 69
Brazil, 242, 249
Brezhnev, 9-10, 12, 25-26, 52, 60, 67, 71, 74, 76-78, 80-82, 85, 86, 89-90, 92, 104, 115, 125, 130, 132-35, 138-39, 152, 168, 170, 173-74, 177, 185, 189-90, 219, 232
Britain, 6, 11, 30-33, 69, 80, 114, 129, 149, 180, 185-86, 223
Brown, Harold, 4, 64, 110, 164-65, 237
Brzezinski, Zbigniew K, 4, 43, 49, 52, 55, 57-58, 59-60, 62-65, 70, 111-12, 116, 126, 145-46, 163-64, 169, 189, 241
Bukti, Akbar Khan, 46
Bulgaria, 78

Index

Burma, 116, 168

CENTO, 11, 142, 197
CIA, 21, 42, 56
COMECON, 229
CPC, 172
Callaghan, James, 58
Cambodia, 62, 166
Canada, 82, 242, 249
Carrington, 127, 184
Carter, Jimmy, 1-11, 16, 18-20, 24, 26, 43, 48, 52, 57-60, 62, 64-65, 70, 77, 81, 86-93, 110-13, 115, 124, 128, 131, 143, 146, 163-64, 166, 172, 179, 183-84, 188-90, 197, 207, 209, 234, 246
Castro, Fidel, 130, 225
Ceausescu, Nicolai, 155
Charnan, Mostafa, 93
Chatty, Habib, 153, 183
Chile, 162
China, 6, 17-18, 20, 39, 41-43, 47-48, 60, 71, 76-77, 79-80, 89, 91, 96-97, 101, 106-9, 114, 118, 120-21, 123, 128-29, 132-33, 135, 138-39, 142, 144, 149-50, 152, 157, 161-64, 166-69, 171, 174, 176-77, 190, 196-97, 199-200, 215-16, 219, 226, 238, 241
  Afghan Crisis, 21
  Diplomacy of Insecurity, 160
Chinese Communist Party, 132
Chou-En-lai, 77
Christian Science Monitor, 225
Christopher, Warren, 111, 126
Churchill, 30-31
Clifford, Clark, 111-12, 126
Cold War I, 3
  II, 2-3, 24, 179, 187
Commentary, 227
Communist Party of India, 215
Communist Party of India-Marxist, 171, 215
Communist Party of the Soviet Union, 13, 47, 67-69, 77-79, 83-84, 86, 104, 191-92
Congo, 49
Congress-I, 107, 202
Council for Mutual Economic Assis-

tance, 77-78
Counterspy, 42
Cuba, 27, 49, 51, 57, 60-61, 74-76, 78, 91, 114, 129-31, 152, 163, 182
Curzon, Lord, 30-31
Czar, 30-31, 33
Czechoslovakia, 15, 35, 78, 97, 109

Daedalus, 231
Dainik Sangram, 205, 214
Dallin, Alexander, 227
Davies, C. Collin, 30
Dawn, 210
Demchenko, A, 38
Desai, Morarji, 171
Disraeli, 30
Djibouti, 63
Dobrynin, Anatoli, 189
Dong, Pham von, 129-30
Dost, Shah Mohammad, 96, 120, 134, 185, 195
Drug Enforcement Agency, 42
Dubs, Adolph, 58, 84
Dufferin, 30
Dupree, Louis, 84
Durand Line, 125, 142, 195

EEC, 163, 183-84
Economist, the 229, 236
Egypt, 4, 18, 38, 41-42, 60, 62, 74-75, 238-39
Eisenhower, 7-8
Encausse, Helene Carrere d', 11
Enlai, Zou, 160-61, 173-74
Estaing, valery Giscard d', 58, 134, 189-90
Ethiopia, 27, 57, 74-76, 78, 80, 239, 242, 245
Europe, 2, 26, 30, 44, 47, 54-55, 58, 80, 105, 115, 164, 182, 190, 223-24, 226, 228, 230
  Eastern, 10, 12, 35, 62, 75, 190, 219, 237, 347
  Western, 2, 8, 11, 42, 48, 55, 60, 69-70, 81, 90, 105, 127, 133, 138-39, 170, 187, 224-25, 229, 231, 248
Evening News, 184

Firyubin, Nicolai, 122, 130, 135
Fontaine, Andre, 11
Ford, Gerald, 7
Foreign Policy, 225, 241
Fortune, 236
France, 2, 12, 32, 57, 69, 80, 86, 114-15, 134, 149, 163, 180, 187, 223, 228-29, 249
French Communist Party, 102

Gandhi, Indira, 2, 14, 16-17, 20, 48, 78, 96, 104, 106-11, 114, 116-19, 121-23, 125-26, 129-30, 132-34, 138-39, 144-45, 148, 152, 155-57, 170-75, 183, 201-2, 204, 210, 212, 216
Gelb, Leslie H., 190-91
Germany, 249
  East, 12, 94
  West, 2, 12, 58, 60, 78, 86, 94, 102, 115, 124, 180, 187, 189-90, 228-30
Ghotbzadeh, Sadegh, 95, 153
Gladstone, 30-31
Glenn, John, 127
Gonsalves, Eric., 126-27, 129, 173
Great Patriotic War, 67
Greece, 2, 239
Grey, 30
Gromyoko, Andre, 12, 86, 88-89, 104, 112, 127, 134-36, 148, 179, 183, 185, 188-89
Guardian, the, 45-46, 211
Gulbzoi, Syed Mohammed, 102
Guofeng, Hua, 115, 132-33, 161-62, 164-66, 170
Guyana, 162

Haqqani, Arshad Ahmed, 210
Harrison, Selig, 20
Hartman, Robert W., 237
Haskar, P.N., 205-6, 218
Heilbroner, Robert, 50
Hekmatyar, Gulsuddin, 44
Hezbe-i-Islami, 44
Hindu, the, 14, 101, 112, 115, 119-21, 125-27, 147, 158, 271, 218-20
Hindustan Times, the 15, 45, 122, 185
Hitler, 33

Hoffman, Stanley, 55
Holiday, 205, 215
Hongkong, 22
Hough, Jerry, 72
Hsiaoping, Deng, 60, 77
Hua, Huang, 43, 144, 163, 169, 172-73, 177
Hungary, 15, 78, 109
Huntington, Samuel, 231
Huq, Shamsul, 204, 213

Iceland, 68
India, 13-15, 17, 19-20, 45, 75, 78, 86, 91, 95-96, 104, 106-7, 109-12, 115-22, 124-26, 128-31, 133, 135-40, 144, 146-48, 155, 157, 160, 162, 169-73, 177, 180, 183, 185, 187, 196-97, 199, 206, 209, 211, 213-14, 218-20, 238, 249
India-Pakistan War 1965, 133
India Today, 220
Indian Express, 10, 15, 40, 111, 120, 122, 185, 206
Indian Ocean, 9, 56, 60, 62, 87, 90, 106, 133, 139, 195, 217, 238-39
Indonesia, 249
International Affairs, 38
International Herald Tribune, 94, 180
International Institute of Strategic Studies, 37
Iran, 1-7, 10, 14, 24, 26-28, 30, 32, 38, 41, 42, 46-47, 50, 58-62, 80, 82, 86, 88, 90, 92, 96, 104, 116-17, 121, 129, 133, 143, 147, 152-55, 163, 176, 180, 182, 191, 193-94, 204, 208, 233, 238, 242-43
Iraq, 4, 58, 74-75, 78, 82, 134, 137, 139, 153, 233, 238-39
Islamic Conference, Islamabad, 44-45, 131, 134-35, 137, 139, 144-45, 153-54, 156, 207, 213
Israel, 10, 58, 60, 154, 159, 239, 242
Italy, 32, 114, 163
Izvestia, 92

Jackson, 11
Jain, Giralal, 15, 206, 218, 220
Jamaica, 162

Index 293

Janata Government/Party, 2, 12, 171, 201
Japan, 8, 55, 58, 60, 76-77, 81, 90, 139, 149, 162-67, 170, 176, 199, 230, 238
Jasarat, 210
Jatiya Samajtantrik Dal, 214
Jerusalem, 10, 241
Johnson, Lyndon, 8, 81, 223
Jordan, 60

KGB, 12
Kampuchea, 4, 15, 21, 47, 76, 78, 119, 130, 160-62, 165, 174, 177, 195, 205
Kant, 2
Kapista, M.S., 135
Karmal, Babrak, 13, 34-35, 37, 39-40, 42, 45, 47, 91, 96-98, 100, 102-103, 120, 126, 130-31, 133-34, 137-38, 154-56, 181, 193
Kennan, George, 227
Kennedy, John, 7
Kennedy, Senator Edward, 2
Kenya, 4, 239
Khalq, 34-36, 40, 84, 102
Khan, Ajmal, 46
Khan, Badshah, 46
Khan, F.M. Ayub, 133, 201
Khan, General Yahya, 18
Khan, Mohammed Daud, 34-35
Khan, Wali, 46
Khomeini, Ayatollah Rohullah, 1, 43, 60, 92-94, 96, 163, 181
Khrushev, 71, 168
Khyber, Mir Akbar, 34
Kirilenko, 12
Kissinger, Henry K., 8, 21, 49-52, 57-59, 61, 83, 112, 160, 165, 191, 203, 231, 241
Kitchner, 30
Korea, 33
 North, 78
Kosygin, 77, 90, 133, 168
Kreisky, Bruno, 155, 183
Kuwait, 10

L'Humanite, 102
Laird, Melvin, 8

Laudsdowne, 30
Laos, 15, 76, 78
Laqueur, Walter, 227
Latin America 75, 225, 238
Le Monde, 228, 235
Legvold, Robert, 241
Lenin, 32-33
Leontief, Wasily, 50
Lewls, Flora, 12, 224
Libya, 4, 75, 91, 134, 154, 239
Louis, Victor, 184
Luttwak, Edward, 10, 231
Lytton, 30

MPLA, 50, 80
Maghribi Pakistan, 210
Malhotra, Inder, 102, 174
Malta, 239
Marxists, 14, 17, 27-28, 33-34, 36, 38, 41-42, 46, 57-58, 74, 76, 78-80, 84, 95, 99-100, 102-103, 131, 142, 180, 182, 186
Mc Mohan Line, 174
Menon, V.K. Krishna, 174
Middle East, 2, 4, 7, 9, 27-28, 51, 60, 62, 74-75, 89-90, 192, 225, 230, 238
Middleton, Drew, 5-6
Mishra, Brajesh, 106
Mishra, S.N., 13
Mondale, Walter, 165
Mongolia, 78
Morocco, 60, 153
Moss, Robert, 231
Moynihan, Patrick, 11, 50
Mozambique, 78-79, 239, 245
Mu, Ku, 163
Mugabe, Robert, 246
Muskie, Edmund, 134, 136, 179, 183, 188-89
Muslim, the, 148, 205, 208

NATO, 11, 25, 57, 60, 63, 86, 182, 206, 226, 236
Nan, Wan Ping, 172
National Awami Party, 46
National Security Council, 60
Nayar, Kuldip, 40-41, 100, 129, 145, 206

Index

Nehru, Jawaharlal, 109, 174
Nepal, 107, 116, 183, 213
New Times, 92, 185
New York Times, 4-6, 8, 10, 12, 19-20, 42-43, 53, 56, 107, 143, 149, 190, 224, 227, 235
Newsweek, 56, 59
Nigeria, 249
Nitze, Paul, 226
Nixon, Richard, 8, 50-51, 55, 81, 160-61, 191, 201, 223, 234
Nonaligned movement, 27, 80, 133
Norway, 230

Ohira, Masayoshi, 164
Oksenberg, Michael, 163
Oman, 4, 63, 163, 239

PLA, 163
Pahlavi, Shah Mohammed Raza, 34, 46, 50, 58-60, 94, 137, 142-43, 163, 176
Pakistan, 1-2, 5-6, 9-10, 14-20, 23-24, 28, 35, 37-39, 41-43, 45-48, 80, 86, 91-92, 95-97, 101-3, 106-9, 111-14, 116-18, 121-29, 131-39, 142-53, 155, 157, 159, 162, 168-69, 174, 176-77, 180-84, 192-93, 195-97, 199, 202, 204, 206-7, 209, 213, 215, 219-21, 238-39, 242
  Diplomacy of Survival, 141
Pakistan Economist, the, 209
Pakistan People's Party, 141, 203, 211-12
Pakistan Times, 158, 208-9, 211
Palestin, 159
Palestine Liberation Organisation, 75, 89, 91, 114, 134, 153-54
Parcham, 34-35, 40, 84-85
Peking, Review, 178
Peng-fei, chi, 163
Peoi, Isidoro Malemiera, 129-30
People's Daily, 23, 175
People's Democracy Party, 22
People's Democratic Party of Afghanistan, 34, 36-37, 39-40, 98
Perey, Charles, 127

Persian Gulf, 1-11, 21, 27, 33, 47, 56, 58-59, 61-63, 81, 87, 94, 104-5, 107, 111-12, 118, 126, 133, 138, 141, 147, 154, 163, 169, 175, 179, 192, 198, 200, 206-7, 210, 216, 218, 225-26, 231-35, 238-40, 242, 246
Petrov, A., 22-23, 94
Philipines, 238
Piao, Keng, 142, 162
Pipes, Richard, 227
Podhoretz, Norman, 240
Poland, 78, 115, 191, 243
Portugal, 80, 223
Pravda, 22-26, 85, 87, 89, 91, 94, 162, 179
Press Trust of India, 103, 146
Problem of the North-West Frontier, the, 30

Quddaji, 10
Quester, George, 225
Rafi, Mohammed, 102
Rahman, Shah Azizur, 205
Rahman, Sheikh Mujibur, 2, 201
Rahman, Ziaur, 183, 203-4, 212-13
Rao, Narasimha, 111, 114-15, 121-22, 130, 134-37, 156, 172, 174
Rapid Deployment Force, 4, 9, 56, 62, 217
Reagan, Ronald, 61, 64-65, 77, 82, 138-39, 177, 189, 192-93, 196, 224, 226, 236-37, 243, 246, 248-49
Reddy, G.K., 115-16, 118, 129, 172
Reston, James, 6-8, 11
Rhodesia, 58
Ripon, 30
Rizzo, Aldo, 224
Rumania, 78, 114-15, 155, 162, 185, 191

SALT, 28-29, 51-52, 61, 63, 190
  II, 53, 57, 60-61, 91, 164, 167, 182, 217, 227, 236
  III, 61
SEATO, 197, 201
SIPRI, 3
Sadat, Anwar, 4, 38, 75, 143
Sadaqat, 208

Sadr, Bani, 93
Sarbuland, Abdul Majid, 40
Sathe, Ram, 13, 116-18, 130, 134, 145-47, 155, 210
Saturday Review, 231
Saud-al-Faisal, 154
Saudi Arabia, 4, 8, 10, 62, 113, 129, 142-43, 147, 149, 154, 158-59, 162, 181, 238, 242
Scandinavia, 229
Schelling, Thomas C, 7
Schlesinger, James R, 234
Sehmidt, Helmut, 58, 190
Sermin, Hang, 21, 174, 177
Shah, Zahir, 142
Shahi, Agha, 131-32, 137, 144, 146, 148, 150-52, 154-56, 169, 192-98
Shapley, Deborah, 227
Shastri, Lal Bahadur, 133, 201
Sholee Javid, 21
Simla Agreement, 117
Singh, Chowdhuri Charan, 2, 13, 15, 107
Singh, J.D., 40-41, 206
Singh, S.K., 120
Singh, Sardar Swaran, 126, 131-32, 210
Sino-US military Cooperation, 4
Smith, Hedrick, 4
Smith, Ian, 58
Somalia, 4, 74, 80, 239
Sonnenfeldt, Helmut, 231
Soviet-Afghan treaty, 13, 39
Soviet Union, 1-3
Soviet Intervention in Afghanistan,
 Indian Reports, 40
 Pakistan Perceptions, 18
 Scrambled images in South Asia, 12
 Western Europe, 11
 World View, 3
Sri Lanka, 116, 183, 213
Stalin, 29, 33, 69, 71-72
Stern, Fritz, 227
Subrahmanyam, K., 205-6, 200, 218
Supreme Defence Council, 36
Suslov, 12
Sweden, 68, 163
Switzerland, 155

Syria, 75, 86, 89, 91, 138, 153, 239

Taiwan, 77, 160
Ta Kung Pao, 22
Tarakki, Nur Mohammed, 22, 34-37, 39, 84-85, 142
Tass, 24, 87, 91, 97, 101, 133, 170, 184
Teja, J.S., 96
Thailand, 4, 76, 239
Thatcher, Margaret, 229
Times, the, 82, 96, 139, 180, 223-25
Times of India, 14, 40, 120, 122, 205-6, 220
Tito, 184, 189
Toha, Mohammed, 214
Tribune, 14
Trinidad-Tobago, 162
Tucker, Robert W., 240-41
Tudeh Party, 8, 94
Turkey, 2. 32, 59, 191, 239
Tunisia, 183

Ukil, Abdul Malek, 214
United Arab Emirate, 10
United Nations, 16-17, 50, 80, 97, 106, 114, 116, 130, 132, 151, 155, **194**, 213
 Charter, 13-14, 23, 93, 195
 General Assembly, 107, 154, 180, 193, 213
 Human Rights Commission, 42
 Security Council, 94, 213
US Asian Fund Organisation, 42
Ustinov, 12, 90

Vance, Cyrus, 9, 11, 57, 115, 184
Vajpayee, Atal Behari, 171-72
Vietnam, 3, **27**, 49-50, 52, 56, 59, 62, 72, 75-76, 78, 103, 114, 118, 129-30, 160-64, 166, 171, 181-82, 223, 225, 239
 North, 15, 81, 149, 223, 242
 South, 223
 War, 1, 74, 79, 81
Viewpoint, 208, 210
Vinogradov, Vladimir, **92**
Voice of America, 101
Vorontsov, Yuri M, 12-13

Wafaaq, 208
Waldheim, Kurt, 116, 195
Wariavwalla, Bharat, 219
Warswa Pact, 61, 73, 77-78, 182, 236
Washington Post, 42, 47, 57, 151
Watanjar, 98
World Bank, 84, 148
World War I, 31, 50, 54, 144
   II, 3, 5, 7, 30, 74, 186, 207, 223, 229
Wranke, Paul N., 55

Xiaoping, Deng, 161-64, 167-68, 170, 174-76, 225

Xinhua, 170

Yemen, 27
Yemen, South, 75-76, 78, 91, 134, 153
Yugoslavia, 78, 162, 183, 185

Zaire, 57, 162-63
Zedong, Mao, 77, 160-62
Zia ul-Haq, 2, 10, 18-21, 43, 46, 92, 96, 115-18, 126, 130-33, 137, 139, 141-59, 169-70, 181, 183-84, 193-95, 197, 201-5, 307-11
Zimbabwe, 58, 79, 246
Ziyang, Zhao, 61